IDEOLOGICAL COALITIONS IN CONGRESS

Recent Titles in Contributions in Political Science
Series Editor: Bernard K. Johnpoll

American Democratic Theory: Pluralism and Its Critics
William Alton Kelso

International Terrorism in the Contemporary World
Marius H. Livingston, with Lee Bruce Kress and Marie G. Wanek, editors

Doves and Diplomats: Foreign Offices and Peace Movements in Europe and America in the Twentieth Century
Solomon Wank, editor

Believing Skeptics: American Political Intellectuals, 1945-1964
Robert Booth Fowler

Locke, Rousseau, and the Idea of Consent: An Inquiry into the Liberal Democratic Theory of Political Obligation
Jules Steinberg

Judicial Craftsmanship or Fiat? Direct Overturn by the United States Supreme Court
Howard Ball

The New Left in France: The Unified Socialist Party
Charles Hauss

The Communist Parties of Western Europe: A Comparative Study
R. Neal Tannahill

France's Vietnam Policy: A Study in French-American Relations
Marianna P. Sullivan

The McNamara Strategy and the Vietnam War: Program Budgeting in the Pentagon, 1960-1968
Gregory Palmer

On the Edge of Politics: The Roots of Jewish Political Thought in America
William S. Berlin

Constitutional Language: An Interpretation of Judicial Decision
John Brigham

IDEOLOGICAL COALITIONS IN CONGRESS

Jerrold E. Schneider

GP Contributions in Political Science, Number 16

GREENWOOD PRESS
WESTPORT, CONNECTICUT • LONDON, ENGLAND

Library of Congress Cataloging in Publication Data

Schneider, Jerrold E.
Ideological coalitions in Congress.

(Contributions in political science ; no. 16 ISSN-0147-1066)
Bibliography: p.
Includes index.
1. United States. Congress—voting. 2. Coalition (Social sciences) 3. Ideology. I. Title. II. Series.
JK1051.S46 328.73'07'75 78-4019
ISBN 0-313-20410-1

Library of Congress Catalog Card Number: 78-4019
ISBN: 0-313-20410-1
ISSN: 0147-1066

First published in 1979

Greenwood Press, Inc.
51 Riverside Avenue, Westport, Connecticut 06880

Printed in the United States of America

10 9 8 7 6 5 4 3 2 1

To SES
and KSS

CONTENTS

	Tables	xi
	Figures	xiii
	Acknowledgments	xv
Part I	**Ideology Versus Pluralism: The Setting and the Problem Specified**	**1**
Chapter 1	Introduction: Perspectives on Congressional Coalitions	3
Chapter 2	Ideology, and the Pluralist and Ideological Theories	11
	The Concept of Ideology	11
	The Concept of Pluralism	20
	Congressional Coalitions: The Pluralism-Ideology Dispute	27
Part II	**Empirical Tests of the Pluralist and Ideological Theories**	**43**
Chapter 3	Foreign Policy and Ideological Consistency	45
	Testing the Ideological-Consistency Hypothesis—Foreign Policy in the Summer of 1970	47

Interview Schedule 47
Interviews 55
Coding of Interviews 58
Liberal and Conservative Foreign Policy Ideologies in 1970 59
Results 62
Foreign Policy Roll Calls—A Reliability Check 66
Continuity and Change: 1970-76 67
The Long-Term Conservative Perspective 73
The Long-Term Liberal Perspective 75

Chapter 4 Analysis of Congressional Coalitions: The Dilemma 91

Comparability Versus Contextual Validation of Indicators 91
A Caveat 93
Congress Experts and Roll Call Analysts 93
Roll Call Analyses from a Contextualist Viewpoint 101

Chapter 5 Congressional Voting Patterns 106

The Data Base 106
Coding Procedures 109
Excluded Vote Categories 111
The Measurement of Cohesion: Cumulating Individual Scores 115
Policy Roll Call Sets 118
Item Direction Assignment 125
An Intercoder Reliability Check 125
Results 126
Discussion 127
Predictability of Congressional Voting 136
Further Comparisons of the Findings with Comparable Studies 138
The Central Finding: Unidimensionality and Its Significance 147

Chapter 6 The "Liberal"-"Progressive" Cleavage over Economic Policy 159

The New Age of Scarcity and the New Congressional Context 163
Progressives, Liberals, and Conservatives 165
Data Sources 166
The Liberal-Progressive Cleavage 167
The Liberal Perspective 168
The Progressive Perspective 176

Chapter 7 Summary and Conclusions: The Ideological Balance of Forces 193

Summary 193

Conclusions: The Ideological Balance of Forces and Its Implications 197

APPENDIX I Roll Call Votes by CQ Number 207

APPENDIX II Response Patterns Obtained in the Congressional Interviews on Foreign Policy 213

Selected Bibliography 235

Subject Index 259

Index of Names 263

TABLES

2-1	Polsby's Determinants of Transformativeness in Legislatures	27
3-1	Constraint of Specific Foreign Policy Attitudes Among Congressmen Interviewed	60
3-2	Average Coefficients—Constraint Among Foreign Policy Attitudes for the Sample of Ninety-seven Congressmen Interviewed	61
5-1	Possible Class Allocation Scores by Roll Call Votes	122
5-2	Results of Inter-Coder Reliability Test	126
5-3	Ninety-second Congress—House (1971-72): Main Findings in Kendall's Tau-B	128
5-4	Ninety-second Congress—House (1971-72): Main Findings in Spearman's r_s	129
5-5	Ninety-second Congress—Senate (1971-72): Main Findings in Kendall's Tau-B	130
5-6	Ninety-second Congress—Senate (1971-72): Main Findings in Spearman's r_s	130
5-7	Ninety-fourth Congress—House—First Session (1975): Main Findings in Kendall's Tau-B	131
5-8	Ninety-fourth Congress—House—First Session (1975): Main Findings in Spearman's r_s	131
5-9	Ninety-fourth Congress—Senate—First Session (1975): Main Findings in Kendall's Tau-B	132
5-10	Ninety-fourth Congress—Senate—First Session (1975): Main Findings in Spearman's r_s	132

5-11 Ninety-fourth Congress—House—First Session (1975) Without First-, Second-, and Third-Term Congressmen: Main Findings in Kendall's Tau-B 133

5-12 Ninety-fourth Congress—House—First Session (1975) Without First-, Second-, and Third-Term Congressmen: Main Findings in Spearman's r_s 133

5-13 Summary of Findings of This Study 134

5-14 Converse's Findings: Summary of Differences in Level of Constraint Within and Between Domains, Elite and Mass 145

5-15 Summary of Differences in Level of Constraint Within and Between Policy Domains 146

FIGURES

3-1 Proportions of the Whole House and of the Original Sample by ADA Ratings 57

3-2 Proportions of the Whole House and of the Reduced Sample by ADA Ratings 57

ACKNOWLEDGMENTS

A number of institutions have made this volume possible. I began this study as a Research Fellow at the Brookings Institution, and, several years later, completed it as a Guest scholar at Brookings, under a "One-Year Fellowship for Independent Study and Research "of the National Endowment for the Humanities. The material support provided by Brookings was secondary to the richness of insight gathered by my years of residence, and extensive interaction with members of the Governmental Studies, Economic Studies, and Foreign Policy Programs. I am most grateful to the Endowment and to Brookings, without whom this study could never have been completed in its present form. I am happy to acknowledge my indebtedness to the University of Delaware for sabbatical leave, a faculty research grant, and many smaller grants for research expenses, and to the Department of Political Science and my students for providing an unusually salutary and gracious atmosphere.

A number of individuals read earlier inchoate drafts and provided important insights and stimulation. Perhaps most effective were the detailed written comments of Philip Converse. Converse's own work was a major influence on this study; Herbert McClosky, Roger Davidson, John Kingdon, Seyom Brown, Herbert Weisberg, James L. Sundquist, Robert Cuthriell, James K. Oliver, Marion Palley, Henry Reynolds, Barbara Hinckley, David and Margaret Karns, Arnold Kantor, Robert Nakamura, Steven Brams, Brian Steinberg and the late K. H. Silvert each provided crucial suggestions and inspired specific changes or additions, for which I am most grateful. At Brookings, I also particularly benefited from discussions with Martha Derthick, Hugh Heclo, Herbert Kaufman, Leon Lindberg, and Gary Orfield.

Among economists, I am especially indebted to Arthur Okun, Charles L. Schultze, Edward Denison, Barry Bosworth, and C. Fred Bergsten for long discussions and rich insights.

Other individuals in Washington to whom I wish to acknowledge my gratitude for sharing knowledge, and for assistance, include Henry Banta, Harrison Wellford, Richard Conlon, Allen Schick, Harrison Fox, Dr. Paul D. Stolley, James P. King, Jr., and Margaret P. King, and the late Wes Barthelmas.

I particularly want to thank Mrs. Doris Miller for secretarial support and sensitivity far beyond the call of duty; Mrs. Barbara Page for unusually precise and thoughtful computer assistance; and Ms. Elizabeth Anthony for extraordinary research assistance.

I am most grateful to the many congressmen, senators, and congressional staff, who gave generously of their time and knowledge. The Inter-university Consortium for Political and Social Research provided a significant part of the data of this study, as originally collected by the Survey Research Center and the Center for Political Studies of the University of Michigan. Although it was many years ago, prior to becoming a political scientist, I cannot but acknowledge the enormous influence on me of being a graduate student at Brown University's Department of Philosophy, and especially the influence of Roderick Chisholm and Richard Taylor.

My wife, Katharine, has been a constant source of balanced judgment, assistance, and support and has unflinchingly shared my commitments. More important, she has been my closest companion. To my mother, I would only say what she already knows, which is ineffable.

Responsibility for errors of fact or judgment is entirely my own.

Jerrold E. Schneider
Newark, Delaware
January 1978

PART I

Ideology Versus Pluralism: The Setting and the Problem Specified

chapter 1

INTRODUCTION: PERSPECTIVES ON CONGRESSIONAL COALITIONS

For at least a quarter-century some political observers and virtually all empirical studies have asserted that the coalitions that structured congressional foreign policy conflicts were quite different from the coalitions which structured cleavage patterns over domestic issues. A few analysts have seen high consistency among cleavage patterns on different domestic issues, but most have not. The latest and most sophisticated analyses have described congressional coalitions, including those occurring on domestic issues, as very flexible, varying widely according to the substance of numerous interests, issues, or policy dimensions. Only a few professional analysts of Congress have believed that a highly consistent (across issues) and continuous (across time) ideological "liberal-conservative" cleavage properly described congressional behavior. This study's central hypothesis is that there exists a very high consistency of congressional coalitions across all major policy domains, foreign and domestic.

The dominant view, often with some ambiguity termed "pluralist," in contrast to the ideological (high consistency) theory, suffers one major *prima facie* disadvantage, namely, that Washington-based journalists and other commentators, as well as congressmen and senators, themselves, make recurrent if somewhat opaque reference to ideological classifications. Perhaps these Washington participants and observers stand too close to see events clearly, but then again perhaps the "pluralist" academics sit too far from things as they are. Clearly nothing less than major perspectives on Congress and on American politics depend upon which theory is right and which is wrong.

In light of complexities of policy and of the legislative process, the sharp disagreements and confusion over various characterizations of congressional coalitions among academic and other political analysts becomes far more understandable. To give a weighty example here of a skeptical position on the durability or propriety of some of the usual ideological classifications, it is interesting to note the remarks of longtime Congress analyst Charles O. Jones, introducing Governor Nelson Rockefeller to the 1973 annual meeting of American political scientists:

> Is he a conservative or a liberal? I have thought about that. Those terms are least durable, in my judgment, when seeking to describe those with lengthy public service. More serviceable are the distinctions between those public officials who are positively directed and those who use their authority in the public interest and those who abuse their authority. . . .[1]

This viewpoint is also heard in the ranks of the working press. Henry Hubbard, *Newsweek* Washington bureau chief, told a panel aduience that when someone on his staff "insisted" on calling the freshmen congressmen of the Ninety-fourth Congress liberals, "I insisted that he take that word out of the account, because I didn't think it applied, . . . and change it to reform minded or something like that, because what the hell do you mean when you say 'liberal'?"[2] Yet these classifications are resorted to by some of the most serious "players in the game," as in, for example, the remarks of Speaker Thomas P. O'Neill when he was asked on CBS-TV-'s "Face the Nation":

> Looking at the Carter program so far, are you finding that President Carter is more conservative than candidate Carter was? *Rep. O'Neill:* No, I don't judge him that way whatsoever. I judged Jimmy Carter from the day that I first met him as a moderate in politics, and I still think he's a moderate in politics. How does he line up as far as the House is concerned? Well, the Democratic party—I'd say two-thirds of the Democratic party are progressives and one-third moderates. But the art of politics has been compromise, and so we're not going to have any difficulties.[3]

For at least some principal political and governmental figures, as well as journalists and academics, the use of ideological classifications are fundamental to their analysis of congressional outcomes. But in the views of some analysts valid and reliable meanings, either in general philosophical or specific policy terms, are *not* conveyed by ideological labels as they are now employed. In a recent special symposium issue of *Commentary,* sixty-five different commentators addressed the question: "What Is a Liberal—Who Is a Conservative?" From this symposium there seems to be as much confusion and disagreement over this subject among those who analyze American politics in general as there is among those who analyze Congress.[4]

Accepting one or another view of the nature of congressional coalitions, or of the validity of various ideological labels in use, has significant consequences. One is the *expectation or anticipation* of quite different outcomes from congressional actions under varying conditions. A second is that the analyst will be led accordingly to see some quite different *causes* for congressional outcomes. Third, different judgments about causes will divert scarce political resources and analytical energies to different *remedies* for perceived public ills.

If all this is true, it would seem that a great deal depends upon how congressional coalitions are construed. Yet Congress is but one element in the configuration of forces whose interactions issue in the exercise of power in the American political system. An incredibly complex interplay exists among forces in the Congress and those outside of it. These include the President, the courts, the political appointee and career layers of the federal bureaucracy, organized interest groups, the media, political parties and other aspects of the electoral system, the economy, the international environment, attentive publics, and public opinion generally. Acceptance of one or another theory of congressional coalitions and cleavages will, however, inevitably constrain our selective perceptions of the *causal weight* to be assigned in any calculus of the relations among these different elements in the American governmental equation. Hence the consequences of accepting one of the rival interpretations of congressional coalitions, from this standpoint, are wider yet.

What explains the often sharp disagreements and confusions concerning ideological labels? We need to account for the fact that widely different views of the matter are held by equally well informed, able, and serious observers and analysts of the Congress. There are a number of *sources of complexity* which obscure underlying bloc structures and help account for such a wide range of different viewpoints on this subject.

One source of complexity derives from a changed atmosphere in Congress reflecting a rapidly changing world. In the post-Bretton Woods world economy, cheap food and energy are apparently out of reach for Americans for the first time, and foreign economic competition seems to threaten advantages enjoyed by the American economy over the past quarter-century. Moreover, the very structure of the international economy has undergone vast changes swiftly. George Ball, in words his usual critics would not dispute, characterized these vast changes as having moved from a period of world economic history structured by "international trade" into a new period of "international production."

> Today a large and rapidly expanding roster of companies is engaged in taking the raw materials produced in one group of countries, transforming these into manufactured goods with the labor and plant facilities of another group, and selling the products in still a third group.[5]

Ball warning of finite resources and exploding demands, urged us to confront the dangers of a "Darwinian debacle on a global scale"[6] a description not out of keeping with perceptions of people who place themselves in very different parts of the ideological spectrum.

In an environment some call "the new politics of resource scarcity," intense arguments over the role of government in the United States have become everyday occurrences structuring the political climate and shaping the terms of a discourse in the Congress. The sharply worsening domestic economic situation in the United States of the 1970s is inextricably enmeshed with the larger changes of the international economic environment, which together cannot but profoundly affect the forces acting on and in the Congress. Complicating these relationships is the emergence of transnational forces and conditions which alarm many observers concerning the physical deterioriation of the planet as a hospitable place for human life.[7]

Another, but relatively new, subtle, and therefore not widely appreciated source of complexity obscuring congressional behavior and the nature of coalitions is change in Congress itself, and the increased activity of Congress in the processes of governing and policy making since the Johnson administration. This activity has spawned an enormous expansion in staff, computer usage, and other aspects of institutional capacity. Joseph A. Califano, Jr., President Carter's Secretary of Health, Education, and Welfare, served in the Johnson administration as "czar" for domestic programs in the White House. Asked to discuss his impressions of the changes in government between 1968 and 1977, he commented:

> One sense I have strongly about what's happened is that there are many many programs now legislated with incredible specificity. . . . The last two administrations were sending up budgets and proposals so out of tune with what the Congress wanted or intended to do that they were outraged. Their programs were being destroyed. They couldn't even administer things, execute the laws that Congress had told them to execute. We still have to make it clear that we will execute those laws.
>
> The tension between the Congress and the executive—which I think we have less of here [in HEW] than elsewhere, at least at the top—is there. It's there in part because the Congress has in many ways been running a lot of these programs for the last few years since Watergate. Now there's an executive [Carter] who's come in and wants to run them, and is saying to the Congress, "All right, you pass the laws, we'll execute them."
>
> Another thing: the staffs on the Hill are much much better and larger than they ever were. And much much more powerful. That's the biggest change that I've noticed since the last time I was in government.[8]

Analysts of the Congress have added much to the understanding of the many changes in attitudes, structures, processes, and analytic capabilities which have strengthened the capacity of Congress as an institution.[9] However, Congress's capacity to develop well-conceived and, above all, integrated policies and legislation does not seem near at hand. The relationships among congressional parties, coalitions, and the institutional capacity of the Congress for integrated policy making deserve a well-specified analysis.[10]

As with Congress, so all elements of the American political equation are becoming more central objects of profound questioning by citizens, practitioners, and scholars alike. Perhaps this reflects an intensification of politics in a period of economic crisis, with greater conflicts over private sector/public sector relationships being ever more tightly woven through escalating arguments over political, economic, and social institutions. Changes in other parts of the American political system, by making greater fluctuations in the forces acting upon the Congress possible, will further obscure the nature of congressional coalitions, as the interplay between proximate and underlying causes becomes more intricate.

In addition there are the complexities built into the American constitutional order, particularly the separation of powers between the Congress and the executive branch,[11] and federalism. These structural complexities not only make responsibility for outcomes harder to assign, but, for the same familiar reasons, obscure the nature of opposing forces in the Congress. Moreover, there is a growing need for "integrated" policy making[12] within and between the Congress and the executive branch, that is, ensuring that a policy designed for one policy area, energy, for instance, does not defeat one's own preferred policies in such areas as inflation and tax reform. This need for integrated policies makes all policy interactions more complex, hence increasing the complexity caused by other factors exponentially. As these complexities grow, there is commensurate increase in the obscurity that cloaks both the nature of congressional coalitions and other variables in the American political equation at any particular time.

Some see the balance of forces in Congress, and between Congress and the executive branch, as the fulcrum on which rests the balancing of all other pressures. Not surprisingly, that is my own bias. What Congress does or does not do, in my judgment, appears, uniquely, the necessary and in many instances the sufficient condition of most political and governmental outcomes. This perspective fits snugly with the views of those who are more impressed with executive branch weaknesses for unilaterally chosen constructive ends, rather than with the views of those who presume overwhelming executive branch advantages of expertise and unity, provided at least the "right" administration with a propensity for activist government is in power. The question revolves around probabilities: The executive branch advocates are unquestionably right for some contingencies and unquestionably wrong for others. Perhaps the central factor shaping the range of possible contingencies is the balance of political forces in Congress, that is, congressional coalitions, or perhaps it is the kind of issue at stake. But certainly congressional-executive branch relationships are increasingly a major source of complexity obscuring the nature of congressional coalitions.

Another reason why congressional coalitions, and their net effects on the larger American political equation, are difficult to understand is the *law of anticipated response,* often referred to as the first law of politics. It is the operation of this "law" which may account for the sharp disagreements among congressional analysts. Simply put, the law of anticipated response states that, howsoever much a senator or a congressman might be disposed to act in one way, he will act in quite another should the configuration of political forces confronting his contemplated actions make failure probable, or raise to an intolerable level the costs of his preferred course of action, either in the near or far future. Congressmen anticipate the President, the other chamber, the changing composition and distribution of power in the next Congress, the political appointee or career layers of the federal bureaucracy, state and local political and government groups, the electorate, and perhaps above all, the press. All of these will constrain what congressmen believe worth an investment of time and effort and what they believe must be written off as desirable but infeasible.

The effect of the operation of the law of anticipated response is that we are all left guessing, on a better or less well informed basis, as to what senators or congressmen would do, or would have done, if political conditions are or had been otherwise than what in fact they are or were. Such questions in the philosophy of science are known as "contrary-to-fact conditional claims" or counterfactuals.[13] As soon as the analyst wishes to know why something happened rather than something else, he is necessarily (logically) involved in making such claims. Applied to the analysis of congressional coalitions, awareness of the difficulties in establishing the truth or falsehood of such claims sharpens the researcher's sense of what he does and does not know, and clarifies the research agenda. Failure to cope with such questions leaves the analyst in the intellectually vulnerable position of assuming, *simpliciter,* that the future will be like what he believes the past to have been. And consequently he will have no systematic way of determining what political forces in Congress and elsewhere would do if the political situation changes, or what would result from a new balance of forces. Hence analyses of causality will be powerfully affected. *If anticipated responses obscure latent tendencies,* tendencies that would become operative if some critical margin of strength were added to one side or another in Congress, then in all likelihood a description of the current situation that ignored such tendencies would be grossly misleading, confusing actors and observers alike about what is possible and probable. Such errors are as easy to make from inside the Congress as from outside looking in. A good example of the operation of the law of anticipated response, embedded in a counterfactual claim, is seen in the following statement by Majority Whip Senator Alan Cranston. Asked whether Majority Leader Robert Byrd's prediction that attempts to repeal 14B of the Taft-Hartley Law ("right-to-work" laws) was dead for the Ninety-fifth Congress, first session, he replied:

I think it probably is. The leadership of the House feels that in light of the experience of [the vote] for site picketing, that there's no point to going through an exercise in trying to repeal 14B of Taft-Hartley. And the Senate is not likely to extend itself and put people on the spot in going one way or the other on either of those issues if in the House there's no prospect of passage of the bill.[14]

In sum, it seems necessary to take account of such sources of complexity if well-founded conclusions are to be achieved concerning the nature of congressional coalitions, and in order to adjudicate between rival "pluralist" and "ideological" theories. These complexities and the general import of choosing among contending theories present a challenge to undertake a systematic analysis of congressional coalitions. That is the purpose of this study. But if the resulting analysis is to have any likelihood of being true, it will have to be well grounded in both observation of the congressional context, and in awareness of different policy analysis perspectives. Hence this study uses a "contextual" modification of the usual approach to analyzing congressional coalitions systematically.

NOTES

1. Address of Governor Nelson A. Rockefeller of New York at the Sixty-ninth Annual Meeting of the American Political Science Association, Fairmont-Roosevelt Hotel, New Orleans, Louisiana, Wednesday, September 5, 1973. Pamphlet.

2. Henry Hubbard, remarks to a plenary session of the National Capital Area Political Science Association, April 19, 1975, chaired by Professor Robert Peabody (personal tape recording).

3. CBS-TV, "Face the Nation," February 20, 1977, CBS, transcript, p. 11. Interview with Speaker of the House Thomas P. O'Neill.

4. A Symposium: "What Is a Liberal—Who Is a Conservative?" special issue of *Commentary* 62, no. 3 (September 1976), with sixty-five individual commentators, including political scientists and other academics, each addressing the question of the title.

5. George W. Ball, "Cosmocorp: The Importance of Being Stateless," in Courtney C. Brown, ed., *World Business: Promise and Problems* (New York: Macmillan Co., 1970), p. 332.

6. Ibid.

7. Cf. Seyom Brown, *New Forces in World Politics* (Washington: The Brookings Institution, 1974); C. Fred Bergsten, Thomas Horst, and Theodore Moran, *American Multinationals and American Interests* (Washington: Brookings Institution, 1978); and Richard J. Barnet and Ronald E. Muller, *Global Reach: The Power of the Multinational Corporations* (New York: Simon & Schuster, 1974).

8. "HEW's Califano: Reflections on a Changing Bureaucracy," *Washington Post*, 29 March 1977, p. A6.

9. There has been an enormous amount of work revealing *change in Congress.* Among a host of congressional documents, four groups of documents merit particular attention: the hearings, prints, reports and compendia of studies by experts for (1) the (Culver) Commission on the Operation of the Senate, (2) the (Stevenson) Temporary Senate Select Committee to Study the Senate Committee System, (3) the (Bolling-Martin) House Select Committee on Committees, and (4) the reports of the Obey Commission, of the Ninety-third, Ninety-fourth, and Ninety-fifth Congresses. *The Congressional Quarterly* and *National Journal* are, as always, rich sources. Some, but by no means all, of the secondary literature in

book form in the field includes: Harrison W. Fox, Jr., and Susan Webb Hammond, *Congressional Staffs* (New York: Free Press, 1978); Roger H. Davidson and Walter J. Oleszek, *Congress Against Itself* (Bloomington: Indiana University Press, 1977); Lawrence C. Dodd and Bruce I. Oppenheimer, eds., *Congress Reconsidered* (New York: Praeger, 1977); Louis Fisher, *Presidential Spending Power* (Princeton, N.J.: Princeton University Press, 1975); Richard F. Fenno, Jr., *Congressmen in Committees* (Boston: Little, Brown and Company, 1973); Harvey C. Mansfield, Sr., ed., *Congress Against the Presidency* (New York: Praeger Publishers, 1975); Morris S. Ogul, *Congress Oversees the Bureaucracy: Studies in Legislative Supervision* (University of Pittsburgh Press, 1976); Gary Orfield, *Congressional Power: Congress and Social Change* (New York: Harcourt Brace Jovanovich, Inc., 1975); Norman J. Ornstein, ed., *Congress in Change: Evolution and Reform* (New York: Praeger Publishers, 1975); Norman Ornstein, ed., "Changing Congress: The Committee System," a special issue of *The Annals of the American Academy of Political and Social Science* 411 (January 1974); Robert L. Peabody, *Leadership in Congress: Stability, Succession, and Change* (Boston: Little, Brown, 1975); Allen Schick's forthcoming volume on the new congressional budget process; and the series of articles on Congress in *Policy Analysis* 2, no. 2 (Spring 1976).

10. Cf. Stanley Bach, "Potential Mechanisms for Integrated and Comprehensive Policy Making by the House of Representatives," unpublished manuscript draft of August 10, 1976.

11. James L. Sundquist of the Brookings Institution is currently at work on a book, *The Decline and Resurgence of Congress*, described as "A reappraisal of the continuing constitutional issue of the executive-legislative balance of power" (Brookings Program 1977, p. 6).

12. Cf. Allen Schick, "Complex Policymaking in the United States Senate," Library of Congress, Congressional Research Service, unpublished manuscript, 1976; Roger H. Davidson, "Breaking Up Those 'Cozy Triangles': An Impossible Dream?" (paper prepared for the Symposium on Legislative Reform and Public Policy, University of Nebraska, Lincoln, Nebraska, March 11-12, 1976), pp. 30-31; Allen V. Kneese and Charles L. Schultze, *Pollution, Prices and Public Policy* (Washington: Brookings Institution, 1975), pp. 112-20. All three of these project a new concept of the role of Congress that hinges on a notion of *integrated policy*; for example, we need alternative energy sources that (1) also meet environmental standards, (2) are not inflationary, (3) are safe, (4) further an energy-intensive American agricultural system, and (5) do not hurt the most vulnerable members of society. Davidson, Kneese and Schultze, and Schick all indicate that the fragmentation of power among the many subcommittees of the Congress works against such integrated policy making, thus weakening the role of Congress as a policy-making institution.

13. Roderick M. Chisholm, "The Contrary-to-Fact Conditional," in Herbert Feigl and Wilfred Sellars, eds., *Readings in Philosophical Analysis* (New York: Appleton-Century-Crofts, 1949); Nelson Goodman, "The Problem of Counterfactional Conditionals," *Fact, Fiction and Forecast* (London: University of London-Athlone Press, 1954). The logical entailment is the elementary modus tolens: $(a \rightarrow b) \rightarrow (\sim b \rightarrow \sim a)$.

14. NBC-TV, "Meet the Press," March 27, 1977 (personal tape recording). Interview with Senate Majority Whip Alan Cranston.

chapter 2

IDEOLOGY, AND THE PLURALIST AND IDEOLOGICAL THEORIES

Contrasting viewpoints characterizing congressional coalitions and cleavages fall into two theoretical categories: the "pluralist" and the "ideological." To understand the fundamental differences between these two bodies of theory, it is necessary to take utmost care to ensure that the issue is neatly joined, that no straw men have been set up, and that the strongest case has been made for all of the conflicting viewpoints. Therefore, this chapter will make three interrelated efforts at clarification: (1) to analyze conceptually meanings and usages of the concept of ideology, and refinements applied in this study, (2) to clarify different senses of "pluralism," and (3) to delineate the existing "pluralist" versus "ideological" dispute on congressional coalitions and cleavages.

THE CONCEPT OF IDEOLOGY

"Ideology" is one of the most frequently used concepts in both politics and political science. Indeed, its usage in economics and other social sciences appears to be equally great. Yet it is a term to which an enormous number of different and often contradictory meanings have been attached. It is important to understand why, despite all the confusion of meanings, the term is indispensable to political analysts. After all, why not simply do away with the term altogether, and use instead new or more precisely understood terms, such as "belief systems," "values," "attitudes," or "political philosophies"?

After perusal of the literature on the concept itself,[1] it appears that when used to analyze actual political systems and behavior, ideology as a theoretical construct is meant somehow to *link beliefs*, whether beliefs about facts or values, *and attitudes*, defined as predispositions to act in certain ways toward certain sets of objects or events, with *behavior*. Neither "beliefs," "attitudes," nor "belief system" is adequate to characterize interrelationships of political forces, whether in Congress, or in the polity generally. This inadequacy may be inferred from the fact that ideology is a concept that continues to be a central object of disagreement, even though it has been haggled over for so many decades by social scientists. Perhaps more convincingly, the concept seems unavoidable in the everyday discourse of political actors and journalists.

Political systems are comparable in terms of similarities and differences at the macro-political and micro-political levels. The effective end of the structural functionalist movement in American political science came when it was realized that it failed to provide a basis for analyzing the differences among political systems and differences between a political system at one point in time and another, which are what especially interest most political analysts. Derivatively, Karl Deutsch has pointed out that the weakness of structural functionalism is its lack of a basis by which to analyze change.[2] The theory failed to provide a framework in terms of which one could effectively compare the underlying causes that would explain, for example, why one political system under severe economic stress turned toward fascism and another did not, or why one had a greater degree of democracy or inequality than another.[3]

Analysis of power configurations in terms of "ideological" forces, with stress on actual and potential beliefs, attitudes, policies, behavior, and the interaction between micro-political and macro-political phenomena, might provide a partial alternative to structural functionalism and Marxism, which have been the only two macro-political theories taken seriously in recent years. The virtual abandonment of structural functionalism has left non-Marxists lacking in macro-political theory. Marxists, according to some analysts, have lacked empirically grounded micro-political theories and analyses, perhaps explaining why they appear to some to be impractical, given their own objectives, when dealing with the analysis of political behavior and policy. Some of the many meanings of ideology will be mentioned in what follows. But the following five considerations would seem necessary bases of a workable concept of ideology.

First, a concept of ideology must allow for verifiable inferences from claims about beliefs and attitudes to claims about behavior, in specific ranges of situations. An adequate concept must permit what is the most difficult kind of judgment to be made about the actions of an individual or of a group, namely: Were those actions opportunistic and expedient or, rather, a matter of perceived strategic necessity, in an area often defined as "the art of the possible"?

Second, the concept should allow clear *comparisons* between elite (including counterelite) and mass political perceptions and evaluations. Comparisons should be possible in situations where elite issues are quite different from issues salient to mass publics and where elite climates of opinion have structures different from those created by and for mass publics.[4]

Third, the concept of ideology must be a tool which assists in the discovery of those areas of belief and behavior that are the latent bases of *potential* coalitions and cleavages at both the elite and mass levels.

Fourth, ideology must be operationalizable in such a way that it is possible to establish empirically that "ideological patterns" per se do *not* in fact fit the range of behavior studied.

Fifth, the concept should allow analyses of the degree of ideational specificity and attitude organization actually attributable to individuals, groups, or the cue setters of cue-following groups of political actors, elite and mass. As a corollary, it should allow specification of problems unaddressed, issues avoided or met in ways that promise no resolution satisfying to others symbolically or materially—in other words, judgments of the form: He (they) *really does not (do not) have a policy* toward Latin America, or, for achieving both long-term price stability and low unemployment. This sort of judgment allows us to say that *what appears* to be a distinct ideology *is not*, since, if given power, adherents of that ideology would not do anything very different from what was done by those they opposed of supposedly contrary ideology. But, on the opposite side, the notion we employ should allow us to be able to discriminate what an ideological group *would do* under varying conditions that determine what is politically feasible, as Ralph Huitt has made exceptionally clear.[5] For example, "with enough support, the liberals would be heavily disposed to do *x*, but lacking such support in Congress they have modified their legislative proposals in such-and-such ways."[6]

From these five criteria the principal utility of a sufficiently specified concept of ideology becomes evident. It must be a concept which relates a number of fundamental notions like democracy, equality, economic growth, human capital, the free market, justice, efficiency, capital supply, freedom, investment, community, transcendental self-realization, economic concentration, cognitive economy, productivity, market entry, and others, to real political behavior in highly contextually specific situations, and to institutions embedded in historically conditioned political experiences and cultures. The concept of ideology must allow the specification of such relationships, in turn, to advance political scientists' fundamental professional responsibility: to describe validly and reliably political forces in such a way as to understand the *net* directions in which a political system is moving, and why. The directions themselves must be described in terms of the broad allocations of values, and in terms of stability, nondisruptive change, conflictual change, or some mix thereof. Above all, ideology should be well enough understood to enable claims to be made validly about how belief and behavior *would* change/or evolve as the *configuration of forces and circumstances* might change.

Analyses of Congress have often seemed to accent continuities over changes.[7] Perhaps this is due to the fact that large changes in Congress are a relatively new phenomena, coming after a quiescent period of several decades. But it does *not* seem that these changes in Congress, particularly in the House, which have occurred in the late 1960s and especially in the 1970s, and the implications of those changes for American politics generally, have been well absorbed into the conventional wisdom of American politics. But with the growing involvement of Congress in every aspect of government policy just at the time when there is an explosion of complexity in policy making generally, with the transformations of the national and international economies now underway, and with the ongoing demythologizing of the American presidency, one might well argue that a new era in American history has begun which will cause a change in the way Congress is analyzed. If so, it seems timely to reexamine our most basic notions of Congress. The concept of ideology as described seems a useful tool for such a reappraisal.

Ideology as a Theoretical Construct

This study relies heavily on Converse's formal construction of the concept of ideology.[8] This construct has increasingly come under attack by some and has been applied by others who have essentially changed the original conceptualization.[9] The attacks have focused on the applications of Converse's model to the analysis of the relationship between elite and mass belief systems. However, there are no criticisms extant of Converse's concept of ideology as applied to elites alone. Therefore, this study need not directly address the cited criticisms of Converse's use of the concept.

The Structural Component—Dimensionality

The structural component, as Converse described it,[10] centers on the notions of "constraint" or "dimensional structuring" over a wide range of political attitudes (rooted in values and empirical beliefs), some more "central" than others, with "contextual grasp" and "levels of conceptualization" sufficient to result in "functional interdependence of attitudes," and especially the interdependence between specific and general idea elements. As Converse stipulated, fully developed ideologies are characterized as those which enable a person to carry on four functions: (1) to attach clear political meaning to events both proximate and remote in space and time, and to see relationships between a specific event or a specific issue and more general issues and political relationships; (2) to make such understandings consistent with other previously held values and beliefs of wide range, and hence;

(3) to absorb and code far more new political information; and (4) to achieve cognitive economies in making political judgments and choices.

A full "ideologue" possesses conceptual yardsticks or "crowning postures"—Converse specified liberalism and conservatism—which can be readily applied to the decision to believe or reject a claim of fact or value with relatively low costs of (cognitive economies in) acquiring additional information, and in validly analyzing that information in order to make such decisions. A person with such conceptual yardsticks and with "contextual grasp" can reliably and validly infer a great deal more from a little bit of political information about a situation at hand. In empirical democratic theory the use of these conceptual yardsticks is most pertinently related to judgment and choice of political candidates and officeholders to be held accountable through the electoral process. Thus knowing a congressman's position on two or more specific issues allows those with fully developed ideologies to predict correctly that congressman's general policy orientations and his membership in a party or ideological faction, and vice versa. From that knowledge such full "ideologues" can infer to many other positions that a politician has taken or will take, with due reference to intervening contextual variables, such as the visibility of the issue and the degree of latitude allowed the politician by his minimum winning base of support.[11]

It is this cognitive economizing advantage which explains why Washington elites seem compelled, according to George Reedy, former Johnson White House press secretary, UPI correspondent for the House, and Senate staffer, to place a "senator who comes to Washington . . . very quickly . . . into the class of liberal, conservative, or moderate (the latter usually meaning nondescript). . . ."[12] What is of central importance here is that some political scientists have challenged the validity of such labels because of findings showing congressmen as much more liberal or conservative in one policy area than another.[13]

It must be emphasized, in relation to the central contention of this study, that if such past findings were correct, *it would not be possible to use the terms "liberal" and "conservative," or any other ideological label, with any clear denotation* regarding general policy orientations of specific congressmen, since with low rank order correlations across policy domains, *most congressmen would be significantly more or less liberal or conservative in one policy dimension than in another.* It would follow that one would be precluded from validly referring to a *unidimensional*[14] liberal-conservative (or left-right)[15] ideological spectrum along which congressmen were arrayed. That in turn would lend support to contrary descriptive and explanatory theories of congressional cleavages, coalitions, and of the nature of the policy differences separating different groups of congressmen, and, most important, *of policy outcomes.* If one cannot discern broad ideological cleavages and coalitions, then all one can discern will be narrower and more fragmented coalitions and cleavages. Hence certain interest group theories,[16] certain versions of pluralist theory[17] and end-of-ideology theories[18] will, by default, be all that remains to refer to in measuring or describing political forces in Congress as a basis for explaining outcomes. Similarly, policy issues would be analyzed on a piecemeal basis, instead of in terms of their cumulative effects, when combined with many other programs, on net systemic and distributive outcomes.[19] End-of-ideology theories would tend to lead one to treating the purely technical aspects of issues, taken one at a time, at the expense of examining overarching integrative value orientations to political and governmental problems.[20]

The Content Component of Ideology—The Policy Cut Points Method

In this study, the policy content of the ideologies of U.S. congressmen is hypothesized as being structured by at most four major dimensions: economic issues, foreign policy, race, and civil liberties and democracy. Commonly referred to in journalistic accounts of Congress, these are the explicit dimensions utilized by the staff of the Americans for Democratic Action in composing their ratings of congressmen.[21] As Clausen points out, the initial selection of dimensions does not preclude the possibility that they can be collapsed into fewer dimensions, if the different dimensions are (1) so highly correlated, and (2) so "substantively coherent" that a single dimension can validly be inferred from two or more of the original dimensions.[22] Indeed, the validity of collapsing all four of the preceding dimensions into a single left-right dimension is the central hypothesis of this study.

The methodology utilized here follows Clausen's own "conceptual" approach, as contrasted to what he calls the "objective" approach.[23] Both the conceptual and objective approaches proceed inductively from the universe of roll call votes actually taken on the floor, but the conceptual approach also employs certain substantive criteria for exclusion from, and classification of, roll call votes in roll call sets. In this study, criteria are provided for both the exclusion and classification of roll calls vis-à-vis roll call sets. Roll call data are related to interview data, and the study links the roll call voting stage of the legislative process to prior stages and the anticipation of succeeding stages. Knowledge of contextual and policy constraints are systematically built into the method of analysis of this study.

This study adds to the conceptual approach what may be described as the "policy-cut-points" procedure. A policy cut point is defined as that difference between two or more adjacent but contrary positions on more or less specific issues, which forces a member to take a clear stand for or against one or another of these positions when questioned, without easily being able to equivocate or disguise his real issue orientation. The procedure is based on the key hypothesis of the ideological model of the study, namely, that there are a very limited number of general and related issues, such as who benefits and who pays for enactment of legislation, that (1) systematically divide the members, and (2) are manifest in a plethora of particular issues and interests across time.[24] These general issues can be delineated in terms of different policy positions (regarding both general policy questions and narrower issues) that are contrary to one another in both the cumulative and proximity scale model senses specified by Herbert Weisberg.[25]

In the first stage of the policy cutpoints procedure, a discrete range of *possible* positions of different congressmen is plotted on salient issues in the four policy dimensions, as derived from congressional documents, public statements of congressmen, and journalistic accounts of the motivations of members supporting or opposing particular legislation or policy approaches. Saliency is similarly derived. Any significant *empirical* association among congressmen's policy positions, especially in their reasoning on, or justification of, positions, implies the likelihood of the latent existence of underlying and more basic policy or ideological dispositions, following Converse. It is these more basic ideological dispositions that are the true hypothetical constructs of the analysis, and these are delineated in the second stage of the procedure. Subsequently, in the third stage, these ideological dispositions are empirically tested for the degree of their actual saturation of individual behaviors and attitudes. They are assumed to be operative whether via elite cue setting, via a member's own ideas, via constituency pressures, or via a combination of all three.[26] The procedure is similar to the approach suggested by the late David Minar: "Another approach to the study of ideology that may yield some of the relevance of the macro-approach and some of the rigor of the micro, proceeds from the study of policy backward through behavior to the ideational antecedents."[27] In other words, in order to differentiate among congressmen, one must be able to differentiate their policy dispositions. Political labels or classifications, like any other form of label, not only permit cognitive economies, they also direct attention to similarities and differences among policies and political actors.

Study of the behavior of any group of elites will be advanced by resort to at least a primary analysis of that elite's own perceptions and evaluations of the acts they perform. The policy-cut-points procedure begins with those perceptions—positions and their justifications—and analyzes how they are applied, adapted, qualified, and contradicted in practice when particular decisions are made. The policy-cut-points procedure is additive to, but may be carried out independently of, analysis of the evolving processes and institutional structures of Congress, and analysis of the balance of political forces within Congress and between Congress and other power centers. Clearly all *three* kinds of analysis must be integrated with a *fourth*, namely, analysis of the electoral process, broadly conceived, for an in-depth understanding of Congress.

Well-informed journalists of the national press, usually those who follow a policy area for a considerable period, use the policy-cut-points method to pin down a congressman or an official who may be trying to duck an issue in order to please opposing constituencies or one who effectively has no policy. Such a journalist has knowledge of the policy area in question in sufficient depth to identify clearly the unavoidable policy choices that must be confronted, their assumptions and expected effects, and the conditions necessary and sufficient for their implementation. The procedure also rests on the understanding that each issue differs in some respect from the larger set of those issues with which it shares properties in common. Well-versed policy analysts will recognize not only those differences but also whether those differences are, or are not, significant enough to a congressman to isolate the issue in his mind from the policy reasoning usually applied to the larger set of issues.

The successful construction of interview schedules and coding of roll call votes according to the policy-cut-points procedure is dependent upon a thorough knowledge of the policy content of the positions taken and the perceived linkages, or differences, among issues as held by Members. The identification of latent policy dispositions and their substantive content requires study of congressional disputes and reasoning in a wide range of issue areas. In the case of Congress there is a record so rich, particularly in the committee hearings, other documents, and the *Congressional Record,* that the investigator is at a great advantage as compared with those studying other elites and mass groups.[28]

The Content Component of Ideology—Refraction

Four recurrent political themes have exhibited remarkable durability over the millennia. They are: (1) war, militarism, and peace, (2) privilege and deprivation, (3) repression and democracy, and (4) racial (or ethnic or religious) conflict. The quarter-century of American history between 1945 and 1970 was marked by conflict-reducing advantages enjoyed uniquely by the United States, which alone emerged from the devastation of World War II relatively unscathed and in a strong financial and economic position. Many events mark the ending of that period of American advantage, no single event more than the action of President Nixon on August 15, 1971, when he suspended the convertibility of the dollar into gold, thereby ending the Bretton Woods system of international finance that had structured international economic relations for that quarter-century.[29] Both the sharp blow administered to all oil-consuming countries by the raising of oil prices by the OPEC cartel, and the changing agenda of international affairs as perceived by some[30] threaten new and unknown dangers for, and constraints on, American politics and governmental institutions. It seems that the literature on Congress has yet to reflect, in any systematic way, the effects of these changes of the 1970s on Congress and its coalitions.

"Ideological" as it is used here refers to core dispositions, which will be discussed, that engage these four recurrent themes as (1) "refracted" through theories of economics and politics, and (2) "refracted" contextually, through perceptions of the political situation at any particular moment. To find ideology manifest in behavior, one must identify the channels of refraction.

With regard to *theoretical refraction*, some close observers identify such refraction in terms of "code words." But behind code words lie more or less specified theories of the economy, polity, society, and world order, and their interrelations. These theories are held with a greater or lesser degree of ideational specificity by those who react to them. But the process whereby some congressmen set cues for other congressmen allows for large differences among congressmen who vote alike and yet vary widely in their grasp of such refractory theories, that is, in the ideational specificity of their mapping of a political issue. The most obvious examples of such a refractory theory are what is constantly referred to inside and outside of Congress as "the trickle down" theory by liberals and "a favorable investment climate" by conservatives in the economic policy dimension.

What is evident from perusal of the *Congressional Record* and other congressional documents are the frequently stated linkages between (1) such theories as referred to by senators and congressmen, and (2) their explicit references to different socioeconomic classes. Contrary to pluralist theories of legislative behavior, ideological theories *focus on* the *linkages* between actual legislation and ideologies based on different dispositions toward privilege and deprivation, domestically and abroad, with special reference to the mediating role of theories of the economy through which different specific issues and behavior are "refracted." What is less obvious, perhaps, is how the four broad dimensions of political conflict—economic issues, race issues, civil liberties-democracy issues, and foreign policy issues—are theoretically and politically enmeshed. This meshing will be discussed in the concluding chapter.

Contextual refraction is another phenomenon that, with theoretical refraction, must be understood in order to reveal ideology. For congressmen, or at least cue-setting congressional leaders, determining the full range of *effects* of a given policy, bill, or legislative package is one major source of contextual complexity. Questions must be answered with regard to who benefits, who pays, who endures new risks, how groups not specifically considered in the formulation of legislation might be affected indirectly (the economists' "externalities"), and what the short- and long-term effects will be on the *structure* of the economy, society, and polity as a whole. Whether or not such determinations are in whole or in part actually accomplished is a major variable in the legislative process.

A second source of contextual complexity is the political context surrounding the legislation. Questions are inevitably raised regarding the political weight of a group with a more or less intense position on an issue, that group's political resources and its capacity and inclination to mobilize others as part of a general all-over calculation of a safe electoral margin of either an individual Member, an ideological faction, or a presidential coalition. Measurement of the relevant variables is very difficult when such questions are raised and adequately specified conceptually.[31] Questions of political feasibility, as described so well by the Huitt article, are stubbornly subtle matters. The presentation of issues to target audiences, and the receptions of, and the reactions to, such presentations, feed back into the legislative process, affecting by anticipations the intent underlying an individual's legislative action and the character of coalition behavior. When in addition such calculations become part of strategies for presenting issues through different channels to different target audiences, and involve how messages sent turn into quite different messages received, we can understand the complexity of the interaction of politics and policy. We must refine our analysis of congressional coalitions accordingly.

There are several factors, some already noted, that allow one to imagine reasonably how strong and persistent ideological regularities can occur in a setting of contextual and policy-related complexities: (1) the division of labor within the committee system, which allows especially House Members (albeit unevenly) to become specialists, with senators hiring professional staff to match House Members in specialization; (2) ideological cueing among Members as the mechanism of coordination at the roll call voting stage; (3) staff coordination; (4) continuity of involvement by interest group and policy analysis communities; (5) committee Member coordination at earlier stages of the legislative process; (6) the role of the elected leadership; and (7) the desire of a legislator to be able to say he voted with his President or his party, or with some group of congressmen that lends *him* credibility.

The problem of analyzing contextual refraction adds to the problem of capturing complexity in a structured analysis of congressional coalitions and cleavages: The problem must be taken into account in any serious effort to solve the problem of adjudicating between the vastly different pluralist and ideological perspectives on Congress. This necessity is rooted in the methodological requirement that unless each and every indicator is correctly classified in terms of the contextual factors that were taken into account by the Members, then Members' statements or acts that we may interpret as indicators of generalized dispositions—including the pluralists' postulated disposition to have no generalized disposition—may well be invalid and unreliable as indicators. In a situation in which indicators are not thus *contextually validated,* one might well expect negative findings.

THE CONCEPT OF PLURALISM

Just as the concept of ideology required clarification, so it is important to recognize (1) that the term "pluralism" has a number of quite different meanings, and (2) that if we fail to distinguish those senses of pluralism which do not contradict the ideological theory from that which does, the reader will quite understandably be confused and perhaps misled.

In one sense, almost all Americans are pluralists: They are fearful of concentrations of unaccountable power in too few hands. The creation of power leads naturally, for most Americans, to questions of how effective and independent *plural* countervailing forces can be created that will prevail through an "open" political process in instances of the abuse or arbitrary exercise of power. In its *academic garb*, this traditional and familiar theory, with emphasis on procedural democracy, the "openness" and "multiple access points" of the American political system, while it seems at this time to be subject to some erosion in surprising quarters,[32] is still a popular academic theory of not only how power *should* be restrained, but also of how power actually is restrained.

A second sense of pluralism has accented the desirability of studying groups in society, including organized interest groups, as a means of better understanding the political system and how it operates. In affirming the limited value of this sense of group theory or interest group focus, there are no dissenters. Extrapolations from such studies are, however, seldom guided by the findings alone, for they are at too low a level of analysis to provide, by themselves, the basis for systemic inferences.

A third, sociological-historical, sense of pluralism is especially American: the awareness of the extraordinary diversity of the political sociology of the United States. This diversity is dimensionalized regionally, racially, ethnically, religiously, economically, and culturally. It is intermixed with a set of partisan attachments based as much on relatively independent and historically idiosyncratic events as on any shared programmatic tendencies. Asynchronous historical developments led the Democratic party to a coalition of southern Bourbon Democrats and immigrant eastern urban Democrats, and led northeastern and midwestern middle-class white Protestants into common Republicanism with financial barons of the twentieth century, found in the great law firms, banking houses, and corporate headquarters of New York, Philadelphia, Boston, Chicago, and a few other great commercial cities.

But countervailing historical developments are overriding the political sociology of the past, as the abundant evidence of national party decomposition indicates sharply.[33] These developments, which cannot help but be reflected in Congress and its coalitions, include the geographical, social, cultural, occupational, and intellectual mobility of Americans since World War II, the economic development of the South and West, the impact of national mass communications media, Vietnam, Watergate, and ever greater interdependence between national and world economies. Particularistic attributes of local political consciousness seem less likely to dominate, though they may well channel, awareness of national and international events. Perhaps they will permanently lose their importance in the face of threats of increased inflation and unemployment, and other economic dislocations and insecurities. Overall, it is most important to emphasize that the relative causal weight of these factors, as they flow through already existing belief systems and political structures, must be *empirically* investigated.

Until now, in part because of these historically ingrained sectional and ethnic habits and isolation from national decision making, broad contemporary national questions may not have had the chance to become linked with stable ideological party identifications with enough strength to overwhelm local particularistic traditions in congressional elections. They still may not. But there has been an avalanche of evidence familiar to political scientists that these traditionalistic bases of party identification have sharply eroded. It seems especially worthwhile to ask whether existing pluralistic particularisms, regional, ethnic, or whatever, are lagged effects of a passing era, or, rather, structural and unchanging constraints on an emerging era increasingly characterized by the saliency of economic issues. Lowi makes the argument compellingly that, "It is wrong to assume that social pluralism (which is an undeniable fact about America) produced political pluralism."[34]

None of the previous senses of "pluralism" is inconsistent with the ideological theory and its description of congressional coalitions and cleavages. It is clear, however, that those pluralists who have denied a significant role to ideology, henceforth simply "pluralists," drew much sustenance and inspiration, indeed understandably, from the preceding *conceptions* of pluralism. The sense of pluralism that concerns us here is what may be called *interest group pluralism*.

Virtually all commentators attribute to James Madison the basic ends and means around which the American constitutional order was originally arranged and which still structure contemporary pluralist thought. Madison emphasizes two main themes, of which one carries over into pluralist thought in our own time. In *Federalist No. 10* he defines the problem of tyranny in government as rooted in "factions," that is, groups "united . . . by some common impulse of passion, or of interest, *adverse* to the rights of other citizens, or to the permanent and aggregate interests of the community" (italics added).[35] And then he asserts two fundamental themes. The first addresses the relation between the *propertied and the propertyless* (the latter including small impecunious farmers): "But the most common and durable source of factions has been the various and unequal distribution of property. Those who hold and those who are without property have ever formed distinct interests in society." The second addresses divisions *among* propertied interests: "A landed interest, a manufacturing interest, a mercantile interest, a moneyed interest, with many lesser interests grow up of necessity in civilized nations, and divide them into different classes, actuated by different sentiments and views."[36] A likely corollary to the thesis of divided property interests was a thesis of divided unpropertied interests, which brings us back to the implicit assumption of Lowi's point cited earlier, that sociological (or economic) pluralism is often taken to imply, *a priori*, political pluralism, without benefit of evidence.

It is the counterpoint between these two relations—the relation of the propertied (clearly the minority in Madison's view) to the propertyless (the majority in Madison's view), and the relations *among* holders of different kinds of property—that has been unclear in many commentaries on early and contemporary pluralist theory.

Without doubt, Madison's principal concern, and indeed, fear, was of majority tyranny, that is, the tyranny of the propertyless majority. He states at the beginning of *Federalist No. 10:* "The diversity in the faculties of men, from which the rights of property originate . . . [is such that] the protection of these faculties is the first object of government." He closes his defense of the new Constitution with its imposition of federal power on the several states as follows: "A rage for paper money, for abolition of debts, for an equal division of property, or any other improper or wicked project, will be less apt to pervade the whole body of the Union than a particular member of it." These statements were not idle rhetoric. Madison spoke of them before the Constitutional Convention,[37] and these themes reflected the experiences of the states under the Articles of Confederation. The main object of Madison's inquiry in *Federalist No. 10* is *how* to contain such threats from the propertyless majority. His strategy, manifest in *his* use of the separation of powers, bicameralism, and federalism, already in vogue, but which might have been superseded when he wrote the Constitution, suited his purpose well. He was not indirect in the statement of his strategy.

> By what means is this object attainable? Evidently by one of two only. Either the existence of the same passion or interest in a majority at the same time must be prevented, or the majority, having such coexistent passion or interest must be rendered by their number and local situation unable to concert and carry into effect schemes of oppression. If the impulse and the opportunity be suffered to coincide, we well know that neither moral nor religious motives can be relied on as an adequate control.

His strategy reflects well his keen understanding of the counterpoint of all politics at all times and places: Divide and conquer versus unite and conquer. But Madison's second theme, that different kinds of propertied men would *divide* against one another, appears to provide an essential balance to the first theme. It is this latter strain that forms the apparent core of contemporary pluralist thinking. This latter strain is the true foil to the ideological theory, even though for Madison it is linked to the prior theme of the conflict of the propertied against the propertyless which seems to reflect the ideological theory. It is important to understand how both views could be held by the same powerful and theoretically acute political leader.

The argument against majoritarianism and its dangers was aimed at persuading those representatives in the states whose task was to decide on the question of ratification of the Constitution. The argument against "leveling" majoritarianism drew the conclusion that new federal power was needed to protect property and stabilize the economy. The second argument, however, that the propertied minority was sufficiently *divided* among different interests that they would not concert their efforts decisively as a faction against the majority, aimed at a different conclusion, namely, that *nothing need be done* via the proposed Constitution to structure power against that possibility. The addition of the Bill of Rights to the Constitution by forces in the states and the swift rise of the Hamiltonian Federalist party and the majoritarian Jeffersonian Democratic-Republican party give evidence that Madison was something less than wholly persuasive with his second argument in his own time.[38]

Contemporary pluralism, in the version dominant among political scientists in the past few decades, has ignored Madison's first theme and accented the second. Current work on Congressional coalitions also reiterates Madison's second them alone. Among the leading pluralist theoreticians in political science have been David Truman, Robert Lane, Nelson Polsby, the last a *doyen* among Congress experts.

Samuel P. Huntington, in describing contemporary pluralists, noted that they saw in pluralism one overriding advantage:

> It was a way of dispersing power and insuring (through cross-cutting cleavages) moderation in politics. . . . *Within the basic ideological consensus of American politics,* the only conflicts which could take place were the relatively minor ones among interest groups over their marginal shares in the economic pie.[39]

Surprisingly, in the very same period that pluralist political scientists were projecting from theory and empirical analyses the second Madisonian theme, they ignored the empirical analyses of the Michigan Survey Research Center. These analyses were perhaps best summed up by Donald Stokes, then a leading analyst of the SRC, when he wrote:

> Indeed the benefit to the Democrats from their party's sponsorship of disadvantaged elements of American society is an antique theme of our party politics. Even in the mid-1950's and the early 1960's, the volume of comment approving the Democrats and disapproving the Republicans in terms of the interests of the common man was impressive.[40]

How the pluralist's theme could be reconciled with the Michigan group's findings has never been made clear, at least at the mass level. Comparisons at the elite level with regard to congressmen will be discussed.

Huntington further noted of the pluralists that they "had no theory of change . . . and also shed little light on the comparisons and contrasts between American politics and that of other societies." He relates how pluralism has come under severe attack from a few essential and familiar arguments: the unequal resources, access, and representation of some groups as compared with others, and the lack of any concept of the public interest that might transcend the interests of any group.[41]

In more familiar terms, pluralism *denied* that class interests, howsoever refracted, explained political behavior, while asserting that pluralistic interests which were essentially *idiosyncratic* in the manner in which they combined in coalitions, *did* "explain" political behavior.

In the history of political thought, from Plato and Aristotle down through Machiavelli, Marx, and Weber, inequality among "classes" has been a crucial notion in terms of which political coalitions and, from a prudential as much as a moral point of view, the stability of society and polity have been analyzed. Too much inequality could lead, it has always been asserted, to instability. Inequality has been conceived of in terms primarily of *absolute* substantive deprivations, and not merely *relative* differences in well-being. The term "class" has had many meanings in the history of political, economic, and social thought, reflecting the complexity of social stratifiction in different societies.[42] But at all times the concept of class has retained a constant core of meaning, referring to broad systematic differences in the distribution of suffering and well-being. Madison, by placing at least equal weight on the thesis that "those who hold, and those who are without property, have ever formed distinct interests in society"[43] was surely invoking the importance of class differences as they have been commonly understood across the ages, despite his being interpreted as the intellectual forefather of the contemporary pluralists of American political science. In these contrasting pluralist and ideological views of the basis of political coalitions there would seem to lie an exposed nerve ending. The ideological theory, as Lowi notes, is rooted in concepts of the class basis of opposing political coalitions.[44] But if one were to sum up the contemporary pluralist interest group theory, whether applied to congressional coalitions or to American politics generally, one could say that its thesis was essentially a negative one, namely, that *there is no coalition,* durable across issues or time, with any clear common characteristic among its members regarding issues of privileged, deprivation, class, the economically powerful or disadvantaged at home or abroad, howsoever refracted. The ideological consistency thesis claims *there are* such stable or consistent coalitions by which the legislative struggle is best described.

Pluralism has a virtue that makes it extraordinarily attractive, and that is its attachment to the *avoidance of conflict.* This virtue is not merely grafted on to the theory but is inherent in it. The pluralist denies that there are any fundamental social or economic cleavages in American society, or even if there are some, like race, transferring the conflict-oriented aspects of such cleavages to American politics would, under most, and probably all conditions merely make the problem worse rather than better. On the supposition that conflict is something most citizens, let alone politicians, would do their utmost to avoid, it should not be surprising that pluralism has had such appeal. It is only in times of widespread deprivation, insecurity, and dislocation that we should expect an increase in ideological politics, at least on a wide basis.

It is a very large question indeed, dealt with in the literature on public opinion, whether the period of the 1960s and 1970s in the United States, marked by the civil rights movement, the Vietnam War, Watergate, and the economic troubles of the 1970s, impressed Americans *deeply enough* to produce the kind of bitter cleavages in opinion that mark the intensification of politics, the conflictual politics we generally call "ideological." Can it now be said with the pluralists that most Americans all want essentially the same structure of economy and society, or perceive a broad consensual foundation available as a basis for reconciling competing interests?

Undoubtedly readers of this study already have strong views on that question. That is good, for these views should therefore provoke them to examine closely the data and analyses here, which *do* suggest an intensification of political conflict, that is, a presence of deep and durable ideological politics at the elite level, specifically in the Congress in the early and mid-1970s. But the reader should bear in mind that, once entered into the arena of elite polities, the modes of conflict take many forms and are obscured in the subtleties of anticipated responses and contrary-to-fact conditional claims.

It was in just the spirit of pluralism described previously that Lyndon Johnson, a masterful politician in all things (except the one time he went in for painful, probably principled conflict in Vietnam), said:

> The biggest danger to American stability is the politics of principle, which brings out the masses in irrational fights for unlimited goals, for once the masses begin to move, then the whole thing begins to explode. Thus it is for the sake of nothing less than stability that I consider myself a consensus man.[45]

To a remarkable extent, that is also what the bulk of the literature in American political science was saying in the 1950s and 1960s, and well into the 1970s. It is subtly being replaced by a cynical school, which, by proclaiming the utter corruption and/or narrow selfishness and egotism of nearly *all* politicians, comes out with a variant of interest group pluralism, namely, hopelessness regarding even enlightened self-interest in politics to the point of hyperbolic and irrational corruption. Such cynicism provides a

TABLE 2-1
Polsby's Determinants of Transformativeness in Legislatures

Independence of Legislature	*Example*	*Parliamentary Organizing Majorities*	*Parliamentary Party Management*	*Successive Policy Majorities*
Highly transformative	United States	Highly coalitional	Very decentralized	Very flexible
Modified transformative	Netherlands	Coalitional	Decentralized	Flexible
	Sweden	Moderately coalitional	Moderately decentralized	Moderately flexible
Modified arena	Germany	Coalitional	Moderately decentralized	Moderately flexible
	Italy	Coalitional centralized	Moderately fixed	Moderately
	France IV	Unstable	Decentralized	Flexible
Arena	United Kingdom	Moderately coalitional	Centralized	Fixed
	Belgium	Narrowly based	Centralized	Fixed
	France V	Narrowly based	Centralized	Fixed

SOURCE: Nelson W. Polsby, "Legislatures," in Fred I. Greenstein and Nelson W. Polsby, eds., *Handbook of Political Science* (Reading, Mass.: Addison-Wesley Publishing Co., 1975), 5:296.

different but no less effective basis for the same avoidance of conflict. Given the cynical view, all principled conflict is ultimately pointless, all political efforts toward idealism or justice, a dumb show, easily stopped by the realities of a uniformly grasping selfishness and corruption, or at least timidity.

CONGRESSIONAL COALITIONS: THE PLURALISM-IDEOLOGY DISPUTE

The political science literature has been marked by sharp disputes over the significance of ideology in congressional behavior and in the American political system.[46] The early work of Philip Converse[47] and recent statements of John Kingdon[48] assign importance to the role of ideology in the belief systems or voting decisions of congressmen, whereas Donald Matthews and James Stimson,[49] along with Aage Clausen,[50] stridently attack what they term the "ideologist theory." Herbert McClosky[51] has gone to great lengths over the years to show, empirically, ideology at work in the American political system generally, and Robert Lane in his classic piece, "The Politics of Consensus in an Age of Affluence"[52] denied its significance. Nelson Polsby, in a review of the literature on legislatures, places the "successive policy majorities" of Congress at the most pluralistic end of a pluralism-ideology continuum, characterizing successive congressional majorities as "very flexible" (see Table 2-1).

The current literature is primarily represented by the well-known studies by Clausen and Matthews and Stimson.[53] These studies involved intensive empirical investigation and, for Matthews and Stimson, immersion in the currents of the congressional context. What follows is only the barest outline of the different positions taken. Further discussion can be found in Chapter 5.

Matthews and Stimson state their position as follows:

> Ideological voting undoubtedly occurs in the House of Representatives, but not often enough to serve as a general model of how congressmen usually make up their minds.
>
> Upon reflection, this is really not very surprising. Congressmen vote on concrete and specific policy proposals rather than on policy in the round. Most bills and resolutions have little or no manifest ideological content, and, when they do, they generally involve several dimensions of conflict rather than just one.[54]

Clausen explicitly refers to and adopts Matthews and Stimson's description and critique of the "ideologist" model and extends that critique. He states:

> I am in full accord with the critique of the ideologist theory. In fact, the policy dimension theory [Clausen's own] is offered as a means of differentiating between different policy concerns currently bundled together in the liberal-conservative dimension. Thus, a policy is labeled as being conservative or liberal and thus the assumption is made that liberals and conservatives will take opposite sides. However, all people labeled as conservatives do not always agree, nor is there some undifferentiated bloc of liberals always taking the same position. *Different alignments form as the policy content changes.* [Italics added.][55]

The italicized sentence restates in different terms the familiar pluralist thesis of evershifting coalitions, or, in Polsby's phrase cited earlier, "very flexible successive majorities."

Certain statements by John Kingdon represent the opposing view of the role of ideology in Congress. It should be noted with emphasis, however, that these statements are made in the spirit of side comments, and cannot be interpreted as central to Kingdon's model of congressional voting, which refers to "policy goals" and "policy attitudes" rather than "ideology." Kingdon has resorted to the very methodology that Matthews and Stimson laud in an earlier work as the most indicative, that is, what they call the direct study of the "intervening processes of decision."[56] Contrary to Polsby, Matthews and Stimson, and to Clausen, Kingdon notes: "Many of the patterns which we have traditionally attributed to institutional factors, therefore, may instead be functions of partisan and ideological conflict or consensus." Kingdon appreciates that partisan and ideological factors are *not* independent, asserting that

> . . . for all practical purposes, congressmen overwhelmingly pick informants from within their party grouping. Once again the most "inbred" group is the Northern Democrats. In keeping with their pivotal position between the two major parties and their small numbers, the Southern Democrats turn to informants in other parties more often than do the Republicans and Northern Democrats.[57]

Kingdon further states:

> Given a legislative environment containing a flurry of contradictory cues and pressures, any mechanism which reinforces and, thus, promotes behavioral stability is of great importance, whether one views such an effect normatively as being a net gain or loss.
>
> There is some *fragmentary* evidence in my data which indicates the importance of this selection of cues *according to ideology.* If one takes all the possible pairs of actors and examines only those cases in which the two actors of a given pair were in conflict, one finds in virtually every pair that liberals (as measured by a relatively high Americans for Democratic Action score) tend to vote with the liberal actor of the pair, and that conservatives tend to vote with the conservative actor, regardless of which actors are involved. While *this tendency to vote with the actor with whom the congressman shares a general ideological viewpoint* varies in strength from one pair to another, *it is nearly always present.* [Italics added.][58]

Authoritative and testimonial support for the ideological view and for a nonpluralist perspective on interest groups comes from Lawrence O'Brien, congressional liaison chief for Presidents Kennedy and Johnson. Commenting on his experience in those assignments in his recent autobiography, O'Brien states:

> I learned in my years on Capitol Hill just how difficult it is to achieve social progress in America. Powerful forces are arrayed against any legislative proposal they think will affect their wealth or influence—for every Medicare, one might say, there is an American Medical Association. Sometimes in my mind's eye I saw two great armies facing one another across a vast field of battle. One army—our army—was led by the President and included in its ranks the forces of organized labor, the urban political leaders, the emerging black political spokesmen, and many of the nation's intellectual luminaries.
>
> Ours was a formidable force, and yet facing us was a no less powerful legislative

army led by such Republican stalwarts as Ev Dirksen and Charlie Halleck, backed by the vast resources of the American business community, the major corporations and especially the oil industry, as well as the medical profession, and important segments of rural and suburban America.

These two armies fought battle after battle on Capitol Hill, with one now gaining the advantage, then the other. In the long view, in terms of my lifetime, the Democratic force has seemed to move ahead, to win more often than it lost, but it was always slow progress, inch by inch, vote by vote, with much bloodshed and heartbreak along the way.[59]

This study tests systematically that proposition for which Kingdon states that he has "fragmentary evidence," which O'Brien clearly indicates, and which Matthews and Stimson, Clausen, and Polsby vigorously deny—that ideology plays a preponderant role in congressmen's voting decisions.

Other previous findings have purported to show that ideology might be operative in some issue domains with some considerable strength while exhibiting little strength in other issue domains, notably foreign policy. This study also tests that proposition.[60]

In their latest work, however, Matthew and Stimson discount the significance of Kingdon's study by noting:

By way of contrast, John Kingdon's ingenious research design could not be applied to decision-making on more than a few roll calls. Since selectivity was inescapable, he chose to confine his attention to highly visible, controversial, "big" votes. *Congressmen's Voting Decisions,* p. 16. His model therefore pertains to a different set of roll calls than ours.[61]

If legislative behavior *can* be described best by an ideological model, then legislatures may be seen to function as a primary arena of a nonviolent struggle over the authoritative allocation of values.

The Lowi distinctions, it may be argued, provide an alternative to both the ideological and the pluralist theories. Lowi's familiar distinctions separating policies—"distributive," "regulative," and "redistributive"—have had a large impact on perceptions of congressional coalitions and cleavages.[62] He states: "Obviously a *distinction* is being made here when a *continuum* is involved." The polar opposites of this continuum are the notions of distributive and redistributive policies. Lowi specifies the three concepts as follows: (1) Redistributive policies fix political actors into "class, ideological" relations, whereas (2) distributive policies and (3) regulative policies involve political actors in relationships which he characterizes as, respectively, "logrolling, mutual non-interference, uncommon interests" (distributive) or "pluralistic" "bargaining" relations (regulative).[63] As such, perhaps it is a *mistake* to assert that either the ideological theory or the pluralist theory is true; *both* might be true for different kinds of policies. But, if the major premise of the Lowi distinctions is false, then that putative mistake is no mistake at all. As Lowi recently stated the theory behind the distinctions: "The perspective of the entire approach is the very opposite of the typical perspective in political science, for it begins with the assumption that *policies determine politics*."[64]

The Lowi distinctions have been widely noted and specifically referred to in the context of legislative behavior by several leading analysts of Congress. Harvey Mansfield, Sr., in his discussion of Congress and economic policy, relies on Lowi's distinctions, noting that they are "based on the premise that policy types make for corresponding types of politics—more than the other way around. . . .[65] Similarly, Duncan MacRae cites the Lowi distinctions as valid in separating out different forms of action in the legislative process, *even* if not distinguishable among floor votes.[66] Randall Ripley and Grace A. Franklin, in a recent book on Congress, structure three chapters to correspond to Lowi's tripartite distinction.[67]

One might accept the utility of Lowi's distinctions for some purposes without necessarily accepting their premise (as Lowi and Mansfield identify it) as a basis for inferring from them to the nonapplicability of ideology to a substantial portion of the legislation acted upon by Congress. Lowi himself suggests one reason for rejecting such an inference:

> In the long run, all governmental policies may be considered redistributive, because in the long run some people pay in taxes more than they receive in services. Or, all (policies) may be thought regulatory because, in the long run, a governmental decision on the use of resources can only displace a private decision about the same resource, or at least reduce private alternatives about the resource.[68]

Moreover, each bill may be seen in relation to similar bills that, taken *together*, have macroeconomic consequences that can be described as redistributive upward or downward. Ultimately, Lowi finds utility in his distinctions primarily because he asserts, without the presentation of evidence, that political actors fail to *see* or are *not concerned with* the long-term cumulative effects that "only from accumulation" from "highly individualized decisions" "can be called a policy."[69]

But the most important argument against the Lowi theory may be stated as follows. The failures just cited are in themselves not a given, not an uncaused cause, but a variable factor among congressmen, which has a frequency distribution which in turn must be explained. Clearly what is crucial is what meaning congressmen, or their cue setters, read into any particular legislative issue. What is involved here is no less than a grand theme of classical political theory: the basis on which particular interests are, or are not, *perceived* to be special interests with *legitimate* claims on the society as a whole. Such claims fall somewhere in the range between those of organized crime and those of orphans. These claims involve, as Converse's original theory showed, no less than the different conceptualizations of, and perceived interrelationships among, issues, which individuals do or do not *accept*. At the data analytical level this problem is captured in the notion of "dimensionality," and at the theoretical level in the notion of "functional interrelationships among attitudes" that is the core notion of Converse's definition and operationalization of the concept of ideology.

Group theorists, of whom Lowi is among the most sophisticated because he is the most qualified in his assertions, often do not explain why certain groups or aggregates of individuals are successful in gaining special treatment or advantage, whereas others are not. Nor do they explain why some groups succeed in creating the relative saliency among voters or among congressmen of some issues to the exclusion of others. This lack of explanation is rooted in the failure to ask, vis-à-vis the social psychology of different groups, why some *issue connections* are made and others are not. This notion of *idea connections* lies at the heart of Converse's conception of ideology and is related to understanding the sources of attitude change, by leading one to ask whether one issue, belief, or valuation is more "central" than another in Converse's sense;[70] or whether an issue is seen by a congressman or a voter as manifesting, in common with other issues, a more general issue; or whether a position on a general issue is seen as manifest in different specific issues. Solutions to such analytical problems may be found in examining possible connections between the power to control policy outputs and the power to control the climate of opinion, such that one issue prevails in saliency over others or makes one definition of a situation drown out others.[71]

With such an approach, the Lowi distinctions may be utilized for analyzing how issues are perceived by different congressmen, but *not* for analyzing how congressmen are constrained *a priori* by the inherent character of legislation to adopt now nonideological, now ideological, positions. It follows from this argument that any issue may be turned into a "redistributive" issue by a congressman, *if he chooses* to note that its import may lie with the *policy* it manifests as to (1) what kind of people are to be aided, or (2) what *precedent* it may establish, reasons quite often invoked by congressmen of all stripes. Rhode, Ornstein, and Peabody provide an excellent example in their account of the actions of Senator Dick Clark and the thirty-one senators who followed his lead:

On March 14, 1974 the Department of Agriculture ordered Mississippi poultry farmers to destroy millions of chickens because they had been contaminated by oils which contained a chemical pesticide. Following the destruction of the chickens Senator James Eastland (D-Miss) introduced a bill to reimburse the poultry firms for their losses, at an estimated cost of eight to ten million dollars. The bill was promptly reported to the Senate by the Agriculture Committee, without hearings and with the support of all members save one.

The one exception was Senator Richard Clark (D-Iowa) the most junior Democrat on the Committee, who had barely completed one year of Senate Service. Clark warned that the bill would establish "a precedent of fully reimbursing businesses which suffer financial losses regardless of how big they may be, regardless of their need and regardless of who is responsible for their losses."[72]

What is particularly striking is that, although the bill itself may not in spirit have been a striking departure from similar special interest legislation, yet it was publicly *construed* as such by Clark. It lent itself to treatment as a merely "distributive" policy, but Senator Clark and his followers chose to construe it as a "redistributive" issue. And once the bill had been so characterized, it became sufficiently embarrassing that the House never took it up, and Eastland lost. Lowi's theory is a subtle attempt to deal with the problem of legitimate and nonlegitimate claims to special privilege. But if the above argument is valid, Lowi's theory will not serve.

Converse sharply illuminates the necessity of studying *empirically* what issue connections of an individual or a group structure belief systems, in his discussion of the psychological and especially of the social sources of constraint.[73] The principal point to be drawn is that *whether or not an issue is characterized by congressmen* as "highly individualized" (Lowi's other term is "distributive") or, instead, is viewed by them as an instance of a general policy which is itself at issue ("redistributive"), depends, contrary to Lowi, in large part on the way congressmen or other political actors choose or happen to construe the particular issue. Particular issues may or may not logically "instantiate" more general issues. The question remains whether or not congressmen perceive or accept such a relationship between specific issues and a general issue. That is an *empirical* question, not an *a priori* matter, as Lowi and Mansfield assert.

The particularities of the policy context and the political context are likely to be crucially intervening. It follows that any methodology which seeks to discover the actual operation of ideological concerns in the context of specific legislative events ought to encompass controls for the refractory effects of intervening *ideologically rooted* contextual variables on the ideological theories of economics, politics, social structure and culture that influence congressmen directly or indirectly. The methodology used in the analysis portion of this study seeks to establish such controls. Ideologically rooted contextual variables can be distinguished by research methods which take into account spurious correlations and alternative causal "paths."[74] It is by reference to the underlying logic of such methodologies that we define "surrogate variables."

Using the concept of ideology derived from Converse, modified by the policy-cut-points method and the understanding of refraction specified previously, the chapters following attempt to resolve empirically the dispute between the ideological and pluralist theories of congressional coalitions and cleavages.

NOTES

1. Cf. Martin Seliger, *Ideology and Politics* (New York: Free Press, 1976); see Seliger's extensive bibliography, which cites almost all articles and books on ideology of which this author is aware.

There have been a number of different uses of the concept of ideology that are *pejorative.* These pejorative uses must now be clearly excluded explicitly from this analysis by their recitation in the following paragraph, lest they become confused with the meaning of ideology specified in this study.

Pejorative conceptions include those that deem ideologies to be (1) systems of belief that are rigid, that is, closed to revision in light of experience or counterargument, or anti-empirical as contrasted to belief systems that are pragmatic. Cf. Giovanni Sartori, "Politics, Ideology, and Belief Systems," *American Political Science Review* 63 (June 1969): 398-411; and the rebuttal by John P. Diggins, "Ideology and Pragmatism: Phjilosophy or Passion?," *American Political Science Review* 64 (September 1970): 899-906; (2) rigid in the sense of precluding political compromise or accommodation to existing political realities; (3) a mere rationalization of the power of the dominant groups of a society; (4) the mere rationalization of the powerless and underprivileged seeking to replace the dominant groups; cf. Joseph La Palombara's and Seymour Martin Lipset's debate, "The Decline of Ideology," *American Political Science Review* 60 (March 1966): 5-18; (5) a set of oversimplified doctrines designed as a social lever for mass manipulation; (6) an absolutist utopia that must become seriously imperfect in any conceivable actualization; (7) oversimplifications at the elite and/or mass levels of complex situations; (8) gross insensitivity to integration of a wide range of goals and objectives into a package that has a reasonable chance of attainment under conditions in which not to accept the package does more harm than good, programmatically and/or politically; (9) the confusion of "technical" problems (i.e., problems of what are the best available means to, or the actual effects of legislation on, a given set of ends) with value questions (i.e., differences over what is desirable or what should enjoy a greater priority than something else).

Ideology in this last sense is the refusal to accept the reality of technical problems, or the insistence that the technical problems are in reality disguised value differences, when such is not the case. Matthews and Stimson, in their most recent treatment of voting in the House, array a number of statements made by congressmen in interviews they conducted in 1969 in which many congressmen utilize the term "ideology" in the latter two pejorative senses, and they themselves seem to share those pejorative uses at times, Donald R. Matthews and James A. Stimson, *Yeas and Nays: Normal Decision-Making in the U.S. House of Representatives* (New York: John Wiley & Sons, 1975). Increasingly, other congressmen such as those interviewed for this study in 1976 utilize the concept fundamentally as it is used in this study. In talking to congressmen, it is far more understandable to them if one uses the phrase "political and economic philosophy," which they readily understand as something that must be modified to fit with, and be achieved within the context of, existing circumstances, legislatively and otherwise.

With these pejorative senses of the concept of ideology clearly designated and declared outside the meaning of the term as it is used here, we can more easily proceed to specify the concept as it is used in this study.

2. Cf. Karl W. Deutsch, *The Nerves of Government: Models of Political Communication and Control* (New York: Free Press, 1963), pp. 57 ff.; and Carl G. Hempel, "The Logic of Functional Analysis," in Hempel, *Aspects of Scientific Explanation* (New York: Free Press, 1965), pp. 287-330.

3. Cf. Sidney Verba, "Some Dilemmas in Comparative Research," *World Politics* 20, no. 1 (October 1967): 111-27.

4. *Symposium Proceedings, Approaches to Elite Analysis,* June 11-12, 1975, Washington, D.C., Mathematica, Inc., Report S-1. The bulk of the papers are evenly divided between academic authors and Central Intelligence Agency analysts.

5. Cf. Ralph K. Huitt, "Political Feasibility," in James E. Anderson, ed., *Cases in Public Policy-making* (New York: Praeger Publishers, 1976), pp. 262-78.

6. Two dimensions of ideology are not dealt with in this study, though they are additive to the policy and politics foci here; their exclusion cannot bear on the validity and reliability of the empirical findings presented here. These two dimensions are: (1) the broader systematic aspects of political culture, including the climate of opinion and beliefs and attitudes that are not specifically about politics or government but are relevant to, or affect, such attitudes and beliefs; and (2) individual psychological typologies. Years of effort by Herbert McClosky will soon culminate in a major study that will illuminate these areas, as has his earlier work.

7. Cf. Barbara Hinckley, "'Stylized' Opposition in the U.S. House of Representatives: The Effects of Coalition Behavior," *Legislative Studies Quarterly* 2, no. 1 (February 1977):5, 6.

8. Philip Converse, "The Nature of Belief Systems in Mass Publics," in David E. Apter, ed., *Ideology and Discontent* (New York: The Free Press of Glencoe, 1964), pp. 206-61. See also Converse, "Public Opinion and Voting Behavior," in Fred I. Greenstein and Nelson W. Polsby, eds., *Handbook of Political Science* (Reading, Mass.: Addison Wesley, 1975), 4:75-169.

9. Cf. Robert Lane, "Patterns of Political Beliefs," in Jeanne N. Knutson, ed., *Handbook of Political Psychology* (San Francisco: Jossey-Bass, 1973). See also George E. Marcus, David Tabb, and John L. Sullivan, "The Application of Individual Differences Scaling to the Measurement of Political Ideologies," *American Journal of Political Science* 18 (May 1974): 405-20; John C. Pierce and Douglas D. Rose, "Non-attitudes and American Public Opinion: The Examination of a Thesis," *American Political Science Review* 67 (June 1974):626-49; Steven R. Brown, "Consistency and the Persistence of Ideology: Some Experimental Results," *Public Opinion Quarterly* 34 (Spring 1970):61-68; and Norman J. Luttbeg, "The Structure of Beliefs Among Leaders and the Public," *Public Opinion Quarterly* 32 (Fall 1968): pp. 398-409; James A. Stimson, "Belief Systems: Constraint, Complexity and the 1972 Election," *American Journal of Political Science* 19 (August 1975):393-418; Michael R. Coveyou and James E. Pierson, *Ideological Perceptions and Political Judgment: Some Problems of Concept and Measurement*, prepared paper delivered at the 1975 annual meeting of the American Political Science Association, San Francisco Hilton Hotel, San Francisco, California, September 2-5, 1975. Cf. Norman H. Nie with Kristi Anderson, "Mass Belief Systems Revisited: Political Change and Attitude Structure," *Journal of Politics* 36 (August 1974):540-91; Arthur H. Miller, Warren E. Miller, Alden S. Raine, and Thad A. Brown, "A Majority Party in Disarray: Political Polarization in the 1972 Election," *American Political Science Review* 70, no. 3 (September 1976): 753-78. Also cf., *inter alia*, Milton J. Rosenberg, Sidney Verba, and Philip E. Converse, *Vietnam and the Silent Majority: The Dove's Guide* (New York: Har/Row Books, Harper & Row, 1970); Herbert McClosky, Paul J. Hoffman and Rosemary O'Hara, "Issue Conflict and Consensus Among Party Leaders and Followers," in William S. Crotty et al., *Political Parties and Political Behavior* (Boston: Allyn and Bacon, 1966), p. 30; Herbert McClosky, "Personality and Attitude Correlates of Foreign Policy Orientation," in James N. Rosenau, ed., *Domestic Sources of Foreign Policy* (New York: Free Press, 1967); Herbert McClosky, "Conservatism and Personality," *American Political Science Review* 52, no. 1 (March 1958); Herbert McClosky, "Consensus and Ideology in American Politics," *American Political Science Review* 58, no. 2 (1964), pp. 361-82.

10. Cf. Converse, "Nature of Belief Systems."

11. Ibid.

12. Cf. George E. Reedy, *The Twilight of the Presidency* (New York: World Publishing Company, 1970), p. 19.

13. See especially Aage R. Clausen, *How Congressmen Decide: A Policy Focus* (New York: St. Martin's Press, 1973), pp. 31 ff.

14. Cf. Herbert F. Weisberg, "Dimensionland: An Excursion into Space," *American Journal of Political Science* 18 (November 1974):743-76; Donald E. Stokes, "Spatial Models of Party Competition," in Angus Campbell, Philip E. Converse, Warren E. Miller, and Donald E. Stokes, eds., *Elections and the Political Order* (New York: John Wiley and Sons, Inc., 1966),

pp. 165 ff., "The Axiom of Unidimensionality"; Gerald Kent Hikel, *Beyond the Polls* (Lexington, Mass.: Lexington Books, 1973), pp. 3-4.

15. Converse identifies the essential synonomy between the liberal-conservative and left-right distinction, with a comparison of the United States and France. See Philip E. Converse, "Some Mass-Elite Contrasts in the Perception of Political Spaces," *Social Science Information* 14, nos. 3-4 (Summer 1975): pp. 49-83.

16. Cf. L. Harmon Zeigler and G. Wayne Peck, *Interest Groups in American Society* 2nd ed. (Englewood Cliffs, N.J.: Prentice-Hall, Inc., 1972), pp. 21-23.

17. For classical references to this theory and its critics, see Peter Bachrach, *The Theory of Democratic Elitism* (Boston: Little, Brown, 1967); Robert A. Dahl, *Polyarchy: Participation and Opposition* (New Haven, Conn.: Yale University Press, 1971); Dahl, *Who Governs: Democracy and Power in an American City* (New Haven, Conn.: Yale University Press, 1961); Robert A. Dahl and Charles E. Lindblom, *Politics, Economics and Welfare* (New York: Harper and Brothers, 1953); Philip Green, "Science, Government, and the Case of RAND: A Singular Pluralism," *World Politics* 20, no. 2 (January 1968): 301-26; Grant McConnell, *Private Power and American Democracy* (New York: Alfred A. Knopf, 1967); Andrew S. McFarland, *Power and Leadership in Pluralist Systems* (Stanford: Stanford University Press, 1969); Michael Rogin, "Non-Partisanship and the Group Interest," in Philip Green and Sanford Levinson, *Power and Community* (New York: Vintage Books, 1970), pp. 112-41; David Truman, "The American System in Crisis," *Political Science Quarterly* (December 1959):481-97; Truman, *The Governmental Process: Political Interests and Public Opinion* (New York: Alfred A. Knopf, 1951); David Truman, *The Congressional Party: A Case Study* (New York: John Wiley & Sons, 1959).

On the theory, first, of elites checking elites in lineal descent from Madison and, then, after the Joe McCarthy years, in his switch to a less optimistic reliance on elite consensus, David Truman revealed the inherent weakness of Madisonian pluralism, according to Bachrach, *Theory of Democratic Elitism*, pp. 49-50.

18. Cf. Chaim I. Waxman, ed., *The End of Ideology Debate* (New York: Simon & Schuster, 1968).

19. Jerrold E. Schneider, "Making Government Work: Political Versus Technical Obstacles to Social Accounting," *American Behavioral Scientist* 17 (March-April 1974):585-608.

20. Ibid.

21. I am indebted to several individuals in the offices of the ADA who are responsible for constructing the ADA roll call set for rating congressmen, and who explained to me the procedure of seeking votes in these four categories. Kingdon points out, "It turns out that when one trichotomizes each of these and cross tabulates them, the ADA and ACA scores are nearly true reciprocals (tau $- b + - .75$; gamma $= -.94$). Throughout the analysis, therefore, I simply used the trichotomized ADA score as the measure of liberalism-conservatism." Cf. Kingdon, *Congressmen's Voting Decisions*, p. 292.

22. Cf. Aage R. Clausen, "Subjectivity and Objectivity in Dimensional Analysis: Illustrations from Congressional Voting," in James F. Herndon and Joseph L. Bernd, eds., *Mathematical Applications in Political Science VII* (Charlottesville: University of Virginia Press, 1974), p. 25.

23. Ibid., passim.

24. This approach owes much to the inspiration provided by Samuel Beer's *British Politics in the Collectivist Age* (New York: Alfred A. Knopf, 1965).

25. Herbert F. Weisberg, "Scaling Models for Legislative Roll-Call Analysis," *American Political Science Review* 66 (December 1972):1306-15.

26. Cf. John E. Jackson, *Constituencies and Leaders in Congress: Their Effects on Senate Voting Behavior* (Cambridge, Mass.: Harvard University Press, 1974).

27. David W. Minar, "Ideology and Political Behavior," *Midwest Journal of Political Science* 5 (November 1961):329.

28. Gary Orfield, in *Congress and Social Change* (New York: Harcourt Brace and Jovanovich, Inc., 1975), p. vi., points out:

> I see Congressional publications . . . as a vast and largely unexploited body of data on how policy is shaped and on the major ideological justifications for policy decisions. . . . Some of the best writers on Congress, from Woodrow Wilson to Ralph Huitt, have based their writings largely on sensitive reading of records that Congress makes easily available to anyone.

The Congressional Information Service now has microfiche of almost all congressional documents, available for purchase by libraries, back to January 1976.

29. Cf. Tom de Vries, "Jamaica, or the Non-Reform of the International Monetary System," *Foreign Affairs* 54, no. 3 (April 1976): pp. 577-605.

30. Cf. Seyom Brown, *New Forces in World Politics* (Washington: Brookings Institution, 1974); and Bayless Manning, "Goals, Ideology and Foreign Policy," *Foreign Affairs* 54, 2 (January 1976).

31. For an excellent example of a minimal calculation that can be applied to such questions, see Robert Axelrod, "Where the Votes Come From: An Analysis of Electoral Coalitions, 1952-1968," *The American Political Science Review* 66, no. 1 (March 1972):11-20.

32. Two former presidents of the American Political Science Association, both Yale professors, whose defense of pluralism in this sense is widely known, have recently shown stunning changes of posture. Robert Dahl has stated:

> Earlier I suggested that this country's commitment to corporate capitalism resulted in at least two such adverse consequences. As to those resulting from the unequal distribution of political resources, a country committed to procedural democracy must (1) either place effective limits on the extent to which economic resources can be converted into political resources, or else (2) insure that economic resources are much more equally distributed than they are in the United States at present. So far we have tried only the first; that approach has largely failed. Perhaps it may prove possible by regulation to reduce the direct and indirect impact on political equality, effective participation, and political understanding of vast differences in income and wealth, *but the record so far is dispiriting. It seems to me time—long past time—to consider the other approach.* Moreover, considerations of substantive distributive justice would seem to require a considerable reduction in inequalities in wealth and incomes. At the very least, the question of distribution of wealth and income ought to be high on the agenda of national politics. [Italics added.]

See Robert A. Dahl, *On Removing Certain Impediments to Democracy in the United States*, prepared for delivery at the 1976 Annual Meeting of the American Political Science Association, The Palmer House, Chicago, Illinois, September 2-5, 1976, p. 27.

In an equally striking change of posture, Robert Lane stated, also in 1976:

> The thesis of the paper is that the market economy (1) continues to break the grip of the collectivity on the individual, providing him with a kind of *sociological release* from group tradition and conformity pressures; (2) in this situation, the market economy does not leave men bereft of capacities to cope with the new problems of choice; rather, it facilitates, at least in the middle class, the cognitive and characterological skills for the requisite *autonomy*; but (3) the market society *erodes the value-giving and value-forming institutions,* misleads men on the relationship between money and utility, and "extrinsifies," thereby reducing, the satisfactions of various activities, especially work. In doing this, the market fosters a "politics of interest" which fails to link the genuine sources of life-satisfaction (friendship, challenging work, a sense of belonging, marital felicity, transcendent purpose) to political life. To support this thesis, the paper draws on cross-cultural

> studies, anthropological reports, surveys, and especially the psychological literatures on subjective well-being, sense of competence and locus of control, and intrinsic and extrinsic rewards.

See Robert E. Lane, *The Effects of the Market Economy on Political Personality*, prepared for delivery at the 1976 Annual Meeting of the American Political Science Association, The Palmer House, Chicago, Illinois, September 2-5, abstract. For perhaps the most brilliant and contemporaneously accurate description of the anti-ideological version of pluralism in theory and practice, see Theodore J. Lowi, "The Public Philosophy: Interest Group Liberalism," *The American Political Science Review* 61, no. 1 (March 1967):5-24.

33. A clear exposition and delineation of party decomposition in Congress is presented by Samuel H. Beer, "The Adoption of General Revenue Sharing: A Case Study in Public Sector Politics," paper prepared for the 1975 Annual Meeting of the American Political Science Association, San Francisco, September 2-5, 1975. Beer, in the section "Party Decomposition" (pp. 33-45), delineates a sharp decline in congressional party cohesion between the 1950s and the 1970s. Similarly, Barbara Hinckley has shown that the "major pattern" is "the decline in Democratic party coalitions over time and the corresponding increase in the bipartisan conservative coalition." See her "Party as Coalition in Legislative Settings: Possible Impermeability to External Effects," paper presented at the Annual Meeting of the American Political Science Association, San Francisco, September 1975, p. 9. Cf. also her " 'Stylized' Opposition in the U.S. House of Representatives: The Effects of Coalition Behavior," in *Legislative Studies Quarterly* 2, no. 1 (February 1977). Cf. U.S. Congress, House Democratic Study Group, Special Report No. 94-7, "Veto Overrides 1956-75," June 23, 1975, which states that comparison of three veto override votes in 1975 "with those of the past two decades shows a sharp decline in the number of Republicans voting against their party position and a massive increase in Democratic defections." Cf. Barbara Deckard and John Stanley, "Party Decomposition and Region: The House of Representatives, 1945-70," *The Western Political Quarterly* 27, no. 2 (June 1974):249-64; and Alan Ehrenhalt, "Can the Democratic Party Survive Victory?" *Congressional Quarterly Weekly Report* (July 31, 1976), pp. 2038-39. Walter Dean Burnham, "Theory and Voting Research: Some Reflections on Converse's 'Change in the American Electorate,' " *American Political Science Review* 68, no. 3 (September 1974):1054-57. On page 1054 he notes that "not since 1910 has a majority of the electorate cast ballots in off-year congressional elections." Burnham notes further that "as Key has pointed out, 'party is the solvent of federalism,' i.e., it permits integration of coalitions and mass demands (if any) across office-specific and geographical boundaries." Burnham, in the Responsible or Parliamentary or Ideological party tradition, likewise sees party as the solvent of congressional-executive branch tensions and disarray. Burnham notes further that party decomposition and the attendant demobilization and "candidate-specific" orientation of elections "will immensely increase the conservative policy effects of the constitutional structure very much along the lines hoped for by Madison in Tenth Federalist" (pp. 1056-57). Converse apparently has no quarrel with Key's and/or Burnham's claims (just cited); indeed, Converse has noted elsewhere:

> In 1958, when there was no presidential ballyhoo to occupy newspaper space, we initiated an analysis of newspaper content relating to local congressional candidates campaigning for reelection. The project was rapidly dropped because examination of newspapers even after the campaign was well under way showed that information about such candidates was printed only sporadically and then was usually buried in such a remote section of the paper that the item would go unheeded by all but the more avid readers of political news. It is no wonder that data that we have collected over the years show a large portion of citizens who fail to be aware of their congressional candidates as individuals at all.

See Philip E. Converse, "Information Flow and the Stability of Partisan Attitudes," in Angus Campbell et al., *Elections and the Political Order* (New York: John Wiley and Sons, Inc., 1966), p. 143. Converse's theory of ideology, in pointing to the different character of elite and mass belief systems, provides the subtlest and most powerful basis for extrapolating to a "manipulated" or "information-and-concept-starved citizen" model than any other available. Cf. William E. Porter, *Assault on the Media: The Nixon Years* (Ann Arbor: The University of Michigan Press, 1976); Thomas E. Patterson and Robert D. McClure, *The Unseeing Eye: The Myth of Television Power in National Politics* (New York: G. P. Putnam's Sons, 1976); and Fred W. Friendly, *Due to Circumstances Beyond Our Control* (New York: Vintage Books, 1967).

34. Cf. Theodore Lowi, "The Public Philosophy: Interest Group Liberalism," *The American Political Science Review* 61, no. 1 (March 1967), p. 22.

35. *The Federalist Papers,* selected and edited by Roy P. Fairfield (Garden City, N.Y.: Anchor Books, 1961), pp. 16-23.

36. Ibid.

37. Saul K. Padover, *To Secure These Blessings: The Great Debates of the Constitutional Convention of 1787, Arranged According to Topics* (New York: Washington Square Press/Ridge Press, 1962), pp. 64-65. "Mr. Madison. . . . The great evils complained of were that the state legislatures ran into schemes of paper money and so forth whenever solicited by the people and sometimes without even the sanction of the people." The line from Madison to Arthur Burns is a linear one through American history, except that new causes of, or different kinds of inflation—for example, food and fuel inflation in a highly mechanized and interdependent society—are now as dangerous to the average person as debt was to the average farmer of the new nation.

38. Cf. Joseph Charles, *The Origins of the American Party System* (New York: Harper Torchbooks, 1961); Noble E. Cunningham, *The Jeffersonian Republicans—The Formation of Party Organization 1789-1801* (Chapel Hill: University of North Carolina, 1957); Manning J. Dauer, *The Adams Federalists* (Baltimore: The Johns Hopkins Press, 1953).

39. Samuel P. Huntington, "Paradigms of American Politics: Beyond the One, the Two, and the Many," *Political Science Quarterly* 89, no. 1 (March 1974):13.

40. Donald E. Stokes, "Some Dynamic Elements of Contests for the Presidency," *APSR* 60, no. 1 (March 1966):20.

41. Huntington, "Paradigms of American Politics," 13.

42. J. A. Jackson, ed., *Social Stratification* (New York: Cambridge University Press, 1968); Reinhard Bendix and Seymour Martin Lipset, eds., *Class, Status, and Power: Social Stratification in Comparative Perspective* 2nd ed. (New York: Free Press, 1965).

43. *Federalist No. 10,* p. 18.

44. Theodore Lowi, "American Business, Public Policy, Case Studies and Political Theory," *World Politics* 16 (July 1964), 690.

45. Quoted in Doris Kearns, *Lyndon Johnson and the American Dream* (New York: Harper & Row, 1976), p. 153.

46. These disputes will be described at length.

47. Converse, "Nature of Belief Systems."

48. Kingdon, *Congressmen's Voting Decisions.*

49. Matthews and Stimson, *Yeas and Nays.*

50. Clausen, *How Congressmen Decide,* p. 31.

51. Cf. note 9.

52. Robert Lane, "The Politics of Consensus in an Age of Affluence," *The American Political Science Review* 49 (1965): 874-95.

53. There are other works that are parties to the dispute, but these are the most widely accepted, most current, and most systematically devoted to the issue.

54. Donald R. Matthews and James A. Stimson, "Decision-Making by U.S. Representatives:

A Preliminary Model," in S. Sidney Ulmer, *Political Decision-Making* (New York: Van Nostrand Reinhold Company, 1970), p. 21.

55. Clausen, *How Congressmen Decide*, p. 31.

56. Matthews and Stimson, "Decision-Making by U.S. Representatives," p. 16.

57. Kingdon, *Congressmen's Voting Decisions*, p. 78.

58. Ibid., pp. 250-51.

59. Lawrence F. O'Brien, *No Final Victories: A Life in Politics—From John F. Kennedy to Watergate* (New York: Ballantine Books, 1974), p. 249.

60. Cf. for example, Converse, "Nature of Belief Systems in Mass Publics," pp. 228-29.

61. Matthews and Stimson, *Yeas and Nays*, p. xii, fn. 9.

62. Theodore J. Lowi's arguments are presented in three articles: "American Business, Public Policy, Case Studies and Political Theory," *World Politics* 16 (July 1964):677-715; "Decision Making vs. Policy Making: Toward an Antidote for Technocracy," *Public Administration Review* 30, no. 3 (May-June 1970):314-25; "Four Systems of Policy, Politics, and Choice," *Public Administration Review* 32 (July-August 1972):298-310. The Lowi distinctions have been frequently attacked on the ground that they cannot be operationalized in a reliable manner.

63. Lowi, "American Business, Public Policy," p. 690.

64. Lowi, "Four Systems," pp. 299, 310.

65. Harvey C. Mansfield, "The Congress and Economic Policy," in David B. Truman, ed., *The Congress and America's Future*, 2d ed., (Englewood Cliffs, N.J.: Prentice-Hall, 1973), p. 154.

66. Duncan MacRae, Jr., *Issues and Parties in Legislative Voting: Methods of Statistical Analysis* (New York: Harper & Row, 1970), pp. 12-13.

67. Randall B. Ripley and Grace A. Franklin, *Congress, the Bureaucracy, and Public Policy* (Homewood, Ill.: Dorsey Press, 1976).

68. Lowi. "American Business, Public Policy," p. 692.

69. Ibid., p. 690.

70. Converse, "Nature of Belief Systems," p. 208.

71. See David E. RePass, "Issue Salience and Party Choice," *APSR* 65, no. 2 (June 1971): 389-401, for a demonstration of how radically issue saliences among the electorate varied with the change from the Eisenhower administration to the Kennedy administration.

As Eileen Shanahan stated in an article in the *New York Times*:

> It is a persistent flaw of journalism that it publicizes the ideas of some individuals more than others. The imbalances of publicity obviously do more harm at some times than at others. The present moment appears to be one of those in which some important national debates are being distorted because one point of view is disseminated by the media over and over while conflicting ones are covered just once, if at all. Debate that is being harmed is the debate over the state of the economy and what to do about it. The problem, in terms of what the public is learning about the issue, is that the opinions of a conservative Administration in Washington (which has real power and thus gets publicized) and those of the mainstream of the business community (which also has real power and publicity) are closely similar or even identical. It therefore often seems that these ideas are the only possible rational ones. What follows is a set of well-publicized beliefs and the under-publicized counterarguments. They are set forth here not necessarily in a spirit of advocacy but with a simple sense that the alternative arguments deserve more consideration than they are getting. Accepted belief No. 1: Cutting the Federal budget is essential to stopping inflation. Counterargument: The budget is not seriously out of balance, but is in fact, running a surplus on the "full employment" basis, which many economists believe is the proper way of determining whether the budget is juicing up the economy or restrain-

> ing it. . . . The prevalence of the belief in all of these questionable propositions brings to mind the warning of the fictional philosopher Mr. Dooley, who once observed that it was not the things he didn't know that got him into trouble but the ones he knew for sure that weren't so.

Quoted from "Equal Time for Economic Ideas" *New York Times*, Financial Section, 1 September 1974. Copyright © by the New York Times. Reprinted by permission of the New York Times.

72. David W. Rhode, Norman J. Ornstein, and Robert L. Peabody, "Political Change and Legislative Norms in the United States Senate," paper delivered at the 1974 Annual Meeting of the American Political Science Association, Chicago, August 29-September 2, 1974, p. 43.

73. Converse, "Nature of Belief Systems," pp. 210-13.

74. Cf. Hayward Alker, *Mathematics and Politics* (New York: Macmillan Co., 1965), pp. 112-129, for a good introduction.

PART II

Empirical Tests of the Pluralist and Ideological Theories

chapter 3

FOREIGN POLICY AND IDEOLOGICAL CONSISTENCY

Whether or not past studies asserted some degree of ideological consistency among domestic policy dispositions of congressmen, that is, consistency of domestic policy coalitions and cleavages in Congress, *none* has asserted that there has been any substantial degree of consistency *within* foreign or *across* domestic and foreign policy dispositions of congressmen.[1] This chapter is concerned with retesting the consistency of ideological cleavages within foreign policy. Chapter 5 will retest the consistency *within and across* foreign and domestic policy.

Past findings which failed to find foreign policy attitudes and behavior the basis of a crosscutting cleavage, vis-à-vis domestic attitudes and the behavior of congressmen, fall into *two* principal theoretical categories. David Truman expressed the first implicitly when he stated:

> But, in a world that not only has become smaller but also has been so polarized as to place in American hands the survival of free institutions everywhere, the special urgency of foreign relations and security policy is not likely to permit a reversal of the tendency (to shift power from Congress to the President).[2]

In this view, the nature of the threat of expansionistic communism was perceived by most congressmen as defining a clear national interest from which might be derived a set of policies affirmed by all reasonable observers. The statement by Clausen that follows best illustrates the second category. He describes domestic issues as being

> . . . close to the homes of most Americans and are concerns of long standing. Consequently, the policy cleavages (of Congressmen) on these dimensions have had time

to form, have had the basis for formation, and have become major features of the political scene. In contrast, the issues making up the international involvement dimension are primarily of post World War II vintage, and thus do not penetrate very deeply into the mass public.[3]

There is little doubt that the Vietnam War radically changed specific foreign policy attitudes and the general perspectives on American foreign policy of large numbers of Americans, some elites and some mass publics, both regarding means and ends. To some, the lesson of the Indochina war is only that the American people will not tolerate the prolonged combat involvement of uniformed military personnel of the United States in any action not directly related to the protection of the physical security and autonomy of the United States. However, such a lesson leaves still available a range of policies that allow for intervention abroad against Communists or anti-American leftists, or leftists generally, in a variety of other ways toward essentially the same ends for which the Vietnam War was planned and carried out. Many in Congress and in the foreign policy community have not changed their attitudes toward a Communist-versus-free-world struggle for the alignment of the developed (Italy, France) and less developed nations. The Angola debate in December 1975 in the Senate, the debate over the nature and implications of the "Euro-Communism" phenomenon, the bitter fights over President Carter's nominations of Theodore Sorensen for CIA director (withdrawn), and Paul Warnke for Strategic Arms Limitations Talks chief negotiator—all of these dramatize the continuity of cold war cleavages among substantially large and influential portions of the Congress, the executive branch, the foreign policy community, and political groups in American politics. Speeches before the 1976 Republican Convention, typified by the speech of Senator Helms (R-NC), bore vivid evidence of the continued militancy and influence of those who see communism versus anticommunism as the most fundamental foreign policy issue.[4]

As noted earlier, an essential aspect of ideology is *consistency*, in the sense that consistency among attitudes and between attitudes and behavior is a necessary (but by no means a sufficient) condition of judging a person or group to be acting out core dispositions, termed "ideological," operative and integrative in a wide range of issues. Such dispositions are sometimes linked to deeply held and highly specified personal beliefs about matters of fact and value, or they may merely reflect ties to certain parts of the society and the polity, mediated by ideological cueing, or there may be elements of both that account for attitudinal and behavioral dispositions of high consistency. But, from the foregoing, it is clear that we are led by past studies to believe that, whether or not ideological consistency was characteristic of domestic policy orientations, at the least, foreign policy attitudes are not related to domestic policy attitudes, or actually constitute a basis of one or more cross-cutting cleavages.

TESTING THE IDEOLOGICAL-CONSISTENCY HYPOTHESIS—FOREIGN POLICY IN THE SUMMER OF 1970

Interviews were conducted on foreign policy issues because roll call data were particularly shallow with regard to the fundamental issue cleavages salient in the Congress at the time the research began.[5] Preliminary perusal also indicated that the documentary record of the Congress would not adequately reflect liberal Members' views. Deference to the White House, Defense Department, and CIA among those who then controlled Congress, as well as a committee assignment process which placed only a few liberals, such as Congressman Donald Fraser (D-Minn), on prestigious foreign policy or the politically influential armed services committees, contributed to the lack of a documentary record. The past seven years have yielded a richer lode.[6] The judgments formed about latent or obscured positions on foreign policy were derived largely from journalistic sources, including network interviews with senators and congressmen, and oblique references in the documentary record implying different perspectives by the minority liberals. Because of the limited amount of time that one could expect a congressman to devote to the interviews, and given that the criterion of *comparability* required that the interview schedule be drawn so as to ensure that all respondents across the ideological spectrum would answer all questions in a codable manner, it was not possible also to interview on domestic policy questions.

Because of the far greater problem of access to U.S. senators as compared with Members of the House, it was decided that it would not be possible to interview a sufficient number of senators to allow a statistically sound design.[7]

INTERVIEW SCHEDULE

The principal foreign policy issues salient in the Congress at the time of the interviewing and around which the interview schedule was constructed were:

1. The Vietnam War.
2. The nature and extent of the threat from communism, especially from the the USSR, the People's Republic of China, and Cuba.
3. Policies toward right-wing regimes.
4. Policies regarding existing and potential left-wing or communist regimes other than the USSR, the People's Republic of China, Cuba, and Eastern European governments, especially in the less developed world.
5. Foreign aid—military aid, economic aid for political purposes, and economic aid for development and humanitarian purposes (not yet being talked about as "international redistribution").
6. Military force structures and spending.
7. Policies toward U.S. private investment abroad.

Several matters were not included in this list that might have been. The role of multinational corporations as distinct from U.S. private portfolio investment abroad was omitted because it had not yet emerged as an issue in its present proportions. Similar reasoning affected the then also still inchoate issues (now more ideological) regarding international distribution of the resources of the oceans and seabeds, nuclear proliferation on a wide scale, and threats to the planet's ecosystem. U.S. support for the United Nations, aside from the general issue of foreign aid, was no longer a serious issue in Congress. Similarly, it was judged that no significant divisions existed in the House over policies toward the Middle East. Though protectionist trade legislation was a serious concern to many Members of Congress, the issue was relatively inchoate in the minds of almost all congressmen. Most believed in free trade but were beginning to feel significant pressures from particular industries and labor groups being hurt by foreign competition. Institutional memory of the effects of the restrictive tariffs of the Depression era was remarkably strong, as the interviews revealed when this issue was raised peripherally at the end of fifty or sixty unhurried interviews.[8] Most congressmen, when asked about this matter, indicated that they had not really made up their minds, and would have to see how the issue developed.[9]

INTERVIEW SCHEDULE

Question 1: Vietnam Consequences. "What do you think the *consequences* would be if there was to be a Communist takeover in all of Indochina, within the next two or three years, for the *security* of the United States?" *Follow-up questions:* "Do you think there would be any domino effect outside of Indochina?" "Do you think there would be any psychological domino effect, that is, do you think Communist insurgencies in different parts of the world would be spurred by a Communist takeover in Indochina?" "You've said it would be bad for U.S. interests even though not vital to U.S. security; how would such a takeover hurt U.S. interests?" "Do you think a takeover would change the balance of power between the U.S. on the one hand and the Soviet Union and/or China on the other?"

Question 2: Vietnam: How Far to Go to Prevent a Communist Takeover. "How far should the U.S. go to prevent a takeover by the Communists?" "How far should the U.S. government go after withdrawal from any combat role in providing support to the Saigon government to help it resist a Communist takeover?"

Questions 3-7: Introduction. "There has been controversy in Congress about U.S. support for a number of different regimes around the world—Greece, Cuba, Brazil, Rhodesia, Taiwan, and others. Looking at these. . . ."

Question 3: Military Aid to Greece. "How do you feel about our military aid to Greece? Do you favor giving Greece military aid, or should it be withheld?" *Follow-up question*: [If respondent mentions regret about the antidemocratic character of the regime without going so far as to say that aid should be cut off to Greece] "Some Members have stated that NATO-related considerations and conditions in the Mediterranean and the Mideast make it necessary to maintain our military aid to Greece, despite the character of the Greek government. How do you feel about that?"

Question 4: Military Aid to Brazil. "There has been controversy in Congress about our aid to Brazil. The government there has been characterized as a particularly repressive one. But our aid levels there have been relatively modest, consisting largely of aid to their police forces and training of their military. Moreover, the situation there is potentially unstable and there is perhaps a danger of a leftist or of a Communist takeover. Given these considerations, or any others, do you favor continuing our aid to Brazil?"

Question 5: Military Aid to Taiwan. "There was an intense argument on the floor last December about an appropriation of $50 million for F-4's for Taiwan. Do you recall how you voted on that and the basis on which you voted? How do you feel about our all-over military aid to Taiwan? Is it about right, is it inflated, or should they be getting more than they are now?"

Question 6: Relations with Cuba. "Some Members have stated that we ought to begin to move toward normalizing our relations with Cuba, perhaps by moving toward ending the trade embargo toward Cuba. How do you feel about that?"

Question 7: The Rhodesian Embargo. "Some Members have urged, for quite different reasons, that we move to end the trade embargo toward Rhodesia. They mention the price of chromium and our need for it, while others, opposing such a move, mention our commitment to uphold the U.N. sanctions and race relations within Rhodesia. Do you feel we ought to continue or end our embargo toward Rhodesia?"

Question 8: U.S. Arms Spending. "There has been controversy in Congress about a number of different weapon systems—ABM and MIRV deployment, the B-1 bomber program, the goal of fifteen modernized aircraft carriers, and a number of others. Have you favored ABM deployment? How about MIRV deployment? Do you favor developing the B-1 bomber? How do you feel about the carrier program? Are there any other weapons systems with which you have some quarrel?"

Question 9: Expropriation. "There has been controversy in Congress about what posture the United States government should take toward regimes that expropriate the property of U.S. private investors. Clearly, there are different kinds of cases and situations, calling perhaps, for different kinds of responses—cases where there is no compensation, some inadequate compensation, full compensation; cases where expropriation takes place only in certain sectors of the economy, as with extractive industries, and so forth. Members of Congress have described to me two rough philosophies that seem to prevail among the Members. The first philosophy leans toward a relatively *harsh* response, coming down hard by imposing trade and aid sanctions with an eye out to discouraging this kind of thing wherever possible. The second philosophy is described as a tendency toward *leniency* in responding to expropriation, a willingness to take into account the development needs of the country, the profit record of the company, the manner in which the company entered the country, and so forth.

First, do you think this characterization of the two prevailing philosophies *does* describe a basic split among the members, and second, would you describe yourself as leaning toward one or the other of these philosophies?"

Question 10: Military and Economic Aids: Goals and Levels. "How do you feel about our military aid programs generally? Are they about right? Are they too high? Or should they be increased in any particular direction or areas?" *Follow-up questions:* "Are there any factors which you feel should lead the United States to cut or to increase its military aid?" "How about our economic aid programs, particularly development aid programs; are they too high, too low or about right?" "Is there anything in particular we should be doing more or less of?"

Question 11: Threats of Communism. "When he first took office, President Kennedy, responding to a speech by Khrushchev about wars of national liberation, stated that the underdeveloped world had become a great battleground between East and West. He stated that outcomes there, whether or not these were Communist takeovers, could well determine the balance of power between East and West over the long run.

"How do you feel about President Kennedy's vision of the place of the underdeveloped world in world politics? Is it essentially correct today, or do you think it does not apply?" *Follow-up questions*: "How do you view Soviet expansionist motives today? How about the Chinese; should we expect them to be seeking opportunities to expand?"

Several points seem notable about the relationship of some of the questions to the underlying dimensions they purport to tap. Those not discussed here are assumed to be obviously valid as indicators of attitude dimensions listed at the beginning of this section. The following reasoning manifests the policy-cut-points method as well as refraction, both contextual and theoretical.

Expropriation

Perhaps the most tenuous relationship between a question and an attitude dimension is between the question about expropriation of U.S. private investment abroad and more general attitudes toward U.S. private investment abroad. It seemed clear that the low knowledge and involvement of most U.S. congressmen with international economic questions of a general character all but excluded widespread interviewing in Congress on these vital matters. The one point where there was some significant congressional involvement had been in the area of expropriation. The passage of the Hickenlooper Amendment and its history were a focal point around which attitudes and the clash of basic orientations seemed to coalesce in a well-defined way. All other questions considered in this area were rejected as being too susceptible to answers in the form: "It depends . . . ," "One would need to know a great deal more about the particular circumstances . . . ," "I'm just not familiar enough with the facts of the Peruvian situation," or "Questions about hypothetical situations are difficult to answer." However, because the Hickenlooper Amendment is law, and because there have been controversies in Congress about the wisdom of invoking it under different circumstances, the question as it appears previously was used.

What is interesting to note in reading over the range of responses to the question is that the responses *did* reflect a basic difference in the degree of respect for the needs and rights of other countries, or disregard of such, in terms of economic justice. Therefore, the question seems to have been successful in tapping the core issue whereby, in terms of doctrines, we can describe attitudes about U.S. private investment abroad. That is, is U.S. private investment abroad equally advantageous to the host country as they perceive it, and to the U.S. investor, or has the benefit of the U.S. investor been the product of political contrivance and/or economic blackmail, and is such advantage taken by U.S. investors unsupportable? Linkages to domestic policy cleavages should be obvious.

Lest it be thought that cries of outrage from Congress over expropriations are only superpatriotic rhetorical flights in which image-mongering congressmen liked to wrap themselves in 1970, there are at least several facts that ought to be pointed out to show the genuineness and sailiency of the expropriation issue. First, there was the rising tide of economic nationalism threatening U.S. interests, particularly in Latin America, which had become a familiar fact of life reflected in the national press. Second, even conservative economists such as Charles P. Kindleberger have pointed out that "as capacity and appetite increase, . . . the host government seeks to renegotiate the initial concession."[10] Kindleberger suggests the prudence of investors who accept the necessity for renegotiating investment conditions, possibly even with specification of the conditions for the full divestment of holdings. Third, the Nixon government, particularly the Treasury Department (in opposition to the State Department), moved in a concerted way to demonstrate the will of the United States government to make as costly as possible any expropriations without "acceptable" terms of compensation. The full announcement of this policy line was reiterated in the *New York Times* on August 14, 1971, but a number of moves, amounting most crucially to a credit "crunch" for such nations, made that policy evident a good deal earlier, in EXIM Bank's refusal of loans, for example, and in White House police announcements.[11] A *Washington Post* editorial pointed out that "Countries that don't pay 'fair' compensation to American companies whose properties they nationalize are now on public notice that the United States will not only halt direct economic aid, but will prevent them from getting aid through the World Bank and regional development banks as well."[12] Also illustrative of pressures used, and perhaps most important of all in terms of the capital needs of precariously balanced foreign economies, are the moves of certain powerful private financial groups. For example, the statements of Jose deCubas[13] demonstrated the concentration of private pressure in opposing the investment code of Bolivia, Chile, Columbia, Ecuador, and Peru, with its rating provisions from A— (will promote foreign investment) to D— (will definitely deter foreign investment). DeCubas said that the most objectionable feature in the code is its "fade out" theory, under which, according to the *Times* account, he said:

> . . . foreigners would have to sell the majority interest in their investment to private investors or to the governments of the Andean countries within 15 to 20 years. . . . "You don't invest to go out of business," Mr. deCubas said. "Also, where would these people raise the money to buy us out?"[14]

If the Nixon administration was forceful in seeking to deter or punish expropriation without "fair" compensation, so was the Congress, though the House has been more forceful in this respect than the Senate. House amendments to the appropriations bills to fund international lending agencies for 1972-74 required that U.S. representatives to the development banks vote against loans to such expropriating countries, and given the proportion of the resources of these banks coming from the United States, it seems natural to infer that the policies of the banks toward such countries are determined to all effects and purposes by the votes of the American representatives. As has been previously pointed out:

> Congressional control through appropriations coupled with U.S. representation in sufficient numbers on the Boards of Directors of both institutions (the World Bank and the Inter-American Development Bank) insures that loans to countries out of favor with the United States will not be granted.[15]

Moreover, it seems worth pointing out that the Council of the Americas, mentioned previously, is the principal lobbyist for U.S. business interests in Latin America:

> Through formal and informal meetings at regular intervals the Council and key U.S. government officials work closely in shaping U.S. policy. The Council's activities and the ability of its members to secure sensitive decision-making positions within the executive branch of the U.S. government assures corporate representation and decisive influence over major governmental decisions in areas which affect them.[16]

The Senate, by way of contrast, defeated an amendment offered by Senator Brock similar to the House strictures vis-à-vis expropriating countries.[17] Speaking specifically to the question of the Allende government's expropriation of Chilean copper, Senator Kennedy stated: "We should halt the tendency to identify U.S. government interests with the interests of U.S. private investment."[18]

Economic and Military Aid

Liberal-conservative cleavages over foreign aid are not revealed in the separate considerations of military aid attitudes on the one hand, and economic aid attitudes on the other, but in patterns of both together. There are some few congressmen, usually highly tenured isolationist conservatives or those who play to "America first" feelings who will oppose both military and economic aid at least on roll call votes, though the genuineness of their opposition to military aid is dubitable. There are a great number of conservatives who favor military aid and oppose economic aid. There are internationalist conservatives who are in favor of a certain amount of altruism in the giving of economic aid, and who, at the same time, wish to strengthen the stability of right-wing governments against forces that might overthrow them. Thus the conservative part of the political spectrum embraces both those who are against all foreign aid and those who are for both present and increased levels of economic and military aid. This pattern may be seen as manifest in the following:

1. All that has been revealed in congressional hearings and reports concerning U.S. intervention in Chile manifests a greater emphasis by successive administrations, backed by a majority in Congress, on defending non-Marxist elements even if they are anti-democratic.

2. Almost all U.S. Foreign Security Assistance at the time of the interviews went to right-wing governments—Vietnam, Laos, Cambodia, Thailand, Korea, Taiwan, Greece, Turkey, Spain, Ethiopia, and the Philippines. This includes DOD-funded grants, MAP grants, foreign military credit sales, and Public Law 480 Common Defense grants.[19]

3. In a typical year, fiscal 1972, the proportion of U.S. foreign aid that went for "development" purposes was $2.7 billion, as compared with the $4.4 billion in Foreign Security Assistance. An additional $450 million was budgeted for welfare and emergency relief. Of the $4.4 billion in Development Assistance, $1.6 billion was budgeted for bilateral aid, which is often questioned as to whether or not it is being used as a political lever. Similarly, the $1.1 billion in multilateral aid,[20] largely given through the World Bank Group and the regional development banks, has fallen under criticism for its support of conservative economic structures abroad. No Member of Congress interviewed mentioned this criticism, as discussed in the study by Teresa Hayter.[21] A number of liberals, however, saw an increase in the "multilateralization" of aid giving as a desirable way at least of avoiding the suspicion of political manipulation that is sometimes attached to bilateral aid giving, and at most actually preventing economic aid from being subordinated to political objectives.

The *coding* of interview responses conjoined certain combinations of attitudes toward economic aid and military aid in order to capture the real liberal-conservative cleavages in this area. A reply that favored both current levels of military aid and economic aid was construed to be a conservative attitude, if (1) military aid was seen as necessary to help conserve the political power of a right-wing government, and (2) the economic aid was perceived as serving largely a political rather than a humanitarian objective. This coding decision reflects the essence of a long exchange between Senator Church and Governor Rockefeller. Senator Church's viewpoint in that exchange is reflected by increasing numbers of liberals in the House who voted against the foreign aid bill, along with certain conservatives who voted against such bills for contrary reasons entirely. In the course of the interviews, liberal congressmen tended to say they wanted to see an increase in economic aid along with a large cut in military aid to dictators or right-wing governments. Given the current set of recipients of U.S. military aid, that would be, in effect, the same as saying they favored a large cutback in U.S. military aid. Many interjected the comment that they wished to be convinced that economic aid was effectively helping the people rather than the government of the recipient countries.

Other Questions as Indicators

As to questions about the relations with left-wing regimes, other than the Soviet Union or China, unfortunately only the one question on Cuba was available as an indicator. The election of the Marxist Allende government in Chile did not occur until after the interviewing had been completed on August 10, 1970. Attitudes toward rapprochement with China, because of the limited character of the rapprochement and the *real-politik* character of that rearrangement vis-à-vis the Soviet-American balance, seems to imply little or nothing as far as general attitudes toward left-wing regimes outside the Soviet Union and China. Moreover, question 11 in the interview schedule explicitly plumbed perceptions of Soviet and Chinese expansion generally and with respect to the less developed world in particular. However, in general, there was no non-Communist left-wing regime over which there was, at the time of the interviewing, a salient congressional policy discussion.

As to questions about right-wing countries, in addition to the questions asked about Greece, Taiwan, Brazil, and Rhodesia, it might have been desirable to have added questions on Spain and South Africa. However, the author was greatly concerned in the construction of the interview schedule to limit the interview to as few questions as possible so as not to count on more than fifteen minutes of a congressman's time, even though the average interview lasted about forty minutes.

The two questions about the Vietnam War were designed to be complementary and not at all covering the same attitude dimensions. This anticipation was confirmed in the interviewing. There were "hawks" who saw little or no domino effect from a Communist takeover in Vietnam but still believed in providing the Thieu government with various degrees of support. Similarly, there were "hawks" who felt we should have bombed North Vietnam much more heavily in the past and could have thereby "won," and that a Communist takeover and a domino effect were likely. But they felt that American public opinion had reached a point of foreclosing any "win" option, leaving no alternative, but to get out quickly and cut our losses. On the other hand, there were those liberals who felt that a domino effect would not take place and that we should cut off all aid to the Thieu government on the grounds of the moral character of that regime.

INTERVIEWS

In all, 108 members of the House of Representatives of the Ninety-first Congress were interviewed between May and August of 1970. Sixty-four percent of the set of Members of whom interviews were requested responded. The 36 percent who either refused to grant an interview or were otherwise unable to arrange an interview were evenly distributed ideologically (ADA ratings).

The interviews lasted an average of forty minutes with some lasting only fifteen minutes, a good number lasting well over an hour, and four or five lasting over two hours. All but about fifteen interviews were taped, the others being recorded by hand, either because the Member refused to be taped or due to machine malfunction.

The sample was selected by the following procedure. First, each of the 435 Members of the House of the Ninety-first Congress was placed in a group with all other members of the same ADA decile; that is, all members with ADA scores of 0 to 10 percent were grouped together, those with 11 to 20 percent together, and so on. The reasoning behind this sampling is presented in Chapter 5. Second, each Member was given a unique number 1 through *n* within each decile up to the number of Members actually in that decile. Third, using a table of random numbers, an equal number of Members (11) was selected from each decile so as to add up to over 100 Members. The figure of 100 Members, or nearly one-quarter of the House membership, was deemed adequate for generalizing from the sample to the whole House. (Republicans were chosen infrequently in the upper deciles of ADA scores, since there were only 6 Republicans with ADA scores of 70 percent or over from the entire Republican House delegation of 188 Members in the Ninety-first Congress, first session.)[23]

The final sample consisted of 63 Democrats and 45 Republicans. The lower number of Republicans reflects (1) the centrality of concern in this study with ideological types (in the House, in this case) rather than the partisanship variable, irrespective of the existing balance of ideological forces in any one Congress, and (2) the fact that, although it may be correct to talk about "liberal Republicans" in the sense of being "more liberal than" other Republicans, except for the anomolous handful of 6, there was no substantial group of liberal Republicans in the House of the Ninety-first Congress.

ADA scores were chosen over AFL-COPE ratings because the latter countenances a narrower range of issues, due to its concentration on what is at issue for labor. The ADA score is specifically based on all four of the major dimensions of liberalism-conservatism concerned in this study: foreign policy, civil liberties and democracy, race, and economic issues.[24]

ACA ratings have been described as the mirror image of ADA ratings. ADA ratings were preferred, however, as a basis for drawing the sample, because they seemed to consciously attempt to tap the four policy dimensions of this study, especially after the 1968 withdrawal of supporters of the Vietnam War from the ADA.[25]

The sample, as it was finally constituted, by design had roughly equal proportions of conservatives, "moderates," and liberals. Using categories of ADA scores of 0-29, 30-69, and 70-100 correspondingly, the sample consisted of 37 conservatives, 28 moderates, and 43 liberals. Figure 3–1 indicates the relationship between the sample distribution and the whole Congress in terms of ADA ratings.

A decision was made after the interviewing had been completed to restrict the roll call analysis portion of this study to roll calls drawn only from the Ninety-second Congress, because of the institution of the Legislative Reform Act of 1970 and its effects, as will be discussed. Nine Members of the sample were thus dropped who were no longer in the Ninety-second Congress.[26] The result was, that of the original 108 Members interviewed, the sample was reduced to 97 Members. The resulting profile of the sample by ADA ratings is shown in Figure 3–2.

Since some of the most politically interesting gradations in the Congress appear among different kinds of degrees of liberals (see Chapter 6), and since the measures used here deal with measures of association among rank orders only, the slightly greater number of liberals in the sample seems interesting and no source of bias.

The aim of the sampling method was *not* to have the sample reflect the same balance among liberals and conservatives as actually existed in the House. Rather, the purpose was to capture, randomly, relatively equal numbers of conservatives and liberals of various shadings, in order to generalize about the differences among them *as political types.* Figures 3–1 and 3-2 should demonstrate that the sampling procedure succeeded in doing that.

Both the interviews and the subsequent coding of responses were carried out by the author.

FIGURE 3-1
Proportions of the Whole House and of the Original Sample by ADA Ratings

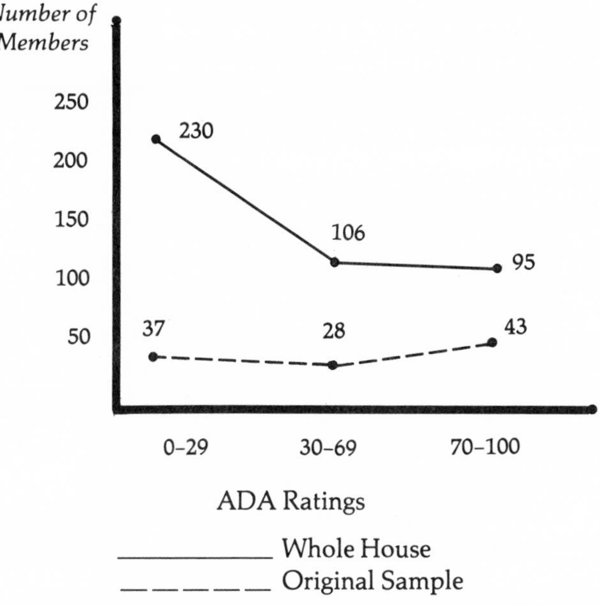

FIGURE 3-2
Proportions of the Whole House and of the Reduced Sample by ADA Ratings

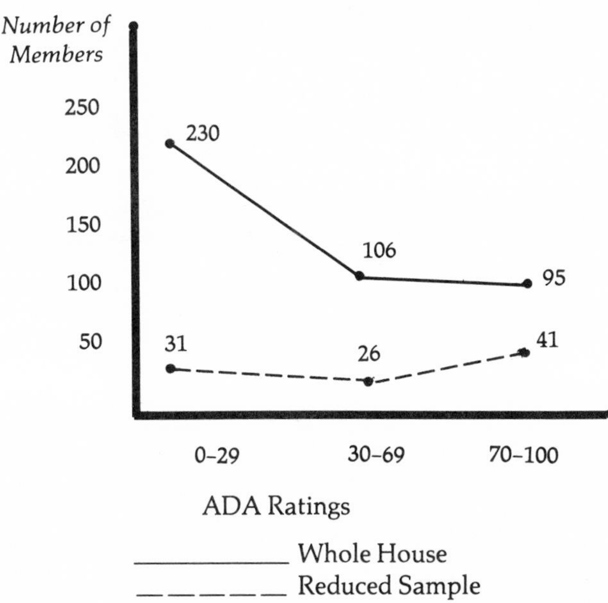

CODING OF INTERVIEWS

The coding of the interviews was structured by a technique built into the interview schedule, namely, the "focused interview" technique utilized by Aberbach, Chesney, and Rockman[27] and described by Galtung.[28] The interview is designed by anticipation of responses to capture the advantages of preset fixed coding categories and rules from open-ended interview questions. The technique is little known, since there are few research contexts in which there is the opportunity to study the belief systems of prospective interview subjects from an extensive documentary record on the subject of the interview. But the study of ideological cleavages in Congress *is* one of those few contexts. Such an approach was consciously sought, bearing in mind Converse's use of the "contextual grasp" and "level of conceptualization" aspects of his concept of ideology. Accordingly, the interview schedule was constructed so that it would capture salient foreign policy issues among different groups of congressmen, the way in which those issues were defined, the idiom and code words in which they were expressed, and the issue linkages that suggested underlying and more general issues, congruent with Converse's conceptualization of ideology.

The focused interview technique, and the coding method appropriate to it, has, as a *sine qua non*, the availability of a great deal of information about the people to be interviewed and their scattered views. The other distinguishing characteristic of the technique is the use of open-ended questions, which appear to allow a very wide range of possible answers which would not be *comparable*, sufficient to achieve reliable coding. But, because of the nature of the subject, and because of immersion in the respondents' idiom, situation, and specific and general dispositions prior to designing the interview schedule, the analyst can narrow to a very small number the expected responses, from which he specifies, prior to the interviewing, the coding categories and rules which, after all, may justify the comparability of the responses actually obtained. The focusing of the questions left virtually no room for varying interpretations of the meaning of the responses given, which should be evident from Appendix II, "Response Patterns Obtained in the 1970 Congressional Interviews." The reader may read Appendix II to ascertain the reliability of the coding procedures on substantive grounds from the congressmen's own words, and to perceive the utility of the "focused open-ended question" strategy of Galtung and of Aberbach, Chesney, and Rockman. As generally understood, the fewer the number of coding categories, the smaller the probability of coding error. All questions except number 10 had only these three coding categories; question 10 had five.[29]

The measurement of similarities and differences among congressmen in the sample was carried out in two stages. First, each interview was coded for each question for all 97 congressmen in one of the three categories for that question (five for question 10), and each verbal response written down to assemble what is found in Appendix II. Second, each individual congressman was assigned a score on each question from 1 to 3 (again, excepting question 10) signifying conservative, vague or evasive, or liberal. The scores for each question were then added, and the result was used to construct individual indices for each congressman on the foreign policy interviews, which indices were rank-ordered and used as the bases of the rank order correlations.

LIBERAL AND CONSERVATIVE FOREIGN POLICY IDEOLOGIES IN 1970

The liberal-conservative cleavage in foreign policy as manifest in responses to the interview schedule had been *hypothesized* to fall along the following lines:

Perceptions of the Threat of Communism

Liberals will reject, whereas conservatives will manifest, a far greater disposition to accept some version of the domino theory. Liberals will not see, in the possible event of a Communist takeover in Saigon, any threat to the security of the United States; conservatives will see such a threat or will refuse to consider that "Vietnamization" is not working, with the implication that it is desirable that it work.

Liberals will tend to see inherent limits in Soviet and Chinese expansionism, whereas conservatives will think the tendencies of Communists to expand are unlimited. Although liberals will manifest tendencies to view nationalism as a countervailing and more powerful force than Communist takeovers, conservatives will not.

Attitudes Toward Right-Wing Regimes

Conservatives will manifest a clear tendency to aid and support such regimes. Liberals will not; nor will they see support as necessary to avoid Communist takeovers, preferring instead the route of genuine reforms in such countries and the attainment of greater equality. Many liberals will see support for right-wing governments as depriving them of incentives to broaden their political base, thereby driving even anti-Communists, like many Buddhists in Vietnam, toward the Communists.

Attitudes Toward Cuba

Liberals will favor accommodation with Cuba and not fear Cuba's "exporting" revolution. Conservatives will oppose accommodation and see Cuba as endangering the hemisphere with the specter of Communist subversion and infiltration.

TABLE 3-1

Constraint of Specific Foreign Policy Attitudes Among Congressmen Interviewed[a]

	Question 1 *Vietnam*	*Question 2* *How Far*	*Question 3* *Greece*	*Question 4* *Brazil*	*Question 5* *Taiwan*	*Question 6* *Cuba*	*Question 7* *Rhodesia*	*Question 8* *Arms*	*Question 9* *Expropria-ation*	*Question 10* *Aid*	*Question 11* *Communist Expansion*
Question 1 Vietnam[b]	—	.596	.449	.564	.678	.558	.512	.649	.461	.551	.631
Question 2 How Far[c]		—	.492	.587	.659	.616	.463	.613	.373	.571	.518
Question 3 Greece			—	.591	.514	.431	.402	.502	.233	.457	.419
Question 4 Brazil				—	.567	.556	.317	.648	.348	.570	.551
Question 5 Taiwan					—	.676	.588	.660	.446	.663	.553
Question 6 Cuba						—	.504	.595	.442	.650	.484
Question 7 Rhodesia							—	.449	.348	.459	.344
Question 8 Arms								—	.416	.674	.590
Question 9 Expropriation									—	.523	.409
Question 10 Aid										—	.609
Question 11 Communist Expansion											

[a]All entries are tau-b coefficients

[b]Perceived consequences of a Communist takeover of Vietnam.

[c]How far to go to prevent a Communist takeover.

TABLE 3-2
Average Coefficients[a]—Constraint Among Foreign Policy Attitudes for the Sample of Ninety-seven Congressmen Interviewed[b]

Total Average coefficient	.522
Without question 7—Rhodesia	.540
Without question 9—Expropriation	.550
Without question 3—Greece	.538
Without questions 7, 9, and 3	.636

[a] All entries are tau-b coefficient averages.

[b] For the foreign policy interview data, a number of different measures were computed measuring the association of responses of members of the sample with other responses. The results were as follows in average coefficients:

tau-a	.324	tau-c	.475	Somer's *d*	.494
tau-b	.522	gamma	.726		

The results were in all cases proportionate to the tau-b results.

Economic Aid

Liberals will support increased economic aid, if such aid can be successfully directed to a genuine humanitarian effort. Conservatives not only oppose increasing such aid, most will favor cutting it back, even from its present low level.

Military Aid

Liberals will favor cutting back military aid, especially to right-wing countries. Conservatives generally will favor present levels of military aid.

Military Spending and Weapons Systems

Liberals will be found to oppose present military spending levels, including outlays for a number of currently advocated weapons systems. Conservatives will support at least the current levels of military spending, including support for the controversial weapons systems specifically referred to.

Private Investment Abroad

Conservatives will indicate their support for American private investment abroad by the strength of their antagonism to foreign governments which expropriate U.S. private foreign investment. Liberals will not oppose expropriation of U.S. private investment abroad, if some compensation is "arrived at." Conservatives will favor severe sanctions against expropriating governments. Liberals will not.

RESULTS

These hypotheses were highly confirmed. The results of the analysis of the foreign policy interviews are presented in Tables 3-1 and 3-2. The average tau-b coefficient for the whole sample, .522, is quite high. Converse obtained a more moderate .37 average gamma coefficient among his 1958 congressional candidates for foreign policy attitudes. The wide discrepancy between Converse's data and that of this study is clearly in the direction of this study having found far greater intra-elite "constraint" (functional interpendency among attitudes) for foreign policy attitudes than did Converse. *The gamma figure I obtained, .726, compares dramatically with Converse's .37.* Since gamma, moreover, overstates the strengths of relationships, especially in the middle ranges, because it takes no account of ties, and since tau-b is, absolutely and relative to gamma, a conservative measure, tau-b is more appropriate, and the divergence between Converse's 1958 findings and those presented here might prove even greater if Converse's data were recomputed using tau-b.[30]

Moreover, dropping the three questions with the lowest average coefficients, the questions about Rhodesia, Greece, and expropriations, the average tau-b coefficient among the eight questions remaining increases to .636. Those[31] three questions have some ambiguity associated with them.

With regard to military aid to Greece, some Members opposed to the Greek regime saw in the threat to Israel and in the Mediterranean, as a result of the buildup of Soviet naval forces, the necessity of giving military aid to Greece for the security of U.S. naval base rights. These Members did not raise the question of the vulnerability of the Soviet forces to other U.S. forces, particularly planes and missiles based on other countries and ships based elsewhere. Nor did they question the assumption that helping the current Greek regime was a necessary condition of having bases in that country. But perhaps some significant proportion of the Members interviewed were unaware of these arguments. The listing of typical responses makes this interpretation possible. Yet even with the relatively middling coefficients (compared with others in Table 3-1) between Greece and the other questions, the relationship is still substantial, with an average coefficient of .446 between attitudes toward military aid to Greece and other foreign policy attitudes.

The Rhodesian embargo issue has an extra-ideological dimension, namely, the infeasibility and impracticality of the sanctions, given that the Soviet Union was buying Rhodesia's chrome anyway and selling it to the United States at about double the price.[32] The issue persisted even into the Ninety-fifth Congress, when at last the liberals prevailed, with aid from the Carter administration. Whether or not to maintain the embargo under such circumstances is then partly an ideological issue—taking a stand in clear sight of all nations against the white minority rule in that country and South Africa—and partly a nonideological issue—whether the mechanics of the chrome embargo is a practical approach to opposing the Rhodesian regime.

The considerations on both sides of this issue make especially clear what is present in a more complex form in all the other questions. As is usually the case in choosing appropriate indicators of ideological positions, proponents and opponents can make plausible and convincing cases for their positions. Indeed, in many instances there is often enough doubt that *the real essense of ideology is the preference to err on one side of a question rather than another,* in which no side can *prove* its case. Of course, the truly responsible "ideologue" (Converse's term and sense) will strive to narrow the range of the unknown as much as possible.

The question, nonetheless, had a substantial average coefficient of association with attitudes on the other questions of .439, though it compares with .540 for the average coefficient of all other questions with the Rhodesian question dropped. The average coefficient of all the questions with only the Greece question dropped is .538.

No such specific mitigating circumstances may be cited with respect to the third question which lowers the average coefficient—the question about expropriation. Yet the nature of the question was such as to present a forced choice between attitudes of a very general nature. The fact is that the operations of *private sanctions,* such as the drying up of credit, or certain marketing and processing monopolies, may have been understood as being sufficiently effective by a number of the Members. Additional U.S. government sanctions would not be required.[33] And so a greater amount of "slack" in the relationship between the indicator (question) and the underlying variable may have occurred in this instance. The average coefficient for all questions with the expropriation question removed is .550. The average coefficient for the expropriation question correlated with each of the other questions is .400.

For the reasons stated, the reader may prefer the *.636 average coefficient, which is based on excluding all three of these questions, as the more reliable figure on the degree of association among key attitudes on foreign policy.* But, in either case, what is indicated is a very strong relationship among attitudes for the sample as a whole. This interpretation seems correct, given the conservative nature of the tau-b measure of association, and the very clear proportional-reduction-in-error interpretation of the meaning of tau-b. The relationships among the foreign policy *roll call votes,* discussed presently, are moreover somewhat stronger still.

We can infer from a set of strong relationships among the data to the claim that there were definite, seemingly distinct, foreign policy ideologies in the Congress in the summer of 1970. One ideology is basically liberal, and one basically conservative.

Generally, the liberal foreign policy ideology that emerged from the interviews seems to have at its core an egalitarian humanism that led liberal congressmen to abhor right-wing authoritarian governments and the inequality of economic and political power seen leading to large-scale human suffering. At the same time, in the face of some pessimism liberals shared with almost all conservatives about the chances for realization of democracy in very many countries, the liberals were distinguished by a relatively live-and-let-live attitude toward left-wing and Communist countries. Liberals tended to perceive threats from various Communist powers as being relatively negligible, as compared with the threats perceived by conservatives. In general, liberals showed a much greater tendency to see a multipolar world with a large variety of interests, an inherent imprecision in the concept of alignments, and inherent limitations in the capacities and ambitions of any country or combination of countries, Communist or otherwise. Nationalism, especially economic nationalism, seemed for the liberals the determinative factor in international relations, far outweighing the significance of communism, ideology, or subversion. The perception of threats from Communist countries as being relatively small seemed to delegitimize, for liberals, the magnitude of current U.S. arms expenditures and current levels of U.S. military aid. At the same time, the humanistic element of their ideology seemed to lead liberals to advocate increasing substantially the extent of U.S. aid aimed at genuinely humanitarian purposes. Most countries, large and small, were perceived as basically preoccupied with internal needs. Liberals saw the United States, the USSR, or the People's Republic of China as possessing a relatively limited capacity to affect profoundly the internal political structures of very many other countries. But liberals deplored U.S. intervention on the side of, and attempts to prop up, right-wing regimes, especially dictatorships.

Abhorrence of right-wing government was not, for the liberals, mitigated by the logic "better a right-wing government than risk a communist takeover," and that abhorrence seemed to lie at the base of liberal assessments of acceptable costs and risks associated with alternative outcomes of the Vietnam War. This set of attitudes follows logically from their view of the world as essentially multipolar, nationalistically self-concerned, and, economically, much more than militarily oriented. In such a world, alignment means little; the "loss" of a Vietnam means little or nothing for international power arrangements; and any form of domino theory seems inconsistent with many facts, especially the Sino-Soviet conflict. Domino theorists were blamed for ignoring the wide variety of combinations of sociocultural, economic, and political conditions in all the different countries of the world. And domino theorists were thus blamed for discounting (1) social injustice as a source of revolution, and (2) the variety of local conditions that affect the susceptibility to Communist takeovers of countries gripped by nationalism, reformist or not. Liberals, in line with their general humanitarian and egalitarian thrust, viewed expropriation from a concern with the needs and rights of the expropriating countries, and from a perception of the greed of some U.S. private investors.

The conservative foreign policy ideology that emerged from the 1970 interviews is the mirror image of the liberal. Conservatives defended right-wing regimes as "friendly allies" or "bulwarks against Communism" and saw Communism as an implacable, unceasingly expansionistic foe, capable of tipping the balance of power until the United States has retreated before falling dominoes into Fortress America. Not only did they perceive a U.S. posture as requiring an ever superior U.S. military force, but also the necessity of continuing present levels of military aid to promote "stability" in vulnerable countries. Vietnam was seen in the context of some version of the domino theory, and therefore any possibility of a Communist takeover in South Vietnam was deemed deplorable. Most of the conservatives were quick to reject, by one argument or another, any role for the United States in providing significant humanitarian aid. A small proportion of conservatives seemed to adopt an apparent beneficent posture supporting humanitarian aid, but largely or exclusively for "free world" right-wing countries. But this economic assistance was urged, mainly in a package with a large emphasis on military aid to such governments.

Some liberals intimated that conservative aid policies of the Rockefeller variety were more politically motivated than humanitarian. This liberal critique depends on reading in some controversial claims about the nature of economic development. That different claims focusing on such matters are explicit in the minds of some liberal congressmen is revealed in the range of liberal responses recorded for question 9 on expropriation (Appendix II). The lack of humanitarian attitudes on aid given among conservatives is also manifest in the correlation in the results, shown previously, between aid and expropriation attitudes. The list of responses reveals that conservative attitudes toward expropriating nations do not reflect any concern for the needs and rights of the expropriating countries. Justice toward the deprived parts of national populations as a value in itself does not emerge as a salient concern among conservatives, but is central in liberal reasoning.

Attitudes toward U.S. foreign investment abroad can be seen, from the responses given, to be bound up in the conservative and liberal ideology with some substantive strength. The data showing the consistency of the attitudes toward expropriation with other foreign policy attitudes might well be interpreted as stronger than the obtained correlation coefficients would indicate, and as implying that attitudes toward large corporations were related to some other attitudes to a greater degree than the coefficients relating to question 9 might suggest. It well may be that the conservatives interviewed believed that the sanctions imposed by private sources of capital, including quasi-public international financial institutions, which threaten to withhold, or actually cut off, capital funds to nations with precariously balanced economies, are sufficient sanctions to combat the rise of leftist governments. Such an interpretation of the obtained correlations alone seems to fit the fact that liberals systematically took significantly more lenient views of expropriation, accenting the needs and rights of other people, whereas conservatives systematically stressed a punishing posture toward expropriating nations, as Appendix II shows.

Strikingly, all of the black congressmen interviewed, who were a majority of the Black Caucus, wanted to see the United States give *more* genuinely humanitarian and development aid, a fact that does not fit well the interest group interpretation of congressional behavior. By that interpretation, the Members of the Black Caucus, in their well-known eagerness for more federal spending on the poor and disadvantaged, should have attacked the vulnerable foreign aid expenditures in order to claim those funds to aid the needy at home. But their opposite reaction was in each case emphatic, revealing a generalized social justice orientation.

FOREIGN POLICY ROLL CALLS—A RELIABILITY CHECK

Among roll calls of the Ninety-second Congress (1971-72), a number of foreign policy roll calls may be used to establish the reliability of the preceding results, which were based exclusively on interview responses. The method of selecting the roll calls and of giving each Member in the sample a cumulative index score, on the basis of which the Members are rank-ordered, is presented in Chapter 5. The reliability test here is based on a tau-b correlation of this rank order of (a) foreign policy roll call votes, and (b) the simple addition of liberal (2) versus vague or evasive (1) versus conservative points (0), for ten of the eleven questions (4, 3, 2, 1, 0, for the aid question), and the resulting rank order of the additions so derived for each Member in the sample.

The resultant tau-b rank order correlation[34] for foreign policy roll calls by foreign policy interview questions was a high .677. The rank order correlation between, first, foreign policy and defense budget roll call votes and the domestic liberalism index of the next chapter, based on roll call votes, and second, foreign policy interview responses and the same domestic liberalism index was very close indeed. They were respectively: .706 (roll call data on foreign policy) and .629 (interview data on foreign policy). In addition, three specific interview questions were given a reliability check against one or a group of roll calls. These were:

1. The Rhodesian question by the vote on Rhodesia *Congressional Quarterly* (CQ) vote 255(T), Ninety-second Congress, first session.
2. A combined and rank-ordered score based on the two Vietnam interview questions by the twelve Vietnam-related votes in the Ninety-second Con-

gress, House (CQ votes 24(T), 25(T), 89(T), 90(T), 91(T), 107(T), 269(T), 320(T), in the first session, and CQ votes, 158(T), 223(T), in the second session).

3. The interview questions on military spending and all defense budget roll call votes.

The results of list items 1-3 are as follows in tau-b coefficients:

1. .679
2. .711
3. .758

This constitutes a very high reliability check from behavioral (roll call) data to attitudinal (interview) data, especially in light of the discussion of the tau-b statistic and of past findings to be discussed.

CONTINUITY AND CHANGE: 1970-76

Despite large change in Congress, and new pressures from changing international political and economic conditions between 1970 and 1976, the congressional cleavages of 1970 in foreign policy endure. Members of the Ninety-fourth Congress voted and were otherwise consistently divided along lines quite similar to those revealed in the 1970 interviews and 1971-72 votes on foreign policy presented earlier. Of the seven dimensions of foreign policy conflict in the Ninety-second Congress, outlined previously, only the issue of the Vietnam War was no longer before the Ninety-fourth Congress in a fundamental way. The six remaining issues continued to be major ones.

The period of 1970-76 encompassed crises over food, fuel, and "stagflation," and overlapped the end of the Indochina war in April 1975. Quadrupling of world oil prices by the OPEC cartel; the sharp rise in food prices in the United States due in part to vast exports of grain; two successive devaluations by the U.S. government in the early 1970s; suspension of the convertibility of the dollar into gold by President Nixon in August 1971, leading to a regime of "managed" floating exchange rates[35] and growing fears of dangerously wide international monetary fluctuations by 1976[36]; accelerating nuclear proliferation, population growth and pollution; evidence of serious deterioration in the world ecosystem; and rising economic tensions between the nations of the Northern and Southern Hemispheres—all of this and more cast the nature of international politics, particularly the Soviet-American conflict, in a very different perspective for some, but by no means all, elites and significant portions of the Congress.[37] For others, Soviet-American rivalry, or communism versus anticommunism and antisocialism, continued to be the central issue of international politics, the previously mentioned problems notwithstanding.

The most compelling evidence of continuity is in the findings prsented in Chapter 5 on cleavages within and across the foreign and domestic policy domains, which occur with the same strength of association in the Ninety-fourth Congress, first session (1975), House and Senate, as in the Ninety-second Congress.

American *policies toward a large number of right-wing regimes* have come under increasingly strident and public criticism in the Congress. The following excerpt, from the *Congressional Quarterly*, shows the continuity and summarizes as succinctly as possible the momentum in this dimension at the end of the Ninety-fourth Congress, second session (1976), *prior to President Carter's inauguration and the launching of his own human rights program:*

Foreign Aid Cutoffs:

Human Rights Violations to Be Reviewed in 1977

Shortly before the 94th Congress adjourned, the Senate Foreign Relations and House International Relations Committees laid the groundwork for debate next year on attempts to terminate U.S. aid to nations that consistently violate internationally recognized human rights standards.

Under the fiscal 1976-77 foreign military aid authorization bill (HR 13680—PL 94-329), Congress declared that no security aid could be granted such nations. Beginning in fiscal 1978, the State Department is required to furnish human rights evaluation reports on each nation designated to receive security assistance, and Congress then can attempt to cut off or reduce the funds by passing a joint resolution of disapproval, requiring the President's signature. (*Background, Weekly Report*, p. 1654)

On Sept. 3 Hubert H. Humphrey (D Minn.), chairman of the Foreign Relations Assistance Subcommittee, wrote Secretary of State Henry A. Kissinger requesting information "already on hand" regarding "17 nations which have been mentioned most frequently as having questionable human rights practices." Humphrey said the background information, including reports prepared by the department in 1976 but never transmitted to Congress, was necessary so his staff "will have some basis of comparison for consideration of next year's reports."

In addition, the House International Relations Committee, at the request of Donald M. Fraser (D Minn.), chairman of the International Organization Subcommittee, asked the State Department for reports on Argentina, Haiti and Peru. Fraser called attention to the "shocking level of violence existing in Argentina . . . the many incidents of kidnapping and killings that have occurred since the military coup on March 24, 1976."

The nations singled out by Humphrey were: Latin America—Argentina, Brazil, Chile, Uruguay and Paraguay; Asia—South Korea, Indonesia and the Philippines; Middle East—Iran; Europe—Spain; Africa—Ethiopia, Nigeria, Mozambique and Zaire; and South Asia—India, Pakistan and Bangladesh.

Over the objections of the Ford administration, Congress in 1976 terminated all military assistance to Chile and placed a $27.5 million cap on economic aid to the nation, an amount that could be doubled if the President certified that the treatment of human rights in the country had improved. Congress also cut off all military aid to Uruguay in 1976. (*Background, Weekly Report*, p. 2708. Reprinted by permission of the *Congressional Quarterly Weekly Report*.)[38]

The Chilean affair and the attempt of the Ford administration, backed by Senate and House conservatives, to involve the United States in the war in Angola, illustrate the *continued cleavage among congressmen with regard to left-wing regimes.* Gains among liberals both in strength and institutional position since 1971 have assisted them in dramatizing their positions. The Chilean affair is a prime example. The continuing cleavage is well illustrated by the character of the statements by individual senators—Church, Mondale, the late Philip A. Hart, Tower, Baker, Mathias, Morgan, Goldwater, and Schweiker—in *The Final Report of the Senate Select Committee to Study Intelligence Activities* (1976). The emergence of the liberal opposition is captured in the posture of the staff conclusion within that *Report* (p. 578), which states:

> In the period 1970 through 1973, in order to prevent a Marxist leader from coming to power by democratic means, the U.S. worked through covert action to subvert democratic processes . . . this interference in the internal affairs of another country served to weaken the party we sought to assist and created internal dissensions which, over time, led to the weakening and, for the present time at least, an end to constitutional government in Chile.[39]

It is difficult to imagine such a staff report being issued in the pre-Watergate political climate.

The congressional dispute over United States intervention in Angola came to a head just before the Christmas recess in December 1975. The battle over the amendment prohibiting all forms of aid serves as an excellent indicator of the continuity of the ideological controversy over *military aid* in the period since 1970. Perusal of the *Congressional Record* for the days preceding the vote shows numerous debates and *Record* insertions on Angola in both chambers, and these statements reflect the intensity among a wide range of Members of the general issue of supporting regimes because of their anti-Communist character alone. If one examines the vote breakdown of yeas and nays on the Tunney amendment, prohibiting U.S. intervention in Angola, one finds a strict liberal/conservative cleavage in the sense that (1) no liberal opposed the Tunney amendment, and (2) only arch conservatives opposed it and supported the administration's position.

Full examination of the debate also clarifies the deep continuity of the cleavage in Congress between 1970 and 1976 *over the long-term dangers threatening the United States from the expansion of communism* (also see note 4). Perusal of that debate indicates that there would have been many more than twenty-two votes against the Tunney amendment if the client Angolan faction of the United States had not already suffered such complete military defeat, and if the issue had not been so highly publicized by the electronic media.

Cleavages over military aid, beyond that already cited during the 1975-76 period, centered on arms sales in general and, as a distinct form of military aid, arose with unusual intensity in the Ninety-fourth Congress. Led by Senators Humphrey, Kennedy, and others, the Congress passed a severe inhibition on future arms sales, a bill that was vetoed by President Ford. The magnitude of U.S. arms sales—government sales alone climbed from $953 million in 1970 to an estimated $9.8 billion in 1976, with total government and private sales above $12 billion—provoked an intensely bitter struggle in the Congress. President Ford's veto of the bill rejected the policy that would have provided the opportunity for a congressional act of disapproval for any sale, credit, grant, or other form of arms transfer on a country-by-country basis.[40]

In the same manner, the battles over individual weapons systems, and over across-the-board cuts in the *defense budget,* filled the roster of recorded votes in 1975 and 1976. The bulk of the votes in the Senate in 1975 was on amendments by the minority liberals to delete funds for particular weapons systems—all soundly defeated. A major vote came on funds to build up a U.S. base at Diego Garcia,[41] some say a potentially dangerous escalation of the confrontation with the Soviets (by extending the rivalry of the two nations into the Indian Ocean). Whereas critics claimed that there was no Soviet base in Somalia, proponents claimed there was, and that therefore the Diego Garcia base was necessary to counter Soviet expansionism in the Persian Gulf and Indian Ocean.

But many more liberals acceded to defense-spending measures that in other years they could have been expected to have opposed. Reasons were threefold:

1. Defense expenditures have been taking and will continue to take an ever *decreasing* proportion of the federal budget.[42]

2. The fall of the Saigon regime to Hanoi, coupled with the events in Angola, according to Senator Culver, led to "a desire (in Congress) not to send out the wrong signals about American will."[43] The *New York Times* reported that: "Asked who or what turned the tide against Pentagon budget cutters," Senator Muskie replied: 'The Angola thing—you could really feel it swing' as the American people got the idea that the Soviets 'had tried their hand at interventionism.'"[44]

3. The widespread unemployment throughout 1975-76 left liberals unwilling to add to it, just when they were trying to force on the administration some degree of fiscal stimulation.

But as made clear in the accounts just cited, the liberals were engaged in a tactical maneuver, not a change in position. The *New York Times* noted Senator Muskie's comment, echoed widely in Washington in 1976, that "We're all sort of marking time" this election year to see who the new leaders will be here and in the Soviet Union.[45]

Thus it would be a mistake to suppose that defense roll call votes of 1975-76 indicated a fundamental or permanent change among the liberals on defense spending.

The economic and humanitarian aid dimension took on dramatic new aspects between 1970 and 1976. The world food problem is so interwoven with other problems—energy, balance of payments, international liquidity, development funding and strategies, bracketed by politics, population growth, and the international economic situation generally—that the intricacy of packaged solutions that possibly could be put into effect shows the simplistic character of much of the thinking about aid in 1970.[46]

In 1975 and 1976, the battle between liberals, who want to create large buffer stocks of food and other commodities, both as a means to hold down domestic inflation and to give as aid to starving people, and conservatives, following the lead of then Secretary of Agriculture Earl Butz, who feared that the government would use such stocks to hold down "free market" commodity prices, has received headline treatment. These positions, from the viewpoint of the needs of the less developed countries (LDCs), parallel the same liberal-conservative split between Nixon administration economic czar George Schultz (at that point, secretary of the treasury) and his liberal critics over the question of making Special Drawing Rights—the new paper money created by the International Monetary Fund—available as a new source of development funding for the LDCs. Schultz, in vivid and uncompromising language, and to the dismay of the liberals, stated at the IMF conference at Nairobi in September 1973 the administration's position that SDRs were *not* to be made available as a new source of development aid. That position was maintained by the Ford administration, over the continued protests of congressional liberals.[47]

In 1975 and 1976, with the United States still suffering from adverse economic conditions domestically, the posture of the congressional liberals on foreign aid was a low-profile one; but votes on replenishment of the funds of the multinational development banks and funds for economic and development assistance passed by wide margins in the liberal House of the Ninety-fourth Congress and survived in the Senate. An amendment by Senator Clark, which would have established a $200 per capita gross national product as a criterion for establishing eligibility as a needy country in the U.S. food sales program, was defeated by a wide margin (36-53), indicating some political intent of the program by the majority conservatives, but a Hatfield amendment to require that 80 percent of all PL 480 commodities sold abroad be allocated to countries with a per capita gross national product of $250 a year was passed by a wide margin (see vote numbers 458 and 459 in Appendix I).

The last major dimension engaging continuing congressional cleavages across the 1970-76 period was *attitudes toward U.S. private investment abroad.* This issue, under the influence of skyrocketing international food and fuel prices, and the large-scale deployment of capital abroad during a period of weak economic growth within the United States, led to the dramatic Church committee hearings on the role of multinational corporations abroad. The substance of these hearings, and the cleavages manifested among congressmen during their unfolding, are too elaborate to summarize here.[48] But even casual perusal of them will lead to the judgment that the underlying dispositions toward U.S. foreign investment manifest in the responses to the expropriation question in the 1970 interviews (see Appendix II) remain fundamental. Thus much remained unchanged in the cleavage patterns over economic and military aid in the period 1970-76.

However, the Seventh Special Session of the United Nations in September 1975 showed that the whole foreign aid area had changed and been ramified in basic conceptualization of how to achieve previously defined ends, setting a new context for the continuing ideological cleavages. With many of the poorer nations only able to service past debts by using half of the amount of new economic assistance, coupled with the hardships brought about by the quadrupling of oil prices, inflation in the cost of manufactured goods, and drought, the growing desperation of the Third and Fourth World nations led them to propose a whole new international agenda of aid. The essential elements of the LDCs' demands, carried over from past UNCTAD meetings, called in effect for a massive international redistribution of income and wealth. The specific demands of the LDCs included: increased development aid funds, debt rescheduling and cancellation, increased access to the markets of the developed countries through trade concessions, technology transfer, massive new infusions of capital in the form of direct grants from government rather than private loans, radically altered terms of trade, including indexation of the prices of commodities from the LDCs to the manufactured products of the developed nations (one proposal would index eighteen raw materials to eighty-nine manufactured products), price support mechanisms for the LDCs' commodities, and buffer stocks of essential commodities to stabilize prices and make available what is needed by the LDCs.[49] The remarkable thing *about the Congress* is that, generally speaking, there has been great continuity of cleavages in the period 1970-76 *about how much more* the United States could or should, or can be or should not be doing for the LDCs, with the liberals claiming that relatively little more money would be needed to have great effect *if* there were substantial transfers of funds now used for supporting questionable political regimes abroad and for defense spending to which the liberals have no attachment. There is hardly an issue of the *Congressional Record* in which one cannot find reference to that essential point made by a liberal Democrat.[50] As Senator Mondale emphasized in the nationally televised debate with Senator Dole when they were vice-presidential candidates, he (and the liberal Democrats) did not seek to vastly increase federal spending, but rather wanted to allocate existing federal spending to serve very different goals and priorities.[51]

It should be noted that the *strongest argument* that there has been *an extraordinarily high consistency of ideological cleavages in Congress within foreign policy across the 1970-76 period,* is in the data presented in Chapter 5.

THE LONG-TERM CONSERVATIVE PERSPECTIVE

A long-term conservative foreign policy world view can be extrapolated from the data of this study. The conservative position is based on the premise that the conflict between communism and the free world has not been essentially altered since at least the late forties, if not 1917 (see note 4). "Detente" connotes for conservatives only a tactical relaxation of tensions, not *an end or an ebbing* of the essentially irrepressible and inherently dangerous worldwide struggle between communism and democratic capitalism. Conservatives do take into account the new forces in world politics, such as the Sino-Soviet conflict, polycentrism, the force of nationalism in Communist as well as non-Communist states and parties, the rise of economic interests and economic nationalism in relations among and between members of the communist camp, the "free world" alliance, and the nonaligned nations. Nevertheless, conservatives see the long-term expansionary thrust of communism as undiminished. Whether democracy shall survive, in this view, depends upon whether capitalism survives, for capitalism alone ensures a pluralistic society, free from the totalitarian control which necessarily flows from socialism, with its government monopoly control over the *resources* of society, especially the resources to mount effective political opposition.[52] Should communism or socialism come to dominate most of the globe, the conservative fears the difficulties of surviving in "Fortress America," given the needs for markets and raw materials.

The added economic and technological power accruing to a greatly augmented socialist camp, they argue, might well be transformed into advantages in military technology which would render the United States defenseless. A highly perfected antisubmarine warfare capability and an effective antiballistic missile system could, after all, tip the balance of terror, if possessed by only one side to the detriment of the other. That Communist powers have not made overt military moves across internationally established borders since the Cuban Missile Crisis, except in Indochina and Czechoslovakia in this view, is attributed to the military strength and credible will of free world military forces to use that strength. Therefore, the United States must not allow its military posture, in either strategic or in conventional forces, to become weakened relative to the Communists, on the mistaken assumption that Communist goals have been altered in any major way. The Communist side seeks accommodation only when confronted with superior force. If free world forces are weakened, if the will to use those forces is not credible, or if the Communists should succeed in a technological breakthrough in the arms race, they will resume an adventurist and highly provocative posture, along with political blackmail, subversion, or "Finlandization" if not overt military takeover of smaller powers. Although the threat of nuclear war requires coexistence with Communist powers, that coexistence should not lull the United States into a false sense of security.

According to conservatives, the Communist powers are now, and have been all along, actively engaged in various forms of subversion in a great many nations. These forms include financing political activities of Communist and other anti-American groups, bribing political elites, shipping arms to, and training, insurrectionary forces, and sponsoring activities aimed at disrupting the economy or political order of the target countries. These countries are seen to be highly unstable politically and therefore quite vulnerable to the attacks of a small, disciplined, and well-supplied Communist cadre of subversive agents, whether indigenous or not. Lest a great many countries fall to communism through subversion, conservatives believe it is necessary for free world forces to engage in systematic *counter-intervention.*[53]

Due to the weakness of existing and potential democratic forces in many countries, the United States is often faced with countering subversion by supporting economically and militarily authoritarian right-wing regimes, which conservatives often see as the only reliable anti-Communist elements available. Regrettable as such support may be, the alternative of letting a country slide into communism is worse, morally and strategically. As countries ruled by right-wing authoritarian forces develop economically, the middle class grows, and democracy follows. Anti-Communist stability is a necessary condition of a favorable climate for attracting outside private investment capital for significant economic development. And economic development is the necessary precondition of social and political development. This development model, much like its domestic "trickle down" theoretical counterpart, finds the self-interests of investment capital and economic nationalism (defined in terms of the investing class of the nation) to be in natural harmony with an altruistic concern for the increased well-being of the LDCs. Viewed in this light, direct humanitarian aid will, for the most part, play too small a role in the alleviation of the general systemic ills of the LDCs to warrant support, especially when added to already swollen federal budgets and deficits of inflationary proportions.[54]

This position places emphasis on the claim that there is a mountain of evidence that Soviet and other Communist leaders also believe that the conflict between communism and capitalism is inherently irrepressible and irreconcilable in the long term.[55]

On the vital question of nuclear proliferation and arms transfers, the conservatives assert that if the United States does not sell what is sought, other major arms suppliers will. Therefore, the United States may as well be the supplier and gain the benefits of the influence and the positive impact on the balance of payments that accrue from such sales.

It is interesting to note that the fundamental cleavage between conservatives and liberals in their long-term perspectives was cast in virtually the same terms by the *New York Times.* On the eve of the debate between President Ford and Governor Carter on foreign policy, at the height of the 1976 election, The *Times* spoke of what that forthcoming debate might be like as follows: "Another fundamental attitude the debates might disclose involves the candidates' perception of the nature of international politics. Is it a politically bi-polar or a politically inter-dependent world?[56]

THE LONG-TERM LIBERAL PERSPECTIVE

Liberals see a new agenda of foreign policy as overshadowing or dampening the very nature of U.S.-Soviet or Communist-anti-Communist rivalry. They see a whole new set of forces in world politics as superseding and to a large degree displacing the bipolar U.S.-versus-USSR or free-world-versus-communism perspective. The major new forces can be outlined as follows:

1. The Sino-Soviet conflict.
2. Technological developments—increased range of strategic weapons, military transport and communications—that enormously erode the value of foreign bases and allies for strategic war.
3. Polycentrism and the rise of centrifugal tendencies within both the Communist and the anti-Communist alliance systems, particularly along economic lines.
4. Growing economic ties between the United States and the Soviet Union, and China's new relationship with Japan and the West.
5. The enormous human suffering in the Southern Hemisphere countries and rapidly increasing North-South tensions.
6. The rapidly rising power of the multinational corporations that threatens to eclipse the nation-state system.
7. The new threats from worldwide pollution of the air and water of the planet, the destruction of the ozone layer, and the cumulative impact of industry on the entire global climate, threatening incredible global transformations.
8. The dangers attendant upon an accelerating rate of nuclear proliferation quite beyond what had been expected by responsible officials.

9. The new issues of the distribution of the resources of the world's oceans and seabeds.
10. The question of the entire distribution and depletion of the world's natural resources as a general issue lending itself no longer to piecemeal treatment.
11. The worldwide population explosion and its consequences.[57]

In this view, new kinds of knowledge as well as a new agenda in American foreign policy are required by the very nature of changing international forces. In many ways these new forces exacerbate the necessity to reach accords with the Soviets so that resources, domestically and globally, may be allocated in ways commensurate with these new forces and the new foreign policy agenda. From this perspective, though the Russians may take some opportunities to extend their influence, as in Angola, they too will be forced to come to grips with the realities of the new agenda.[58] The challenges of a new age of scarcity and of the international spread of weapons, technology, population upheaval, transnational corporations, communications, and terrorism are irreversibly transforming the globe.

Among those who do see the new agenda of foreign policy as overshadowing or channeling Soviet-American rivalry, there are significant differences. In attaching primary importance to new forces in world politics, the liberals are led to a fundamental reinterpretation of the nature and threat of communism. Soviet and Communist capabilities are, for the liberals, far less powerful relative to the contingencies likely to arise than either Communists or conservatives may believe. Indeed, the liberals perceive the new agenda as requiring unprecedented changes in the scope and character of government and the organization of society.

With regard to strategic force structures, liberals tend to believe that the United States has spent far too much money on weapons systems, such as the B-1 bomber and the Trident submarine, which do not significantly protect or increase the second-strike capability of the United States for "assured destruction." In making this judgment, they take into account possible advances in technology or force levels of the Soviets and other powers and allow for a "first-use" (as opposed to a first-strike) deterrent function of nuclear forces vis-à-vis superior conventional forces. Liberals deny the argument that a weapons system should be developed or deployed because it serves as a bargaining chip in slowing down the arms race. They argue, to the contrary, that the bargaining-chip approach only serves to escalate the arms race.[59]

With regard to conventional force structures, liberals on the whole see Soviet forces, particularly those of the air and ground, as basically defensive in their overall structure, although they wish to consider each proposed U.S. conventional capability on its merits against plausible contingencies. They view the possibilities of a limited conventional war involving the major powers, at least outside the Middle East, as unlikely given (1) Western European unity, (2) the Chinese threat preoccupying Soviet attention, (3) the greater Soviet interest in economic and technological development, and trade with the West as a means to that end, and, as the *keystone* of their whole position, based on estimates of past Soviet behavior and attitudes, (4) the inevitable risks of any conventional war escalating into full-scale nuclear war, and (5) the belief that the Russians fully appreciate those risks, with the memory still fresh of 20 million Russians killed in World War II.

Liberals see worldwide expenditure on arms as a diversion of the very resources needed to combat the problems of the new agenda. In this sense they become "ideologues" in their privately admitted preference to err on the side of less military force than might be useful for contingencies of what they see as remote possibilities in favor of large expenditures for contingencies that have already arisen.

Liberal attitudes toward Soviet and Communist subversion are complex. Generally speaking, they seem to vary with regard to how extensive they believe the subversion to be. Yet there appears to be a set of common responses regarding the importance of such subversion. They generally believe that not many countries are vulnerable to internal subversion, due to countervailing forces in those countries which have great incentives to resist control by any foreign power. Even if a country did "fall," there would be little effect on the balance of power among the United States, the Soviet Union, China, Western Europe, Eastern Europe, and Japan. If a major LDC country, such as Brazil or Indonesia, became controlled by local Communists, there is now every reason, liberals believe, to assume that its power would not be *additive* to the military threat posed to the United States by other Communist powers, especially as the new military technology—in transport, communications, and the range of strategic forces—makes the need for bases and staging areas in foreign countries for central war contingencies less necessary.

Moreover, if a country goes Communist, it does not entail that that country will have any the less incentive to trade with the United States. Domestic economic pressures will force these countries to trade where the trading is best, ideology notwithstanding, the more so since the Soviet Union and countries of Eastern Europe have already set such a pattern.

Since the strategic and economic reasons for counterintervention seem slight, there remains only the moral justification for intervention, that is, to prevent a people from falling under the rule of an oppressive totalitarian or authoritarian Communist dictatorship. Generally speaking, liberals would favor selected measures to support democratic forces, such as economic aid and strengthened trade relations. Increasingly, liberals believe that the United States is poorly equipped to attempt to influence political configurations in other countries, even for highly moral reasons, because (1) of the intractability of the multivariate interactions of forces within the countries, and (2) the agencies of the U.S. government are not reliable instruments, either in expertise or bureaucratic imperative, for political intervention on the side of democratic forces.[60]

What is perhaps the greatest cut point between the liberals and conservatives in the area of intervention, however, is the adamant aversion of liberals to support repressive and exploitative right-wing authoritarian regimes, whatever the reason. This division had become wider and deeper since 1970, in large part because of Vietnam, because of the revelations of U.S. intervention in Chile, with the bloodiness of the reactionary repression there and its protracted nature, and because of events of a similar nature in Argentina, Uruguay, Greece, and elsewhere.[61]

Some liberals are caught ambivalently between (1) the desire to help less fortunate people around the world, as evidenced by their uniformly high support for that humanitarian and economic aid which is not politically diverted to anti-Communist objectives, and (2) a moral aversion to intervention in other countries' politics. Of course, intervention consistent with their principles entails supporting only those regimes or groups which are both egalitarian and democratic. In the instance where the only choice is between authoritarian forces on the right and authoritarian forces on the left, some liberals would opt for noninvolvement and a few would favor aiding repressive left-wing forces, if, and only if, they had demonstrated a genuine will and competence to serve all of their own people and develop their societies.

With regard to the role of U.S. private investment in the LDCs, liberals tend to believe that such investment plays a significant role in development, but that some or even much of that investment has been exploitative. Therefore, some of the investment deserves to be nationalized, some should be nationalized but with compensation, some should be renegotiated, and some should be subject to explicit agreement on divestiture between the host and investing countries. Some liberals tend to be optimistic about the increasing power of the LDCs to forge the will and implements necessary and sufficient to become independent of external economic interests.[62] Others are deeply pessimistic about the economic leverage available to the LDCs, especially of the Fourth World. Some purpose, others revolt against, "triage."

Liberals evidence a larger concern with nuclear proliferation than do conservatives. It appears that the liberals would, if in power, seek to negotiate with those countries that are the sources of nuclear proliferation to limit to the maximum degree possible such proliferation, and liberals seek greater guarantees and security machinery to ensure that weapons-grade nuclear materials will not be acquired from nuclear technology transfers for peaceful purposes.

One group of liberals differs from the foregoing in only three respects, namely, in their active concern for the creation of effective supranational agencies for controlling (1) the effects of the growth of multinational corporations, (2) shocks to the ecosystem from worldwide industrialization, population growth, and pollution, and (3) the distribution of the world's resources, including nuclear technology and materials, the resources of the seabed, natural energy resources, development capital, and food, for the maximum well-being of the planet as a whole, and in a *much more equitable way* among the people of the world. Those holding this position perceive dangers of failing to institute such controls in the near term as catastrophic for everyone, not for only the less powerful and less advantaged. Yet they tend to resign themselves to the conclusion that the nations of the world, developed countries included, are not yet ready, politically, intellectually, or bureaucratically, to integrate and rationalize their own economies with a world economic order, which meets the previous three concerns.[63] Those of this persuasion find their role to be to educate elites as to the dangers of international anarchy and to the opportunities for international cooperation, and to formulate policies that take advantage of the opportunities available in a piecemeal fashion.

Another group of liberals begins where the previous group leaves off, asking *why* the world is not ready to enter into the kind of cooperation that may well be vital to the survival of the planet itself, and surely is vital to the survival of hundreds of millions of disadvantaged people in both the underdeveloped and the developed worlds, that is, those "marginals" without access to the benefits of the existing economic systems. The answer to the question for this group is that the great multinational corporations, in their tendency to protect and extend existing investments, cannot be reconciled with such progress as this group believes necessary. In an extraordinary parallel of reasoning, this group agrees with conservatives that the conditions present in many less developed countries make any democratic development remote. Therefore, they conclude, the only choice available to those who would influence the political destiny of those countries is between an authoritarian regime of the right and an authoritarian regime of the left. But by and large, some liberals would be attracted to any genuinely progressive democratic forces in the LDCs which would build a mass base of genuine support, and would eschew authoritarian political movements. These congressmen show a deep cultural antipathy to any form of authoritarianism, except where the alternative was continued lack of development with the mortality rates that accompany such failure.[64] Whereas conservatives see an irrepressible conflict between the two forces of capitalism and communism, this group of liberals sees a repressible conflict between the three forces of radical corporatism, communism, and democratic socialism. To this group of liberals, there is a vast difference between a strong government of unaccountable bureaucrats of the communist variety, and strong government of politicians in a democratic parliamentary socialist system, held accountable through a perfected electoral process by a well-informed citizenry, governing with the help of a higher civil service possessed of neutral competence.[65]

Another group of liberals see modern corporatism as an irreconcilable obstacle to the development of conditions which foster freedom, community, and a decent standard of living for all the people both of developed and less developed countries on two planes—the economic and the political. This group points to the conservative model of development (creating a "favorable investment climate" and its prerequisite political stability)[66] and asks whether that model does not in good faith demand of conservatives active political intervention in countries around the world to prevent socialism, if conservatives are sincere about their beliefs concerning the efficacy of uncontrolled capitalism as a model for development.

This group believes that only the collective efforts of many nations operating through supranational organizations will be able to destroy effectively the power of the multinationals, but unlike others, believes that only an international order of "progressive" governments would be willing to construct such supranational agencies. As long as the multinational firm can easily transfer much of its capital and other resources to countries which afford the most favorable treatment, and as long as the multinationals control goods and services essential to modern economies, it is not clear that even nationalization within any one country, even the United States, would significantly alter the problem, in this view.

The central problem of international politics for liberals is how to bring about the institution of strong democratic and progressive regimes in the United States and Western Europe and in the LDCs, in order to end wide-scale human suffering and save the planet from both nuclear war developing out of nuclear proliferation, and from destruction of the environment and the world's natural resources, through international cooperation and redistribution. The liberal believes that in an advanced democratic society the bulk of the people are willing to make mature sacrifices so long as the sacrifices appear necessary and equitable, and if they believe that those who administer the government have a deep sense of responsibility to all the people.[67]

NOTES

1. Clausen's work, besides being currently the most influential, asserts unequivocally the total independence of foreign policy issues from domestic policy issues in the voting patterns of congressmen. Moreover, he asserts that "foreign trade and foreign aid involve different policy concepts. Defense policy is independent of both. Immigration policy involves yet a

different concept. Let me emphasize, here, that these are not findings based only on this study; they appear in other studies in some historical depth" [no footnote], *How Congressmen Decide* (New York: St. Martins, 1973), p. 41. I concur with Clausen's judgment of past findings, vis-à-vis congressmen. Among the many other studies that obtained similar results *within* foreign policy and *across* foreign and domestic policy, perhaps the most influential vis-à-vis congressional candidates, were the findings of Philip Converse. His findings were as follows:

Converse's Findings: Summary of Differences in Level of Constraint (Attitude Consistency) Within and Between Domains, Elite and Mass

	Average Coefficients[a]		
	Within Domestic Issues	*Between Domestic and Foreign*	*Within Foreign Issues*
Elite	.53	.25	.37
Mass	.23	.11	.23

[a]Entries are average gamma coefficients. Converse's coefficients, though identified as "tau-gammas" (*sic*), are in fact gamma statistics. I am indebted to Converse for communicating to me what measure was actually used. The misprint was due to a terminological confusion at the time of Converse's publication; cf. p. 228.

SOURCE: Philip Converse, "The Nature of Belief Systems in Mass Publics," in David E. Apter, ed., *Ideology and Discontent* (New York: The Free Press of Glencoe, 1964), p. 229.

2. David Truman, *The Congressional Party* (New York: Wiley, 1959), p. 2.

3. Clausen, in *How Congressmen Decide*, pp. 41-44, 77, 78, 82-84, 100-104, denies the claims of this chapter and Chapter 5 in relationship to consistencies within foreign policy and across foreign and domestic policy. Other studies that found no significant relation within foreign policy attitudes or behavior or across foreign and domestic attitudes or behavior include Duncan MacRae, *Dimensions of Congressional Voting: A Statistical Study of the House of Representatives in the Eighty-first Congress* (Berkeley: University of California Publications in Sociology and Social Institutions, 1958), p. 213; Charles D. Farris, "A Scale Analysis of Ideological Factors in Congressional Voting," in Heinz Eulau and John C. Wahlke, eds., *Legislative Behavior: A Reader in Theory and Research* (Glencoe, Ill.: The Free Press, 1959); George M. Belknap, "Scaling Legislative Behavior," in the same volume. Duncan MacRae notes in *Dimensions of Congressional Voting* (1958), p. 213:

> In the study of Congress, the foreign-policy dimension is most readily distinguished. Gage and Shimberg, using cumulative scales for the first time in application to legislative roll-call votes, analyzed the *New Republic's* selection of roll-call votes for the Senate in the Seventy-ninth and Eightieth Congresses; in both Congresses it was found that foreign-policy and tariff issues created a disproportionate number of nonscale types and had to be eliminated from the scales. Belknap, in a more thoroughgoing analysis of the Senate in the Eightieth Congress, found four major scales and examined their intercorrelations; one outstanding result was the relative independence of the foreign-policy scale (dealing with the Marshall Plan, Greek-Turkish aid, and CARE) from the other scales dealing with domestic issues. Findings presented below serve further to confirm the distinctness of foreign-policy issues from domestic issues in Congress, at least in the period immediately following World War II. Once foreign policy has been isolated as a distinct dimension (or set of dimensions), it is possible to discern in almost every study a general dimension of domestic liberalism—conservatism related particularly to the conflict between labor and

> management. Such a dimension has been found in several closely related forms by Belknap, in Harris's factorial study of the Senate in the Eightieth Congress, by MacRae in an analysis of the Massachusetts legislature, and by Okusu in a study of the California legislature.

Clausen's theory is contradicted by the evidence presented earlier by RePass, which showed that in 1960 about 65 percent of Americans said that a foreign or defense policy issue was "most important" and only about 35 percent said a domestic policy issue was. David E. RePass, "Issue Salience and Party Choice," *American Political Science Review* 65, no. 2 (June 1971): 389-401. Curiously, Clausen makes no reference to, let alone arguing against, RePass's findings, despite the wide attention given to the RePass article.

4. Cf. James A. Nathan and James K. Oliver, *United States Foreign Policy and World Order* (Boston: Little, Brown, 1976), pp. 126-36, the discussion of National Security Council Policy Paper No. 68, produced in early 1950 by Acheson and Nitze, which became an overarching conceptual framework for America's foreign policy in the cold war. Perhaps the most articulate expression of the viewpoint that the threat of expansionist international communism in 1976 is no different from the way it was as earlier perceived to be by strong anti-Communists in the United States, as originally expressed in NCS-68, is Norman Podhoretz's 1976 article, "Making the World Safe for Communism," *Commentary* 61, no. 4 (April 1976):31-41. For a brilliant description of Kissinger's reactions to the perceived threat of a Communist regime taking power in Portugal, if true, and of how Ambassador Carlucci, whose right-wing credentials in a variety of domestic and foreign assignments in the Nixon administration were beyond reproach in those quarters, frantically attempted to prevent Kissinger from overreacting, cf. Tad Szulc, "Lisbon and Washington: Behind Portugal's Revolution," *Foreign Policy*, no. 21, Winter 1975-76, pp. 3-63. For further examples of how little the Vietnam War affected fundamental beliefs about the nature of the threat of communism and how that threat should be identified and dealt with, see the "Speech by Assistant Secretary Schaufele to the House International Relations Subcommittee on Africa," February 6, 1976, pp. 11 and 16 (obtained from the Department of State):

> We are told that we are over-reacting—that the Africans will never be communists and we should not worry about what the Soviets are doing. This argument misses the whole point of Moscow's strategy in less developed areas like Africa. When the Soviets speak about changing the "correlation of forces" in the world, they are talking about extending their influence in countries where it has not been strong before, and conversely neutralizing Western influence in countries where it was previously dominant. It is true that Moscow claims to see this as a long, slow process growing out of internal social and other conflicts. It also believes, however, that communist countries have a certain role to play as "midwives of progress" assisting leftist forces in each country. . . .—And in the last analysis we risk bringing on other confrontations in the future under conditions less advantageous to us and more dangerous to all. . . .

Similarly, W. Averell Harriman, in testimony before the Subcommittee on Future Foreign Policy Research and Development of the Committee on International Relations, House of Representatives, 94th Cong., 1st sess., July 15, 1975, p. 5, stated in the same vein:

> . . . I believe on the one hand we are spending too much money on our new nuclear weapons systems, perhaps giving too little attention to our conventional military equipment and strength. On the other hand, we are neglecting the need to face Soviet support for so-called liberation movements. . . . The functions of the CIA are now under critical review. All abuses at home and abroad must be protected against in the future. However, the continued activity of this agency is of real importance to our security both in its intelligence activities and in its ability to help nations counter subversive actions against them.

(Now Senator) Daniel P. Moynihan, "The United States in Opposition," *Commentary* (March 1975), states at page 39:

> The great darkness could yet consume us. The potential for absorption of these states into the totalitarian camp is there and will continue to be there. This is perhaps especially true where one-party states have been established, but even where multi-party democracy flourishes, the tug of the "socialist countries," to use the UN term, persists. . . . The outcome will almost certainly turn on whether or not these nations, individually and in groups, succeed in establishing sufficiently productive economies. If they do not, if instead they become permanently dependent on outside assistance, that assistance is likely more and more to come from the totalitarian nations, and with it the price of internal political influence from the totalitarian camp through the local pro-Moscow, or pro-Peking, Communist party. For everywhere there are such parties. . . .

But, as we shall see, the entire Angola debate showed that, for a majority of the Senate, the events in Indochina changed nothing regarding the perception of the threat of communism or the need for U.S. intervention against left-wing regimes short of U.S. combat involvement on the ground. *Congressional Quarterly Weekly Report* 34, no. 34, August 21, 1976, p. 14, notes: "Much of the conservative wording (of the Republican Platform) on foreign policy was the work of Senator Jesse A. Helms of North Carolina." See especially the portion of the Republican Platform under the title of *United States-Soviet Relations* and the portion devoted specifically to Angola.

5. Many Members, during these interviews, commented on the fact that not a single roll call vote on the Vietnam War had been held on the floor of the House as of that time (Summer 1970).

6. The quote that follows, from Congressman Donald Riegle, then a Republican congressman from Michigan, now a Democratic senator, could as well be applied to foreign affairs and armed services committees in 1970, especially the more important ones:

> The Democratic leadership has another built-in bias that reflects itself in terms of committee assignments. Often, the more conservative Democrats will assign liberals to such "liberal" committees as Education and Labor. They know that, as long as they control the appointment of Members to the Appropriations Committee, they can put on the brakes at that point. Both Democrats and Republicans have gone to great pains to screen out from the Appropriations Committee those who spend more for domestic needs. I'm a fluke. If the Republican leadership had a second chance, they probably wouldn't appoint me to Appropriations. I'd more likely get Education and Labor. [Donald Reigle with Trevor Armbrister, *O Congress* (New York: Popular Library, 1972), p. 176]

7. I was aided in forming this judgment by interviews with Pat Holt and Roland Paul of the Senate Foreign Relations Committee Staff, who were generous with their time in long interviews, and by David Karns, who had only weeks before tested the routes of access.

8. Cf. C. Fred Bergsten, "Crisis in U.S. Trade Policy," *Foreign Affairs* 49 (July 1971):619-35.

9. The following criteria determined the formulation of questions constituting the interview schedule:

> 1. Each question should successfully evoke answers expressing the policy cleavages actually existing in the Congress on the underlying dimension which the question purports to tap.
>
> 2. Each question should easily evoke clear and equivalent understandings of what is being asked.
>
> 3. The questions individually and taken together should seem to all respondents to be a genuinely neutral attempt to understand the differences that divide the members on foreign policy, as the letter requesting interviews described the purpose of this study.

4. The questions should be phrased in the language in which the issues were ordinarily posed in the Congress, so that time would not be wasted, nor resistance of the respondents provoked, over the definition of the issue or policy alternatives.

5. The choice of questions should involve issues familiar enough to minimize any unwillingness to answer or disposition to answer invalidly. Familiar issues presume that the Member would have been more likely to have taken a position or been identified with a position already in other contexts.

6. The latter condition of familiarity with the issues should hold both for Members who do not sit on national security policy related committees and for those who do.

The advantage involved in interviewing congressmen on politically salient issues is almost unique. By examining congressional hearings and documents, reading the press closely and listening to interviews with congressmen on television and radio, a political analyst can become familiar, without significant pretesting, with the congressional idiom, and so fulfill these six criteria.

10. Charles P. Kindleberger, *American Business Abroad: Six Lectures on Direct Investment* (New Haven, Conn.: Yale University Press, 1969), p. 148.

11. Tad Szulc, "U.S. Retaliating for Foreign Seizures," *New York Times*, 14 August 1971, p. 3.

12. "The White House vs. Latin America," *Washington Post*, 21 January 1972, p. A22.

13. DeCubas was then president of Westinghouse Electric International and president and chairman of the Council for the Americas, which represents the association of 210 companies with about 85 percent of U.S. private investment in Latin America.

14. Gerd Wilcke, "Business from U.S. Fears Loss of Capital," *New York Times*, 4 April 1971, III, p. 15. Compare the account of the credit "crunch" by the Nixon government, especially through the Treasury Department, on expropriating foreign governments, in Stanley Hoffman, "Will the Balance Balance at Home?" *Foreign Policy*, no. 7 (Summer 1972): p. 65; James F. Petras and Robert LaPorte, Jr., "Chile—No," *Foreign Policy*, no. 7 (Summer 1972): 132-58.

15. Petras and LaPorte, Chile—No," p. 148.

16. Ibid., p. 153.

17. Ibid., p. 148.

18. Ibid., p. 146.

19. Charles L. Schultze, Edward R. Fried, Alice M. Rivlin, and Nancy H. Teeters, *Setting National Priorities: The 1972 Budget* (Washington, D.C.: The Brookings Institution, 1971), p. 122.

20. Ibid.

21. Teresa Hayter, *Aid as Imperalism* (Baltimore: Penguin Books, 1971). This study was originally commissioned by the World Bank itself through the Overseas Development Institute, which later tried to suppress the result, according to documentation supplied in the book itself.

22. U.S. Congress, Senate, *Rockefeller Report on Latin America, Hearings* before the Subcommittee on Western Hemisphere Affairs of the Committee on Foreign Relations, 91st Cong. 2nd sess., November 20, 1969. See the discussion in Chapter 7.

23. I am indebted to several individuals in the offices of the ADA who are responsible for constructing the ADA roll call set for rating congressmen and who explained to me the procedure of seeking votes in these four categories.

24. ADA scores were taken from *They Grade the Congress* (Washington, D.C.: Chamber of Commerce, 1971).

25. Cf. Judith G. Smith, ed., *Political Brokers: Money, Organizations, Power and People* (New York: Liverwright/National Journal Book, 1972), p. 19, by the editors and reporters of the *National Journal*.

26. The nine included three Members who became senators—Beall (R-Md), Stafford (R-Vt), and Taft (R-Ohio)—two who died in office—Andrews (D-Ala) and Corbett (R-Penn)—and four who were defeated in primary or general elections in the 1970 election—Cohelen (D-Calif), Foreman (R-NM), Langen (R-Minn), and Lowenstein (D-NY). In addition, one Member of the

sample had to be dropped because his interview was unintelligible on the tape due to machine malfunction, and an eleventh member of the sample was dropped because he expressed an unfamiliarity with the bulk of these issues.

27. Joel D. Aberbach, James D. Chesney, and Bert A. Rockman, "Exploring Elite Political Attitudes: Some Methodological Lessons," *Political Methodology* 2 (1975): pp. 1-28; Aberbach et al. give far more detailed attention to the questions treated here in their 1974 paper delivered at the Midwest Political Science Association meeting, April 25-27, which is also the University of Michigan Institute of Public Policy Studies Discussion Paper No. 60. References to Aberbach et al., such as the following quotation, are *from the convention paper*:

> When a *very high* degree of focus can be attached to the question, it usually makes sense to structure the range of answers as well. *As has been repeatedly argued here*, this structuring should occur when expectations can be made rather precise as a result of a considerable degree of background knowledge. [P. 40, fn. 15; italics added.]

28. John Galtung, *Theory and Methods of Social Research*, rev. ed. (New York: Columbia University Press, 1969), pp. 119-21.

29. Cf. Ole R. Holsti, *Content Analysis for the Social Sciences and Humanities* (Reading, Mass.: Addison-Wesley, 1969), p. 138; Aberbach et al., 1974 convention paper, p. 42, fn. 26, p. 138.

30. Converse concurs in this interpretation of the impact of using the two different statistics on the discrepancy in the findings of the two studies.

31. An anonymous reviewer for this book, in a review of an earlier version, has pointed out that I categorize "a person's position on economic and military aid as liberal or conservative in part on the basis of the kinds of regimes for which the military aid would be used. But does this not create a contamination that would artificially raise the correlation between the question on support for right-wing nations?" I think this is a perceptive criticism, pointing to a source of contamination that I did not anticipate. However, since only part of the response as coded reflected military aid, and since the argument might be made that the Members on the whole are in far greater contention over the economic aid portion, especially since military aid to Israel is an especially sensitive issue to the liberals vis-à-vis military aid in general, the extent of this possible contamination might be negligible. To test this, the average of the coefficients from Table 3-1 was recalculated after dropping all correlations between the aid question (question 10) and all other questions. The effect was slight—the average coefficient dropped from .522 to .513.

32. Cf. U.S. Congress, House, 92nd Cong., 1st sess., November 10, 1971, *Congressional Record* 117, no. 176, pp. 10855-66.

33. Cf. Theodore H. Moran, "New Deal or Raw Deal in Raw Materials," *Foreign Policy*, no. 5 (Winter 1971-72):119-36. As Moran points out, the vertical integration of many commodity enterprises of the underdeveloped countries in world markets makes the gesture of expropriation in many cases little more than a mere show of economic nationalism. This is particularly the case where the credit for exploiting the natural resources, the technology and resources for processing and transporting them, and the economic relationships for marketing them, make ownership a relatively unimportant fact of life. This, of course, varies from commodity to commodity and industry to industry.

34. All Kendall tau-b correlations from here on have two properties not shared by those previously: (1) many more categories, 33 as opposed to 3, and (2) for what it is worth, levels of significance testing that established each of the following correlations as significant at .001 level of significance. See Blalock, *Social Statistics* (New York: McGraw Hill, 1972), pp. 441-42, for a brief discussion of Reynolds's findings on the effects of categorizations. For an understanding of the logic of when tests of significance might be worth something, perhaps after all relevant correlated biases have been controlled, see Hanan C. Selvin, "A Critique of Tests of Significance in Survey Research," *American Sociological Review* 22 (October 1957):408-14;

cf. Leslie Kish, "Some Statistical Problems in Research Design," in Edward R. Tufte, ed., *The Quantitative Analysis of Social Problems* (Reading, Mass.: Addison-Wesley Publishing Co., 1970), p. 394, for a critique of Selvin's stringent attitude toward significance tests, along the lines of "the perfect is the enemy of the good."

35. Tom de Vries, "Jamaica, or the Non-Reform of the International Monetary System," *Foreign Affairs* 54, 3 (April 1976):577-605.

36. C. Fred Bergsten, "Let's Avoid a Trade War," *Foreign Policy* 23 (Summer 1976):3-23; Hobart Rowan, "Witteveen Cites Need to Dampen Wide Swings in Exchange Rates," *Washington Post*, 18 June 1976, p. D11; Andrew D. Crockett and Morris Goldstein, "Inflation Under Fixed and Flexible Exchange Rates," *International Monetary Fund Staff Paper* (November 1976). I am grateful to Morris Goldstein for an early opportunity to examine this paper. Seven recent projects at Brookings reflect the new foreign policy agenda. They are part of a series on worldwide inflation and include: *World Inflation and World Money* (Walter S. Salant); *Inflation and World Commodity Markets* (Barry Bosworth); *A Comparative Evaluation of National Stabilization Policies in Industrial Countries, 1972-75* (Gardner Ackley); *The Balance-of-Payments Adjustment Process, National Efforts to Export Inflation, and World Inflation* (C. Fred Bergsten); *Japan and the International Transmission Mechanism* (Lawrence B. Krause and Sueo Sekiguchi); *A Comparative Evaluation of National Incomes Policies in Industrial Countries in the 1970s* (Lloyd Ulman and Robert J. Flanagan); *World Inflation and the Less-Developed Countries* (William R. Cline).

37. Seyom Brown, *New Forces in World Politics* (Washington, D.C.: Brookings Institution, 1974). Brown's book is probably the best overall treatment of the components of the new agenda confronting American foreign policy.

38. *Congressional Quarterly Weekly Report* 34, no. 42 (October 16, 1976):3022-23.

39. Cf. U.S. Congress, Senate, "Staff Report: Covert Action in Chile—1963-1973," *Select Committee to Study Governmental Operations with Respect to Intelligence Activities*, and *Hearings*, December 4, 1973, *Foreign and Military Intelligence, Book I, Final Report of the Select Committee to Study Governmental Operations with Respect to Intelligence Activities, United States Senate, Together with Additional, Supplemental, and Separate Views*, 94th Cong., 2d sess.; cf. Petras and LaPorte, "Chile: No," pp. 132-58; Paul E. Sigmund, "The Invisible Blockage and the Overthrow of Allende," *Foreign Affairs* 52, no. 2 (January 1974):322-40; William P. Bundy, "Dictatorships and American Foreign Policy," *Foreign Affairs* 54, no. 1 (October 1975):50-60. Petras and LaPorte, and Sigmund have had clashing points of view published before the facts were made fully known.

40. *Congressional Quarterly Weekly Report* 34, nos. 6, 18, 19, 20, 41, and Richard D. Lyons, "U.S. Arms-Sales Rise Stirs Capital Concern," *New York Times*, 19 October 1975, p. 1, first in a series of articles on arm sales; cf. Senator Edward M. Kennedy, "The Persian Gulf: Arms Race or Arms Control," *Foreign Affairs* 54, no. 1 (October 1975):14-36.

41. Cf. Robert F. Ellsworth, "Diego Garcia: A Stabilizing Impact," *Washington Post*, 31 July 1975, p. A18; cf. Barry Blechman's article in the *Washington Post*, 20 July 1975, to which Ellsworth, who was assistant secretary of defense for international security affairs, replies.

42. According to Leslie H. Gelb, "Move for Big Cuts Wanes: Liberals and Moderates in Congress Want to Avoid Signaling Isolation," *New York Times*, 6 May 1975, p. 1; cf. James K. Oliver, *Congress and the Future of American Seapower: An Analysis of United States Navy Budget Requests in the 1970s*, a paper delivered at the 1976 Annual Meeting of the American Political Science Association, The Palmer House, Chicago, Illinois, September 2-5, 1976; cf. Charles L. Schultze's figures in Owen and Schultze, eds., *Setting National Priorities: The Next Ten Years*, especially Tables 8-14, 8-15, 8-16.

43. George C. Wilson, "Pentagon Cashes In: Hill Budget Leaders Unsuccessful in Cuts," *Washington Post*, 15 May 1976, p. 1.

44. Leslie H. Gelb, "Liberal Democrats Retreat on Pentagon's Budget," *New York Times*, 3 June 1976, p. 29.

45. Gelb, "Liberal Democrats Retreat. . . ," *New York Times*, 3 June 1976, p. 29.

46. Lester R. Brown and E. P. Eckholm, *By Bread Alone* (published for the Overseas Development Council by Praeger Books, New York, 1974); Lester R. Brown, *The Politics and Responsibility of the North American Breadbasket*, Worldwatch Paper Series, 1975; Alan Berg, "The Trouble with Triage," *New York Times Magazine*, 15 June 1975, pp. 26-35; I. M. Destler, "United States Food Policy: Reconciling Domestic and International Objectives," paper delivered at the 18th Annual Convention of the International Studies Association, 1976, p. 14; Raymond Hopkins and Donald Puchala, "Global Food Policy: Economic and Political Forces," prepared for the 1980's Project of the Council on Foreign Relations; Emma Rothschild, "Food Politics," *Foreign Affairs* 54, no. 2 (January 1976), pp. 285-307; Emma Rothschild, "A Reporter at Large: World Food Economy," *The New Yorker* (May 26, 1975):40-76; Fred H. Sanderson, *The Great Food Fumble* (Washington, D.C.: The Brookings Institution, 1975); *Scientific American*, special issue on Food and Agriculture, vol. 235, no. 3 (September 1976).

47. Article, "Schultz Hits Any S.D.R. Tie to Poor-Land Aid," *New York Times*, 28 September 1973, p. 43; editorial, "Monetary Deadlock," *New York Times*, 28 September 1973, p. 30.

48. Cf. U.S. Congress, Senate, *Multinational Corporations and United States Foreign Policy*, *Hearings* before the Subcommittee on Multinational Corporations of the Committee on Foreign Relations, 93rd Cong., 2nd sess., June 17, 19, and July 17, 18, 19, and 22, 1974, Part 10; U.S. Congress, Senate, *Multinational Corporations and United States Foreign Policy*, *Hearings* before the Subcommittee on Multinational Corporations of the Committee on Foreign Relations, 93rd Cong., 2nd sess., June 5 and 6, July 25, and August 12, 1974, Part 9; U.S. Congress, Senate, *Multinational Corporations and United States Foreign Policy*, *Hearings* before the Subcommittee on Multinational Corporations of the Committee on Foreign Relations, 94th Cong., 1st sess., 1974, Part 8: Appendix to Part 7; U.S. Congress, Senate, *Multinational Corporations and United States Foreign Policy*, *Hearings* before the Subcommittee on Multinational Corporations of the Committee on Foreign Relations, 94th Cong., 1st sess., January 29, February 5, 14, 20, and 26, March 11 and 18, 1975, Part II; U.S. Congress, Senate, *Multinational Corporations in Brazil and Mexico: Structural Sources of Economic and Noneconomic Power*, *Report* to the Subcommittee on Multinational Corporations of the Committee on Foreign Relations, by Richard S. Newfarmer and Willard F. Mueller (Washington, D.C.: U.S. Government Printing Office, 1975).

49. Ann Crittenden, "Doubt Is Voiced on Impact of U.S. Plan on Poor Lands," *New York Times*, 19 September 1975, p. 1; and the illuminating report by Michael T. Kaufman, "U.N. Trade Talks: The Have-Nots Demand a Fair Share," *New York Times*, 19 September 1975, p. 1.

50. Cf., for example, the extended and representative remarks of liberal Senator Pell on the rationales for and against further U.S. involvement in Angola at the height of the Angolan debate in the Senate, *Congressional Record*, 121, no. 189, Part II (December 13, 1975):S23055-56; cf. *Congressional Quarterly Weekly Review* 33, no. 52 (December 27, 1975):2898; cf., for example, the equally extended and representative remarks of conservative Senator Buckley on the same issue, *Congressional Record*, 121, no. 189, Part II (December 13, 1975):S23053; it should be crystal clear from these and countless other debates to be found in congressional documents that, save for acknowledgment that no uniformed U.S. military personnel should be committed publicly in a Vietnam-type conflict again, nothing has changed the deep ideological conflict of liberal and conservative perspectives on foreign policy.

51. Cf. transcript of the Dole-Mondale debate, *New York Times*, 16 October 1976, p. 1.

52. Milton Friedman, *Capitalism and Freedom* (Chicago: University of Chicago Press, 1962); at p. 8, Friedman states: "A society which is socialist cannot also be democratic, in the sense of guaranteeing individual freedom."

53. Cf. the testimony of Harriman before the Subcommittee on Future Foreign Policy Research and Development of the Committee on International Relations, House of Representatives, 94th Cong. 1st sess. July 15, 1975, p. 5:

> . . . we are neglecting the need to face Soviet support for so-called liberation movements. . . . The functions of the CIA (are) of real importance to our security both in its intelligence activities and in its ability to help friendly peoples counter subversive activities against them.

See also Rockefeller's testimony discussed in Chapter 7 and the *Rockefeller Report.*

54. Cf. the Church-Rockefeller exchange in Chapter 7.

55. Cf. Harriman's testimony, cited in note 53.

56. *New York Times,* "The Week in Review," Section 4, Sunday, 3 October 1976; cf. *Congressional Quarterly Weekly Review* 34, no. 41 (October 9, 1976):2901-14, for the full text of the debate.

57. Seyom Brown, *New Forces in World Politics.*

58. While certain analysts of American politics and society accent the theme of the apparent lack of cultural assimilation of certain groups of Americans, without any clear-cut criteria of what constituted assimilation in a functional sense, they ignored how very much greater were the problems of hard-core unassimilated nationality groups in the Soviet Union, which dwarf the problems in the United States; cf. Edward L. Keenan, "A Majority of Suppressed Minorities: Soviet Time Bomb," *New Republic,* August 21 and 28, 1976, pp. 17-21. Keenan is director of the Harvard Russian Research Center.

59. Cf. testimony of Marshall D. Shulman, then director of Columbia University's Russian Institute, before the Senate Foreign Relations Committee's Arms Control Subcommittee, July 14, 1971, as reported in "For the Record," *Washington Post,* 25 July 1971, p. B6.

60. Indeed, if one is to believe then CIA director William E. Colby, in testimony before a number of congressional subcommittees, according to Leslie H. Gelb, then diplomatic correspondent for the *New York Times*: "Sources paraphrased Mr. Colby as saying that, in the present world, the United States is not seriously threatened by communist undercover activities and that both sides see little advantage in such ventures for now." Cf. Leslie H. Gelb, "For Congress Overseeing the CIA Is No Easier Now," *New York Times,* 20 July 1975, p. E3. Whether or not Colby's remarks were intended for a cosmetic effect proffered to deflect forces bent on greater scrutiny and control of the CIA is not important here. What does seem important is that (1) either he made the claim in good faith, (2) or the array of forces that were taking positions against the CIA was a far different array than had defined the agency's political environment in the past. It is not unreasonable to surmise that changes occurred in congressional attitudes toward the agency *because* Soviet-American rivalry was obscured beneath the issues of the new global agenda. This argument may or may not be true. It would be a serious mistake in judgment to believe it was true when in fact it was false, from the liberal's perspective. But what is clear is that such an argument has been made an explicit and substantively coherent position, available to the Congress at this time.

61. Hans Morgenthau stated the liberal position with clarity and force:

> *Repression's Friend*
>
> To the Editor: The storm that has broken over our intervention in Chile has obscured what seems to me to be the crucial issue transcending this particular intervention: With unfailing consistency, we have since the end of the Second World War intervened on behalf of conservative and fascist repression against revolution and radical reform. In an age when societies are in a revolutionary or prerevolutionary stage, we have become the foremost counterrevolutionary status quo power on earth.
>
> Such a policy can only lead to moral and political disaster. While we wax indignant or apologetic over our most recent antirevolutionary intervention, we might do well not to

> lose sight of the political root of the problem. [Hans J. Morgenthau, "Repression's Friend," *New York Times*, 10 October 1974, p. 57]

62. C. Fred Bergsten, "Coming Investment Wars?" Brookings General Series Reprint 299 (Washington, D.C.: The Brookings Institution, 1975).

63. Brown, *New Forces in World Politics*, p. 201.

64. Robert L. Heilbroner, "Counterrevolutionary America," *Commentary* (April 1967): 31-38; cf. Senator Church's comments in the Hearings on the Rockefeller *Report* (cf. Chapter 7).

65. To this group of liberals, there *is* a vast difference between the unaccountable bureaucrats of communism and politicians in a democratic parliamentary socialist system held accountable through a perfected electoral process by a well-informed citizenry. This issue has crystallized around the question of whether or not the new European or "Euro-Communism" is genuine or merely tactical in adherence to parliamentary democracy. The saliency of the issue is indicated by the recent front page treatment by the *Washington Post* in a five-part series on "Euro-Communism." Reported by Jim Hoagland of the *Washington Post*, September 19-23, 1976, all five articles appeared on page 1. A litmus test that some consider valid as to the genuineness of the attachment of "Euro-Communism" to parliamentary democracy is open public intraparty democracy. According to an account in the *Washington Post* by Sari Gilbert, Thursday, October 21, 1976, p. A17, "Italian Communists Clash on Government Support," the Italian Communists seem now to be meeting this test for the first time with the painfulness attendant upon intraparty battles everywhere. The *Post*'s treatment dealt with questions such as (1) whether there is genuine aversion to Soviet-style bureaucratization, (2) strong dislike of repression based on the experience of living under it during the Fascist episodes of the 1920s, 1930s, and 1940s, (3) recognition of the need for material incentives and efficiency in the economist's sense, even in nationalized industries, and indeed the backing off from nationalization as a cure-all or a litmus test of one's political position.

In a fascinating interview between Zygmunt Nagorski, Jr., a staff member of the Council on Foreign Relations, and Sergio Segre, foreign minister of the Italian Communist party, that became the "Segre affair," an unnamed correspondent, claiming to represent the council, pointed out to Segre that the three grounds on which Western liberals oppose Communist parties coming even to share power were: "links to Moscow, totalitarianism and a tendency to nationalize everything." After denying all three charges and giving the historical background of how Italian Communists had arrived at their antipathy to these positions, Segre is reported to have said: "The important point is that the state takes the power to direct investment and consumption." If the attachment to parliamentary democracy and a pluralistic party system is genuine, then there is an intriguing similarity, on the one hand, of Segre's statement that control of investment and consumption patterns is the goal of political power, and, on the other hand, to the last paragraph of the Brookings Institution's *Setting National Priorities: The 1974 Budget*, in which the authors of that volume, Edward R. Fried, Alice M. Rivlin, Charles L. Schultze, and Nancy Teeters state:

> The chief distinctions we have drawn in this book, stated in perhaps oversimplified form, hinge on the extent to which the federal government goes beyond providing funds to persons or governments [income support and revenue sharing with states and localities] and intervenes in decisions about the demand or supply of particular goods and services.

Moreover, as we shall see in Chapter 5, ideas about credit allocation and capital allocation have been put forward in Congress by figures such as Senator Hubert Humphrey and Congressman Henry Reuss. These proposals seem highly suggestive of deep-rooted tendencies of change.

66. Robert Dahl pointed out in 1971:

> If Dr. Allende fails and the United States Government is known to have contributed to his failure, two lessons will be obvious to Latin Americans, and indeed to the world:
>
> (1) Although it supports dictatorships that oppose basic reforms, the United States Government is unwilling to support, and will probably oppose, democracies that attempt structural changes even by democratic and constitutional means.
>
> (2) Since the American Government opposes fundamental reforms even if these are brought about by democratic processes, and since fundamental reforms are, in the best of circumstances, enormously difficult to achieve through democratic processes, the optimal strategy for bringing about basic reforms in Latin America is by means of a revolutionary dictatorship, as in Cuba or Peru.
>
> It is my impression that most informed Latin Americans are already strongly predisposed to believe these two propositions. By its actions toward Chile, the Administration may erase any lingering doubts—and hopes. ["Letter to the Editor," *New York Times*, 3 December 1971, IV, p. 10]

67. For an authoritative and illuminating view of the sharp cleavage among American elites over Russia, cf. George F. Kennan's article in the Sunday "Outlook" section of the *Washington Post*, 11 December 1977, p. D1, entitled "A Plea by Mr. X 30 Years Later: George F. Kennan Urges a New Vision of Russia as We Near SALT Crossroads."

chapter 4

ANALYSIS OF CONGRESSIONAL COALITIONS: THE DILEMMA

The previous chapter, Chapter 3, confirmed very high ideological consistency ("constraint") *within* the domain of foreign policy issues. The following chapter, Chapter 5, specifically tests coalition and cleavage patterns within domestic policy, and across foreign and domestic policy, using analysis of roll call voting patterns. By using roll call votes, this study confronts an obstacle to *any* systematic analysis of Congressional coalitions and cleavages. That obstacle, most clearly stated as a formal logical dilemma, is the subject of this chapter, and must be resolved first, prior to proceeding to the analysis in Chapter 5.

COMPARABILITY VERSUS CONTEXTUAL VALIDATION OF INDICATORS

1. Because of the requirement of data comparability, any systematic analysis of Congressional coalitions and cleavages must use roll call analyses, if systematic interviews cannot be used, which they often cannot, given the range of issues and contexts involved.

2. But, for a variety of reasons, which will soon be stated, roll call votes are often false, misleading, or opaque, as indicators of the operative intent of a given Member or group of Members casting a particular vote. Yet it is that intention which must be identified, in order to discover fundamental dispositions—ideological, pluralistic, policy dimensional (Clausen) or whatever. If such fundamental dispositions can be isolated empirically, they can be used to support inferences to latent and manifest coalitions and cleavages structuring the outcomes of congressional action and inaction. But if the objects of inquiry are coalition structures in Congress, we must

not fall into the trap of identifying ideology with rigidity, that is, of expecting practical politicians to take rigidly uncompromising stands. Hence we must expect to find such dispositions, and the intentions they manifest, mired in the complexities of tactics and strategies, ambiguities and ambivalences about many levels of compromise, in a kaleidoscopic world of shifting political and policy contexts. Robert Putnam's delineation of decreased political or tactical rigidity and hostility, coincidental with constant ideological thinking in Britain and Italy, underscores this point.[1]

3. Contextually rich and intensive analyses of particular events, including case studies of battles over particular policies, leadership fights, and analyses of changes in congressional structures and processes, often reveal far more about operative intentions and behavior of Members, and seem intuitively more effective in "explaining" congressional events, than do roll call analyses.

4. But, from such non-roll call sources alone, it does not seem possible to be sure that one is seeing the forces at work proportionately. The question must always remain: Did the case study reliably represent the way congressmen and senators behave in the universe of their actions? Moreover, case studies will tend to accent manifest over latent forces, and areas of opportunity for action rather than structural forces that constrain legislative behavior. Most important, case studies do not allow one to establish *the comparability* of the actions or intentions of one legislator or legislative group with any other. Hence one cannot infer reliably from such contextually rich accounts to any *generalizations*, even spatio-temporally bracketed generalizations. And hence it does not seem possible, from such accounts, to lend controlled empirical confirmation to conflicting theories about forces or coalitions in Congress as a whole, nor to establish the validity of claims about what *would* happen if any particular set of conditions changes, particularly change in the political balance of forces in Congress.

Clearly, it is necessary to surmount our own prejudices of judgment or experience, howsoever much graced by a close contextual knowledge of Congress. That knowledge is of necessity selective, based on our own best understanding as to what is important, and sometimes merely based on what happened to come to notice by chance, bias, prior training, or institutional location, whereas much else is ignored! The kind of perspective that we must strive to achieve, if analyses of Congress are not to lead to proliferation of contrary and irreconcilable interpretations, is one which provides a sound basis for adjudicating among those interpretations, which of necessity brings us into the realm of social science. To do less is to ensure that we shall select interpretations to fit our preconceptions. What is required is a perspective that is not out of proportion, nor unwittingly time bound, nor overwhelmed by the particular to the point of not seeing the general. We should instead formally state and investigate generalizations which are implicitly assumed in major viewpoints about Congress, and about Congress as an element of the larger political equation.

Despite the low repute, deserved or not, that roll call analyses have attained among many trained academics and others who know Congress well,[2] the sole hope of attaining valid and reliable generalizations about congressional coalitions and cleavages will be found in some use of roll call analyses. However, these analyses must *somehow* be made to fit a research strategy that reflects the fact that many votes are not what they seem, and, because of actions influenced by anticipated reactions, may be a poor reflection of the congressional balance of forces working its will on the outcomes of the legislative process. Only such a research strategy offers a promise of escape between the horns of the dilemma.

The great advantage of roll call votes as data lies with their comparability: comparability of all legislators with all others on the same votes; comparability of all issues voted on with all other such issues by reference to the same legislators; and comparability of both issues and legislators over time to reveal patterns of stability or change in issue dispositions of legislators, or change or stability of issues over time.

A CAVEAT

All general claims made in this study about roll call analyses and analysts pertain *ONLY to roll call analyses focused on congressional coalitions and cleavages.* There are, of course, other analytic purposes to which roll call analyses are put, such as examining the relationships between various kinds of constituencies and legislative voting. The specific problems predicated of roll call analyses in this study are *not* attributed here to those other analytical purposes or uses of roll call analyses.

CONGRESS EXPERTS AND ROLL CALL ANALYSTS

Congress experts specialize in contextual knowledge: studying actual events involving Congress, congressional structures, processes, personalities, some policy areas and outcomes, congressional subcultures, the substance of legislation and its subsequent modification and implementation, incentive structures, and change in the institution over time. The vast majority of these studies add, cumulatively, to the understanding of congressional behavior. However, the real cumulativeness of these studies might be less than what is desired, once finely honed analytical questions, of the kind that have spurred the development of social sciences generally, are raised. Once surreptitious *causal* claims and inferences are brought out into the open, and formally stated, confidence in the understanding provided by the existing literature may be reduced. Close Congress watchers, academic and otherwise, know that within their own ranks many disputes have continued over years, and indeed decades,[3] regarding the actual role and institutional capacity of the Congress. At a time of great change in Congress itself, and when the relations between government in general and the private economy and society are coming under more urgent scrutiny, past disputes can only be intensified. Causal and counterfactual claims, as already indicated, set the only fully acceptable test of the adequacy of the unfolding research enterprise. But generally it is not facts, at least individual facts, that science explains, but rather, patterns. Bertrand Russell used the example of the stone and the avalanche: Science will never predict where a particular stone at the top of a hill will land at the end of an avalanche, having collided with many others on the way to the bottom. But science will explain the general conditions under which avalanches occur, with ever higher degrees of probability of successful prediction, and explanation of the conditions which prevent avalanches.

This study offers a pattern analysis from which, elsewhere, causal analysis can subsequently proceed. By analyzing the nature of congressional coalitions and cleavages, whether a pattern of ideological dispositions or a pattern of pluralistic dispositions, we shall at least know what to expect from the Congress, even if we do not explain in this study why those patterns exist. Other studies, building on analyses such as this, can explain *why* an ideological or a pluralist pattern best fits congressional attitudes and behavior. But the pattern analysis must be done first. That is the task of this study.

Roll call analyses of congressional coalitions and cleavages have their own special problems. The particular.virtue of a social science approach is touted to be the comparability of the data, in terms of which patterns of variation in attitudes and or behavior are described. But one cannot assume, *a priori*, that because a given datum of congressional history is a roll call vote, that it is comparable to another roll call vote, just because they are called the same thing; for example, both called a vote on foreign aid, or both named a congressional reform bill. Foreign aid in 1949 engaged very different preconceptions and intentions and, indeed, recipient countries, than aid in 1977. Similarly, the congressional reorganization of 1946 was a very different matter than congressional reform bills of the early and mid-1970s, which were instigated by liberals eager to weaken their conservative opponents (the Stevenson bill of early 1977 excepted). On reflection, it may be obvious that simply to *assume* such comparabilities is far too casual for adherence to rigorous social science standards.

A second major problem of roll call votes is that differences exist among them with respect to their *reversibility*, that is, the extent to which a vote can be undone by another vote, or by action or inaction in other parts of the legislative and administrative processes. Some votes *are* truly decisive, that is, strictly determinative of a policy or political outcome which cannot be undone. The vote on the Tunney amendment barring United States intervention in Angola in December 1975 is a good example. The vote did indeed determine an outcome that, given the beliefs and dispositions of the Ford administration and Secretary Kissinger, would have been quite different, had either the Tunney amendment failed of passage, or if there had been no vote either way. But among those who have seen many such votes, no one will fail to appreciate how many votes are *not* decisive, that is, how many do something that is actually undone, or could easily be undone, and often, as is the point here, are *meant* to be undone.

George Aiken, the highly respected Republican senator from Vermont, discussing his "sins" on the occasion of his retirement, noted:

> During the 34 years of my tenure as a United States Senator, I have committed many sins.
>
> I have voted for measures which I felt were wrong, comforting myself with the excuse that the House of Representatives, the conference committee, or, if necessary, the chief occupant of the White House would make the proper corrections.
>
> At other times I have voted for measures with which I did not agree for the purpose of preventing the approval of other measures which I felt would be worse.[4]

No one would call his behavior at all unusual.

In addition to questionable comparability and reversibility of different roll call votes, there are other reasons why such votes often are not what they appear to be. Every close observer of Congress has been in the gallery of the Senate when a clerk of the Senate has called out, after a preliminary announcement of the vote tally, "Does any Senator wish to change his vote?" Of course the *Congressional Record* prints no account of such happenings—not the initial vote tally, not the vote changes—and, after the real test of strength has occurred, not that some senators will change their votes to satisfy some attentive public, nor that others simply hold back until it is known whether their vote is needed by their leaders.

An example was provided the author in the course of interviewing one senator. He left to vote after receiving a note from his staff aide watching the floor for him. He read the note and told the author, "Kennedy has just introduced an amendment to add a billion dollars to the education budget" (on the grounds that if the Senate was going to deny funds to bus children to compensate for unequal educational opportunity, then it was responsible to provide that compensation in some other way).

Another senator was asking that the senator being interviewed come to the floor and vote against the Kennedy amendment on the grounds that it was "budget busting," that it would disrupt the liberal-conservative agreement that existed, with great fragility, and derived from very different motives, to make the new congressional budget process work. In explaining his vote afterward (he had voted for the Kennedy amendment), the Senator said: "It became clear that the Kennedy amendment was not going to receive more than thirty votes [it did not][5] and since there was no danger to the budget ceiling, I felt it appropriate to show that there was sentiment in support of doing more of that kind of thing."

There are a number of other sources of complexity affecting the valid interpretation of roll call votes as indicators, leading to a great deal of room for honest disagreement as to appearances and reality in the round.[6] There are significant differences between the rules of the Senate and the House. Relationships among committees, the elected leadership, and the full membership assembled on the floor vary between the two chambers, and within them as well. A wide variety of tactics and situations also may serve to obscure the real intent of those voting, or their cue setters. Tactics include tacking on riders to bills in committee that will divide otherwise cohesive groups; adding an amendment that destroys a carefully contrived but fragile compromise package; passing a bill in full knowledge that appropriations will *not* also be voted to make a program effective or a regulation enforceable, to mention only a few of many tactics.

Many if not most bills voted on in Congress are such that their real content is opaque, that is, not easily understood, sometimes even from a careful reading of a bill by professional staff. In other words, the manifest bill content is very often opaque as to what that bill would actually do and to whom if it were to take effect. Much of what goes on in the legislative process hinges on that fact. The struggle to understand such effects, or enable others both within and outside the Congress to be alerted to the impact of a piece of legislation, or, on the other side, to obscure such understanding or prevent its dissemination, is a large part of the political process generally, and the legislative process regularly. One must understand who is affected directly, who indirectly, via changes in the political, economical, or social system as a whole rather than only in its parts, and understand effects that take place in the long run as well as in the short run. Much legislation has indirect effects that no one foresees, *but* which could have been foreseen if the resources necessary to finding out had been committed. But that commitment is a quintessentially political act.[7]

Ideology has usually involved justifications of claims that manifest the classic theme of equality versus privilege, at home and abroad, which in our own day is refracted through economic theories of, and data or lack of data on, economic growth, capital supply and allocation, investment behavior, savings behavior, consumption behavior, labor markets, theories of the causes of inflation, and the social stratification of various kinds of well-being and deprivations, all enmeshed in an international economic setting. It is peculiarly these matters which are so opaque, often even to professional economists outside their fields of specialization. Yet so much of what the Congress votes on directly and indirectly involves these matters, whether through the mechanism of direct allocations or through the manipulation of incentive structures,[8] that it is no wonder, if such matters are the stuff of ideology, that ideology has been particularly opaque to political scientists. It is quite difficult to acquire knowledge of how economic theories are meshed with economically implicative legislation, sufficient to identify ideology at work in the Congress in particular contexts.

If one were to restrict one's understanding of forces in Congress to the roll call stage of the legislative process, one would be likely to uncover mostly conservative themes being played through the roll call voting process. This restricted understanding would be highly misleading and invalid. By comparison, examination of evidence from committee documents and journalistic sources reveals the existence of *other minority political positions* not evident at the floor voting stage. Minority and majority coalitions' cohesiveness can only be empirically demonstrated with roll call votes and/or interviews. The appropriate research strategy is to formulate hypotheses regarding political forces from the more revealing committee stage of the legislative process, and *then* test those hypotheses with data from the roll call stage, *suitably coded*. The reader may peruse the statements of congressmen in hearings before the Joint Economic Comittee, for example, and then examine the body of actual roll call votes on economic (including, in Lowi's term, "distributive") legislation. What will emerge from such a comparison is a keen sense that the agenda voted on on the floor in Congress is a *truncated agenda* of economic issues and presents a sharply distorted picture of what minority liberals in Congress represent programmatically. Their program would emerge to view only if, by becoming a sustained majority, they could shape the agenda of House voting, or if the coverage of congressional committees by the press were far different from at present. This truncated agenda of voting results from a systematic preponderance of the conservative coalition, which has used such devices as the closed rule in the House[9] and unanimous consent agreements in the Senate[10] to prevent much legislation of a liberal character, especially on economic policy and campaign practices, from ever reaching a floor vote. The truncated character of the body of roll call votes might mislead analysts who rely solely on roll call votes as data for many of the inferences they wish to draw.

The truncated agenda of roll call votes also results from a number of other factors. First, liberal congressmen, at least until very recently, have been systematically assigned to the less powerful committees, as Senator Donald Reigle has pointed out.[11] Indeed, to use a rough indicator, perusal of the ADA ratings of the Members who serve on key committees—Appropriations, Ways and Means, and Rules in the House, 1971-72—shows that these committees have been overwhelmingly dominated by arch conservatives. Even in the liberalized Ninety-fourth Congress, conservatives had a firm margin over liberals on those committees. Nor can seniority alone explain this phenomenon. The new Budget Committee of the Ninety-fourth Congress, that emerged from the new committee assignment process, had a median ADA score among *Democrats alone* of only 65 percent and a mean of 51 percent (not including the one Ninety-fourth Congress freshman, who is very conservative). With the scores of the Republican members averaged in, the ideological center of gravity of the Budget Committee would be *far* lower yet.[12] By way of comparison, the mean ADA rating of the last five congressmen who have served as chairmen of the Democratic Study Group of the House was 88 percent and the median was 87 percent.[13]

Second, staff resources are unevenly distributed, with entrenched committee and subcommittee chairmen enjoying a disproportionate share of these pivotal resources. Relatively lacking in significant staff support, liberal Members in the House have been in a poor position to clarify their views on many issues, or to bring forward supporting evidence so as to make their views salient to the press or to the academic analysts of Congress who concentrate on roll calls alone. Without staff support, even with an opportunity to introduce an amendment for the purpose of building a record, it would be most difficult to compose well-conceived legislation whose implications would be understood. The one opportunity would be to propose across-the-board cuts or increases on money bills, but there have not been many such opportunities on bills shepherded on the floor of the House by the Ways Means and Appropriations Committee Members, often under closed rules. Indeed, it is difficult without professional staff to even find out what has been effected by the passage of a tax bill of more than a thousand pages, as the gargantuan tax battle in the Senate all through the summer of 1976 made abundantly clear.

Third, given conservative predominance on the floor, liberal efforts at amendment have been mostly futile, especially when even hard-won concessions are removed in conference committees dominated by conservative Members who in the recent past have been routinely appointed to them in the House in disproportionate numbers.[14] Hence liberal Members have had disincentives for attempting to make a record on the floor other than one of opposition to conservative legislation and support for what little liberal legislation does reach the floor.

Fourth, the process of assigning legislation on the basis of committee jurisdictions, an enormously complex, important, and evolving matter, combined with the fact that legislation is primarily brought to the floor by Members of a committee of jurisdiction in an already overburdened legislative schedule, and added to pressures and norms of committee specialization, have further restricted the opportunities of liberal forces to make their weight felt on the floor proportionate to their numbers.[15]

Fifth, not even a President can necessarily change this situation regarding the agenda of floor voting. Indicative in this regard is President Kennedy's remark regarding his attempt to push his legislative program through a conservative-dominated Congress: "There is no use in raising hell and then not being successful. There is no sense in putting the office of the Presidency on the line and then being defeated."[16]

If, then, the roll call stage of the legislative process is so mired in misleading factors, what value can accrue to studying patterns of roll call voting as a means of measuring forces in Congress? The answer is complex. If, and only if, one can identify significant clusters of congressmen whose cohesiveness and cleavage patterns are clearly evident among carefully *coded* votes on different issues, then even though the views of congressmen in a minority are not reflected in the legislative agenda that reaches the stage of floor voting, we can identify the shared characteristics of those minority forces once isolated by cluster analysis.[17] We can then examine the committee positions of Members of minority clusters. Admittedly, this is not as satisfying as drawing inferences from the purportedly ideal "hard" data of actual roll call votes, but it is a more valid procedure. For if the earlier reasoning is correct regarding the misleading character of many votes, and on the truncated agenda of legislative voting, then roll call vote patterns are not at all "hard" data, at least from the viewpoint of the theoretical significance and methodology of measuring coalitions in Congress. Moreover, if roll call voting patterns are found statistically to be highly consistent across policy domains, what else could, in the sense of overarching dispositions, "explain" such consistencies but shared ideologies as described previously and commonly held with more or less ideational specificity, flowing through the cue-setting process?

That little-known liberal positions and understandings exist in the Congress does not necessarily imply that liberals are a significant or cohesive political force in the legislative process. By what criteria do we determine that an ideological group exists as a significant political force in Congress if that group currently reflects no clear agenda of its own in the roll call voting on the floor of the House? The first criterion is the demonstration of consistency of coalitions and cleavages across policy domains. That criterion is met by the analysis that follows.

The second criterion is that any static analysis of politics in a single slice of time should lend itself readily to expansion into a dynamic analysis across time. From this concern springs the preference for longitudinal analysis over cross-sectional analysis. However, there is the danger that many longitudinal analyses are questionable on a contextual basis as to the actual equivalence of different indicators *taken* to indicate the same policy disposition at different points in time. But if that problem can be faithfully treated, there can be no question as to the greater value of longitudinal analysis over cross-sectional analysis. Surely, only longitudinal analysis will provide a basis for inferences about the dynamic evolution of an institution and to the evolving balance of power of political forces in that institution. Clearly the latter question applied to Congress is one of the most important we can ask. But there is another approach to the problem of the evolution of coalition and cleavage patterns over time than using roll call votes alone.

A dynamic analysis of Congress, and of the balance of political forces across time, naturally leads to the question of whether a clear and distinct minority force can become a majority or enter into a coalition that can become a majority that is significantly different *in policy terms* from the majority it replaces. It is hypothetical answers to that question which determines whether or not we treat an ideological group in Congress as an analytically significant political force. After the election of the Ninety-fourth and Ninety-fifth Congresses, for example, many analysts and Congress watchers wondered whether the strength of the liberals would increase sufficiently in the House over the next few elections to become the dominant coalition in the Congress in both institutional controls and absolute numbers.[18] It would seem that the next logical question to be raised analytically must be: What would be the programmatic thrust of such an emergent coalition under various conditions, particularly under a prolonged and severe economic crisis? But if we *cannot* establish that such forces are now cohesive across policy domains, it would be pointless to ask the programmatic questions vis-à-vis the future! On the other hand, if we *can* establish a high degree of consistency of ideological forces in roll call voting patterns across policy domains, *then* we can turn to data about Congress from sources other than roll call voting patterns. Such data, lacking the cited liabilities of roll call data, *when linked to* voting patterns demonstrating Members as belonging to specified coalitions, allow analysis of what a coalition, especially its cue setters or opinion leaders, has been doing or saying about how its Members perceive the world differently from an opposing coalition, and what their programs would be *if* their coalition comes to enjoy greater power. Such a dynamic analysis must, however, take into account potential sources of fragmentation of existing coalitions that would appear only when Members had to take positive action together in ways that would require them to suffer the consequences together. But by linking the two kinds of data, one can perceive much more clearly the minority coalition's world view and substantive policy dispositions.

If roll call analysis is to hold the promise of *comparability* of data, unlike the more intensive studies of the Congress experts, that promise is less easily fulfilled than many have taken it to be. Eulau has written:

> There has always been trouble with studies of legislative behavior that rely solely on roll calls. . . . More statistical and methodological sophistication will not change the inherent weaknesses of the roll call as an indicator of either a legislator's "position" (vis-à-vis other legislators or on issues) or others' "influence" on his position. Simply too much happens in the legislative game before the yeas and nays are counted to

make the roll call anything more than a starting point for inquiry. To treat the roll call as the end point . . . is to invite failure. The failure is to confuse an explanation of roll call outcomes with an explanation of the preceding legislative process. Roll call analysis is at best an auxiliary strategy and cannot be substituted for more direct research using interviews, committee hearings, and reports, news accounts, and other documentation.

Eulau concludes his review by raising again the long-noted and unsolved problems of measuring power, and the unlikelihood that "mechanistic" roll call analysis will contribute to solving these problems.[19]

ROLL CALL ANALYSES FROM A CONTEXTUALIST VIEWPOINT

The previous section argued that a new method was needed (1) to capture the property of comparability possessed only by roll call votes (in the context of this study's focus) in order to state and verify generalizations of the kind made about congressional coalitions and cleavages; (2) but a method would need to be designed to avoid the many pitfalls of misconstruing roll call votes, by failing to understand how they were perceived in the act of voting and its context.

The basic outlines of *a new contextualist method* are proposed here, to remove sources of contamination and code votes according to procedures to be detailed shortly. Underlying conceptual devices for formulating this new method were described in Chapter 2—the policy-cut-points method, and refraction—contextual and theoretical. Much of what follows in Chapter 5 is an elaboration and operationalization of these devices and methods, with Converse's conceptualization of ideology as the keystone.

The new contextualist approach to roll call analysis presented in this and the following chapters is a response to a generic issue in the social sciences, the same issue that divides the habits of Congress experts and roll call analysts. The issue has been defined as whether greater understanding and/or truth, in the strictest sense, is conveyed by the "nomothetic" (generalizing), or by the "ideographic" (singularizing), approaches to social knowledge. The issue has been neatly summarized by Johan Galtung.[20] Congruent with the approach of this study, Galtung asserts the untenability of this dualism.

Despite all the arguments adduced about the weakness of roll calls as indicators,[21] it must be concluded that, *if* properly interpreted in the terms in which different Members, especially cue setters, *perceived* the purpose of their vote, roll call votes alone will allow a systematic test of the cohesiveness of opposing political forces on many different issues, and of the consistency of the cleavages from one issue or set of issues to another. Determinations of cohesiveness or consistency of opposing forces on a number of issues, or the lack thereof, is how it is determined whether certain political forces exist as such in the Congress, from which can be extrapolated, theoretically, explanations of past or future legislative, governmental, and political outcomes. Hence from both the practical and theoretical viewpoints of wanting to know where power is located, as described in terms of *dispositional claims,*[22] *but not causal claims,* the stakes in discovering whether or not there are certain patterns of cohesion—coalitions, cleavages, cross-cutting cleavages, and so on—are very great. If Polsby and others are correct about "very flexible" coalitions in Congress, it follows logically that one really can make no such judgments about the Congress. Yet people do every day, some with very high success rates in predicting outcomes. Causality enters in by explaining coalition and cleavage patterns that *have* been demonstrated by a prior analysis, as in the focus here. Such causal analysis lies outside the scope of this study.

It is necessary for this study to analyze the universe of roll call votes, rather than rely on one or another of the many key-vote approaches used by lobby groups, which use one or two dozen votes encompassing a rather narrow range of contexts. One of the most frequent complaints heard from congressmen about the key-vote ratings by lobby groups, such as those published by the ADA, the ACA, the AFL-CIO (and the many narrower ratings that seem to be proliferating for measuring how good or bad each legislator is on a certain kind of legislation, such as votes to aid the elderly, the environment, poor farmers, a hawkish national security rating, and many others) is that "one can prove anything one wants if one chooses the right votes." There is some element of truth in this complaint. There are other reasons for suspicion regarding key-vote approaches. A mistaken judgment on the character of one or two votes can significantly skew such a rating. There is also the danger that a legislator will try to build a record on highly noticeable votes, but will take a far different position on other more intricate votes on the same matter that might be much less visible. Moreover, there is the entire reasoning set forth for multiple indicators by Blalock and others.[23]

Key-vote approaches of the global kind, that is, ADA, ACA, and COPE ratings, also tend to lack explicit *substantive coherence* that allows the user to see clear relationships among specific and general issues, and lack explicit criteria to guide the choice of their few indicators—for example, "liberalism" in the ADA ratings and the specific votes chosen to indicate "liberalism."

NOTES

1. Cf. Robert D. Putnam, *The Beliefs of Politicians: Ideology, Conflict and Democracy in Britain and Italy* (New Haven, Conn.: Yale University Press, 1973).

2. People who are interested in politics, government, and political configurations in Congress (i.e., the balance of forces described in policy terms) have learned to view analysis of the academic literature that focuses on roll call voting patterns with deep suspicion. Such reactions often come from Congress experts with good to excellent training in social science method-

ology, statistics, and the philosophy and history of science, and who are well qualified to criticize specific applications of quantitative techniques. For a vivid example, cf. a review by Heinz Eulau, a student of Congress and a recent past president of the American Political Science Association, and certainly someone who fits the description of a scholar steeped in knowledge of social science. Whether Eulau's review of this study is accurate or not, what is of interest here are his reasons for attacking the book under review, which was grounded in the standard kind of roll call analysis characteristic of the roll call analysts described in the text. Eulau's criticisms of roll call analysis as generally structured are stated in the text. Cf. Heinz Eulau, review of *Constituencies and Leaders in Congress: Their Effects on Senate Voting Behavior*, by John E. Jackson (Cambridge, Mass.: Harvard University Press, 1974), pp. xi-217, in the *American Journal of Sociology* 81, no. 4 (January 1976): 953-55. For an excellent critique of coarse inductive operationalism, cf. Hubert M. Blalock, Jr., "The Measurement Problem: A Gap Between the Languages of Theory and Research," in H. M. Blalock and Ann B. Blalock, eds., *Methodology in Social Research* (New York: McGraw-Hill, 1968).

3. Cf., for example, Charles A. Beard, "Whom Does Congress Represent?—The Problem Behind the Lobbies," *Harper's Monthly Magazine* (January 1930):145-52, and contrast this article with pluralists as described previously.

4. Clifton Daniel, "Aiken Admits 'Sins' in Farewell," *New York Times*, 12 December 1974, p. 40.

5. Cf. the *Congressional Record*, May 11, 1976, pp. S6945-54.

6. Cf. Robert L. Peabody, *Leadership in Congress: Stability, Succession, and Change* (Boston: Little, Brown and Company, 1976), pp. 480-82; and Richard F. Fenno, Jr., *Congressmen in Committees* (Boston: Little, Brown and Company, 1973), pp. 190-91; Lewis A. Froman, Jr., *The Congressional Process: Strategies, Rules and Procedures* (Boston: Little, Brown and Company, 1967); Lewis Deschler, *Rules of Order* (Englewood Cliffs, N.J.: Prentice-Hall, 1976); Roger H. Davidson and Walter J. Oleszek, *Congress Against Itself* (Bloomington: Indiana University Press, 1977); *Ruling Congress: A Study of How the House and Senate Rules Govern the Legislative Process*, the Ralph Nader Congress Project, Ted Siff and Sean Weil, directors (New York: Grossman Publishers, 1975), and the forthcoming book-length treatment of House and Senate floor procedures by CRS analyst Walter Oleszek.

7. Cf. Jerrold E. Schneider, "Making Government Work: Political Versus Technical Obstacles to Social Accounting," *American Behavioral Scientist* 17 (March-April 1974):585-608.

8. Cf. Charles L. Schultze, *The Public Use of Private Interest* (Washington, D.C.: Brookings Institution, 1977).

9. I am grateful to Kenneth Bowler of the staff of the House Ways and Means Committee for clarifying that the closed rule, which had been the *bete noire* of the liberals in the late sixties and early seventies, has been "defanged." Only the changing character of the ideological balance within the Democratic delegation to the House, via changes in use of the Democratic Caucus and DSG, changing structures, processes, and leadership, explains why the closed rule emanating from a reconstituted Rules Committee, which has become an arm of the leadership, has lost much of its bitter edge for liberal Democrats. Cf. Arthur G. Stevens, Jr., "The Democratic Study Group and the House Democratic Party: Sixteen Years of Change," paper prepared for the 1974 Annual Meeting of the American Political Science Association, Chicago, August 29-September 2.

10. Cf. Robert Keith, "The Use of Unanimous Consent in the Senate," *Congressional Research Service*, unpublished manuscript, Summer 1976. I am indebted to Allen Schick for illuminating this matter for me.

11. Donald Riegle with Trevor Armbrister, *O Congress* (New York: Popular Library, 1972), p. 176.

12. *They Grade the Congress: A Summary of Ratings of U.S. Senators and U.S. Representatives Serving in the Second Session of the 94th Congress Based on Their Past Voting Records* (Washington, D.C.: Chamber of Commerce of the United States, February 1972 and 1976

editions). "Group Ratings: Trend to Liberalization Seen," *Congressional Quarterly Weekly Report* 33 (February 22, 1975):387; "Committee Assignments for the 94th Congress," *Congressional Quarterly Weekly Report* 33 (February 8, 1975):295.

13. Ibid.

14. Cf. David J. Vogler, *The Third House: Conference Committees in the United States Congress* (Evanston, Ill.: Northwestern University Press, 1971).

15. Cf. Roger H. Davidson, "Representation and Congressional Committees," pp. 48-62, and Richard Bolling, "Committees in the House," pp. 1-14, the *Annals of the American Academy of Political and Social Science* (January 1974).

16. Arthur M. Schlesinger, Jr., *A Thousand Days: John F. Kennedy in the White House* (Boston: Houghton-Mifflin Co., 1965), p. 709.

17. Cf. Brian Everitt, *Cluster Analysis* (New York: John Wiley & Sons, 1974), pp. 43 ff.

18. David W. Rohde, Norman J. Ornstein, and Robert L. Peabody, "Political Change and Legislative Norms in the United States Senate," paper delivered at the 1974 American Political Science Association Annual Meeting, Chicago, August 29-September 2.

19. Cf. Eulau's review of Jackson, *Constituencies and Leaders in Congress*, pp. 953-55.

20. Cf. Johan Galtung, *Theory and Methods of Social Research* (Oslo: Universitetsforlaget; New York: Columbia University Press, rev. ed., 1969); see pp. 22-29 for his discussion of the *untenability* of the "ideographic-nomothetic" dualism. Clearly, the differences between what are named here "the Congress experts" and "the roll call analysts" are neatly fitted to this distinction. The research strategy utilized in this study synthesizes the nomothetic and the ideographic with specific procedures. The earlier discussion of refraction—theoretical refraction and contextual refraction—embodies by design this synthesis.

The metamethodological problem of systematically integrating the contextual (ideographic) with the generalizing (nomothetic) is receiving increasing attention. Cf. Adam Pzeworski and Henry Teune, *The Logic of Comparative Social Inquiry* (New York: John Wiley & Sons, 1970), pp. 124-31; Aaron Wildavsky, "The Analysis of Issue Contexts in the Study of Decision-Making," in *The Revolt Against the Masses and Other Essays on Politics and Policy Making* (New York: Basic Books, 1971), pp. 139-54; Sidney Verba, "Some Dilemmas in Comparative Research," in *World Politics* 20, no. 1 (October 1967): 111-27; David C. Leege notes:

> In asserting that contextualism needs to be the subject of concentrated attention, we are seeking a systematic exposition of the ways in which variance in social, economic, and political behavior is accounted for by individual effects and by context. There must be a middle ground between individual choice models and Durkheim. To some extent Commons sought this. The article by Siegal and Meyer, "The Social Context of Political Partisanship" is a suggestive illustration of this. The current NSF-funded mathematical work of political scientists, Sprague and Pzeworski, is addressed to this. The sociologist, Coleman, has done considerable theorizing on it, also from a mathematical perspective, as have political scientists, Hibbs and Tufte.

The quote is taken from "Is Political Science Alive and Well and Living at NSF? Reflections of a Program Director at Midstream," delivered at the 1975 Annual Meeting of the American Political Science Association, San Francisco, California, September 2-5, p. 25. Cf. John G. Gunnell, "Deduction, Explanation and Social Scientific Inquiry," *The American Political Science Review* 63, no. 4 (December 1969):1233-46; Arthur S. Goldberg, "On the Need for Contextualist Criteria: A Reply to Professor Gunnell," *The American Political Science Review* 63, no. 4 (December 1969):1247-62.

Cf. David A. Karns, "Legislative Context and Roll Call Analysis: Foreign Policy Voting Behavior in the Senate" (Cornell University, November 1972, unpublished manuscript).

21. For an analysis of the relationship between concepts, dimensions, and indicators that is excellent for all purposes except in showing the nature of contextually, as well as theoretically,

establishing the validity and reliability of the indicator-dimension relationship, see Paul F. Lazarsfeld, "Evidence and Inference in Social Research," in Daniel Lerner, ed., *Evidence and Inference* (Glencoe, Ill.: Free Press, 1958), pp. 107-17. The means of contextually establishing indicators is somewhat better reflected in Blalock's conception of an "auxiliary theory." Cf. Hubert M. Blalock, Jr., *Theory Construction: From Verbal to Mathematical Formulations* (Englewood Cliffs: Prentice-Hall, 1969), pp. 151-54. The epistemic understanding of these relationships is best grounded in the work of W. V. O. Quine. See his *Word and Object* (New York: John Wiley& Sons, 1960).

22. For a powerful analysis of the logic of *dispositional claims* about states of mind, see Stuart Hampshire, review of *The Concept of Mind*, by Gilbert Ryle (London: Hutchinson's University Library, Senior Series, 1949), *MIND* 59 (1950):237-55, and Ryle's volume itself. Hampshire's piece is an effective refutation of Ryle's main claim, but both illuminate the logic of dispositionals. Cf. also, Carl G. Hempel, "The Logical Analysis of Psychology," in Herbert Feigl and Wilfred Sellars, eds., *Readings in Philosophical Analysis* (New York: Appleton-Century-Crofts, Inc., 1949), p. 373:

> I now (1947) consider the type of physicalism outlines in this paper as too restrictive; the thesis that all statements of empirical science are *translatable*, without loss of theoretical content, into the language of physics, should be replaced by the weaker assertion that all sentences of empirical science are *reducible* to sentences in the language of physics, in the sense that, for every empirical hypothesis, including, of course, those of psychology, it is possible to formulate certain test conditions in terms of physical concepts which refer to more or less observable physical attributes. But these test conditions are not asserted to exhaust the theoretical content of the given hypothesis in all cases.

23. Cf. for example, H. M. Blalock, Jr., "Multiple Indicators and the Casual Approach to Measurement Error," *American Journal of Sociology* 75 (September 1976): pp. 264-72; Stuart W. Cook and Claire Selltiz, "A Multiple-Indicator Approach to Attitude Measurement," *Psychological Bulletin* 1 (1964):36-56; H. M. Blalock, Jr., "Estimating Measurement Error Using Multiple Indicators and Several Points in Time," *American Sociological Review* 35, No. 1 (February 1970); and H. M. Blalock, Jr., "Correlated Independent Variables: The Problem of Multicollinearity," *Social Forces* (December 1963); John L. Sullivan, "Multiple Indicators: Some Criteria of Selection," in H. M. Blalock, Jr., *Measurement in the Social Sciences* (Chicago: Aldine Publishing Company, 1974), pp. 243-70. But see Aage R. Clausen and Carl E. Van Horn, "How to Analyze Too Many Roll Calls," draft prepared for Conference on Mathematical Models of Congress, Aspen, Colorado, June 16-23, 1974, especially pp. 10-17, and p. 19.

chapter 5

CONGRESSIONAL VOTING PATTERNS

Highly consistent ideological cleavages holding across *all* policy areas, and bound together by common overarching beliefs or attitudes in the manner made clear by Converse's treatment of "ideology," are at one end of a *continuum* of possible intra-legislative group patterns. At the other end are ever-shifting coalitions, or Polsby's "very flexible successive majorities." Between these two ends of the continuum (a non-well-ordered one, logically) are (1) highly cohesive coalitions within a small time span; (2) a highly cohesive coalition across time, but restricted to some policy areas and nonoperative in other policy areas; (3) one or several crosscutting coalitions; (4) the patterns given in Polsby's and Lowi's typologies, described in Chapter 2. And there are other possibilities.[1]

The following empirical analysis of voting patterns in Congress, beyond those patterns analyzed in Chapter 3, reexamines what pattern, if any, is characteristic of Congress as a whole, across all issues and among all senators and congressmen, in the period 1971 to 1976.

THE DATA BASE

The data base of this chapter consists of all of the roll call votes from the Senate and from the House of the Ninety-second Congress (January 1971-January 1972)[2]—and all of the roll call votes from the first session only of the Ninety-fourth Congress (1975), both in the Senate and the House. In the Ninety-fourth Congress, first session (1975), there was a total of 1,214 votes, 602 in the Senate and 612 in the House. In the Ninety-second Congress for *both* sessions (1971-72), there was a total of 1,604 votes, 649 in the House and 955 in the Senate.[3] The overall total of votes analyzed in this chapter sums to 2,818 roll call votes, each analyzed by itself. The great increase in the number of floor votes in the Senate, reflected in the numbers just cited, according to one key Senate staff person who is also a highly respected political scientist, has been due to increased ideological cueing and decreased following of cues from Senate committee members. This phenomenon in the Senate and in the House results from the increase in staff resources and information-retrieval capabilities. The increase has also been stimulated in part by younger, better-educated, and more liberal Members who have steadily increased their demands for information and analysis in a context of rapidly eroding deference to the White House, to the bureaucracy, and to more senior Members on matters of policy.[4] What one finds in both Houses is a very substantial growth in the number of floor amendments, revealing far more substantially the character of coalitions and cleavages.

The recorded teller vote reform, instituted in the Ninety-second Congress, has had major effects on the measurement validity of all vote analyses of the House. This study's analyses of House roll calls rely exclusively on post-teller vote reform roll call data. The virtue of this later data is that the reform cut absenteeism in floor voting dramatically, and in ways that reveal a systematic bias in analyses that use earlier data.

As the *Congressional Quarterly* pointed out, "voting participation on major issues by Members of the House doubled during the first seven months of 1971 over the comparable period in 1970."[5] Prior to the institution of the recorded teller vote reform, one estimate is that at least 150 Members could be counted on to be absent from any unrecorded teller vote.[6] Before the Legislative Reorganization Act went into effect, fewer than 285 of the 435 possible Members voting were recorded on 34 key issues. Of the 41 recorded teller votes taken up to the August recess under the new recorded teller vote rule in 1971, 7 votes had a turnout of 400 Members voting and the smallest number of Members voting was 308. Only 3 nonrecorded teller votes taken prior to the institution of the Reorganization Act reforms had as large a total vote as the lowest taken subsequently.[7] The demand of only 20 Members is sufficient under the Legislative Reform Act to bring about the recording of who voted yea or nay on a teller vote.[8]

Clearly, if the number of Members' positions available to public scrutiny has sharply increased due to the reform, so has the number of different issues voted on by different legislative blocs. Thus the real structure of coalitions and cleavages could be examined vis-à-vis a larger range of issues in the Ninety-second Congress (House) than before that first session under the Reorganization Act. The number of recorded votes taken increased more than 30 percent, from the average of 223 roll calls during the five preceding years, and has tripled since.[9] Moreover, it is the distinct impression of this author that in both foreign and domestic affairs, many of the demands for a recorded teller vote came from liberal Members anxious to increase public scrutiny of Members' positions on bills or alternatives suppressed in other parts of the legislative process by conservatives.

Under the new rule, a large number of issues that divided the Members emerged from obscurity (notably the Vietnam War, which prior to this Congress had never been voted on in the House). In the words of the *Congressional Quarterly*:

> . . . the immediate effect of the voting reform has been to make accessible to the public a more accurate picture of the divisions in the House. The survey showed that the conservative bloc still is in control on most issues but that liberals are stronger than appeared from the roll call votes in earlier years before voting on amendments was made public.[10]

The explanation of the difference between the findings here and those of other analysts, particularly Aage Clausen, may lie in part, at least for the House, with this unique difference between the House of the Ninety-second and subsequent Congresses and the House of all previous Congresses. Clausen's analysis is based on six Congresses, both the Senate and the House, up through the Ninety-first, the *last* to operate *without* the recorded teller vote reform. Matthews and Stimson's data are also limited to pre-1970 data but from the House alone,[11] and suffer from the same liability.

What this discussion illuminates is the far greater validity and reliability for analyzing blocs of the Ninety-second Congress (1971-72) and subsequent House roll call data as compared with all previous House vote data, as utilized by Clausen, Matthews and Stimson, and others. No such factor, however, affects the analysis of Senate voting. Other sources of discrepancies between this study and past findings are discussed later in this chapter (see the discussion of further comparisons with past findings).

The great diversity of the data base of this study is derived from the following: (1) the number of roll call votes used, 2,828; (2) the fact that votes analyzed are from both the Senate and the House; (3) that the period covered, 1971 to 1976, spans a tremendous turnover in membership;[12] (4) also encompassed are the enormous changes in the political situation domestically, including the end of the Vietnam War, Watergate and the economic crisis of 1973-76, and (5) remarkable structural and procedural changes, at least in the House;[13] (6) the cross-tabulation of *attitudinal* data (the foreign policy interview data of Chapter 3) with *behavioral* data (with each of the domestic policy roll call data sets from the Ninety-second Congress, with certain combinations of them, and with foreign policy roll call data). This cross-tabulation provides an independent test of validity and reliability, especially when viewed in light of the near perfect stability in the order of magnitude of all of the relationships across the time period studied, as reported next, despite the changes cited in (3), (4), and (5). With approximately 2,000 roll calls utilized in this study, and with 535 senators and congressmen voting (omitting, of course, the relatively low absenteeism in the period studied), this analysis utilizes approximately 1,070,000 individual acts of voting.

The advantages provided by this diversity of the data base should be uppermost in mind in evaluating the validity of the analysis that follows. Over 50 percent of House Democrats in the Ninety-fifth Congress that began in January 1977,[14] when President Carter was inaugurated, were newly elected in the *two* previous congressional elections (1974 and 1976). This change, by itself, may cause congressional experts to rethink some of the most accepted textbook generalizations carried over from the 1960s.

CODING PROCEDURES

The following is a schematic outline of the procedures used in coding. They are presented here in this form so that the reader may quickly survey them in a concentrated way. Some of the procedures are discussed in greater detail after this section.[15]

1. Bloc structures were observed in the *Congressional Quarterly's* breakdown of the vote tally by Southern Democrats, yea and nay, Northern Democrats, yea and nay, and Republicans, yea and nay.[16] In most instances, this is a very quick guide to the character of a vote, with Southern Democrats, barring only a handful of exceptions, voting with most Republicans on most matters.

2. Bloc structures were also observed by examining the individual votes of approximately 100 to 150 Members of the House whose basic dispositions were well known to this investigator before the coding ever began and who were divided into liberals, "moderates," and conservatives. Bloc structures in the whole Senate were scrutinized in a similar fashion. Unusual patterns were noted (see the later discussion of excluded votes and both-ends-against-the-middle votes.

3. *Congressional Quarterly*'s brief description of each vote was scrutinized for complex policy or political matters, especially if steps (1) and (2) indicated substantial deviations from expected patterns of ideological voting.

4. Where such deviations or complex matters were apparent or suspected by divisions among usual allies, even if only a few in the House and one or two in the Senate, the *Congressional Quarterly*'s discussion, if given, was carefully examined. This often involved reading back through earlier issues of *CQ*.

5. If there still was any serious doubt as to what any group of congressmen might perceive to be the implications of their vote, the debate in the

Congressional Record was carefully read, from which may be derived further reasons that might direct the voting of a group of Members.

6. Utilizing the policy-cut-points method and the concept of refraction (see Chapter 2), distinct policy positions and their manifestation in the parliamentary situation of a particular vote were observed or inferred from information acquired in the previous steps. The few votes in which ambiguity, ambivalence, or confusion seemed to be operative were also identified by this and the previous steps.

The foregoing six steps were aimed at maximizing the possibility of a sensitive analysis of what each individual roll call vote meant to all of its participants, bearing in mind that the need for cognitive economizing in an arena of unusual complexities required a regularized cueing process. Interviews with Senate staff led to the belief that a similar cueing process worked in the Senate as well, though many senators' personal staff watch the floor and often explain a vote to a senator arriving on the floor. A "hanging together" mood also can be observed from the documentary record among ideological groups that answer to similar constituencies. That regularized cueing process, undergirded by the desire of congressmen not to make a politically vulnerable vote when they can seldom know directly the implications of what they vote on, accounts in part for the persistent voting regularities expected here.

7. Each roll call was assigned to one of five categories: (a) foreign policy; (b) race; (c) civil liberties and democracy; (d) economics (economic policy and class allocation—see later discussion); and (e) excluded roll calls. Assignment of a vote to the excluded category was decided only when carried out in conjunction with step (8).

8. Each roll call was assigned an "item direction" as it is usually called, that is, liberal = yea or liberal = nay.

9. For the House of the Ninety-second Congress, the sample from the foreign policy interviews (see Chapter 3) was used; for the House of the Nineth-fourth Congress, a second stratified random sample (also ADA percentages—0-10, 11-20, 21-30, etc., to 100%) was drawn with equal numbers from each of these ten percentage groups. No sample was necessary for the Senate, and analysis utilized all senators' votes from the sessions analyzed. The necessity of using a sample of the House rather than the whole, derived from the simple fact that the state of the art in computer technology does *not* allow for a program analyzing pairwise comparisons (a parsimonious and here appropriate form of cluster analysis) of a matrix as large as 435 × 435 (for the 435 Members of the House). However, pairwise comparisons of 100 × 100 matrices (for the 100 senators) can be analyzed by computer with existing technology.[17] A discussion of the logic behind the sample selection is presented in the later discussion in this chapter of further comparisons with past findings.

10. Liberalism index scores were computed for each senator in each of the sessions analyzed, and for each congressman in a sample, in each of the four policy categories of step (7). The absolute score of each senator (or congressman) was derived by simple addition of the number of liberal votes cast in each one of the four policy categories. Senators (or congressmen) were then rank-ordered by their total absolute liberalism score, ignoring missing data[18] in each of the four policy categories or dimensions.

11. Rank order correlations were computed among all the different combinations of the four policy sets of rank-ordered individual scores, giving the final results of the analysis in terms of tau-b (see Tables 5-3 through 5-13, presented later in this chapter.

12. An intercoder reliability test was administered, under stringent conditions, of the two coding steps (7) and (8).

EXCLUDED VOTE CATEGORIES

Roll call analysis generally employs at least one or two exclusion categories. The two most common are (1) unanimous and near unanimous votes, and (2) votes with high absenteeism. The latter category is not applied in this study because, first, most absenteeism was eliminated in House voting in the Congresses studied by the introduction of the recorded teller vote reform; second, in the Senate absenteeism was quite low, since none of the years studied encompassed a presidential nominating contest; third, the missing-data procedure that was used ignored missing votes, although it included Members' positions recorded as paired or announced.

The common exclusion of the category of unanimous and near unanimous votes has been defended on the grounds that, as Clausen and Van Horn state, "omitting roll calls with extreme splits [is desirable] because they are relatively weak tests of dimensionality."[19] This statement implies that *not* to exclude such votes would have the effect of invalidly obscuring dimensionality that actually exists in the roll call voting. Otherwise, why not simply ignore them rather than exclude them? This reasoning is extended next to other exclusion categories.

Unanimous and near unanimous votes excluded in this study were identified, following the usual practice, as those in which 10 percent or less voted in opposition (44 votes in the House and 10 votes in the Senate). This category totaled 838 votes, or 22 percent of a universe of 2,818 votes. The remainder of coded votes totaled 1,980. Clausen and Van Horn suggest that for some analytic purposes it might be appropriate to use a 15 or 20 percent cut point.[20] However, if one makes assumptions such as are implicit in the drive for public financing of congressional campaigns, about the unrepresentativeness of the electoral process, then to exclude votes of 20 percent *might* be equivalent to eliminating a segment of opinion that represented a much larger portion of public sentiment than would be apparent from that segment's weight in the Congress. The customary 10 percent cut point seems, therefore, appropriate.

In addition to unanimous votes, several other categories of votes were excluded in this study. These additional categories reflect the contextual approach of this analysis, and may be seen as an expanded application of the reasoning customarily attached to the exclusion of unanimous and near unanimous votes. The additional categories may also be seen as following Clausen's affirmation of the inevitable reliance on "manifest content criteria,"[21] as an extension of his "conceptual approach" for which he argues against the "objective approach,"[22] and as a further application of MacRae's reliance on content coding.[23]

The following are the categories of excluded votes added in this study:

1. Votes to recess or adjourn.
2. Votes on the partisan organization of the House and Senate at the beginning of the first session of each Congress. These votes ought not to be related to other partisan votes, because it has been demonstrated by Samuel Beer and by Deckard and Stanley that party unity scores in the 1970s have declined sharply.[24] Party voting on policy matters, then, is quite a different phenomenon than party voting on the organization of a Congress at its beginning, primarily because of the wide ideological differences within the House Democratic delegation and within both parties in the Senate.
3. Votes on unusually particularistic minor bills involving no funding or tiny amounts of money in budgetary terms. These votes often occur in the House under suspension of the rules (requiring a two-thirds vote for passage), and would not be described by policy analysts as interest group votes exemplary of any wider pattern of voting. Examples include an appropriation for an administrative assistant for the Chief Justice, increases in pensions for widows of Supreme Court justices, designation of a day to commemorate the 1915 massacre of Armenians by Turks, authorizing a monument to Mary McCleod Bethune, amendments concerning the American Revolution Bicentennial, and so on.
4. Votes in which a substantial issue of House rules, norms, committee prerogatives, House-versus-Senate prerogatives, or congressional-versus-executive-branch prerogatives were explicitly raised in floor debate in such a way as to be clearly independent from either policy or ideological considerations.

It should be evident to those familiar with congressional voting that the preceding four categories of excluded votes involve a very small proportion of the total voting universe. The following three additional categories also, as a matter of fact, involved an equally small proportion of the total votes analyzed.

5. Votes on legislative "packages," that is, votes on bills with a large variety of provisions, all with the effect that at the time of the vote, there existed no practical parliamentary possibility that a Member could single out a particular provision or program to vote against. For example, some of these packages were the product of delicate compromises between liberals and conservatives, reached in committee, and some packages reached the House floor under a rule which prohibited all or many significant kinds of amendments. Voting against such packages would under the circumstances not only be legislatively useless, but also uninterpretable to those who later scrutinize the vote on the whole package in order to understand the policy intent or content underlying a vote against such a package bill. Prominent subcategories of this exclusion category include (a) votes on supplemental appropriations for several departments in a single vote, such as for the Commerce, Justice, and State Departments; (b) votes on "final passage" in which Members are uncomfortable voting against a broad category of legislation, for example, for Defense Department appropriations as a whole: (c) votes on the adoption of conference reports under certain conditions.[25] Votes to pass such bills are often tantamount to expediting the flow of legislative business, where opposition would be fruitless. Such votes are always near unanimous. When they are not unanimous, they would probably be so counted under Clausen and Van Horn's suggested 15 or 20 percent cut-point criterion. Regarding (b) and (c), the test votes which reveal the "will" of the chamber have occurred earlier, making further efforts to bring about another vote useless and time wasting.
6. Votes that manifest confusion on the floor at the time of voting.[26] Operational criteria for determining the existence of floor confusion are: (a) when questions are raised in floor debate about the uncertainties of actual impact of the bill, questions that would trouble any responsible person;[27] (b) reference made on the floor to deliberate tactical obfuscation (some Members seeking to alert others),[28] often resulting in appeals for clarification from the parliamentarian; (c) amendments offered spontaneously from the floor during a long floor battle, attempting a compromise, satisfying none of the contending forces, generally offered predictably by a few uninfluential senators or congressmen, and which seem to be offered primarily out of a desire to expedite a recess. Invariably met with unanimous or near unanimous votes, such amendments are voted for by only a few predictable Members.
7. Last, votes manifesting an ideological dilemma. Such votes can be seen to be clearly ideological votes from the comments made in floor debates

invoking broad ideological principles by the opposing sides. But the actual votes must be excluded, because, if one took the vote talley at face value, one would invalidly infer from the vote pattern that Members who voted together did so for the same or at least compatible purposes, which from the debate can be seen as opposite to the fact. Such votes have been classified by others, such as Philip Converse and Duncan MacRae, as both-ends-against-the-middle votes.[29] These votes involve the dilemmas of whether a compromise is more desirable than defeating a bill altogether, that is, whether a bill's good outweighs the harm *from an ideological standpoint.* The propriety of excluding such votes is obvious, because they involve groups *voting together for contradictory reasons.* An example is when some conservative Members voted against a welfare reform bill because it gave too much to the recipients, whereas liberal Members also voted against the bill, but rather because it provided too little. Supporters included conservatives who voted in favor of the bill because it emanated from President Nixon, and liberals who saw it as a "thin edge of a wedge."

To deny the necessity of excluding ends-against-the-middle votes (or votes manifesting a dilemma as to whether the good outweighs the bad) *would be equivalent to defining ideology* as some scholars do, as a term denoting voting that is *rigidly doctrinaire and oversimplistic.* Hence *without* this exclusion category, an implicit assumption would be inserted, that if in general Members voted along ideological lines, they would not perceive any situations or choices that presented ideological dilemmas, which is clearly contrary to fact.

Readers will quite naturally pose two critical questions regarding the effects of adding, in this study, the seven additional categories of excluded votes. First, the question will be raised as to whether the added categories account for discrepancies with past findings. I shall address this question in the comparison of the findings of this study with those of Clausen. Second, a question will be raised by some readers, despite what has been said, as to whether the additional seven categories introduce a systematic form of bias in favor of confirming the ideological consistency hypothesis of this study, and against the interest group pluralist thesis of ever-shifting coalitions, or "very flexible successive majorities," or Clausen's claim that in Congress "different alignments form as the policy content changes."[30]

First, the simplest answer to this second question is as follows. The exclusion of unanimous and near unanimous votes is almost universal practice, and the reasoning for this is generally unchallenged. Those who would claim that the first six additional exclusion criteria used here introduce a systematic source of bias should indicate for any or each of the additional categories why they are not a simple extension of the same reasoning as supports the accepted exclusion of unanimous votes, and must explain why Clausen's defense of the "conceptual approach" does not also justify the added exclusions. (The seventh category is defended in its description earlier and the attendant notes.) Second, the reliability of applying the exclusion criteria of this study is submitted to a stringent test of intercoder reliability, as will be seen. Third, if excluded votes are cited as a source of bias here, the reader must decide whether any significant number of the excluded votes fit the first of two categories, rather than the second. The first category encompasses votes which manifest strong but *nonideological* concerns with interest groups or other nonideological policies, in which case the criticism of bias in this study *would* be true. The second category encompasses votes which either (1) have no *policy* content or (2) whose exclusion is based solely on the fact that they obscure or misrepresent the operative intentions of different groups voting together on a bill for opposite reasons. In either case the criticism of bias in this study linked to the exclusion of nonideological votes would not be true. In deciding whether a group of excluded roll call votes should be seen as better fitting the first or second category, it is necessary to bear in mind the central task of this analysis: to ascertain the coalition and cleavage structures operative in Congress without contamination by votes that invalidly obscure bloc structures, or to use Clausen and Van Horn's phrase, that "are . . . relatively weak tests of dimensionality." Finally, in all, approximately 30 percent of the total universe of nonunanimous votes were excluded, leaving roughly 70 percent (see Appendix I).

There was one other category of votes that was excluded, which does marginally qualify the scope of the ideological consistency hypothesis. This is a set of regional votes. Few in number and small in overall impact as compared with the significance of the other legislation voted on, either in budgetary terms or in all-over distributive effects, regional votes, particularly on jobs, some aspects of energy policy, and revenue-sharing legislation, did involve a coalition that was not isomorphic with the coalition behavior manifest in the other congressional voting encompassed in this study. But in the larger scheme of things, such voting is a minor phenomenon.[31]

THE MEASUREMENT OF COHESION: CUMULATING INDIVIDUAL SCORES

Cohesion is commonly understood as the opposite of fragmentation, and since the bulk of the voting in the legislative struggle involves opposing sides rather than unanimity, cohesion entails cleavages. The set of cleavages, delineated at the data level, to be theoretically (or practically) interpretable, must be located by some valid description of preferences of legislative groups in terms of issue orientations (including ideologies) or "operational codes" (in Alexander George's sense),[32] as adapted to a particular context. Legislative coalitions are objects of interest only when operative over a variety of particular efforts, including floor votes, that are bound together by some principle of interest. To say that a coalition lacks a certain degree of cohesion with regard to its putative principle of cohesion is, to that degree, to deny that it is a coalition at all. Such a principle can be a substantive policy orientation of greater or lesser generality, or it can be a *modus operandi* for harmonizing efforts in support of unshared interests. The essential pluralist paradigm postulates that actually observable coalition behavior involves unshared interests in the strictest sense: that is, those which together *cannot* be found to share some common element of policy significance. For example, all and only the interests primarily represented by the coalition are wealthy, even though various as to the source of wealth.[33] This example is an instance of Madison's first major theme (class conflict) with the subordination of his second major theme (the balancing, politically, of opposing forms of property interests), as noted in Chapter 2.

Cohesion of factions, as opposed to parties, is frequently measured by one of two methods, either (1) dispersion around a group mean,[34] or (2) indices of intragroup cohesion based on measures of interpersonal agreement using pairwise comparison of each possible pair of legislators.[35] As such, pairwise measures of agreement are a much more sensitive measure of cohesion and fragmentation. This second method is appropriate to "noncategoric groups," or "empirically defined groups,"[36] such as liberals and conservatives.

This study introduces a new method of measuring bloc cohesion, which is a modification of the technique of pairwise comparisons of legislative votes *bill by bill*. Following the assignment of an item direction (liberal = yea or nay) and of a particular vote to a policy roll call set, each legislator analyzed was calculated by simple addition to have a specified *percent* liberalism score within each of the policy roll call sets.[37] The senators or congressmen analyzed were then *rank-ordered* by their computed percentage liberalism scores for each roll call set or, in the case of economic policy votes, by the percent economic liberalism *index scores.* These latter scores were achieved by *adding* the liberalism score of each legislator from each of the three class allocation sets, for reasons that will be described, these new scores *then* being rank-ordered. Rank order *correlations* were then computed among the four resulting rank orderings (foreign policy, race, civil liberties and democracy, and economic policy including class allocations). This computation involved *pairwise* comparisons in the manner specified by the logic of the statistics used.[38]

This new procedure, as a variation on the usual pairwise comparison of votes on each bill as a technique for measuring cohesion, has the following advantages: (1) It permits the use of the economic liberalism index scores, which in turn permits a direct test of the class-conflict versus the-many-unrelated-interest-groups voting theories, according to the logic arrayed in the next section; (2) duplication of roll call votes, of which there are a substantial number, will have no effect on the rank ordering under this method, as they will with other procedures which might have been used, and which might have had the effect of artificially *inflating* the magnitude of the correlations obtained;[39] (3) scalar relationships that do exist will be sensitively reflected to reveal "constraint" (Converse's sense) of the scalar type as well as the correlational type, as Converse has pointed out.[40] The number of possible categories of the rank ordering are as many as encompassed by 100 percentage points (300 for the economic liberalism index scores). The procedure used permits the legislators' positions vis-à-vis one another within the roll call sets to assume their "natural" scale positions without what, under some analytic situations, would amount to the less parsimonious intervention of the investigator in eliminating nonscale roll calls by nonsubstantive and often methodologically tenuous criteria, and usually without any analysis of residuals that is substantively coherent. Nor will the liabilities of factor analysis and the techniques that rely on it be required to be endured; in other words, the analysis can be carried out without making arbitrary judgments through continuous rotation from an infinite number of possible solutions, as to the nature and number of the factors, and as to what is too low a factor loading to justify desired inferences.[41] Overestimation of the number of factors by such methods has been established by Coombs and Kao, as well as Ross and Cliff, among others.[42] Problems of arbitrariness in choosing or justifying positioning of the axes seem especially to lend an arbitrary character to such procedures when measurement of *two-way* association is used, as is necessary if the goal is to produce inter-individual analysis, as it is in the study here.[43]

As MacRae notes, "However elegant the standard methods of factor analysis may be, they do not yield single clear-cut dimensions for identifiable issue clusters, and *they fail especially in this respect when extreme divisions are analyzed*" (italics added).[44] The sensitivity of the measurement of cohesion used here of "constraint" of the scalar as well as the correlational type is made more likely still by virtue of the quite wide range of variation in both legislators and issues included in this analysis (see the previous discussion of the diversity of the data base).

As MacRae also points out, a simple additive index of one of the more familiar varieties, that might have been used, does not reveal the agreement and disagreement within a legislature in ways that reflect whether or not repeated disagreements separate the same or different sets of legislators. He notes:

> In the former case, we may have a stable structure of antagonistic blocs; in the latter, a set of shifting and cross-cutting factions. This distinction is well known in political sociology and corresponds to superimposed versus pluralistic cleavages, respectively. However, indices that make this distinction for legislatures are rare.[45]

MacRae does not cite any instance of such an index in the more difficult nonparty situation at question here. In this study the measure of cohesion developed is aimed precisely at analyzing the data in terms derived theoretically from this distinction, as may be obvious from what has already been said.

Other techniques and measures might have been used for the purpose of this study's measurement of cohesion. However, two principal considerations prevailed in the decisions made. First, using simple rank order correlations is preferable on grounds of parsimony, of correspondence with the correct level of measurement (ordinal), of isomorphism to the nonparametric nature of the situation here, and of clarity of interpretability in terms of the proportional-reduction-in-error (P.R.E) logic of the tau-b rank order statistic.[46] Second, resort to more complicated measures, particularly nonmetric multidimensional scaling, are usually justified as preferable to the simpler measures used here, either because (1) tau-b or similar rank order (ordinal) nonparametric measures tend considerably to *understate* relationships that do in fact exist, under some conditions; or (2) by virtue of an analytical purpose involving causal inferences.[47] With regard to (1), it is enough to say that, *if* using tau-b or a similar measure, strong relationships *are* demonstrated, the objection to using tau-b stated in (1) is simply obviated. Regarding (2), this study involves no causal inferences from data patterns other than purely theoretical inferences, and hence resort to such measures as might otherwise be appropriate is not necessary.

POLICY ROLL CALL SETS

Economic Policy and a Class Allocation Index

It should be obvious that different legislative parties or factions will likely disagree as to whether or not problems of class conflict in society are serious enough, in terms of existing deprivations, to deserve a central place in politics. In our own society an understanding of such beliefs of politicians is complicated by the fact that such assertions are *refracted* through the discussion of macroeconomic policy in all its complexity and ambiguity. Further complication stems from the fact that most Members follow cues on such complex subjects, and that many and perhaps most of those who observe and report about politicians seldom convey the rudiments of basic alternative arguments and positions in this most determinative of policy areas. Yet an intelligible analysis of ideological attitudes or behavior by politicians must necessarily involve macroeconomics.

However, familiarity with congressmen who have more than a two- or three-year tenure on Capitol Hill will assure the observer that even the most district-oriented congressman knows that he and those whose cues he takes fall in step with a general macroeconomic posture represented by certain economists—Milton Friedman and Arthur Burns, or Arthur Okun and Charles Schultze, or John Kenneth Galbraith, Robert R. Nathan, and Lester Thurow. In reality, one may best discover which economists are most influential by observing who among them testify before certain congressional committees with the greatest frequency on the most implicative economic matters. Congressmen and senators are generally aware that they might face the electorate when the level of unemployment and inflation will crowd out other issues with a possibly critical effect on their electoral margins. They correctly infer that their electoral fortunes may ride on decisions made several years prior to an election. Perhaps the clearest case, untangled from other factors, is the recession of 1958 and the very liberal class of 1958 elected to the Senate.

The language of economic policy is the language and the logic of social science, and that fact places much of the dialogue about economic policy beyond the ken, though not beyond the gut reactions, of almost all senators and congressmen. By comparison, though they might never have read Arnold Wolfers, Inis Claude, Lenin, or Raymond Vernon, foreign policy matters do *not* similarly inhibit or elude the active reasoning of Members of Congress. Only a theory of cueing makes it plausible to ask about congressional postures on economic matters.

The question that must be of concern here is whether, with regard to macroeconomic policy and social stratification, or class generally, there exists in Congress anything like a clear situation of "regime and opposition." That is to say, is it possible to discern clearly contending ideological coalitions in dispute systematically over economic policy and possessed of clashing perspectives on the distribution of privilege and deprivation?

The fundamental question is best phrased another way. Is there a systematic struggle within the Congress over basic questions regarding the intervention of government in the economy to affect *what is invested in, what is produced, and what is consumed*? In 1973, then Brookings authors Fried, Rivlin, Schultze, and Teeters, in the summary paragraph at the close of their analysis of the 1974 federal budget, put the question this way:

> The chief distinctions we have drawn in this book, stated in perhaps oversimplified form, hinge on the extent to which the federal government goes beyond providing funds to persons or governments and intervenes in decisions about the demand or supply of particular goods and services. . . . But if one looks five years ahead, the budget is not uncontrollable. . . . The projections that show little room for new initiatives in the foreseeable future are only extrapolations of current priorities.[48]

It is true that persons of apparently shared values can and do disagree as to whether, for example, certain "incentives," such as investment tax credits, will actually do more for the deprived (unemployed in this case) than measures that take privileges away from the privileged. But perhaps the most indicative characterization of the situation has been made by President Johnson's chairman of the Council of Economic Advisers, Arthur Okun, who stated:

> Our philosophical and ideological positions are part of our professional (economists') views and our potential contribution. One has to search hard for professional controversies—even on purely theoretical or empirical issues—that are independent of differing ideologies. . . . Most of the key policy controversies among economists reflect different philosophies about government's role in the society and the economy, and about the relative priority attached to various objectives that we all value to some degree. There is no logical necessity for economists who place a particularly heavy weight on the goal of price stability also to favor a minimum size and scope of the federal budget, or to emphasize the importance of the balance-of-payments equilibrium. Yet empirically this association exists. If you knew the views of an unidentified economist on half a dozen controversial issues, you could make a good estimate of his positions on six other issues.[49]

Moreover, Okun stated: "Nobody comes out of graduate school with a Ph.D. in priority setting or applied political ideology. And yet these are the major tasks in the executive's policy making."[50] Furthermore, if the latter was true of the presidency in the 1960s, it might also be true of the emergent activist Congress of the 1970s, amid what has been called "the new politics of resource constraint," responding to the cues of the economists Okun describes.

The question clearly then arises, how can a measure be derived which would validly and reliably test for systematic and opposing forces vis-à-vis this central focus within the Congress? This general question with regard to the *structure or form* of existing coalitions is addressed in *this* chapter. Chapter 6, based on the results of this chapter, sets out to determine whether "regime and opposition" on economic matters exists in any sharply distinct way substantively, that is, in the character of the opposing beliefs and policies held or preferred by opposing coalitions within Congress.

The Class Allocation Index

If we give positive scores for allocations to votes purportedly for legislation that would benefit middle-income and lower-income groups and for taking away values from upper-income individuals and particularly wealthy producer groups, and, moreover, if we give negative scores for the opposite behavior—that is, increasing allocations to upper-class groups or preserving their privileges, macroeconomic theories aside, and for denying values to middle-income and lower-income groups—the resulting index should reveal a rank ordering that shows high consistency with other liberal positions on foreign policy, race, and civil liberties and democracy.

The mechanics of constructing the index are straightforward. In each of the three class data sets described previously, each Member in the House samples and every senator in the two Congresses analyzed was given a total liberal score for the number of liberal votes he cast. The three scores from the three data sets, both positive and negative scores, were *added* to create a class allocation liberalism index score for each Member (in the two samples) or senator.

It is now time to introduce a *linguistic convention.* Henceforth we shall make a distinction in certain contexts between "Liberals" and "Progressives," while retaining the word "liberal" with the lower case *l* as a generic term including both "Progressives" and "Liberals." Table 5-1 gives an operationalized meaning to the terms distinguished.

The hypothetical typology in Table 5-1, expressed in terms of conflicting patterns of class voting preference, is constituted from the idealized patterns of voting on allocations to different social classes. The table delineates the maximum possible index scores that can be attained by the different hypothesized ideological types.

The substantive character of the positions that distinguish Progressives, Liberals, and Conservatives on matters of economic policy, class, and political economy will be delineated in Chapter 6. Hopefully, by associating each of these categories with the three economists signified in Table 5-1 (Galbraith, Okun, and Friedman), the reader will be sufficiently informed for the purpose here.

It is, however, necessary to illuminate the fourth category of the table, "Brokers."

Brokers were determined from the roll calls to exist as a significant minority, but not in numbers which would conclusively affect any interpretation of the ideological consistency hypothesis. The criterion for placing a Member in the Broker category was that he did not vote for or against any of the three classes at least 75 percent or more of the time; that is, he voted for all classes between 25 and 75 percent of the time. These kinds of cut points are inevitably arbitrary and cannot be established by any theoretically significant criterion, given the truncated agenda of voting, discussed earlier, and the lack, therefore, of a wide enough range of variation in class allocation indicators to establish theoretically significant cut points at the data level.[51] However, because of their stringency, the arbitrary percentage cut points used here will serve the purpose of roughly discriminating Brokers from ideologues (the other categories). Given the broad opportunity provided by the width of the category "Brokers," namely, 25-75 percent, and the large number of votes on economic matters alone (see Appendix I), if the number of Brokers as opposed to ideologues is a small minority in the sample here, then empirically establishing that it *is* a small minority establishes the pertinency of the class allocation index described in Table 5-1. In fact, only twenty of the ninety-six members[52] of the sample for the Ninety-second

TABLE 5-1
Possible Class Allocation Scores by Roll Call Votes

		From[a] *Corporations and Upper Class*	*To Middle Class*	*To Lower Class*	*Maximum Possible Index Scores*
liberals	Progressives (Galbraith)	100%	100%	100%	300
liberals	Liberals (Okun)	0%	100%	100%	200
	Conservatives (Friedman)	0%	0%	0%	0
	Brokers	25-75%	25-75%	25-75%	75-225

[a]"From" means here "vote to take away from," *or,* "vote against increased allocations to."

Congress, House, did *not* vote for or against one class over 75 percent of the time, that is, were Brokers. Of the twenty Brokers, almost all may be understood as Conservatives because all but a few had combined class allocation index scores (upper + middle + lower) below 60 percent liberal.

This finding by itself lends confirmation to the ideological theory as opposed to the pluralist theory.

The cut point between middle and lower class, utilized here, was $6,960 per year in 1970, as borrowed from Congressman Brademas's discussion of the Bureau of Labor Statistics' low figure for a moderate budget for an urban family of four. Approximately one-third of the American people fell below this income amount in 1970.[53] Congressman Brademas was attempting to establish that families between the $4,320 poverty line and $6,960 income per year ought to have free resort to the proposed comprehensive child care programs.[54] Since no tax legislation was voted on in the Ninety-second Congress and since all the votes directly affecting people with incomes over $25,000 a year were votes on matters affecting large and very wealthy industries and firms, there was no need of an income cut point in categorizing votes affecting primarily upper-income groups. Scrutiny of the data for the Ninety-second Congress, Senate, and the Ninety-fourth Congress, House and Senate, seems clearly to be in accord with the preceding analysis.

As we have seen, great confusion has been generated in the attempt to discern political forces by the failure theoretically to discriminate what the term "liberal" denotes. The categories of Table 5-1 are an operationalized version of a political typology based on theoretical and observed empirical considerations. The difference in the weight of the combined scores of Progressives, Liberals, and Conservatives ensures clear theoretical meaning on a perfectly nonarbitrary weighting basis. Despite the difficulties of operationalizing types of class allocations voting in Congress, there can be no question that an analysis of legislative groups in such terms ought to be undertaken, if we are to continue to think of politics in terms of Lasswell's "who gets what"—of power vis-à-vis distribution.

For purposes of the intercoder reliability test, to be specified shortly, it was determined that designation of a roll call vote as properly assignable to one of the three class allocation sets was somewhat arbitrary, in that a bill could be construed as *helping* one class more than it *hurt* another. Therefore, the only theoretically necessary coding in the class of economic roll calls was that (1) a roll call vote *was* a matter of economic policy with determinative class allocative effects, and (2) the other coding requiring an intercoder reliability check was the coding of the item direction according to the basic logic laid out previously, which cumulated in the index scores along the lines indicated by Table 5-1, and specified in some detail in Chapter 6. It is from this reasoning that further discussion of economic roll calls will be labeled as belonging only to the "economic roll call set," thus collapsing the three allocative vote sets into one. But the core class conflict categorization is retained in the reasoning behind the coding of the item direction, which heuristically was enhanced by having at least to attempt a crude categorization of the class effects of a vote. Thus a class conflict pattern is allowed to emerge if actually existent in the data, but is disconfirmable if either low intercoder reliability obtained or low correlations among economic votes and the other votes indicated a lack of substantive coherence. That is, the pattern is disconfirmed if a lack of commonalities is demonstrated with the other roll call sets, and which commonalities could alone be explained by a class conflict theory. This theoretical linkage, especially with regard to the explanation of the high degree of association across foreign and domestic ideological positions, is explicated in the concluding chapter.

Race Policy

The race dimension is at once simpler and more complicated than the two previous dimensions of economic and foreign policy. First, it is simpler in that the reasoning of racial policy questions as they occur legislatively involves no subtle underlying and complex logic of a policy community, such as the economic policy community. The legislative issues—among them, busing, equal employment, open housing, voting rights—merely require choosing one or the other side to varying degrees. The complexity lies in the origin of the race issue politically. Unlike economic and foreign policy, race policy options are close to popular experience and concern, and legislators feel mass constituency pressures to be keener on well-exposed racial questions.[55] Second, a large part of the race issue falls within the province of the judiciary. Third, and most important, racial equality is intimately bound up with problems of economic equality.

Sustained full employment, along with an increase in the supply of goods and services necessary for an adequate standard of living, seems to be the primary answer to the economic plight of blacks and other minorities, in the view of liberals. Arthur Okun, for example, has presented evidence that the quality as well as the quantity of employment is raised by higher levels of overall economic activity. He notes that a tight labor market enables workers to move into higher-paying and more productive jobs.[56] Therefore, it can be argued that furthering those conditions which create sustained full employment is an important strategy for attacking the economic deprivations of racial minorities, and others as well. Additionally the argument has been made that once full employment has been achieved in that manner, racial tensions would be greatly reduced, if there were widespread expectation among both whites and racial minorities that sustained full employment would endure, and they would not be competing for the bottom rungs of the ladder.

From the foregoing analysis it follows that at least a great part of the domain of race issues is, via economic policy, part of the domain of class issues. But the two categories, inductively, were kept separate here. The nature of the specific race issues are sure to be sufficiently familiar to the reader as to require no delineation of major positions.[57]

Civil Liberties and Democracy Votes

In many ways this dimension most of all reveals, in its particulars, the intensity of political conflict of an ideological nature in the Congress. Only if the particular legislation, and more significantly the committee hearings, are placed in the context of knowledge of the nature and scope of actual governmental activities, and media quality, viewed from the perspective of a finely drawn empirical democratic theory, will the centrality of this dimension be grasped. This is not the place to describe such a theory of democracy and explicate such relationships. Rather, it is sufficient here to list some of the major aspects of this dimension in order to illuminate its special quality.

In the area of democracy issues, congressional cleavages have occurred over the following in the period covered by this study, and readers not familiar with the specific issues of this period may consult the appropriate votes under the civil liberties-democracy category in Appendix I.

1. Efforts to affect the electronic mass media or print media.
2. Matters pertaining to the electoral process and campaign practices seen to affect the democratic character of the electoral process.
3. Matters pertaining to the access of the whole citizenry to information

about, and understanding of, contrary viewpoints on government practices, policies, and politics.

4. Matters pertaining to the procedures of the Congress affecting the balance of political or ideological forces in ways that affect the representational character of the legislature.
5. Matters pertaining to government actions vis-à-vis political dissidents not accused of violating the law, including the legally defined "chilling effect."
6. Matters pertaining to the relation between church and state.
7. Matters pertaining to the broadening of access to the electoral process of various groups other than racial minorities.

In the area of civil liberties, the three salient aspects before the Congress have been:

1. Equal rights for women.
2. Matters pertaining to individual privacy in nonpolitical areas.
3. Matters pertaining to the rights of defendants in criminal investigations and proceedings.

These issues, as policies in contention, are familiar to readers of the daily press.

ITEM DIRECTION ASSIGNMENT

Based on some years of observing Congress and congressmen and senators in various policy contexts, a list of very liberal, moderately liberal, moderately conservative, and very conservative congressmen and senators was constructed. Then, after observing the *Congressional Quarterly* summary vote tally by Northern Democrats, Southern Democrats, and Republicans, and reading the description of the vote given with the vote talley, each individual vote was scrutinized to see whether the very liberal, moderate, and very conservative Members were voting together uniformly as should be expected if the ideological theory is true. In most cases the expected regularities were observed, allowing a *pro forma* item direction assignment. If there were irregularities, then the procedures outlined earlier were carried out (see the preceding discussions of excluded votes and the outline of procedures). The same list of those who should be expected to vote together was used for the intercoder reliability test.

AN INTERCODER RELIABILITY CHECK

The problem, and the procedure fitted to it, of an intercoder reliability check in this kind of a study is best stated by Converse, who described the method used here vis-à-vis his own work on "levels of conceptualization" in his classic "The Nature of Belief Systems in Mass Publics." He has noted the following:

I felt it was very important to dig below the superficial level of easily-score answers, to try to capture the vast differences in more qualitative response textures beneath the surface. Context, you might say. I did not dare to farm out that coding, because it was too complex, and I did all 2000 interviews myself. I knew just what I wanted, and I never would have trusted any coding team off the street to understand all of the perceptions I was bringing to my evaluations. However, when I finished, I felt strongly that there had to be some demonstration of replicability, or the whole business might not be suitable for presentation. Still despairing of explaining the millions of nuances to our normal coding staff, I went to my colleague Warren Miller, spent several hours "training" him, and then turned him loose on an independent recoding of a subsample of the same protocols.

The point is that the criterion of replicability does not mean that anybody can be dragged off the street and duplicate things. The point is "are the criteria adequately communicable interpersonally?" where the *alters* may have to be at some reasonably equivalent level of sophistication about the material.[58]

The same reasoning applied here, with James K. Oliver in the role of the sophisticated second coder played by Warren Miller.[59] The results of Oliver's coding replication, following Converse's method and rationale, are shown in Table 5-2.

TABLE 5-2
Results of Inter-coder Reliability Test

Congress	*Concordant and Discordant Pairs of Votes as Coded by Oliver and the Author*
(1) 92nd Congress, House: 1971-72	Concordant pairs = 89.2% Discordant pairs = 10.8%
(2) 92nd Congress, Senate: 1971-72	Concordant pairs = 89.4% Discordant pairs = 10.6%
(3) 94th Congress, House: 1975	Concordant pairs = 90.0% Discordant pairs = 10.0%
(4) 94th Congress, Senate: 1975	Concordant pairs = 98.3% Discordant pairs = 01.7%

The sharp increase in the similarity of coding in the fourth category in Table 5-2, over the previous three, is not susceptible to any clear explanation of which either Oliver or I am aware. The results overall, however, are gratifying.

RESULTS

The results from carrying out the procedures outlined in this chapter follow in Tables 5-3 through 5-12. The measure of domestic liberalism is simply an index composed of the addition of the scores for each Member in all of the domestic roll call sets, including (1) the class allocation index, (2) race, and (3) civil liberties—democracy.

DISCUSSION

A number of features of Tables 5-3 through 5-12 lend internal evidence of the validity of the findings and the reliability of the procedures used. If one compares, in Table 5-13, correlations ("constraint)" *across foreign and domestic issues* for (1) the House in the Ninety-second Congress (1971-72), (2) the Senate (1971-72), (3) the House for the Ninety-fourth Congress, first session (1975), and (4) the Senate (1975), the corresponding figures are, respectively (in tau-b), .734, .822, .620, and .626. The *differences* among these four correlations fit well with congressional realities. It was only after the post-election saturation bombing of North Vietnam, including Hanoi and Haiphong (in tandum with the first mining of Haiphong harbor), and the loss of fifteen B-52 bombers, between December 18 and December 30, 1972,[60] that a peace agreement was reached between the United States and North Vietnam, marking the end of the U.S. combat mission in Vietnam. We should expect very high ideological conflict across foreign and domestic policy between 1971 and 1972. This conflict was domestic in origin as well, since it was in this same period that the Nixon government's "abuse of power" occurred. By the beginning of the much liberalized Ninety-fourth Congress in 1975, with Ford in the White House and the end to the fighting and to "Vietnamization" in April, Congress had the bit in its teeth.[61] We should expect the correlations of 1975-76 to reflect some systematic falloff in intensity of ideological conflict form the 1971-72 period. The correlations obtained indicate just that.

But, the figures fall off to what are, nonetheless, historically high levels of ideological "constraint," as compared with past findings. That the figures in Table 5-13 do signify very high levels of constraint should be apparent, bearing in mind (see note 46) that Reynolds notes a tau-b of .3 or higher is moderately strong, whereas .5 or above is very strong when the number of categories is large, as is the case here.

The continued high levels reflected in the 1975 data are consistent with a number of salient factors in the congressional environment. First, 1975 encompassed the most severe economic crisis—very high inflation and unemployment simultaneously—since the depression of the 1930s. Second, congressional emotions, intensified during the Vietnam War and the Nixon incumbency, were unlikely to be dissipated during President Ford's occupancy of the White House, given public reaction to the Nixon pardon, and, under Ford as President, a continuation in office of essentially the same administration with the same fundamental dispositions and perspectives in broad policy terms. With all of Gerald Ford's geniality, the most objection-

TABLE 5-3
Ninety-second Congress—House (1971-72): Main Findings in Kendall's Tau-B

	Foreign Policy Interviews Rank Order	*Foreign Policy-Defense Roll Call Rank Order*	*Domestic Liberalism Roll Call Rank Order*	*Class Allocation Roll Call Rank Order*	*Race Roll Call Rank Order*	*Civil Liberties-Democracy Roll Call Rank Order*
Foreign Policy Interviews Rank Order		.676	.672[c]	.629	.542	.682
Foreign Policy-Defense Roll Call Rank Order			.734[c]	.706	.578	.711
Domestic Liberalism Roll Call Rank Order[a]						
Class Allocation Roll Call Rank Order					.623[b]	.754[b]
Race Roll Call Rank Order						.622[b]
Civil Liberties-Democracy Roll Call Rank Order						

[a]Domestic liberalism equals the rank order based on the added index scores of class + race + civil liberties-democracy.

[b]Average Kendall tau-b coefficient among the three domestic roll call sets' rank orders = .666.

[c]These numbers indicate the results of the two tests of the claim that ideological cleavages are consistent across foreign and domestic policy.

able aspect of the Nixon administration's posture, other than its Vietnam policy, was manifest to the liberals in Congress by the Ford government in its push for passage of the much publicized Senate bill S.1. This bill to codify the criminal code included provisions that many in Congress considered inordinately repressive, and which was condemned in parts by the conservative American Bar Association.[62] Nor were foreign policy issues subsiding in the concerns of Congress. The intensity with which liberal Democrats fought the conservatives in Congress and in the Ford administration over foreign policy was evident in issues such as the battle over aid to Angola, in the battle over arms sales, in the intensification of the human rights issue, and in the general ongoing confrontation over the nature and extent of the threat from communism in general and Russia in particular. If one returns

TABLE 5-4
Ninety-second Congress—House (1971-72): Main Findings in Spearman's r_s

	Foreign Policy Interviews Rank Order	*Foreign Policy-Defense Roll Call Rank Order*	*Domestic Liberalism Roll Call Rank Order*	*Class Allocation Roll Call Rank Order*	*Race Roll Call Rank Order*	*Civil Liberties-Democracy Roll Call Rank Order*
Foreign Policy Interviews Rank Order		.837	.835[c]	.805	.707	.837
Foreign Policy-Defense Roll Call Rank Order			.904[c]	.890	.770	.898
Domestic Liberalism Roll Call Rank Order[a]						
Class Allocation Roll Call Rank Order					.804[b]	.922[b]
Race Roll Call Rank Order						.804[b]
Civil Liberties-Democracy Roll Call Rank Order						

[a]Domestic liberalism equals the rank order based on the added index scores of class + race + civil liberties-democracy.

[b]Average Spearman's r_s coefficient among the three domestic roll call sets' rank orders = .877.

[c]These numbers indicate the results of the two tests of the claim that ideological cleavages are consistent across foreign and domestic policy.

to the 1970 foreign policy interview schedule in Chapter 3, it will be apparent that all of the questions except those on Vietnam and Greece divided the Congress as least as intensely in 1977 in the Ninety-fifth Congress as in 1970, witness the battles over the Warnke and Sorensen nominations.

Moreover, the reactions of the American public to the economic crisis, and to the attack of conservatives on "big government," was not what one would expect from many accounts by the press and some analysts of public opinion. According to a poll presented to Hubert Humphrey before the Joint Economic Committee by pollster Peter D. Hart, a majority of Americans (58 percent) believe that "public officials in Washington are dominated by the country's big corporations"; by a margin of 57 to 35 percent, a majority of the public felt that "both the Democratic and Republican parties are more in favor of big business than the average worker"; and that by a mar-

TABLE 5-5
Ninety-second Congress—Senate (1971-72): Main Findings in Kendall's Tau-B

	Foreign Policy-Defense Roll Call Rank Order	*Domestic Liberalism Roll Call Rank Order*	*Class Allocation Roll Call Rank Order*	*Race Roll Call Rank Order*	*Civil Liberties-Democracy Roll Call Rank Order*
Foreign Policy-Defense Roll Call Rank Order		.822	.811	.633	.695
Domestic Liberalism Roll Call Rank Order					
Class Allocation Roll Call Rank Order				.637	.740
Race Roll Call Rank Order					.508
Civil Liberties-Democracy Roll Call Rank Order					

TABLE 5-6
Ninety-second Congress—Senate (1971-72): Main Findings in Spearman's r_s

	Foreign Policy-Defense Roll Call Rank Order	*Domestic Liberalism Roll Call Rank Order*	*Class Allocation Roll Call Rank Order*	*Race Roll Call Rank Order*	*Civil Liberties-Democracy Roll Call Rank Order*
Foreign Policy-Defense Roll Call Rank Order		.822	.811	.634	.695
Domestic Liberalism Roll Call Rank Order					
Class Allocation Roll Call Rank Order				.637	.740
Race Roll Call Rank Order					.508
Civil Liberties-Democracy Roll Call Rank Order					

TABLE 5-7
Ninety-fourth Congress—House—First Session (1975): Main Findings in Kendall's Tau-B

	Foreign Policy-Defense Roll Call Rank Order	*Domestic Liberalism Roll Call Rank Order*	*Class Allocation Roll Call Rank Order*	*Race Roll Call Rank Order*	*Civil Liberties-Democracy Roll Call Rank Order*
Foreign Policy-Defense Roll Call Rank Order		.620	.608	.619	.596
Domestic Liberalism Roll Call Rank Order					
Class Allocation Roll Call Rank Order				.659	.746
Race Roll Call Rank Order					.538
Civil Liberties-Democracy Roll Call Rank Order					

TABLE 5-8
Ninety-fourth Congress—House—First Session (1975): Main Findings in Spearman's r_s

	Foreign Policy-Defense Roll Call Rank Order	*Domestic Liberalism Roll Call Rank Order*	*Class Allocation Roll Call Rank Order*	*Race Roll Call Rank Order*	*Civil Liberties-Democracy Roll Call Rank Order*
Foreign Policy-Defense Roll Call Rank Order		.817	.806	.791	.794
Domestic Liberalism Roll Call Rank Order					
Class Allocation Roll Call Rank Order				.815	.908
Race Roll Call Rank Order					.720
Civil Liberties-Democracy Roll Call Rank Order					

TABLE 5-9
Ninety-fourth Congress—Senate—First Session (1975): Main Findings in Kendall's Tau-B

	Foreign Policy-Defense Roll Call Rank Order	*Domestic Liberalism Roll Call Rank Order*	*Class Allocation Roll Call Rank Order*	*Race Roll Call Rank Order*	*Civil Liberties-Democracy Roll Call Rank Order*
Foreign Policy-Defense Roll Call Rank Order		.626	.608	.566	.636
Domestic Liberalism Roll Call Rank Order					
Class Allocation Roll Call Rank Order				.630	.658
Race Roll Call Rank Order					.645
Civil Liberties-Democracy Roll Call Rank Order					

TABLE 5-10
Ninety-fourth Congress—Senate—First Session (1975): Main Findings in Spearman's r_s

	Foreign Policy-Defense Roll Call Rank Order	*Domestic Liberalism Roll Call Rank Order*	*Class Allocation Roll Call Rank Order*	*Race Roll Call Rank Order*	*Civil Liberties-Democracy Roll Call Rank Order*
Foreign Policy-Defense Roll Call Rank Order		.825	.793	.760	.824
Domestic Liberalism Roll Call Rank Order					
Class Allocation Roll Call Rank Order				.813	.834
Race Roll Call Rank Order					.814
Civil Liberties-Democracy Roll Call Rank Order					

TABLE 5-11

Ninety-fourth Congress—House—First Session (1975) Without First-, Second-, and Third-Term Congressmen: Main Findings in Kendall's Tau-B

	Foreign Policy-Defense Roll Call Rank Order	*Domestic Liberalism Roll Call Rank Order*	*Class Allocation Roll Call Rank Order*	*Race Roll Call Rank Order*	*Civil Liberties-Democracy Roll Call Rank Order*
Foreign Policy-Defense Roll Call Rank Order		.556	.537	.621	.576
Domestic Liberalism Roll Call Rank Order					
Class Allocation Roll Call Rank Order				.640	.727
Race Roll Call Rank Order					.582
Civil Liberties-Democracy Roll Call Rank Order					

TABLE 5-12

Ninety-fourth Congress—House—First Session (1975) Without First-, Second-, and Third-Term Congressmen: Main Findings in Spearman's r_s

	Foreign Policy-Defense Roll Call Rank Order	*Domestic Liberalism Roll Call Rank Order*	*Class Allocation Roll Call Rank Order*	*Race Roll Call Rank Order*	*Civil Liberties-Democracy Roll Call Rank Order*
Foreign Policy-Defense Roll Call Rank Order		.739	.722	.782	.746
Domestic Liberalism Roll Call Rank Order					
Class Allocation Roll Call Rank Order				.804	.897
Race Roll Call Rank Order					.760
Civil Liberties-Democracy Roll Call Rank Order					

TABLE 5-13
Summary of Findings of This Study[a]

	Congressional Incumbents, 92nd Congress 1971-72		*Congressional Incumbents, 94th Congress, 1st Sess., 1975*		*Congressional Incumbents* without *First-, Second-, and Third-Term Members, 1975*
	House	*Senate*	*House*	*Senate*	*House*
Within Domestic Issues	.666	.628	.648	.644	.649
Within Foreign Issues	.636				
Across Foreign and Domestic Issues	.734	.822	.620	.626	.556

[a]Figures are average tau-b coefficients, and are derived from Tables 5-3 through 5-12, except for the last column.

gin of 72 to 24 percent, the public felt that "profits are the major goal of business even if it means unemployment and inflation," with 61 percent of the opinion that "there is a conspiracy among big corporations to set prices as high as possible."[63] Those who followed the financial news in this period will be aware that many business leaders accepted the validity of the claim that there was widespread and deep antagonism to large corporations among the American public. The advertising campaign of the oil companies was only the most salient effort to "educate Americans about this country's economic system," with many such efforts by business appearing in 1975 and 1976.[64] In such an environment, would it be plausible to expect correlations lower than those arrayed? The intensity of ideological conflict in Congress on domestic issues was just as large during 1971-72 as in 1975, during the economic crisis, as reflected in the preceding correlations. What is clear from even casual perusal of congressional documents from the committee stage of the legislative process is that most of the issues that came to be markedly salient to mass publics, or parts thereof, only with the economic crises in the post-1972 environment, were well-articulated issues in the records built by committees such as the Senate Antitrust and Monopoly Subcommittee, the Senate Small Business Committee, the House Antitrust Subcommittee, the Joint Economic Committee and others, *prior to 1973.* The correlations obtained for constraint within domestic policy (expressed in tau-b) were for the same four groupings, House and Senate (1971-72 and 1975), .666, .628, .648, and .649.

Though intraforeign policy constraint was measured only for the interview data in Chapter 3, one can reasonably infer from the stability and high levels of tau-b's obtained for both (1) intradomestic issues, and (2) between-foreign-and-domestic issue domains, that the high constraint within foreign policy, demonstrated from the summer 1970 interviews recorded in Chapter 3, was maintained through 1976.

Internal evidence of the validity of the procedures utilized is also conveyed by comparing the three House figures in Table 5-13, "across foreign and domestic policy," which were .734 (1971-72—all incumbents), .620 (1975—all incumbents), and .556 (1975—without first-, second-, and third-term congressmen). These differences are exactly what one would expect, if one takes into account the membership changes recorded in note 12, and the context of the conflict over the Vietnam War in the periods described by the data. The high .734 figure includes the freshman class of the Ninety-second Congress, which was the first Congress that saw large numbers of conservative congressmen, who had previously supported the war, accept the inevitability of the American withdrawal, as public opinion moved inexorably in that direction. These conservatives were, however, distinguished from their liberal opponents by their support for the Nixon-Kissinger withdrawal policy, which liberals suspected was predicated at best on what was called "the decent interval" strategy, and at worst, in the liberal view, on shoring up the Saigon government as much as public opinion and Congress would allow. The liberals, to the contrary clamored for a negotiated but very expeditious withdrawal policy predicated on a tacit admission of the inevitability of North Vietnamese control of South Vietnam, from which they drew the conclusion that it was pointless if not immoral to continue further bloodshed. The polarization of the Congress over the character of a withdrawal policy was extreme, not surprisingly. The effect of this polarization is reflected in the .734 (House) and .822 (Senate) figures in columns one and two of Table 5-13 for the 1971-72 period preceding the 1972 election. The peace agreement is reflected in the dimunition of the figures just cited to the figures .620 and .626 for the House and Senate, respectively, during 1975 across foreign and domestic policy. That this dimunition did reflect the decreased salience of the Vietnam issue after the end of the U.S. combat role, prior to the total collapse of the Thieu government in Saigon in April 1975, is further supported by the significantly lower figure, .556, for congressmen who were *not* first elected in 1970, 1972, or 1974. These three freshmen groups, as might be expected, increased the "across foreign and domestic policy" constraint significantly, in part because they constituted roughly 49 percent of the House of the Ninety-fourth Congress (approximately 12 percent, 16 percent, and 21 percent respectively—see note 12).

The foregoing description of some of the internal contours of the data, in relationship to the larger aspects of the real context of the data, should persuade the reader to some substantial degree that the procedures of this study which were used to organize and analyze the data enjoy considerable verismilitude to the process modeled, and substantive coherence between the findings of analysis, on the one hand, and independent evidence of beliefs and action on the other.

The choice made to also array the even larger findings expressed in Spearman's r_s depended on the following reasoning. The advantages of Kendall's tau-b over Spearman's r_s are specified in note 46. It was also pointed out there that, in r_s, a discordance or disagreement in ranking appears as the *squared* difference or disagreement between the ranks themselves over individuals, and thus there is a somewhat different weight on particular inversions in order, whereas, in tau measures, all inversions are weighted equally by a simple count.[65] *However*, on *theoretical* grounds, it could well be argued that squaring the differences is *more valid* than representing the differences as equals. The argument is that by squaring the differences, r_s gives greater weight to the tails of the distribution than the center, thus compensating for the truncated agenda of voting described earlier, and giving, as well, greater representation to trends early on, before they become fully manifest.[66] For example, there is the growth in power of the liberal Democrats in the House between the 1960s and the mid-1970s. However, the reader may have his choice: The more conservative tau-b tables nonetheless show extraordinarily high constraint, but according to the previous argument it *does* seem more reasonable to represent the true relationships with Spearman's r_s. Both Spearman's r_s and Kendall's tau-b are equally powerful in rejecting H_o, since they make equal use of all the information in the data. And both statistics have efficiency of 91 percent as compared with Pearson's r, in the sense that tau-b and r_s are approximately as sensitive tests of the existence of association between two variables in a bivariate normal population with a sample of 100 cases as is Pearson's r with 91 cases.[67] However, I shall restrict my argument to what may be inferred from the more conservative tau-b statistics obtained.

PREDICTABILITY OF CONGRESSIONAL VOTING

The predictability discussed in this section relates *only* to aggregate predictability, *not* to predictability of a particular vote of a particular legislator on one bill, and *not* to the predictability of the outcome of one vote by all the Members voting. The kind of aggregate predictability discussed here is specified as follows.

Unlike other studies, the pairwise comparisons of this chapter are of rank order positions of index scores of Members within four policy roll call sets, not pairwise comparisons of votes themselves. Prediction in this chapter is based on inference from any one rank ordering to any of the other rank orderings, each of which has at least 101 possible ranks (0-100 and 0-300 for the economic policy set). Predictability is predicated on the rank order position of a Member in any one of the four policy dimensions from the rank order position of that Member in any one of the other three policy rank orderings. But the ability to predict successively from one ranking order to each of the other three is not an end in itself in this study. Rather, by establishing a high degree (size of obtained tau-b correlations) of predicability in inferring from any one of the four rank orderings to any of the others, we thereby to that degree determine whether or not these four rankings can be statistically fitted to a single left-right or liberal-conservative dimension. That question alone structures the concept of predicability that arises here. A discussion of the *principal finding of unidimensionality and its significance* is presented next.

Herbert Weisberg has formulated an extremely important, and I believe correct, argument that applies to most analyses of voting in Congress and legislative voting behavior generally, but *not* to this study. In particularly, Weisberg applies his argument to the previously cited studies by Clausen, Matthews and Stimson, and the study by Cherryholmes and Shapiro.[68]

The central contention with which Weisberg begins his analysis is the following:

> Dichotomous votes can be predicted with considerable success by a simple chance mechanism. If every bill received equal numbers of yes and no votes, one could achieve 50 percent prediction simply by always predicting an affirmative vote. Even if the vote totals were not all tied, at least 50 percent prediction would be expected on a chance basis. *That 50 percent is the obvious floor in predicting legislative votes.* The models which have achieved 80-90 percent success *have implicitly compared their success with that floor* when claiming that their models have been vindicated by analysis. [Italics added.][69]

I am in full agreement with Weisberg in this characterization of the studies to which he applies his central contention, as well as his subsequent analysis. However, it is most important, if the findings of this study are not to be misconstrued, to realize two points. First, *this study* does *not* implicitly compare its success to the 50 percent floor Weisberg identifies, simply because dichotomous votes are not the unit of analysis in this study. *The rank orders* within four policy groups are the unit of analysis. Second, the correlations between and among the four rank orderings are measured by the tau-b statistic, which is a proportional-reduction-in-error statistic. By chance alone, tau-b would approximate zero, not 50 percent. It follows that, *to the degree represented by the magnitude of the tau-b coefficients obtained,* one can proportionally reduce one's errors in prediction over what predictions would be obtained by chance alone. In the case of a rank order, this reduction in error would be equivalent to one divided by the number of possible ranks multiplied by 100 percent. Since there are at least 101 ranks, the magnitude of tau-b expresses the increase in predictability over 1/101 times 100 percent, or .009900990 percent. Hence the increase in predictability between any two rank orders in the tables of this chapter, over chance alone, is the tau-b recorded in the cell of the matrix minus .009900990. For example, looking at Table 5-9—on the Ninety-fourth Congress, first session (1975), Senate—the tau-b correlation between the foreign policy roll call rank order and the class allocation rank order is .608. Hence the increase in predictability over chance is .608 minus .009900990 (see note 46).

By way of contrast, the studies analyzed by Weisberg including Clausen's and Matthews and Stimson's, are based on models, he argues, where there is a floor, that is, a minimum possible correlation, of 50 percent. Hence, if the stated predictive capacity of these models is between 80 and 90 percent, their real predictive capacity is 90 percent minus 50 percent or 80 percent minus 50 percent, or real increases over chance of between 30 and 40 percent. The tau-b's of this study range between roughly .50 and over .80. *And that implies, if Weisberg's argument is correct, that the predictive success of this study, albeit directed to its own theoretical purpose, surpasses by a very considerable degree, taking into account the two different "floors," the predictive (or postdictive) success of other extant studies of congressional behavior in the aggregate.*

FURTHER COMPARISONS OF THE FINDINGS WITH COMPARABLE STUDIES

The significance of the findings of this study will be better appreciated if placed in perspective of other comparable studies in the field. There is little doubt that, for many readers, Clausen's *How Congressmen Decide* will be the principal point of comparison. Clausen's findings have been identified here as negative findings with respect to relationships among policy dimensions. These dimensions are differently derived from those in this study, leading Clausen to deny unidimensionality (the liberal-conservative or left-right dimension) among the policy dimensions that fit congressional behavior as he measured it.

The question that is necessary to answer is how one might account for the differences between the findings of this study and Clausen's findings. One possible answer lies with the very different time periods studied. Clausen's data are from the period 1953-64, to which he has added data from the Ninety-first Congress (1969-71). The reader will recall the earlier mentioned argument concerning the invalidity of roll call data from pre-Ninety-second Congresses, on the grounds that prior to the institutionalization of the recorded teller vote reform in the Ninety-second Congress, absenteeism was so great that the real bloc structure in the House was obscured, as the *Congressional Quarterly* analysis cited previously pointed out. That analysis also pointed out that the minority liberals were seen under the teller vote reform to be a more considerable force than had been previously recognized from roll call voting patterns. There was a good reason for this systematic bias. Liberals, knowing that they were a badly matched minority, did not come to the House floor to vote on nonrecorded teller votes they knew they would lose anyway. So House roll call data from before the institution of the reform is systematically biased. *But* Clausen's data are also derived from the Senate, and his findings are apparently the same as his findings for the House. Therefore, the difference between his findings for the Senate at least and those here need to be accounted for by other reasons.

A second possible source of discrepancy is that conditions changed. This alternative is suggested by a number of factors, including large membership changes, procedural and structural changes in both Houses, the Vietnam War, the effects of the civil rights movement, the inflation and unemployment that were so central to the experience of the 1970s, and the Nixon presidency itself. However, there can be no denying that there are substantial differences in the methods and procedures utilized here and those used by Clausen. It seems proper to suspend judgment until the concluding chapter as to how much changed conditions account for discrepancies in the findings of the different studies, until methodological and theoretical sources of discrepancies have been specified.

Third, the argument has been made that, if a pattern can be demonstrated among roll call data, the procedures can be interpreted as embodying a set of hypotheses about the procedures themselves, hypotheses that are confirmed by the demonstration of the pattern. Thus Duncan MacRae has stated:

> The use of *a priori* indices must therefore be considered as corresponding to the hypothesis stage of research; but the hypothesis that the index or category measures something must be tested. Again, methods such as scale analysis and cluster analysis provide a possibility for this test. They are not the only test since the verification of substantive hypotheses also supports by implication the measures of the variable used.[70]

In the classic beginning text in this field, Lee Anderson and his associates have stated: "If the voting behavior of legislators is indeed capable of description according to a single dimension or variable . . . this fact will be revealed by the pattern or configuration formed by the votes on the roll calls."[71]

And in the same vein, Leslie Kish has stated: "There are extraneous variables which are *controlled*. The control may be exercised in either or both the selection and the estimation procedures."[72] The key words here are "either" and "or."

As previously argued, Clausen's findings about voting alignments changing as one turns from one of his policy dimensions to another, can be interpreted as *negative findings* (no pattern found) vis-à-vis the claim of high ideological consistency across policy domains (unidimensionality). It follows that either (1) Clausen's findings must be judged as valid but not indicative of the later period covered by the findings of *this* study, or (2) the patterns discovered in this study must be shown to result from a systematic source of bias, or (3) Clausen's own research design must be found to be flawed. There are two major differences between Clausen's research design and that of this study: (1) differences stemming from the use of samples in this study; and (2) differences in the subset of roll calls used. It is necessary to consider each of these in turn.

Use of Samples

Whereas Clausen's study reflects the actual composition of the Senate and the House in the Congresses he studied, this study, by design, did not. Rather, the two samples of the House were drawn so that there would be roughly equal proportions of Members from each 10 percent of ADA percent liberalism scores, that is, 0 percent (very conservative) to 100 percent (very liberal). If there was not at least a rough balance in the proportion of ideological types across the ideological spectrum in the Congress, then there would be a large probability (equal to the proportion of conservatives and, perhaps, "moderates," in the House as a whole in the Congresses sampled) that there would *not* be included in the sample a sufficient number of liberals to allow all four of the policy roll call sets to reflect the range of variation in policy positions in all four that the House actually contained. In general, the greater the variation in x the greater the magnitude of r_{xy}. By failing to provide, in his design, for the same degree of representation of different policy proclivities, Clausen necessarily and invalidly lowered the relationships he obtained among different policy dimensions. However, in this study, the results obtained for the Senate, which involved analyzing all senators and not samples as was done for the House, were the same as the results obtained for the House (see the tables of this chapter). Hence it is likely that the sampling procedures of this study's analysis of the House cannot be a source of systematic bias, but clearly might account for the discrepancy between findings. The unidimensionality question is equivalent to asking if different Members are equally liberal or conservative in all policy dimensions. But how can that question be answered by reference primarily to conservatives and the differences among them, as is in effect the case when Clausen failed to equalize proportions of senators and congressmen of different policy proclivities?

Differences in the Subset of Roll Calls

These differences in all likelihood account for some portion of the discrepancies in the findings of Clausen and this study along with the sources already discussed. This study excludes kinds of roll call votes that Clausen does not exclude; *but Clausen's procedures lead to exclusion of roll calls not excluded in this study.* The earlier discussion on excluded votes describes and defends the roll calls excluded here. Barbara Deckard Sinclair has analyzed Clausen's methodology as follows:

> Clausen first classifies roll calls into issue domains on the basis of their substantive content. He then applies a type of cluster analysis to the roll calls within each issue domain. This procedure produces several homogeneous issue dimensions from the votes within each domain. Clausen uses the most comprehensive dimension to represent each domain in later analysis. The strict clustering criteria used insure that the roll calls constituting this primary dimension are homogeneous, *but, at the same time limit it to the comprehensiveness of the primary dimension. Thus, on the average, 35% of the roll calls in the economic and welfare domains are not included in the primary dimensions.* If voting alignments are undergoing a secular change, these included roll calls and the secondary dimensions may be important precursors of what, in the future, may constitute the primary dimension. Clausen's procedure is capable of locating gross changes after they have become fully manifest. It is not sensitive to the earlier stages of a secular trend. To identify a trend in its early stages, *a procedure which stays closer to the data than the sophisticated clustering and scaling techniques do is needed.* The smoothing of the data which these techniques accomplish is likely to smooth out just what one is looking for. [Italics added.][73]

If the reader accepts the reasoning for excluding votes in this study, then he should, I submit, conclude that if Clausen's findings on unidimensionality among his policy dimensions were negative, it is very likely because in part Clausen *did not exclude those categories of votes and did exclude others.* The reader is referred back to the intercoder reliability test of this chapter regarding the reliability of the exclusions. Clausen's method for excluding votes, on the other hand, is an artifact of his method of identifying dimensions, and is thereby arbitrary regarding reasons for the exclusions on their own grounds, as Sinclair indicates.

Clausen provides a clear reason that may well underpin his orientation to the subject of ideological behavior. In Chapter 2, pluralism and its end-of-ideology and interest group variants were described as having deep appeal because they denied fundamental overarching and persistent value conflicts, and such pluralists could be comforted with a nonconflictual view of politics. Clausen illustrates this theme graphically when, in describing those who explicitly or implicitly advocate the Responsible Party model of the American Political Science Association lore, he defends the desirability of ideologically amorphous parties as appreciative "of the compromises that are made *because* the parties avoid the bloody drama of ideological warfare." What is striking is that Clausen does not conceive of ideologically intense electoral conflict in a democratic mold as a means between the extremes of bloody conflict and no political conflict at all. That he excludes such a conception is but one example of a widespread attitude, one that has perpetuated the controversy over the role of ideology in American politics over the last quarter century, and underpins disputes over the constraints upon, opportunities for, and dangers of, an ideological mass-based party system in the United States.[74]

The discrepancy between the findings of Matthews and Stimson in their *Yeas and Nays: Normal Decision-Making in the U.S. House of Representatives*, previously cited, and those in this study, insofar as roll calls are the basis of their inferences, may be explained by, first, the criticisms arrayed by Weisberg, regarding the predictive aspects of their cueing model, with its 50 percent minimum possible floor. Second, it is difficult to understand how, on the one hand, Matthews and Stimson can deny a role to ideology so categorically, as cited previously, and on the other hand, cite as cue givers the following: the President, the state party delegation, the party leadership, the committee chairman, the ranking minority member, the Conservative Coalition, the Democratic Study Group, the party majority, and the House Majority. It is difficult to understand how these cue setters are not ideological, insofar as they are effectively setting cues.

These authors' analysis suffers from two other weaknesses. First, they also rely on roll call data which is exclusively the systematically biased preteller vote reform House roll calls (they go no farther than 1969 House roll call data). Second, they attempt to persuade us that congressmen are not behaving ideologically because, when asked about "ideology," they identify ideological thinking with rigidity and various other simplistic failings (see the reference to Putnam given earlier). However, the interview data they utilize allow congressmen to interpret the term "ideology" as they wish, and the term *does* carry for many congressmen the *connotation* of intellecutal rigidity, unwillingness to compromise, and a tendency to ignore contextual factors that ought to affect judgment. But what if, instead, Matthews and Stimson had asked the congressmen they interviewed in 1969 about the role played by their basic *political philosophy* as adapted to specific situations? Might they have obtained quite different responses? And furthermore, many congressmen have a need to appeal to opposing constituencies, and are loathe to clarify publicly their operative philosophies.

There is one line of thought presented by Matthews and Stimson regarding the role of ideology which is very interesting and provocative. This may be termed the "nonapplicability of ideology" theory, which they stated most stridently in an earlier version of their study,[75] and which they stated in a more elliptical fashion in *Yeas and Nays*.[76] In its earlier version, their nonapplicability theory was presented as a refutation of what they described as the "ideologist theory." Matthews and Stimson's description of the ideologist theory implies more or less explicitly that there are some general principles, which they do not identify, that constitute ideologies, and that these general principles cannot logically be, and/or in fact are not taken by politicians to be useful as a basis for, voting decisions. This nonapplicability of ideology, they argue, is due to the fact that congressmen must make a "very large *number* of decisions on very *complex, specific,* and *technical* policy proposals in a *wide range of subject matter areas* in a very *limited amount of time.*"[77] Indeed, all students of Congress agree that the need to reduce great information costs is characteristic of all congressmen and, of course, is the underlying logic of legislative specialization which inspired the committee system.

Matthews and Stimson array five questions on which roll call votes were in fact taken and defy the reader to imagine how any general ideological considerations could possibly be used to decide in favor of or against one or another side of any of the five legislative issues. The five issues are: (1) whether $92 million should be allocated for a California water project; (2) whether farmers in the same county should be permitted temporarily to lease, sell, or transfer acreage allotments for peanuts; (3) whether to authorize a 12.5 percent Social Security increase in a bill which also includes restrictions on welfare eligibility, payments to unemployed persons refusing job training, or payments to families with absent fathers; (4) whether the United States should reduce some foreign cotton imports in general and also cotton imports from countries that have severed diplomatic relations with the United States; and (5) whether the model-cities program should be funded at a level of $237 million or at $537 million.[78]

The answer that Matthews and Stimson find impossible to imagine is simply stated: It depends on who benefits and who pays for the benefits. It is a complex task to determine the distribution of benefits and costs that would result from passage of a piece of legislation. If Matthews and Stimson intend to imply that such matters are difficult to ascertain from the face reading of a bill, no one could argue, but that is not their assertion. For example, if it was determined that the bulk of net benefit would be gained by upper-income and wealthy interests primarily, as, for example, Charles L. Schultze's 1971 analysis[79] of the distribution of farm subsidies established, the applicability of ideology becomes straightforward. Whether a water project or a peanut acreage allotment transfer benefited those who least needed help, either as individuals or as a component part of the economic situation in the nation, may be a complex matter. But the albeit complex determination of that matter is an essential part of the legislative struggle. Once such a program can be and is publicly identified as primarily benefiting the wealthy, unless there is an all-things-considered overriding and otherwise unfulfillable national production need, that program's chances of passage may be proportionately diminished. A useful illustration is provided by the example, cited in Chapter 2, of the attempt by the very powerful Senator Eastland to get a federal compensation for wealthy Mississippi chicken producers and the junior Senator Clark's successful opposition. Such opposition might well entail analysis with the professionalism of Schultze's study, but that is why the enormous staff development within the Congress has been going on, and by all accounts will continue.[80] Matthews and Stimson's thesis is tautological, since they equate ideology with being simplistic, and then find ideology too simple to structure the understanding of complexities.

In their most recent effort, they state: "Such difficult problems are commonplace, and their complicating effects on decision-making erode the possibilities for *simplification* of decision-making by ideology." As discussed in Chapter 2, the "cognitive economizing" benefit of ideological decision making is what Converse has seen as the underlying advantage of the liberal-conservative yardstick made available principally to elites. What Matthews and Stimson fail to take into account is that the complexities are examined by those possessing the resources of analysis to see what and who is advantaged in the contrived or expected result, and that those few who carry out such examinations cue philosophically like-minded congressional confreres. In *that* way does complexity and time-bound specificities of particular contexts fit with the structure of ageless struggles over privilege and deprivation.

It should be noted in passing that the presumed nonapplicability of ideology to what are supposed to be purely "technical" issues has been linked to a major macropolitical implication, the decline of legislatures, which Matthews and Stimson cite:

> A major cause of the "decline" of Congressional power is usually thought to be its inability to cope effectively with this malignant glut of evermore perplexing problems. "The growth of governmental action," Dahl and Lindblom state in one presentation of this point of view," has required decisions that in sheer number, detail, prerequisite knowledge, and dispatch cannot be made by legislatures. . . ."[81]

This theme, generalized into a series of questions about the institutional capacity of Congress in the American political system, probably should become even more of a centerpiece of research than it has been in the early and mid-1970s. By way of contrast with what seems an overwhelming context of complexity, one should note the *Congressional Quarterly Weekly Report*'s article on the use of computers by the Congress to monitor activities in the bureaucracy and their impact on the nation:

> The implications of such a system on the balance of power between the legislative and executive branch are profound . . . every time an executive agency issued a regulation, spent or collected money, or took other action, it would be noted in the Congressional computers.
>
> Committees or Members interested in a specific program could then dial into the computer and receive an up-to-date accounting of actions taken. Rose says that such a system would revolutionize Congress's oversight role. . . .[82]

If Matthews and Stimson's conceptualization of ideology was the only guide, we would be compelled to see ideology and matters of complexity as mutually exclusive. In fact, if anything, the opposite is the case. Complexity, if it is not to be overwhelming, must be structured in perception by a well-integrated, but open-ended, set of beliefs about matters of fact and valuation.

Other past findings of note provide a sense of the sharp differences between the findings of this study and the findings of studies from several decades ago. The study that is most theoretically isomorphic with this study was carried out in Converse's classic, "Nature of Belief Systems in Mass Publics," to which we have already referred. Converse's findings, in part, are shown in Table 5-14:

TABLE 5-14
Converse's Findings: Summary of Differences in Level of Constraint (Attitude Consistency) Within and Between Domains, Elite and Mass

	Average Coefficients[a]		
	Within Domestic Issues	*Between Domestic and Foreign*	*Within Foreign Issues*
Elite	.53	.25	.37
Mass	.23	.11	.23

[a]Entries are averaged gamma coefficients, though identified as "tau-gamma." I am indebted to Converse for communicating to me what measure was actually used. The misprint was due to a terminological confusion at the time of Converse's publication.
SOURCE: Converse, *The Nature of Belief Systems in Mass Publics,* p. 229.

A direct comparison with the findings of this study appears below in Table 5-15.

It should be noted that the findings of this study are expressed in gamma for purposes of the comparison with Converse's data. Though there is no difference betwen the findings expressed here in gamma or tau-b, one should not be misled. For a readily accessible example of how severe the differences can be between relationships expressed in gamma as compared with tau-b, one may look at Richard Boyd's article[83] in the *American Political Science Review* on the 1968 election, Appendix I. Boyd arrays his findings in Kendall's tau in the upper diagonal of the 15 × 15 matrix, and in gamma in the lower diagonal. The differences are striking. Some of these differences are as follows (the first figure of each of the following pairs is gamma, the second, Kendall's tau): 59-35; 47-28; 65:26; 60-35; 67:35; 42-23; 50:14; and 61:36. Clearly then, given these figures, and what has been widely accepted as the propensity of gamma to overstate relationships *in the case of a few coding categories,* it would be most interesting to rerun the Converse data in tau-b for a direct comparison. However, it should be noted that the period

TABLE 5-15
Summary of Differences in Level of Constraint Within and Between Policy Domains (Schneider, 1971-76, and Converse, 1958)

	Within Domestic Policy	*Within Foreign Policy*	*Across Foreign and Domestic Policy*
Converse, congressional candidates, 1958	.53	.37	.25
Schneider, congressional incumbents, 1971-1972 and 1975, House and Senate	.64	.73[a]	.70[b]

[a]Ninety-second Congress, House only.

[b]Based on roll call data alone. Substitution of the interview data on foreign policy also leads to a gamma of .70. All of the data on domestic policy are roll call data. Entries are average gamma coefficients. The elite data were borrowed by Converse from the Miller-Stokes *Representation Study*. I am grateful to Professor Converse for conveying this fact to me.

between the time Converse's data were gathered and the time period of the interviews and roll calls of this study was marked by the Vietnam War. It is difficult to believe that the war did not reflect itself in the striking differences between Converse's findings and my own in the second and third columns of Table 5-15.

Large increases in mass constraint parallel to the congressional increases noted in Table 5-15 have been asserted by Nie and Anderson,[84] lending corroboration. What emerges as distinguishing congressmen in the early and mid-1970s from those of the 1950s is much higher constraint within the foreign policy issues domain and across foreign and domestic policy domains.

A number of other studies of Congress from the 1950s found no significant relation with foreign policy attitudes or behavior, or across foreign and domestic attitudes or behavior.[85] In *Dimensions of Congressional Voting,* MacRae noted:

> In the study of Congress, the foreign-policy dimension is most readily distinguished. Gage and Shimberg, using cumulative scales for the first time in application to legislative roll-call votes, analyzed the *New Republic's* selection of roll-call votes for the Senate in the Seventy-ninth and Eightieth Congresses; in both Congresses it was found that foreign-policy and tariff issues created a disproportionate number of nonscale types and had to be eliminated from the scales. Belknap, in a more thoroughgoing analysis of the Senate in the Eightieth Congress, found four major scales and examined their intercorrelations; one outstanding result was the relative independence

of the foreign-policy scale (dealing with the Marshall Plan, Greek-Turkish aid, and CARE) from the other scales dealing with domestic issues. Findings presented below serve further to confirm the distinctness of foreign-policy issues from domestic issues in Congress, at least in the period immediately following World War II. Once foreign policy has been isolated as a distinct dimension (or set of dimensions), it is possible to discern in almost every study a general dimension of domestic liberalism-conservatism related particularly to the conflict between labor and management. Such a dimension has been found in several closely related forms by Belknap, in Harris's factorial study of the Senate in the Eightieth Congress, by MacRae in an analysis of the Massachusetts legislature, and by Okusu in a study of the California legislature.[86]

THE CENTRAL FINDING: UNIDIMENSIONALITY AND ITS SIGNIFICANCE

Two contending theories of congressional coalitions have been tested in this study: the pluralist and the ideological theories. A very clear answer has emerged, namely, for the period 1971-76: The pluralist theory in no way fits the data, and the ideological theory receives overwhelming support from the findings. This result is underscored by the very large increment in the *predictive* capability of the ideological theory, as operationalized here, compared with the studies previously cited. The latter studies *appeared* to enjoy high predictive capability of Senate and/or House voting behavior. But Weisberg's analysis showed that they were based on a "floor," that is, a *minimum possible* correlation of 50 percent. In contrast, this study's predictive "floor" approximates zero, that is, if there was no association between or among the legislators' policy positions—in foreign policy, economic policy, race, and civil liberties and democracy—the correlations obtained would have been about zero.

The high correlations obtained verify that a *single dimension*—perhaps recognizable as the left-right dimension characteristic of European politics—structures congressional voting and foreign policy attitudes in the period 1971-76. The most direct implication of this finding is that one *can* validly and reliably refer to clusters of congressmen and senators in terms of the ideological labels which they apply to themselves, and which are often applied to them by the Washington press corps and other close observers. *This in turn allows, in the aggregate, congressional and indeed governmental outcomes to be explained by reference to the ideological balance of forces in Congress.*

It must be emphasized that, if the preceding findings had resulted in low correlations, then this study would have confirmed the pluralist claim of ever-shifting or very flexible coalitions structuring congressional behavior. It would not have been possible, in other words, to claim, on the basis of this study, that terms like "liberal," or "conservative," or any other ideological classification, *did validly and reliably denote* distinct clusters of congressmen and senators in terms of broad policy predispositions in sharp contrast to other broad predispositions of other Members. Rather, had the correlations of this study been less than very high, to that degree it would have been necessary to conclude that, at best, most congressmen and senators were *significantly more or less liberal or conservative in one policy dimension than in another, as Clausen asserts. Consequently, explanation of congressional outcomes could not,* then, have been based, even in part, on reference to an ideological balance of forces.

In summation, it should be noted that (1) *predictive success* is only one of seven criteria used at various points of this analysis to validate the thesis of unidimensionality. The other six include: (2) theoretical integration (3) verisimilitude to the context and process modeled; (4) parsimony; (5) adequacy of procedures used as operationalizations of the theory; (6) contextual validation of indicators; and (7) substantive coherence, including political and policy coherence.[87]

There are a number of other major implications of the findings of unidimensionality in the period studied here. These are discussed in the conclusion (Chapter 7). But there is a question remaining that has not yet been addressed, and which must cast into doubt the practical and theoretical significance of the findings regarding unidimensionality. Chapter 6 focuses on that question.

NOTES

1. For one of the best abstract discussions on coalitions, cleavages, and crosscutting cleavages, see James L. Sundquist, *Dynamics of the Party System* (Washington, D.C.: Brookings Institution, 1973), pp. 11-25. Cf. also E. W. Kelley's brief and uniquely valuable discussion of the problems of operationalizing ideology in "Utility Theory and Political Coalitions: Problems of Operationalization," in Sven Groennings, E. W. Kelley, Michael Leiserson, eds., *The Study of Coalition Behavior: Theoretical Perspectives and Cases from Four Continents* (New York: Holt, Rinehart, and Winston, Inc., 1970), pp. 474-77; cf. also William Riker, *The Theory of Political Coalitions* (New Haven, Conn.: Yale University Press, 1962), and the large literature flowing from Riker's work, including articles in the *American Political Science Review* by Steven Brams, David Koehler, Eric Uslaner, and others; Douglas W. Rae and Michael Taylor, *The Analysis of Political Cleavages* (New Haven, Conn.: Yale University Press, 1970), chap. 2; G. Bingham Powell, Jr., "Political Cleavage Structure, Cross-Pressure Processes, and Partisanship: An Empirical Test of the Theory," *American Journal of Political Science* 20, no. 1 (February 1976):1-23. See also the discussion of "dimensionality" in Chapter 2.

2. In the case of the roll call votes of the House of the Ninety-second Congress, the last few months of the second session, from the beginning of the August recess through the end of the session, were dropped for reasons extrinsic to the research design, but no source of bias suggests itself, the more so as the relationships demonstrated are the same as those for the Senate for the whole two sessions and for the Ninety-fourth Congress, first session, both Senate and House (see the tables of this chapter).

3. Cf. *Congressional Quarterly Weekly Report* 34, no. 34 (August 21, 1976):2276.

4. Cf. *inter alia*, the statement quoted in Chapter 1 by Joseph Califano; and Norman J. Ornstein, "Legislative Behavior and Legislative Structures: A Comparative Look at House and Senate Resource Utilization," paper presented at a seminar on Mathematical Models of Congress, Aspen, Colorado, June 16-23, 1974.

5. "House Voting Participation on Major Issues Doubles," *Congressional Quarterly Weekly Report* 29 (September 25, 1971): 1968.

6. Ibid., p. 1968.

7. Ibid.

8. Ibid. I am indebted to Judy Kurland, at the time administrative assistant to then Congressman and now Speaker Thomas P. O'Neill, for much valuable information about this reform. Congressman O'Neill played a major role in the passage of the Reorganization Act.

9. "Democrats to Study Changes in Recorded Teller Voting," *Congressional Quarterly Weekly Report* 30 (January 22, 1972):152.

10. Cf. *Congressional Quarterly Weekly Report* 33 (August 21, 1975):2276.

11. Cf. Aage Clausen, *How Congressmen Decide* (New York: St. Martins, 1973); the Matthews and Stimson study published in 1975 is based on 100 interviews with congressmen in 1969 and all roll calls cast by House Members from 1965 to 1969. Cf. Donald Matthews and James Stimson, *Yeas and Nays: Normal Decision-Making in the U.S. House of Representatives* (New York: John Wiley, 1975), p. 13.

12. Change in House and Senate membership can be seen from the following figures, taken from tables compiled by the Office of the Clerk of the House. I am indebted to Ben Guthrie of that office for making the tables available to me.

Change in Membership

House			
Congress		*Number of New Members*	*As Percent of the House*
95th	1977	67	15
94th	1975	92	21
93rd	1973	68	16
92nd	1971	51	12
91st	1969	39	9

Senate			
Congress		*Number of New Members*	*As Percent of the Senate*
95th	1977	17	17
94th	1975	10	10
93rd	1973	13	13
92nd	1971	12	12
91st	1969	11	11

13. See Chapter 1, note 9.

14. Cited in Lou Cannon, "The Independent Democrats," *Washington Post*, 23 May 1977, p. A1.

15. The list of decisions to be made in constructing an analysis of roll call votes outlined by Herbert Weisberg in his study, *Dimensional Analysis of Legislative Roll Calls* (University of Michigan, 1968: Ph.D. dissertation, unpublished), pp. 43-44, helped to structure the original

version of this study. In addition, the following other works have influenced this study's analysis of roll call voting: Herbert F. Weisberg, "The Inherent Predictability of Legislative Votes: The Perils of Successful Prediction," *Social Science Working Paper*, California Institute of Technology, April 1976; Weisberg, "Models of Statistical Relationship," *American Political Science Review* 67 (December 1974): pp. 1638-55; Weisberg, "Dimensionland: An Excursion into Spaces," *American Journal of Political Science* 18, no. 4 (November 1974):743-776; Weisberg, "Theory Development in Congressional Research," paper delivered at the Research Seminar on Mathematical Models of Congress, Aspen, Colorado, June 16-23, 1974; Weisberg, "Scaling Models for Legislative Roll-Call Analysis," *American Political Science Review* 66 (December 1972): 1306-15; Duncan MacRae, Jr., "Spatial Models for the Analysis of Roll-Call Data," in James F. Herndon and Joseph L. Bernd, eds., *Mathematical Applications in Political Science* (Charlottesville: University of Virginia Press, 1971), pp. 51-69; MacRae, *Issues and Parties in Legislative Voting: Methods of Statistical Analysis* (New York: Harper & Row, 1970); MacRae and Susan Borker Schwarz, "Identifying Congressional Issues by Multidimensional Models," *The Midwest Journal of Political Science* 2, no. 2 (May 1968):181-201; MacRae, "Indices of Pairwise Agreement Between Justices or Legislators," *The Midwest Journal of Political Science* 10, no. 1 (February 1966):138-41; MacRae, "A Method for Identifying Issues and Factions from Legislative Votes," *American Political Science Review* 59, no. 4 (December 1965):909-26; MacRae, with Fred H. Goldner, *Dimensions of Congressional Voting: A Statistical Study of the House and Representatives in the Eighty-first Congress*, Publications in Sociology and Social Institutions, vol. 5, no. 3 (Berkeley: University of California, 1958), pp. 203-390 (reprinted by University Microfilms on demand); Aage R. Clausen, "Subjectivity and Objectivity in Dimensional Analysis: Illustrations from Congressional Voting," in Herndon and Bernd, *Mathematical Applications in Political Science* (vol. 7, 1974), pp. 15-39; Clausen and Richard B. Cheney, "A Comparative Analysis of Senate-House Voting on Economic and Welfare Policy: 1953-1964," *American Political Science Review* 64, no. 1 (March 1970):138-52; Clausen, "Measurement Identity in the Longitudinal Analysis of Legislative Voting," *American Political Science Review* 61, no. 4 (December 1967): 1120-1235; Clausen, "The Measurement of Legislative Group Behavior," *The Midwest Journal of Political Science* 2, no. 2 (May 1967): 212-24; Mark S. Levine, "Standard Scores as Indices: The Pitfalls of Not Thinking It Through," *American Journal of Political Science* (November 1973): pp. 431-40; Allen R. Wilcox, "Indices of Qualitative Variation and Political Measurement," *Western Political Quarterly* 26, no. 2 (June 1973):326-43; David M. Olson and Cynthia T. Nonidez, "Measures of Legislative Performance in the U.S. House of Representatives," *The Midwest Journal of Political Science* 16, no. 2 (May 1972):269-77; Thomas W. Casstevens, "Linear Algebra and Legislative Voting Behavior: Rice's Indices," *Journal of Politics* 32 (November 1970):769-83; Alan L. Clem, "Variations in Voting Blocs Across Policy Fields: Pair Agreement Scores in the 1967 U.S. Senate," *Western Political Quarterly* (1970):530-51; E. W. Kelley, "Techniques of Studying Coalition Formation," *The Midwest Journal of Political Science* 12, no. 1 (February 1968):62-84; Thomas A. Flinn and Harold L. Wolman, "Constituency and Roll Call Voting: The Case of Southern Democratic Congressmen," *The Midwest Journal of Political Science* 10, no. 2 (May 1966):192-99; John G. Grumm, "The Systematic Analysis of Blocs in the Study of Legislative Behavior," *Western Political Quarterly* 18 (June 1965):350-52; Cleo H. Cherryholmes and Michael J. Shapiro, *Representatives and Roll Calls* (Indianapolis, Ind.: Bobbs-Merill, 1969); Fred I. Greenstein and Elton F. Jackson, "A Second Look at the Validity of Roll-Call Analysis," *Midwest Journal of Political Science* 7 (1963):156-66; Wilder Crane, Jr., "A Caveat on Roll-Call Studies of Party Voting," *Midwest Journal of Political Science* 4 (1960):237-49.

16. Cf. John Kingdon, *Congressmen's Voting Decisions* (New York: Harper & Row, 1973), p. 78.

17. I am indebted to David Karns, Lon Mackleprang, and Herbert Weisberg for confirming this point for me.

18. Missing data procedures will be discussed later in the chapter.

19. Aage Clausen and Carl Van Horn, "How to Analyze Too Many Roll Calls," a paper presented to the Conference on Mathematical Models of Congress, Aspen, Colorado, June 16-23, 1974. p. 21.

20. Ibid.

21. Clausen, "Measurement Identity," p. 1022.

22. Clausen, "Subjectivity and Objectivity," pp. 15-39.

23. MacRae, *Dimensions of Congressional Voting*, pp. 315 ff.

24. Samuel H. Beer, "The Adoption of General Revenue Sharing: A Case Study in Public Sector Politics," *Public Policy* 24, no. 2 (Spring 1976):151-57. Barbara Deckard and John Stanley, "Party Decomposition and Region: The House of Representatives, 1945-1970," *Western Political Quarterly* 27 (1974):249-64.

25. Regarding norms vis-à-vis conference committee reports, Senator Kennedy stated the matter as follows:

> . . . the report of a conference committee ordinarily deserved and received the highest respect and regard of Members of both Houses of Congress. A conference report carries with it a presumption of merit, for it normally represents the good faith efforts of Members of each House, who had supported respective versions of a measure, to design a common bill which follows the parent bills insofar as they are consistent, and affords a compromise between them insofar as they conflict.

Quoted in James MacGregor Burns, *Edward Kennedy and the Camelot Legacy* (New York: W. W. Norton & Co., Inc., 1976), p. 141. Similarly, Congressman Reuss stated to Members on the House floor, assumedly to those prepared to follow his cue, that a conference committee home-buying credit provision was "the least harmful compromise which could have been made," and such reasoning will seldom cause a philosophically like-minded Member to second-guess his committee fellow to the contrary. Quoted in *Congressional Quarterly Weekly Report* 33, no. 15 (March 29, 1975), p. 633. Cf. David J. Vogler, *The Third House: Conference Committees in the United States Congress* (Evanston: Northwestern University Press, 1971); and David L. Paletz, "Comment on Vogler's Article Concerning Congressional Seniority," *Polity* 3, no. 3 (Spring 1971).

26. Elizabeth Drew has given an excellent account of confusion on the House floor.

> At that point, watching the House floor is like watching a sporting event more intricate than any real sporting event: amendments, amendments to amendments, and parliamentary maneuvers—the substance and implications of which must be quickly grasped by the major participants—come in rapid succession. The rules are complicated, as they must be in order to move complex legislation through a legislature made up of four hundred and thirty-five individuals. Ambushes and sudden reverses can take place. Floor managers of major bills must be foresighted and quickwitted, and sometimes even that doesn't help. Moreover, the place can become rowdy and emotional—particularly if it meets long hours on controversial legislation—and that can affect the final substance of the legislation.

Elizabeth Drew, "A Reporter at Large: The Energy Bazaar," *New Yorker* (July 21, 1975):65.

27. In the Ninety-second Congress, for example, serious question was raised as to whether the federal legislation as proposed might undo some state laws that were relatively more advantageous economically to lower-income and middle-income women workers. For the Ninety-fourth Congress roll calls, however, women's rights legislation was coded, since the reason just given seemed to have been resolved.

28. An example of how tactical use of the rules and the parliamentary situation can be used purposely to create confusion on the floor is well indicated by the following statement by former Representative Madden (D-Ind), who soon after became Rules Committee chairman.

> There are no provisions in this legislation for payments to farmers and this $20,000 limitation amendment is completely remote and not germane from the purpose for which this bill should be enacted.
>
> The sponsors know that if it is attached to the bill the bill will never be passed and, of course, if the bill is not passed the amendment will not become law either. So on the face of it, it is just a political move and gimmick to try to get the bill into cross-currents and result in killing it.

See U.S., Congress, House, Representative Madden speaking against an amendment to limit agricultural subsidies to $20,000 per year, 92nd Cong., 1st sess., December 8, 1971, *Congressional Record*, vol. 117, p. H12012.

29. This kind of vote is salient to Members themselves, as is illustrated by a letter from Senator Edward Kennedy to the *New Republic*, and the editors' reply. Senator Kennedy objected to the use by the *New Republic* of a particular vote on campaign finance reform as one of twelve Senate votes used in its rating of senators in the Ninety-third Congress. Kennedy explained that, in the parliamentary situation of the time, the motion voted on was made by a loyal supporter of full public financing (Senator Cannon) and was "an effort to block a weaker proposal." Senator Kennedy went on to explain that "this particular vote was hardly a useful referendum on the basic issue, because it reflected an unusual parliamentary 'squeeze play,'" and asserted that full understanding of that vote involved "an even more complex situation than a full TNR article [could] explain." He concluded that the use of this vote was to "lump together the principal sponsors . . . and the most diehard opponents of public financing." The editors replied: "We agree with Senator Kennedy" (November 9, 1974, pp. 48-49).

MacRae points out, "one type of roll call that cannot be easily detected by pairwise comparisons is the alliance of both extremes against the middle on a compromise proposal." Inclusions of these votes, though they constitute only a small fraction of all votes, if not excluded, would proportionately weaken invalidly the correlations obtained from measurement of voting bloc structures as they are actually operative. See Duncan MacRae, Jr., *Issues and Parties in Legislative Voting: Methods of Statistical Analysis* (New York: Harper & Row, 1970), p. 51.

Philip Converse, in an ongoing analysis of the French National Assembly, has been systematically weeding out such votes. He describes "ends-against-the-middle votes [as those] which surely are more corrosive of meaning of final scales (as usually interpreted) than anything else I can think of." With regard to the French case, Converse notes: "In weeding out ends-against-the-middle votes, most of these are very grossly and replicably flagged at first glance by the manifest behavior of the five groups as blocs, and nobody can question it" (personal communication, letter of December 17, 1976, pp. 5-6, quoted by permission).

A similar situation occurs here. Using *Congressional Quarterly*'s breakdown of each vote by the vote within the Northern Democrat, Southern Democrat, and Republican blocs, one can easily discern whether an ends-against-the-middle vote has occurred by the oddity of the voting pattern; an example would be to find Senators Stennis, Eastland, Nunn, Baker, Curtis, Garn, and Laxalt voting with Senators Kennedy, Humphrey, Mondale, Bayh, Gary Hart, and Muskie, together against Senators Chiles, Gravel, Bentsen, Ribicoff, Biden, Javits, Schweiker, Bumpers, and Leahy. A similarly obvious ends-against-the middle selection of congressmen of similar hues could be easily made by any reader close to the Congress. Converse is dealing with an apparently less fluid situation, because of the much greater party discipline and multiparty situation of the French Assembly. But any continuous perusal of the *Congressional Quarterly*'s three-part breakdown (Northern Democrats, Southern Democrats, and Republicans) would surely reveal that Converse's analytic situation is not really less fluid than the problem in the congressional setting. Ends-against-the-middle votes are easily flagged at a glance in Congress as well, with newspaper articles identifying some of them as "unnatural alliances" or improbable temporary coalitions. Cf., for example, Spencer Rich, "Liberals,

Conservatives Join to Kill New Withholding Tax," *Washington Post*, 1 July 1976, p. A6. One could not wish to exclude such roll calls without reference to some operational criterion. The operational criterion used here was that, either in the discussion of the bill in *Congressional Quarterly*, or in the debate on the floor as recorded in the *Congressional Record*, either a congressman or *Congressional Quarterly* analyst explicitly referred to (1) an alliance of ends against the middle, and (2) reasons fitting an ends-against-the-middle model motivating the split among members of an ordinarily cohesive group. By adhering to this criterion, the coding procedure constitutes a replication of judgments already made in the record.

For example, vote 29(T) in the second session of the House, Ninety-second Congress, an Upper Class roll call, saw some liberals and some conservatives on both sides of the issue. The vote pattern was ignored and the vote coded, since it was a bill to delete pollution abatement grants (rather than taxes, fines, or regulation by guidelines) to profit-making institutions. Cf., Allen V. Kneese and Charles L. Schultze, *Pollution, Prices and Public Policy* (Washington, D.C.: The Brookings Institution, 1975). *Thus if an interest group theory was better fitted to the data than an ideological theory, that better fit would be apparent in the results of this analysis!*

A second example, roll call vote 282(T) from the Ninety-second Congress, House in the first session under the civil liberties and democracy category, was given a liberal=nay item direction despite the fact that a large number of liberals voted for it. Their vote was purely self-serving as 282(T) called for eliminating the provision in the bill to require that "copies of reports on campaign contributions and expenditures be sent to the clerks of the federal district courts of the districts and the states in which each election was held." In other words, each congressional candidate's sources of campaign contributions would have become much more publicly exposed locally, where the congressman would be most vulnerable. It would have decreased the influence of special interests in their ability to influence congressmen, hence increasing voter influence.

30. Clausen, *How Congressmen Decide*, p. 31.

31. Cf. Martin Tolchin, "Congressmen from Northeast and Midwest Establish Economic Coalition," *New York Times*, 2 September 1976, p. 17.

32. Cf. the various treatments of this well-known concept by George in a variety of his publications and papers, and Alexander L. George and Juliet L. George, *Woodrow Wilson and Colonel House* (New York: John Day & Co., 1956).

33. Cf. Sundquist, *Dynamics of the Party System*, pp. 11-25, chap. 2, "Some Hypothetical Scenarios"; and Kelley, "Utility Theory," especially pp. 474-77.

34. Cf. Thomas E. Mann, Arthur H. Miller, and Arthur G. Stevens, Jr., "Mobilization of Liberal Strength in the House, 1955-1970: A Look at the Democratic Study Group," prepared for delivery at the 1971 Annual Meeting of the American Political Science Association, Chicago, Illinois, September 7-11, pp. 15-21, and the published version of this paper in *The American Political Science Review* 68, no. 2 (June 1974):667-81.

35. It should be emphasized that the state of the art in computer technology still does not allow pairwise comparison of the 435-×-435 matrix appropriate to the House with its 435 Members; hence a sample of the House must be used, though the entire Senate can be analyzed by pairwise comparison. For the underlying logic, cf. Sidney Siegal, *Nonparametric Statistics for the Behavioral Sciences* (New York: McGraw-Hill, 1956), pp. 202-23, and especially pp. 214-15.

36. Cf. Lee F. Anderson, Meredith W. Watts, Jr., and Allen R. Wilcox, *Legislative Roll Call Analysis* (Evanston, Ill.; Northwestern Universtiy Press, 1966), especially chaps. 3 and 4, for this elementary distinction.

37. The missing-data procedure used was to calculate the number of liberal votes over the total number of votes cast by each legislator, dropping from the calculation of each individual liberalism score any vote missed by a congressman. Though laborious in terms of computer work, this procedure is clearly the most parsimonious of the missing-data procedures. Cf. Weisberg, *Dimensional Analysis of Legislative Roll Calls*, p. 39. No procedure was used to

drop legislators altogether due to high absence rates (1) because the institution of the recorded teller vote in 1971 so radically narrowed absenteeism, (2) because scrutiny of the votes generally convinced the author that few, if any, congressmen were absent very often, though a number of senators would be in the year of an open presidential election, and (3) because even a few votes in the case of any odd legislator with a higher absentee record than his fellows would indicate reliably the direction of his proclivities, given the findings marshaled in this study, and hence would indicate what side he would join in a close vote when the whip system would pull him in. Mann et al., "Mobilization of Liberal Strength in the House, 1965-1970: A Look at the Democratic Study Group" (paper presented at Annual Meeting of the American Political Science Association, Chicago, September 7-11, 1971), p. 3.

38. Cf. Siegal, *Nonparametric Statistics.*

39. Cf. MacRae, *Issues and Parties in Legislative Voting,* p. 177.

40. Cf. Converse, "Nature of Belief Systems in Mass Publics," p. 228, Table VII, note a.

41. Cf. among the many critiques of factor analysis, R. E. Bonner, "On Some Clustering Techniques," *IBM Journal of Research and Development* 8, no. 1 (January 1964):28; and cf. Raymond B. Cattell, "Factor Analysis: An Introduction to Essentials," Parts I and II, *Biometrics* (March 1965):190-215, and (June 1965):405-35.

42. Cf. Weisberg, *Dimensional Analysis of Legislative Roll Calls,* pp. 134-38.

43. Cf. ibid., pp. 108-10, 132, 143-45.

44. MacRae, *Issues and Parties in Legislative Voting,* p. 287.

45. Ibid., p. 181.

46. Cf. Herbert L. Costner, "Criteria for Measures of Association," *American Sociological Review* 30, no. 3 (June 1965):341-53, and H. T. Reynolds, *Making Causal Inferences with Ordinal Data* (Chapel Hill: University of North Carolina, 1971).

All entries relied upon are tau-b coefficients of the correlation between rank orders according to the formula:

$$t_b = \frac{N_C - N_D}{\sqrt{N_C + N_D + N_{TX}}\ \sqrt{N_C + N_D + N_{TY}}}$$

where N_C = the number of concordant pairs between the two rank orderings, and N_D = the number of discordant pairs between the two orderings, and where N_{TX} and N_{TY} are the number of pairs tied only on X and Y, respectively. The interpretation is easily understandable. Two variables are likely to have no order association (*zero score*) if a pair of observables is (by chance) as likely to be concordant as discordant. See also William L. Hays, *Statistics for Psychologists* (New York: Holt, Rinehart, Winston, 1963), pp. 647-55, and Siegal, *Nonparametric Statistics,* pp. 213-23. See Blalock, *Social Statistics, 2nd ed.* (New York: McGraw-Hill, 1972), pp. 441-42, 470, for a discussion of Reynolds' findings with simulated testing of tau-b, especially in relation to other ordinal measures. See Weisberg, "Models of Statistical Relationship," *supra,* n. 15.

Tau-b was chosen because, in part, it is a nonparametric measure of association suitable to the ordinal level of measurement characteristic of the data of this study. It is preferable in the circumstances of this study to other nonparametric measures. It is preferred over Spearman's r_s, uncorrected for ties, and tau-a, which do not attain their maximum value $\pm$ 1.0, when there is a significant number of ties, as may be the case here, even if the underlying variables are perfectly correlated; for tau-a its value can be as low as .754 under conditions of actual perfect correlation. (Cf. Reynolds, *Making Causal Inferences with Ordinal Data,* pp. 77-80, 133.) Moreover, tau-b is a more conservative measure than r_s, since, as Hays points out, in r a discordance or disagreement in ranking appears as the squared difference between the ranks themselves over the individuals, and thus there is a somewhat different weight on particular inversions in order. On the other hand, in tau measures, all inversions are weighted equally by a simple frequency count. In general, a Kendall's tau type measure is usually preferred to Spearman's r_s because tau measures (1) have simpler interpretations, (2) provide better estimators of the population coefficient, and (3) have more fully worked-out sampling distributions. (See Hays, pp. 647-51, and Reynolds, especially pp. 80-88.

Tau-b is preferred to tau-c in this study because tau-c was constructed for cases in which the number of columns and rows are unequal, which does not obtain here, and tau-c has less clear interpretations and statistical tractability (Reynolds, pp. 80-81, 133), Somer's *d* is an asymmetric measure of correlation which does not fit the noncausal pattern analysis of this study. Moreover, Somer's *d* ignores ties on the independent variable. Kendall's coefficient of concordance suffers from having unworked-out sampling distributions, and hence is difficult to interpret. Gamma likewise presupposes no tied pairs. I am indebted to my colleague Henry Reynolds for assistance in determining these judgments.

Reynolds, it should be pointed out, states: "If one wishes to be cautious or conservative, he would pick tau-a or tau-b" (p. 83). He points out that a tau-b of .3 or over is a degree of association of medium strength, whereas anything above .5 in tau-b should be considered quite strong. He indicates also that if the number of response categories were low and if the actual degree of association between two variables were .5, tau-b would probably be .3 (personal communication, cf. Reynolds, p. 144). Although there is some question about it, the standard interpretaton of tau-b is as a proportional-reduction-in-error measure, that is, *a measure of the increase in success of prediction* by the addition of the knowledge of the value of another variable. I am also indebted to Henry Reynolds for clarifying the point for me. Reynolds points out in his *Making Causal Inferences with Ordinal Data*, pp. 102-3, that "as the number of categories decreases, the number of ties increases, and most measures decline in absolute value." Similarly, Blalock points out, "In most instances it will not be possible to categorize X and still retain differences in variation in X which are commensurate with the differences that might have been obtained with less crude measurement techniques. Generally speaking, the greater the number of categories that can be retained, the more likely that one can measure such differences accurately." See his *Causal Inferences in Nonexperimental Research* (Chapel Hill: University of North Carolina Press, 1961), p. 124. This implies that the results in Table 3-1 in the present study are understated by an amount of .15, except for correlations with the questions on arms and aid, which will be understated by a smaller amount.

Cf. Richard J. Niemi, "A Note of Clarification on the Term Tau-Beta," *Social Science Information* 7, no. 6 (December 6, 1968):195-97. Surprisingly, Niemi denies that Kendall's tau-b allows a proportional-reduction-in-error (P.R.E.) interpretation of tau-b. Wilson, on the other hand, asserts that interpretation. Cf. Thomas P. Wilson, "A Proportional Reduction in Error interpretation of tau-b is as a proportional-reduction-in-error measure, that is, *a measure of* tique of Ordinal Variables," in H.M. Blalock, Jr. (ed.), *Causal Models in the Social Sciences* (Chicago: Aldine-Atherton, 1971), pp. 415-31. This author has been convinced by Wilson's argument. Tau-b provides exact agreement for ordered categories for a perfectly reliable measure. The tau-b statistic is especially sensitive to linear monotonicity. It is a conservative measure of association, since its computing formula treats all observations outside of the main diagonal of a matrix equally.

47. Cf. Hayward R. Alker, Jr., "Statistics and Politics: The Need for Causal Data Analysis," in S. M. Lipset, ed., *Politics and the Social Sciences* (New York: Oxford University Press, 1969); see especially pp. 266 ff., "A. The Search For Latent Types: Cluster Analysis," and pp. 295ff., "C. Some Priorities in Data Analysis."

48. Edward R. Fried, Alice M. Rivlin, Charles L. Schultze, and Nancy H. Teeters, *Setting National Priorities: The 1974 Budget* (Washington, D.C.: The Brookings Institution, 1973), p. 441.

49. Arthur M. Okun, *The Political Economy of Prosperity* (New York: W. W. Norton & Co., 1970), p. 23.

50. Ibid., p. 19.

51. Cf. Edward R. Tufte, "Improving Data Analysis in Political Science," in his *Quantitative Analysis of Social Problems* (Reading, Mass.: Addison-Wesley, 1970), pp. 440-41.

52. One congressman was dropped in the roll call analysis stage from this sample by the computer for entirely mysterious reasons.

53. I am indebted to Marian Palley for this calculation from the 1970 census figures.

54. Cf. U.S., Congress, House, Debate on Economic Opportunity Act Amendments 1971, HR 10361, 92nd Cong., 1st sess., September 30, 1971, *Congressional Record*, vol. 117, pp. H8884-90.

55. Warren E. Miller and Donald E. Stokes, "Constituency Influence in Congress," *American Political Science Review* 57, no. 1 (March 1963), reprinted in Angus Campbell, Philip E. Converse, Warren E. Miller, and Donald E. Stokes, *Elections and the Political Order* (New York: John Wiley & Sons, Inc., 1966), pp. 351-72.

56. Arthur M. Okun, "Upward Mobility in a High Pressure Economy," in *Brookings Papers on Economic Activity*, 1:1973 (Washington, D.C.: The Brookings Institution, 1973).

57. Cf. the following by Gary Orfield: (1) *Must We Bus? Segregated Schools and National Policy* (Washington, D.C.: Brookings Institution, 1978); (2) "Congress, the President, and Anti-Busing Legislation, 1966-1974," *Journal of Law and Education* 4, no. 1 (January 1975):81-139; (3) "How to Make Desegregation Work: The Adaptation of Schools to Their Newly-Integrated Student Bodies," Brookings Reprint 312 (Washington, D.C.: The Brookings Institution, 1976); and (4) *The Reconstruction of Southern Education* (New York: John Wiley & Sons, 1969).

58. Personal communicaton, letter of December 17, 1976, pp. 6-7; quoted by permission.

59. Oliver read a draft of the procedures followed and was given a list of the cue setters of the liberal, moderate, and conservative Members. A third party, using a table of random numbers, selected for Oliver a stratified random sample of 10 percent of the roll calls, 282 votes in all constituting the sample. The sample was stratified so that equal numbers of votes were drawn from each session of each chamber analyzed in this study. Oliver was given a two-page set of instructions directing him to specially selected parts of the manuscript to be read alone, that would illuminate his purpose, and directing his attention to important data that should guide his coding, especially excluded vote criteria and the reasoning behind assignment of item direction. We discussed for several hours some of the nuances.

Cf., James K. Oliver, *Congress and the Future of American Seapower: An Analysis of United States Navy Budget Requests in the 1970's*, a paper delivered at the 1976 Annual Meeting of the American Political Science Association, The Palmer House, Chicago, Ill., September 2-5; James A. Nathan and James K. Oliver, *United States Foreign Policy and World Order* (Boston: Little, Brown and Company, 1976). The brief review of this volume in *Foreign Affairs* 55, no. 2 (January 1977):432, reads as follows: "A superior eclectic blend of several theories of American behavior in an effort to understand the American image of international reality since 1945. This book would be an effective text in historically-oriented college courses in American foreign policy." *The Wilson Quarterly* (Spring 1977) noted on page 141 that "Few other books on the U.S. world role have been so readable and balanced in perspective, satisfying both scholar and layman." See Oliver and Nathan, "Political Change and Political Choice: A Review of Some Introductory American Government Texts," *Teaching Political Science* 3, no. 4 (July 1976):445-60. Oliver has in the past taught courses on Congress.

60. "Inching Toward an End to a Long and Costly War," *Congressional Quarterly Weekly Report* 31, no. 3 (January 20, 1973):86-90; "The Vietnam Bombing: Senate Opposition Grows," *Congressional Quarterly Weekly Report* 30, No. 52 (December 23, 1972):3171-2: "War Costs: Budget Figures Easy, Others Impossible," *Congressional Quarterly Weekly Report* 31, no. 4 (January 27, 1973):148-52.

61. "Congressional Government: Can It Happen?" *Congressional Quarterly Weekly Report* 33, no. 26 (June 28, 1975):1331-52.

62. Mary Link, "Subcommittee Approves Criminal Law Reform," *Congressional Quarterly Weekly Report* 33, no. 45 (November 8, 1975):2385-97.

63. U.S., Congress, Joint Economic Committee, *Pollsters Report on American Consumers and Businessmen, Hearing,* Part 1, before the Joint Economic Committee, 94th Cong., 1st sess., October 30, 1975, pp. 150-54. Cf. Joan Huber and William H. Form, *Income and Ideology: An Analysis of American Political Formula* (New York: Free Press, 1973); Norman H. Nie, with Kristi Anderson, "Mass Belief Systems Revisited: Political Change and Attitude Structure," *Journal of Politics* 36, no. 3 (August 1974):540-91; and Norman H. Nie, Sidney Verba, and John Petrocik, *The Changing American Electorate* (Cambridge, Mass.: Harvard University Press, 1976).

64. Cf. the large banner headline battle over the effort of business groups, such as the Advertising Council, the J. Walter Thompson Company, and others, to "educate" the public. Cf. Jack Egan, "Networks Balk at Ad Campaign," *Washington Post,* 23 July 1976, p. D1; Philip H. Dougherty, "Advertising: Two Sides of Textron's T.V. Ads," *New York Times,* 16 July 1976, p. 29, and "Advertising: Simplifying the Dismal Science," *New York Times,* 1 August 1975, p. 39. There are of course, in addition, the regular radio broadcast series of Paul Harvey, Ronald Reagan, and like-minded efforts especially in certain media markets. Cf. also, Tom Wicker, "Corporate Populism," *New York Times,* 16 May 1976, p. 19. William Chapman, "Corporate Power Campaign Issue," *Washington Post,* 29 February 1976, p. E1. The nature and extent of this "educational" effort would make a worthwhile doctoral dissertation, and even a trade book.

65. Siegal, *Nonparametric Statistics,* p. 203.

66. Compare the widening of the tails of the distribution in "Figure 4. Self-Locations on the left-right continuum (1967)," on page 60, in Philip E. Converse, "Some Mass-Elite Contrasts in the Perception of Political Spaces," *Social Science Information* 14, nos. 3-4 (Summer 1975): 49-83.

67. Siegal, *Nonparametric Statistics,* p. 223.

68. Weisberg also refers to a study by Koehler, but fails to provide a citation.

69. Weisberg, "The Inherent Predictability of Legislative Votes: The Perils of Successful Prediction," p. 2.

70. MacRae, *Dimensions of Congressional Voting,* p. 302.

71. Anderson, et al., *Legislative Roll Call Analysis,* p. 90.

72. Leslie Kish, "Some Statistical Problems in Research Design," in Tufte, *Quantitative Analysis of Social Problems,* p. 392.

73. Barbara Deckard, "Political Upheaval and Congressional Voting—The Effects of the 1960's on Voting Patterns in the House of Representatives, paper delivered at the Midwest Political Science Association, 1975, pp. 2-3. Compare her shortened version of this paper (same title) in the *Journal of Politics* 38, no. 2 (May 1976):326-45.

74. Burns, *Edward Kennedy and the Camelot Legacy,* pp. 302-7, "The Promise of Party"; Clausen, *How Congressmen Decide,* p. 88.

75. Donald R. Matthews and James A. Stimson, "Decision-Making by U.S. Representatives: A Preliminary Model," in S. Sidney Ulmer, *Political Decision-Making,* p. 15.

76. Matthews and Stimson, *Yeas and Nays,* pp. 34-37.

77. Matthews and Stimson, "Decision-Making by U.S. Representatives," p. 15.

78. Ibid., pp. 14-15.

79. Charles L. Schultze, "The Distribution of Farm Subsidies: Who Gets the Benefits?" Brookings Institution Staff Paper, 1971.

80. Harrison W. Fox, Jr., and Susan Webb Hammond, *Congressional Staffs* (New York: Free Press, 1978).

81. Matthews and Stimson, "Decision-Making by U.S. Representatives," p. 15.

82. Thomas P. Southwick, "Computers Aid Congress in Work, Politics," *Congressional Quarterly Weekly Report* 35, no. 22 (May 28, 1977): 1049.

83. Richard W. Boyd, "Popular Control of Public Policy: A Normal Vote Analysis of the 1968 Election," *American Political Science Review* 66 (June 1972):429-49; cf. Appendix I.

84. Nie and Anderson, "Mass Belief Systems Revisited."

85. MacRae, *Dimensions of Congressional Voting*, p. 213; Charles D. Farris, "A Scale Analysis of Ideological Factors in Congressional Voting," in Heinz Eulau and John C. Wahlke, eds., *Legislative Behavior: A Reader in Theory and Research* (Glencoe, Ill.: The Free Press, 1959); George M. Belknap, "Scaling Legislative Behavior," in the same volume.

86. MacRae, *Dimensions of Congressional Voting*, p. 213.

87. Weisberg, "Inherent Predictability of Legislative Votes," passim.

chapter 6

THE "LIBERAL"-"PROGRESSIVE" CLEAVAGE OVER ECONOMIC POLICY

The purpose and methods of this chapter are quite different from previous ones. The purpose arises out of (1) a purely analytical problem, and (2) a contextual situation structuring arguments within the liberal part of the now established unidimensional left-right, or liberal-conservative, dimension. The analytical problem can be stated as follows. Even if the analysis of the preceding three chapters did establish unidimensionality of congressional coalitions, it does not follow that the differences between the liberal part of the liberal-conservative dimension and the conservative part are significant in policy terms. In other words, it is possible that one end of the ideological spectrum in the Congress is more similar than different from the other end, with differences more matters of degree than of a philosophy which would cause sharp departures in policy if the minority faction was to become a majority. This problem is evident in the semantical hesitancy over how to describe the ideological spectrum: People are reluctant to identify the liberal-conservative dimension of American or congressional politics with the left-right dimension of European class politics. Only Converse, to the best of my knowledge, has recently asserted such a similarity based on empirical data.[1]

Given the nature of the American party system, particularly its federalist structure, and the absence of anything analogous to the powerful Communist, Socialist, or, some say, the Social Democratic parties of Western Europe, it is reasonable to question whether, on matters of economic policy there really is any "opposition to the regime."[2] No empirically grounded theory of ideological coalitions in Congress can be of importance if it would make little difference, in terms of the impact of policy on all social classes, whether or not one ideological coalition or another dominated Congress. It is necessary, therefore, to examine the substantive nature of the differences of opposing groups on the congressional ideological spectrum. Differences over foreign policy have already been delineated. Those occurring over race and civil liberties and democracy issues are familiar to the reader of the daily press and were listed in the previous chapter. It is apparent from the preceding discussion that there is a bimodal distribution of policy orientations on each of these three policy dimensions among Members during the period covered by this study.

Economic policy, on the other hand, is a more complicated issue domain. Close examination of economic dispositions in Congress revealed that the economic crises of the 1970s had led to a *trimodal* polarization of congressional opinion.[3] This contextual situation, the complexity of economics, and a general unfamiliarity of most political scientists and political observers with the issues and cleavages in the economic policy community, all indicate the need for careful delineation, if the essential differences among the various segments of the ideological spectrum in Congress are to be grasped. The need to be more exacting about economic policy differences than other differences is underscored by Eileen Shanahan's authoritative description of the skewed dissemination of economic news (Chapter 2, note 65). American politicians do not and will not use transplanted foreign slogans and rhetoric, but that should not, as some conservatives point out, prevent us from appreciating comparable philosophies with direct policy implications. At this point it is necessary to recall the *linguistic convention* of the previous chapter, *using the lower-case "liberal" as a generic term to denote both "Liberals," such as Arthur Okun, and "Progressives," such as John Kenneth Galbraith,* in relation to the differences to be defined in this chapter.

The very different methods of this chapter from previous chapters must be noted with emphasis here. The interviews carried out for this chapter, and the results of the document search as well, were not structured as the interviews on foreign policy and the roll call analysis were—they did not attempt to be systematic in a social scientific manner. The purpose of this chapter is meant to be *suggestive rather than conclusive.* But the chapter is not merely impressionistic, being both theoretically derived and based on systematic exposure to the gamut of perspectives and policy dispositions in Congress and in the economic policy community. And given the findings earlier of a systematic liberal/left coalition, the policy dispositions arrayed in this chapter can be taken as indicative of core dispositions of that coalition, the more so given the prominence of those whose views are represented in what follows. In other words, having established very high cohesion among the liberal bloc in previous chapters, it therefore becomes appropriate to study in depth policy leaders or cue setters from within the identified liberal cluster, with data from interviews and, because of the truncated agenda of floor voting previously described, with evidence from the often more revealing committee stage of the legislative process, and other documentary sources.

Two other notes on methods must be made clear. First, for the all-important purpose of credibility, I have departed from accepted stylistic practice in presenting quite a number of long quotes from congressional documents and from statements of certain economists who are extraordinarily influential and active in advising key congressmen and senators. For those not familiar with recent developments, mere paraphrasing might well have provoked skepticism.

Second, there is a notable asymmetry in the presentation of the views that follow, justified by a fact about the policy-making context. When delineating the views of what I classify as "Progressives," I largely quote congressmen and senators. However, the views of what are termed "Liberals" are represented primarily by quotes from leading economists. The contextual reason for this asymmetry derives from the fact that "Progressives" in the Congress have departed from the conventional theories of Liberal economists upon whom they had formerly relied, but have no comparable group of "Progressive" economists versed in policy and the Washington subculture to whom they turn. Consequently, they are forced to speak for themselves, despite the fact that they must challenge trained professional economists to do so. The "Liberals" on the other hand, continue to rely on familiar Keynesian reasoning as carefully presented by economists, rather than trying to state their own views formally. When confronted by "Progressive" reasoning, they retreat into generalizations that often take shape in utterances such as "I believe in the market" or "Either you believe in the market or you don't." Such remarks were made frequently in the interviews for this chapter. But the Liberals leave economic reasoning to their economists, including much reasoning about the political aspects of economic policy. It is after all, easy to sound illiterate in this area, an unwelcome posture for congressmen and senators. Nor do they like to make statements which they believe might be picked apart by knowledgeable opponents or journalists. It should be noted that although Members may have some strong convictions that divide them, this is not to say that they lack implicative uncertainties, ambiguities, and volatile beliefs. However, the uncertainties, ambiguities, and volatilities are not random, but are structured along lines that can only be described as ideological in a Conversian sense. That is to say, such matters show significant belief system structuring even when loosely specified or unrelated to problems of political feasibility of preferred remedies. One can, after all, know a great deal about what should not be done, without knowing what to do, if for no other reason than the fact that actions would need to be fitted to conditions at the time. One can know what may have to be accepted as desirable, because it is a politically feasible option, without knowing what other options might be feasible that have not been legislatively developed or widely discussed.[4] What is important to derive from knowledge of such uncertainties is an understanding of what policy options would not be seriously considered if those who now constitute the minority came to have preponderant political power, that is, what options a new majority would be unwilling to develop, and what options would be left available for choice.

As stated in Chapter 1, the most important claims that need to be made and verified in science, including social science, are contrary-to-fact condition claims—claims in the subjunctive mode about what would occur (have occurred) if conditions were (had been) otherwise than in fact they are (were). That is indeed the character of the central question of this chapter. The problem to be addressed is: *In what directions would economic policy, especially macroeconomic policy, be different, if the minority liberal coalition in the Congress, established in the previous chapter as a cohesive and consistent force in opposition to conservatives, were to come to power*? Readers of this study may include those who believe nothing would be very different because, once faced with the sobering responsibilities of power, those who now enjoy the luxury of attacking current policies, without having to take responsibility for the consequences, would be forced to confront the constraints imposed by economic realities. Whatever the readers' views, surely the tension of these questions exists in the American polity in the 1970s, and will no doubt continue beyond this decade.

One should not be misled by traditional terminological descriptions of opposition of the liberal/left. Specifically, if one goes in search of "opposition to the regime" with preconceived notions derived from foreign contexts or, worse, from symbolic representations of what the opposition ought to look like, one surely will not find an opposition. In particular, it would be wise to avoid searching for some simplistic opposition that labels itself socialist, or insists on immediate full-scale government planning of the economy, presumably by the federal bureaucracy, or that assumes the advocacy of nationalization is a litmus test for those who are genuine about political and economic control of corporate power, while being relatively indifferent to problems of bureaucratic unaccountability and entanglement with special interest groups. Freed from such shibboleths of past and foreign contexts, we shall be in a far better position to discover the presence of an authentic "opposition to the regime." Possibly an opposition will be discovered that is quite different from what is reported by the press, if such does in fact exist in Congress. Even stock phrases such as "being for greater government intervention in the economy" are misleading, as Ralph Nader's use of the phrase "corporate socialism" betokens. We shall need, therefore to understand different professional assessments of economic policies and realities if we are to have any hope of discovering political opposition by those who actually contend in the arenas of power, particularly in the politically sensitive Congress.

THE NEW AGE OF SCARCITY AND THE NEW CONGRESSIONAL CONTEXT

In this section a number of views will be presented which together may explain why a wholly new assessment of the character of regime and opposition in the Congress is desirable.

As early as 1974, the *New York Times*, in a lead editorial entitled "An Age of Scarcity," declared:

> With regard to each of these critical problems—famine, energy, inflation—the facts and portents are plain to read. Men have not transcended the limits imposed by the finite resources of a small planet. It is not neo-Malthusian doctrine but mere common sense that impels men everywhere to come to terms with a new age of scarcity.
>
> Each of the critical problems has an American as well as a worldwide dimension. America is the breadbasket of the world, but this country's farmers cannot help feed the world and also produce the surpluses that once kept food prices low here at home. Yet the United States has no food policy, either for building a reserve for further domestic needs or for feeding the hungry overseas on a consistent basis.
>
> Americans are 6 per cent of the world's population but consume 35 per cent ot the world's energy. In moral terms, Americans have no right to pre-empt so large a share of the world's resources; in practical terms, the economic costs and strategic risks are too great. . . .
>
> Rapidly rising prices for food, for oil, for raw materials are the economic signs that people everywhere are bidding even higher for scarce resources. This country's industrialized trading partners in Western Europe and Japan cannot get their inflation under control until the United States, the most powerful economic force in the free world, gets a grip on its own economic problems.[5]

Elizabeth Drew, writing in the *New Yorker*, in a case study of Congress, noted:

> . . . the country is confronting a third generation of issues involving government intervention. These issues have several common characteristics: they are technological and highly complicated; they are not subject to resolution by spending; they cut across the interests of a wide variety of interest groups; and they concern economic resources that are seen to be shrinking rather than expanding. They cannot be settled by the traditional method of buying off (doing a little something for) the various competing interests. . . . The new issues—food, raw materials, energy—have brought us to a new kind of politics: a politics of what might be called resource constraints. A great deal rests on how—even on whether—we figure out ways to resolve these issues. There is already some serious questioning about whether a democratic society can do so.[6]

Roger Davidson, one of the most perceptive analysts of congressional processes, and recently a participant observer in both the House and the Senate,[7] expressed as clearly as anyone the effects of the new politics of resource constraints on the Congress and its processes. Davidson notes:

> One long-term social phenomenon looms as a deterrent to the clientele-centered politics of the past political era. That is the declining attractiveness of the distributive policy-making mode upon which clientelism rests. The *seriatim* distribution of benefits by semi-autonomous decision-making arenas was made possible by a high level of resources relative to demands, and the consequent belief that individual group benefits were of little over-all consequence. In a world of costly resources, this belief cannot be maintained. The "people of plenty" (Potter, 1954) have been transformed into a people of scarcity. In such a world, tradeoffs must be examined more carefully, for people are aware of the ultimate zero-sum character of societal allocations ("there ain't no free lunch"). One manifestation of this new politics is the sudden popularity of the "small is beautiful" philosophy, and its seemingly successful enunciation by a number of aspiring politicians. Another manifestation is the unprecedented attention being given to priorities questions through recent Capitol Hill budgetary innovations (P. L. 93-344). Clienteles are by no means on the wane, but in the future it may be harder for them to maintain closed decision-making arrangements in the face of widely-recognized system-wide constraints. Whether this brave new world of resource scarcity will foster more rational or equitable public choices, the skeptical observer may well doubt. One thing, however, is certain: in an environment where allocations are "tough," the politician's life will be a most unhappy one indeed.[8]

At the very least, the changes in the economic context and in the congressional context, reflected in the passages just quoted, should impel a reexamination of whatever intellectual baggage has been carried over concerning Congress from the quite different context of the 1960s. Reappraisal of Congress in the new contexts of scarcity should include the search for the possibility of more intense ideological conflict. As the recent evolution of theories of economic growth makes evident,[9] and given the centrality that theories of growth have had in the conceptions of leading economists and congressional leaders (to be delineated later), the relationship between the new resource constraints and ideological coalitions in Congress might well become increasingly clear, particularly regarding the changing character of "opposition to the regime."

The "regime" is, of course, the "market" model of economic behavior, in those of its aspects which are held in common by Liberal economists such as Okun, Heller, Samuelson, Klein, on the one hand, and conservative economists such as Friedman, McCracken, Fellner, and Haberler, on the other hand. There is here no need to delineate the market theories of the regime, since readers of this volume are likely to be well acquainted with the basic features of market theories, that is, of theories that economic activity basically does conform to the model of free competition operative under the laws of supply and demand, and responsive in the aggregate to the freedom of "consumer sovereignty," and that the allocation of capital and other resources is best left on the whole to market forces rather than government. This is, of course, vastly oversimplified, but sufficient to indicate the bench mark against which Liberal and Progressive deviations may be compared.[10]

PROGRESSIVES, LIBERALS, AND CONSERVATIVES

Conservatives are distinguished by any one of the following beliefs, or combinations of them:

1. The public sector should not be expanded, as it is too large now, because government cannot successfully, let alone efficiently, solve the many problems which liberals believe it can and should solve.
2. Expanding the public sector occurs at the expense of growth in the private sector, upon which America's unique prosperity and technological supremacy are based.
3. Private-sector growth will in time produce the prosperity which will lead indirectly to the elimination of the problems which liberals address, insofar as those problems are not overstated, or problems which only individual self-confidence, initiative and a sense of responsibility can resolve.

Liberals and Progressives agree and disagree in several areas. They agree that there is an outstanding social agenda that must be met by government policies and programs. This agenda is seen as fitted to serious and widespread deprivations, in health care, education, housing, income security, problems of aging, the family, abandoned children, pollution, transportation, and a surprisingly long list of other problems. Second, they agree that the private sector cannot enter these areas in a profitable and equitable way, and that government, and only government, can successfully deal with these problems, and is morally obliged to do so. They also believe that government is responsible for managing macroeconomic problems, particularly unemployment, inflation, and the international economic situation of the U.S. economy.

But it is in this latter area that the principal differences between Liberals and Progressives are found. What many congressmen and senators, and many political scientists, find difficult to understand are the arguments over what constraints on fiscal policy, that is, on the acceptable costs of meeting the social agenda, may be imposed by macroeconomic conditions.

At root are fundamental differences of perspective on the role and nature of market forces. These differences are the subject of the remainder of this chapter. Many observers of economic policy making believe that the Liberals have been moving rapidly toward the conservatives because of macroeconomic policy concerns that cause the Liberals to abandon *effective* governmental action on the social agenda. Some observers have asserted that the Liberal center is vanishing as a group with a coherent program and hence as a politically viable coalition. That is certainly arguable. But such assertions cannot be comprehended unless the fundamental disagreements between Liberals and Progressives over market forces are delineated. By doing so, the remainder of this chapter hopefully will contribute to a better understanding of the recondite matter of the underlying character of the liberal/left opposition in Congress.

DATA SOURCES

The following is an outline of the data base of this chapter.

1. In-depth interviews with eleven U.S. senators, each lasting from one to three hours, several stretching over two successive interviews.
2. In-depth interviews with eighteen key liberal Democratic congressmen, lasting for the most part at least one hour, and many lasting two to three hours, occasionally in two successive interviews.
3. Extensive interviews and reinterviews with roughly a half-dozen key staff experts from both Houses.
4. Extensive interviewing and reinterviewing with leading Democrat economists who are constant advisers to Democratic leaders.
5. A luncheon held by the author on the effects of economic concentration on inflation, involving three leading Democrat economists and three key staff members of the Senate Antitrust and Monopoly Subcommittee of the Senate, all lawyers, along with one political scientist, Gary Orfield, who performed the function of sharing impressions after the luncheon of the differences and similarities that existed among the participants. *All* 1976 interviews and the luncheon were tape-recorded and transcribed.
6. In addition to background reading in economic policy and economic affairs, including the works of some of the experts interviewed, systematic analysis of congressional document sources—over 200 different hearings, reports, and so on—plus debates in the *Congressional Record* on key economic conflicts in 1976, were carefully selected and used as a basis for the remainder of this chapter.[11]

The following interview schedule was sent to each senator and congressman with the letter requesting the interview.

CENTRAL QUESTIONS OF THE INTERVIEW

Leaving aside the economic situation at the present time and, rather, looking past the 1976 election to the economic problems of the future:

Question 1. What do you see as the major economic problems that will face the American economy both internally and internationally over the next decade or two? What do you see as their underlying causes, and/or what do you think are the major policies that should be pursued if people of your political philosophy were actually to gain control of both Houses of Congress and of the executive branch?

Question 2. Let us suppose that Congress and/or the White House is in the control of "conservatives," as you understand that term, over the next decade. What do you think would be the consequences for the economy and the society as a whole and for the international economic order? What do you think would be the effects on domestic American politics?

Question 3. More and more, debates over economic policies are talked about in terms of the market—what the market is, what it does, what it does not do, what happens to the market when government intervenes in certain specific ways, and in general what should be the role of government in relation to the economy. What are your own views about the role of the market and the role of the government in the economy, leaving aside the effects of politics on what is or is not politically feasible to think about at the present time?

In the course of discussing these questions I would hope you will indicate your general perceptions regarding problems and/or policies relating to as many of the following as you deem appropriate:

a. Consumer, worker and environmental safety;
b. The role of government in providing universal health care, low- and middle-income housing, more and better education, and mass transportation;
c. Government power to audit corporate profits and assets and the lending practices of financial institutions;
d. Government regulation to effect credit allocation in line with legislatively determined national priorities;
e. Whether government deficits or industry practices, particularly administered pricing, are root causes of the inflation we should be most on guard against.
f. Whether government-induced recession is an effective and/or an acceptable means of fighting inflation;
g. Where, if at all, government spending should be cut—the social services sector of the federal budget or elsewhere;
h. If the antitrust laws should be more vigorously enforced and in what areas, and with what effects;
i. The interrelated problems of food, energy, population, international monetary and trade policies, manpower policy, and regulation of the multinationals;
j. What, if any, the government's role should be in long-term economic planning;
k. The dangers of bureaucracy as an alternative to the unregulated operation of the market; and
l. An increase in the power and capacity of Congress as a third alternative to corporate and bureaucratic centers of power.

THE LIBERAL-PROGRESSIVE CLEAVAGE

The economic events of the early and mid-1970s had a much larger impact on sentiment within the Congress than this author had any reason to suspect. Although this study itself offers no basis for supposing that change occurred, since it includes no evidence of economic attitudes in Congress from the 1960s, nonetheless it seems difficult to imagine the kind of responses that follow occurring in the relative calm of the economy in the 1960s. What does seem clear is that a gulf between Liberals and Progressives now exists in ways that, should the Liberals fail demonstratively in their prescriptive and diagnostic roles, presages a widening gulf of polarized opinion among those who, in the name of common values, oppose the conservatives.

The next sections will delineate the substance of existing Liberal-Progressive cleavages in a number of categories, including unemployment, inflation, economic growth, and the agenda of social programs.

THE LIBERAL PERSPECTIVE

The Liberal view of unemployment manifests sharply a difference in empirical judgments in a context of what appears to be shared values. Charles L. Schultze, prior to his appointment by President Carter as Chairman of the Council of Economic Advisers, made clear the great value he placed on full employment, that is, "tight labor markets."

The occasion was an extremely dramatic moment in the spring of 1976, before Governor Carter had secured the nomination, and with many of the more liberal elements in the Democratic party rallying to Senator Humphrey. Schultze delivered withering testimony directed at Humphrey's chief legislative effort at that time, the Humphrey-Hawkins Full Employment and Balanced Growth Act, bill S. 50. He began by indicting why he shared the value of full employment to the same extent as the bill's sponsors.

> The emphasis that S. 50 puts upon the goal of full employment is, in my view, quite proper. We are a society in which not only economic rewards but status, dignity, and respect depend heavily on a person's place in the work force. The single most important contribution toward solving the major social problems of this generation—deteriorating inner cities, inequality among the races and between the sexes, high and still rising crime rates, poverty, insecurity, and hardship for a minority of our citizens—would be a high level of employment and a tight labor market.
>
> However valuable some of the federal government's manpower training and other social programs may be, they cannot hold a candle to the efficacy of a tight labor market. Necessity is the mother of invention. When 4 million business firms are scrambling for labor in a highly prosperous economy, it suddenly turns out that the unemployable become employable and the untrainable trainable; discrimination against blacks or women becomes unprofitable. In World War II, to choose a dramatic example, we pushed the unemployment rate below 2 per cent. And the result of that tight labor market was revolutionary. Black-white income differentials shrank faster than in any subsequent period; the income distribution became sharply more equal; employers scoured the back-country farm areas and turned poor and untrained sharecroppers into productive industrial workers, whose sons and daughters became the high school graduates of the 1950s and whose grandchildren will shortly begin to enter college in droves.
>
> The importance that S. 50 attaches to high employment, therefore, is not misplaced.

The nation cannot afford over the next decade to settle for a relatively sluggish economy and a high unemployment rate.

But Schultze went on, dramatically, to declare that the Humphrey-Hawkins bill was dangerously inflationary with its provision that the government be the employer of last resort. His reasoning is so fundamental to the Liberal position, and in contrast to the Progressive position, that it is imperative that its main outlines be stated here. Schultze's testimony went on as follows:

What stands in the way of full employment?

The basic problem with achieving and maintaining full employment is not that we lack the economic tools to generate increased employment. The traditional weapons for stimulating economic activity—easy money, tax cuts, and government spending for worthwhile purposes—are perfectly capable of generating an increased demand for public and private goods and services, thereby inducing employers to hire more workers. Moreover, we do not need to have the government hire people directly on special programs of public service employment as a long run device to reduce unemployment. The real problem is that every time to push the rate of unemployment toward acceptably low levels, by whatever means, we set off a new inflation. And, in turn, both the political and the economic consequences of inflation make it impossible to achieve full employment or, once having achieved it, to keep the economy there.

With unemployment now at 7.5 per cent, the problem is not an immediate one. A rapid recovery could continue for the next year and a half or so, pushing the unemployment rate down steadily, without setting off a new inflation. But experience in the postwar period to date strongly suggests that once the overall rate of unemployment edges below 5.5 per cent or so, and the rate of adult unemployment gets much below 4.5 per cent, inflation will begin to accelerate.

Inflation can occur for other reasons—as it did from crop shortages and oil price hikes in 1973. And inflation, once started, can persist stubbornly for a while even when unemployment has risen sharply. Despite these complications, it is still highly likely that pushing the adult unemployment rate to the 3 per cent target of S. 50 would generate substantial inflation in the absence of major new tools for inflation control.

There is, among economists, a division of opinion about whether the resultant inflation would be a high but steady rate or an ever-accelerating rate. If the latter view is correct, then keeping employment to the 3 per cent target would eventually become impossible, since no economy could stand an ever increasing rate of inflation. One of the reasons we do not know the answer to this controversy is that the political consequences of inflation have been such that the nation has never persisted in holding adult unemployment to 3 per cent for many years running.

I believe, therefore, that a realistic view of both the economics and the politics of inflation and unemployment lead to one central conclusion: The stumbling block to low unemployment is inflation; the supporter of a full employment policy must of necessity become a searcher for ways to reduce the inflation that accompanies full employment.

The central problem is that when the overall unemployment rate gets down into the neighborhood of 5 per cent, the job market for experienced prime age workers becomes very tight. There are many unfilled job vacancies and not many unemployed in this age group. The large number of younger unemployed workers do not move in to fill these vacancies. As a consequence, wages are bid up sharply and prices begin to rise, even though the overall unemployment rate is still high.

One approach to this problem lies in the whole panoply of job counseling, training and placement services for youth. Federal efforts in this direction should be continued and expanded. And a carefully structured public service program for youth could also contribute. (Strangely, the "employer-of-last-resort" program in S.50 is restricted to adult workers.) But in all honesty, the record of recent years does not warrant a confident hope that such programs can be the principal solution to the problem.

Sec. 206(d) of S.50 establishes a major new policy—the federal government is pledged to become the employer-of last-resort for those who cannot find work elsewhere. Sec. 206(e)(4) provides that a person shall be eligible for an employment opportunity under this section if, among other things, he or she has not refused to accept a job that pays whichever is the *highest* of either the prevailing wages for that job or the wage paid in the government-created "employer-of-last-resort" job. In turn, Sec. 402 sets up a standard for wages in the "last-resort" jobs that is bound to be highly inflationary.

Under Sec. 402(c)(i), for example, the wage paid for a "last-resort" job in which a state or local government is the employing agent must be equal to that paid by the same government for people in the same occupation. But in states or cities with union agreements for municipal employees, and in many cases even without union agreements, the wage for a low-skill or semi-skilled municipal job is often higher than the wage paid for the same jobs in private industry. Given the provisions of Sec. 206(d), a person can turn down a private industry job and still be eligible for a "last-resort" job, so long as the latter pays more than the former, and in many cases it will. An unskilled laborer earning, say, $2.50 an hour in private industry can afford to quit, remain unemployed for four to six weeks (or whatever time might be needed to be eligible), then claim a "last-resort" job paying (on municipal wage scales)$3.50 to $4.50 an hour, and come out way ahead.

This would show up in heightened form in any "last-resort" jobs created in construction work, since Sec. 402 requires Davis-Bacon wages, which in practice are set at the construction union wage scale in the nearest large city.

It is clear that in any area where municipalities or non-profit institutions pay higher scales for relatively unskilled or semi-skilled labor than does private industry, the wage scales in private industry will quickly be driven up to the higher level. Otherwise there would be a steady drain of labor away from private industry into "last-resort" jobs. A new and much higher set of minimum wages would be created!

The direct and indirect effects of this on the inflationary problem would be extremely serious, once the bill was in full operation. Labor would become very scarce over a broad range of semi-skilled and unskilled jobs in private industry. Wage rates would rise sharply and prices would follow; the size of the government's job programs would grow rapidly, as workers left lower paying private jobs for the higher wages stipulated in Sec. 402.

Once you begin to ask how to correct this problem, the dilemma of any "government-as-employer-of-last-resort" provision becomes clear. When the unemployment rate is below 5 or 5.5 per cent, most unemployment is *not* long term. Among adult males, unemployment often consists of a period of four to eight weeks after a layoff before a new job is found. Among many teenagers unemployment in such times is not a steady thing, but a period between two relatively low paying jobs. What wages do you pay in the "last-resort" jobs? If you pay low enough wages so as not to attract many people from their existing jobs, you have a very unattractive program. Many private jobs are low-paying, and the only way to avoid attracting people from private industry is to set the "last-resort" wages very low indeed. But then, except in periods of high unemployment, when even very low paying jobs aren't available, who wants the program? If you set the wage somewhat higher—even if not absolutely high—it will still exceed the wages of many people with a current job in private industry. If so, it will begin to cause an exodus from private industry, and drive up wages and prices.

Special public service employment during periods of recession is a useful tool of counter-cyclical policy. Government-financed summer employment for school age youths makes sense. And, in good times, public service employment, paid at unemployment compensation rates, may be the most appropriate way to provide for that relatively small number who have exhausted their unemployment compensation. (This would, however, imply unequal pay for equal work.) But the concept of government as employer of last resort is not a workable method of pushing the overall unemployment rate down to very low levels.

I think that there would be merit in reorganizing the bill so that it jointly addressed the inflation and unemployment problems, and explicitly pointed in the direction of preventing the inflation acceleration that goes with low unemployment.[12]

Another major aspect of Liberal reasoning with regard to policies toward unemployment is what is known as Okun's Law, formulated in 1961 and apparently confirmed by economic behavior with unfailing regularity. It describes the relationship between changes in the unemployment rate and changes in the level of overall economic activity. Its central thesis is that it takes approximately 4 percent real growth in the gross national product just to keep unemployment from rising, and for every one percentage point that real gross national product grows beyond the 4 percent trend rate, unemployment drops by one-third of a percentage point. On the downside of the business cycle, the same relationship exists, that is, the same three-to-one ratio holds. In other words, if the economy is in a situation in which there is 7.5 percent unemployment, to lower that to the 5.5 percent figure that Schultze cited in the previous quote, it would be necessary (but difficult to imagine) to stimulate the economy to a growth rate of 4 *plus* 5 percent, or 9 percent real gross national product growth in one year.[13] More realistically, reduction of unemployment from the high 7.5 percent level would take several years of carefully targeted stimulation, if inflation is not to be re-ignited, in this view. The idea that one is making a value choice in preferring a lower inflation rate to a higher unemployment rate, a view often attributed to the Liberals by congressional Progressives, is countered by Liberals with the argument that, by a variety of transmission mechanisms, reigniting inflation by inhibiting investment would have the effect under some conditions of *increasing* unemployment, and hence efforts to alleviate unemployment that also increased inflation would be self-defeating. Liberals would remind their audience that roughly 70 percent of all costs of production are labor costs.

The essential Liberal approach to curing the unemployment problem is predicated on aggregate macroeconomic stimulation of aggregate *growth* in real GNP. The reasoning stems only in part from the relative lack of success of targeted manpower programs during the Kennedy-Johnson years. Liberals, though skeptical of such efforts, are willing to see them tried anew, if better designed. But their skepticism is rooted in an analysis that also leads to their preferred remedy.

The essential reasoning has been summed up recently by Okun with unusual clarity and brevity:

> The deep recession and incomplete recovery have had a very uneven impact on employment across industries. At one extreme, in service industries, employment is doing fine, moving along a normal trend path. It has also stayed on trend in state and local governments, partly because of federally subsidized public service jobs. In other industries, like retail trade, employment today is considerably higher than it was three years ago, but has grown at an unusually slow rate as a result of the weakness of business. As in the case of every recession and incomplete recovery, the big problems are in manufacturing and construction: these two sectors account for about five-sixths of the nation's job short-fall, even though they employ only about one-fourth of the entire labor force. . . .
>
> Because a majority of workers in factories and in construction are adult males, this group experiences the bulk of the cyclical increase in unemployment. In 1973, less than 40 percent of the unemployed were males aged twenty and over, but they account for over half of the increase in unemployment from 1973 to 1976. Similarly, the changing phase of the business cycle alters the major cause of unemployment. In 1973, less than 40 percent of the unemployed had lost their last job, while the majority were people who were newly entering or reentering the labor force or else had quit their job voluntarily. Of the increase in unemployment between then and 1976, however, nearly two-thirds were job losers, mainly people laid off from factory and construction jobs. Some laid-off workers find stop-gap employment elsewhere, but most are essentially waiting to get back to their old jobs—where their earnings reflect their skills and experience. The same uneven pattern also shows up geographically, as cities and states that depend heavily on manufacturing show especially high unemployment rates, while those based on service industries may be virtually unscathed.
>
> Recognizing the uneven pattern of unemployment, some observers become enthusiastic about pin-pointed ways to create jobs—programs that would do something special for manufacturing or construction, or for particularly high unemployment

regions, or for people on layoff. Such well-intentioned suggestions are, I submit, basically misconceived. A weak economy is like an underinflated tire. A flat tire is flat only at the bottom, but there isn't any way to pump up merely the bottom. On the other hand, increasing the pressure in the entire tire brings the bottom back into shape.

Of course, even with the uneven incidence of recession, unemployment rates for teenagers remain far higher than those for adult males. So we hear another set of well-intentioned suggestions to pinpoint job opportunities for teenagers—or for other high-unemployment groups like unskilled women and minorities. Over the years ahead, the country must find ways of solving the special job problems of disadvantaged groups. But in the immediate future, any program aimed at that laudable objective faces a huge obstacle. How can one hope to find jobs for people who are chronically at the back of the hiring line while so many skilled breadwinners are still in that line waiting to get their jobs back?

Thus, the first task must be to pump the tire back up. And we know how to do that: tax cuts and easier money are reliable ways to increase overall pressure in a soft economy. Their success has been proven again and again—in 1964, in 1971, and in 1975. To be sure, it is not a panacea: we don't precisely know how to find the ideal amount of additional pressure; in particular, we have to guard against overinflating the tire, and thus intensifying price and wage increases; and finally we have to recognize that one application of additional pressure may not last forever, as the weakening of the recovery in the second half of 1976 revealed.

Both the outgoing Ford administration and the incoming Carter administration are emphasizing lower taxes as the main way to bring the economy up and the unemployment rate down. The infusion of purchasing power will increase the pressure throughout the system and bring the flat parts back into shape. Anybody who has ever encountered a soft tire should understand the nature of the process.[14]

Schultze's position was an effective representation of the congressional Liberals when it mattered most, particularly as it is supplemented by Okun's reasoning (just stated), and Okun's own frequent congressional testimony. It is no small part of the influence of these economists that they are generally respected on the Hill as sincere, even by those who disagree with them, in caring very much to better the condition of the poor and less advantaged in the United States. But as should be evident from the preceding quote their views on *the sources of inflation and on economic growth* are highly determinative of their views on remedies for unemployment and, as we shall see, determinative of their agendas for government programs in a variety of social service areas.

The Liberal view of inflation takes into account that there are different causes of different periods of inflation, and various mixes thereof. The Liberals readily admit that so-called administered pricing by oligopolistic firms occurs in some proportion, and acknowledges that a variety of other causes of inflation can explain some significant increases in the inflation rate at various times. But the cause of inflation which preoccupies Liberals is wage inflation. The Liberals as often as not are preoccupied with combat against conservatives who wish to decrease the money supply and increase interest rates to control inflation by slowing down the economy, and Liberals and Progressives alike accuse conservatives with cold-blooded indifference to the unemployed. The Liberals hope to steer a middle course between inflation and recession, using devices of governmental intervention from tax cuts, government spending, and control of the money supply, as well as negotiation directly with labor and management (jawboning, and, in the past and perhaps the future, a more severe incomes policy, possibly involving controls of some kinds and durations). The management by government of complex international economic relationships, so crucial in the international transmission of inflation and unemployment, international commodity prices, and international liquidity, is now as never before a crucial part of the Liberal program for walking the tightrope of economic well-being. Against threats of foreign oil boycotts and international commodity shortages, the Liberals seek to build large reserves, not only to avoid political blackmail, but to guarantee supply and stabilize prices when commodity demand is excessive, relative to supply. Moreover, the Liberals show a strong disposition to use government policy to provide incentives to the private sector to avoid supply bottlenecks and generally increase capacity in areas deemed essential to the overall health and stability of a growing economy. The congressional Liberals, perhaps because they did not have the votes, seemed to have lowered their demands substantially on the private sector to pay the costs of worker, consumer, and environmental safety. But in part that lowering of demand is related to perceptions of what is necessary to induce the private sector to invest in economic growth at rates deemed necessary to meet employment, productivity, and inflation targets. Yet, taking all of this into account, the fact remains that the Liberals place the Phillips curve—the trade-off between unemployment and inflation—even a flattened curve, at the center of the reality they see, as noted in the Schultze testimony earlier. To avoid inflation, it will be necessary in this view to have something less than tight labor markets, lest wage demands kick off the inflationary spiral to ever higher levels, as workers flow into and out of jobs, ratchetting up wage rates in their wake.

It should be noted that the Liberals are clearly distinguished from conservatives, who espouse the budget deficit theory of inflation, whereby large federal budgets cause inflation, and who claim the necessity of cutting federal government programs, largely in the areas of what they deem the less essential social services areas. The Liberals respond with the concept of the "full employment budget," arguing that as has been recently the case, the inflation aspect of the simultaneous occurrence of high unemployment and inflation cannot be put at the door of federal budget deficits, since the entire amount of recent deficits is equal to the total of the amounts paid out by the U.S. Treasury for unemployment compensation, added welfare payments, and especially lost revenues that would have accrued to Treasury coffers under conditions of full employment. The figure used by Schultze is $22 billion lost to the federal Treasury for every one million people unemployed.[15]

Growth as the core Liberal objective can be understood in part from some of the preceding, but must be sharply delineated if Liberals are to be distinguished from Progressives. For the Liberals, growth in real GNP has as its immediate effect the increase in jobs, and as its indirect effect, through increases in federal tax revenues, increased funds for undernourished federal programs already in existence, and new federal programs such as national health insurance and welfare reform as well. This fiscal dividend is thus obtained through growth without increasing, proportionately, the tax burden on anyone, and without engaging in class conflict with the privileged. Previous discussion of the "new politics of resource constraint" delineates the perspective that has made some observers more skeptical that this nonconflictual best-of-all-possible-worlds situation can be achieved.

The important question that follows is: *What kinds of things should the government do to stimulate growth*? It is in the answers to this question that we begin to see that political controversy over economic policy lies just beneath the surface of what had appeared to be unobjectionable, if perhaps underspecified and simultaneously unattainable goals. There are basically three kinds of things that can be done to stimulate the economy, and a Liberal government's program is apt to involve elements in all three categories, though the mix is the subject of the bitterest kind of fighting that can go on within an administration and between an administration and a Congress. The three forms of stimulation have a distinct class character, and include (1) increased incentives to business to invest, including investment tax credits, accelerated depreciation allowances, and many more devices that perhaps only a few specialists know well; (2) transfer payments from the Treasury to lower-income and middle-income taxpayers and the poor, including cash allotments, rent subsidies, food stamps, and increased tax credits and/or deductions; and (3) increased government spending on government programs involving hiring large numbers of government employees, including minimal, temporary public service jobs, CETA jobs, and public works programs, (4) most controversially, a permanent shift of resources to the public sector for large-scale increases in the production of public sector goods and services (as one economist put it, less beer, whitewall tires, and cosmetics for more public health measures, education, and so forth).

The social programs agenda of the Liberals is the last area of controversy between the congressional Liberals and Progressives considered here. As should be evident from the foregoing, the Liberals are committed in principle to additional efforts in the areas of health, education, welfare, housing, urban redevelopment, and so on, but are constrained by overall budgetary ceilings arrived at by calculations as to the effects of total government expenditures on capital investment in the private sector, in part as a function of what are taken to be calculations on the part of investors regarding the inflation rate and its stability. The Liberal position looks forward to funding the social programs through expanded fiscal dividends emanating out of economic growth, realizing that prior to achieving such fiscal dividends, and even when they are achieved, under the most optimistic assumption, there will not be available enough money to fund what it would be socially and humanly desirable to fund. Schultze's reference to political constraints as well as economic constraints, in the previously quoted testimony, should be noted with emphasis, and one might easily read into the conception of such political constraints the ideological balance of forces in Congress, if one will but imagine the fate of a bill to restrict the independence of the Federal Reserve, or an attempt to pass a capital or credit allocation bill.

THE PROGRESSIVE PERSPECTIVE

The Progressives' view of *unemployment* is bound to their strenuous objection to the Liberals' fear of the inflationary effect of full employment or "tight labor markets." They disagree with Liberals as to the causes of the current *inflation*, and therefore about the inflationary effects that might occur if there were tight labor markets. A number of senators and congressmen have made it plain that their disbelief in the methods, data, theories, and lack of awareness of the role of politics in economic behavior of empirically oriented economic analysts could not be greater, and it follows, as they see it, that what is taken to be empirical confirmation of the Phillips curve trade-off (of unemployment and inflation) (1) is the product of the unreliable theories and methods of the economic guild, as proved by the existence of "stagflation" (high levels of inflation and unemployment simultaneously) and by the failures of economic forecasting in the 1973-76 period,[16] and (2) is incompatible with patterns of pricing in periods of slack demand that was sharply at variance with what "market" theories of the laws of supply and demand allowed.[17]

The different view of the *causes of inflation* that separated the Progressives from the Liberals in the Congress, very much as a result of the events of the economic crisis of 1973-76, was well represented by the statements of Senator Proxmire, chairman of the Senate Banking Committee. The reader might note that no one has sung the virtues of the free enterprise system more emphatically than has Senator Proxmire. What follows is representative of the views of roughly one-third of the U.S. Senate in 1976, and about one-fourth of the House, in the judgment of several of the senators and congressmen interviewed. Senator Proxmire expressed himself as follows:

[Senator Proxmire.] Mr. Greenspan, I am very disturbed, in fact I am shocked at the complete absence in your statement of any recognition of the effect of industrial concentration, administered prices, the lack of competition reflected in these tremendous price increases in the big, concentrated industries. Anybody who has observed the steel industry as long and as thoroughly as you have must realize that prices really are not determined in the usual competitive way.

Prices rarely go down. In fact, I have an analysis here that shows that since 1930, in no year have they gone down as much as 2 or 3 percent, and in very few years have they gone down at all. In this past year they have gone up 44 percent.

You give some general explanations here: One, shortage of capacity; two, oil price related; and three, past thrust of cost. But I can find nothing and we have studied this for the last 2 weeks very intensively to find out how these factors might contribute to the immense size of that price increase.

Take shortage of capacity. We are producing less steel now than we were a year ago, and that has been true almost every week for the past several months. Capacity is now greater than it was a year ago, but they will not tell us what the capacity is, and we have to subpoena those facts. We have now subpoena power in this committee, and we are going to go after them. But we do not know what the capacity is.

If you do know, would you please tell us?

You have attributed half of the increase to capacity shortages. If you do not have the data, how do you know?

So I wish you would tell us what part, if any, you think administered prices and the power of industrial concentration has had on these very, very big increases, 44 percent for steel, and 45.3 percent for nonferrous metals, and 62 percent for industrial chemicals, and 87 percent for petroleum.

Mr. Greenspan. Let me first make a couple of technical points, Senator.

One, the capacity to produce steel involves a balance between coke, blast furnaces, steel furnaces and rolling mill capacity.

One of the problems that we have had in this country with respect to steel availability is that in the past year or so that steel mill product shipments have been maintained only by drawing down inventories at the steel mills.

I think that deferred maintenance may also have added to the difficulty of maintaining production schedules. That is my understanding.

Senator Proxmire. They say that, but that is pretty hard to believe. I have talked to one of the biggest manufacturers in the country, who happens to have headquarters in my State, and they have great skepticism about the justification for these enormous increases in steel price.

Mr. Greenspan. I was not referring to prices. I was referring strictly to shipments, I would come to that in just a moment.

Senator Proxmire. All right.

Mr. Greenspan. I am merely indicating that capacity problems at the moment are real, they have been running down inventories for some time, and they are having difficulties maintaining schedules.

So far as the price increases—I would certainly agree with you, that we are getting into areas of rapid and dramatic price changes—as you have cited, it is very difficult to know what the impact is. I said in my testimony that the studies that I did earlier this year indicated to me that the level of steel prices in the early spring, was too low in the sense of being well below what the market would have been.

I cannot comment on what have been the causes of the price index changes over above—

Senator Proximire. The principal thing is that they have had an enormous increase.

Mr. Greenspan. Yes, I do not know how much it is—frankly, I cannot answer your question, because I do not know the underlying facts. But what I would say to you. . . .

Senator Proxmire. Let me just interrupt to say that is this not something that we ought to find out? You are the number one professional economist in our government, the President's No. 1 adviser. It seems to me that we ought to find out because steel is so important to our economy and has such a profound effect on the prices of everything else, and I think we have a duty to get that information.

It is conceivable that there is some justification other than sheer power. But I think we ought to have the facts, we ought to know. We ought to have a clear analysis of precisely where the cost increases, if they are cost increases, are coming from. We know that their profits have gone up enormously.

In the second quarter this year the steel industry is enjoying better than an 18 percent return on equity, which breaks all their records and exceeds that on the average of other industries, which is something new for that industry. . . .

In the first place, as far as cost is concerned steel is very proud of the fact, and understandably so, that it is requiring about 30 percent less manpower to produce steel than it did in 1970. They have had a tremendous increase in productivity. That holds down their labor costs. So they admit that labor costs, in spite of the wage increases, are quite stable, number one; and number two, they are very highly integrated.

As Senator Humphrey notes, they get a lot of ore out of his State, they own the ore, and they own mines, and they own almost every aspect of it. They do have to buy scrap at sharply increased prices. And scrap is relatively less in the whole picture than all these other cost elements are.

So it seems to me that their costs are relatively stable, and there is just no way that you can justify a 44 percent increase in a year. I have gone back to previous years, and there has never been a year in which they have increased prices more than 22 percent, and this year 44 percent.

As was said in an article in *Business Week*, they are surprised that there has been very little criticism of it. That is the problem. We ought to criticize, we ought to raise the dickens about it unless they can explain it because, as I say, this is a big element in inflation.

Let's move to nonferrous metals, up 45 percent, How about that? Is there any explanation there for all the metals, except steel going out of sight in prices?

Mr. Greenspan. I think it is much the same problem.[18]

Senator Proxmire has gone even further to state:

Two-thirds of the inflation has been caused by a handful of industries who exercise enormous economic power—steel, chemicals, non-ferrous metals, food processors and distributors, and oil. Anti-inflation legislation should be tailored to the precise inflationary problem we face rather than a shot-gun approach which would attempt to control every Mom and Pop grocery store, the prices of every small farmer at the local feed lot or country elevator, or the profits of every small foundry or clothing store.[19]

Senator Proxmire has been outspoken on what he and many other Members see to be the ruthless exercise of raw economic power:

What I think are outrageous price increases in some concentrated industries will result in the American consumer paying higher prices for years to come. There is no cost justification for most of these increases other than the use of pure market power to increase profits, and the corporations have certainly been more successful in increasing their profits.

The pretax profit rate of stockholders' equity was about 14 percent in the petroleum industry during the 1960's and early 1970's. For the first quarter of 1974, the return on stockholders' equity has risen by more than two-thirds to 25.4 percent. In primary metals the average return in the past decade was about 14 percent. The figure for the first quarter of 1974 was one-half again as large, rising to 21.2 percent. The chemical industry has increased its return on equity from the 1970 through 1972 average of 21 percent up to a whopping 30 percent for the first quarter of 1974.

While costs have indeed increased in all these industries, it is clear that prices have increased even faster in order to achieve these incredible profit rates. The indications are that when all the profit figures are in for the second quarter of 1974, the first quarter figures will be just the beginning of the bonanza. For anyone who wonders where all of the money is going in this inflation, and who wonders who is getting rich when so many are getting poorer, these profits are a substantial part of the answer.

The *Wall Street Journal* of Friday, September 6, reported on a study of the salaries of top corporate executives. Last year the top executives of major companies enjoyed their largest gain in total compensation in 5 years. Why? As the report showed, there is a strong correlation between changes in executive pay and changes in company profits and 1973 was a good year for profits.

It appears that 1974 will be a very good year for profits and corporate executives, and a very bad one for workers and consumers.[20]

Let me just give you a quick example. I doubt very much if you would classify oil as a concentrated industry. There are 23 majors. And there are many thousands of other companies in the oil industry. I doubt if you could call the oil industry a concentrated industry under these circumstances. And yet, because of their vertical integration, and because there are some very large companies, and because of the tradition of international cooperation, perhaps, they have followed a policy of pricing which seems to be based on power rather than on supply and demand, inasmuch as they continue to maintain and to increase prices, while the supplies available and increasing should lower prices.[21]

Let us just confine our remarks to oil for the time being. As I understand it, the oil companies had a great deal of crude oil available, more than they had last year at this time. But they were not refining it at the same rate in July and August as they did last year. They were restraining their production of gasoline. They had the supply available, and the price was enormously inviting. They could make a big profit at the price, but they restrained it. Why? So they could maintain and reinforce that enormously high price.[22]

It is just a matter of sheer economic power. It has nothing to do with supply and demand, it is related to the fact that they have the power to get whatever price they want.[23]

Senator Humphrey, whom, likewise, few identify with left-wing views, was substantially radicalized by the economic events of the early and mid-1970s. Taking into account Senator Humphrey's political standing, his remarks, which follow, should be especially indicative of how far the thinking of Congressional Liberals has transformed them into Galbraithian Progressives in economic perspectives. It should also be clear from what follows that wage inflation is not what Senator Humphrey is particularly worried about, as are Schultze and Okun:

Unemployment drains billions of dollars out of our economy in lost production and revenues, and bleeds away millions more in welfare, unemployment compensation and other transfers.

But it costs more than that.

It adds up to a terrible price in broken families, in the attitudes of our children, in the rising crime rate, in skills forgotten and work habits never formed, in permanent alienation from society and—perhaps worst of all—in loss of self-respect.

Of course, there are those who are telling us that we will simply have to pay that price and more-because there just isn't any room for the unemployed in the system.

But let me tell you something. If the greatest free nation in the history of mankind has to get down on its knees in fear of something as abstract and as arbitrary as these so-called "free market forces," well, then we're through. We might just as well haul down the flag, lock up the Capitol, go home and admit that we don't have the courage or the imagination to govern ourselves.

But I don't think the American people are going to stand for that. They know that market forces aren't written up on any stone tablets somewhere. They know that they're not supernatural powers which we have to worship. The figure of 7.3 percent unemployment isn't written into the Constitution or stamped on the Liberty Bell.

But, a lot of people have been telling us that the maximum of three percent adult unemployment is unrealistic, that it is idealistic, that it can't be reached without intolerable levels of inflation. Well, I don't believe that—and I believe the figures bear me out.

But let me tell you something that the critics *don't* mention.

When someone comes along and says that five percent unemployment is the best we can do, you and I know what that means—it means *ten* percent or more unemployment for blacks and other minorities.

But the critical problem is that the critics just seem to be fiddling with their slide rules and calculators and saying more jobs cannot be found—it can't be done.

I'm here to tell you that it *can* be done. With the right kind of incentives for private-sector hiring, with carefully coordinated monetary and fiscal policies, with targeted anti-recession assistance programs, and with productive public service jobs when and where we need them, we *can* assure every American the opportunity for a piece of the action, *without* fueling the fires of inflation.

And we can't stop there, either—because, as you know, our young people have special employment problems. And it will take special policies to meet them. But if we can't get that job done—and done soon—we stand to lose an entire generation to the streets.

Now, there are those who have called this plan "alarming." Well, I wish they would take a walk with me through some of our cities. I'd show them something really alarming.

Like the fact that the richest nation on this planet is willing to sacrifice the suffering of millions of Americans to some notion of "price stability" for the wealthy.

Like the fact that black family income has sunk to a mere 58 percent—little more than half—that of the average white family.

Like the fact that in this country of two-car garages and matching sets of lawn furniture, there are children crying from hunger and families broken by poverty.

Like the fact that in this land of hot-lather shaving machines and electric can openers, there are millions of Americans who have never seen the inside of a decent school or a doctor's office.

My friends, if you want to see something *truly* alarming, you don't have to look very far.

So full employment is the broad base on which to build our progress. But there is much more to be done.[24]

Just how far Senator Humphrey has moved is indicated by his own depiction of what corresponds to the Conservative, Liberal, and Progressive positions set forward here. He stated:

Why are all these prices accelerating in a slack economy that is in the throes of a recession? . . .

With respect to the economic summit, it seems to me that the Nation must choose between *three* packages of economic prescriptions.

The first package of policies is what has commonly come to be called the old time religion—drastic cuts in the Federal budget accompanied by very tight monetary policy. I reject this position because there is no evidence to show that our current inflation has arisen from profligate fiscal action by the Federal Government, and extremely tight monetary and fiscal policy at this time could throw the nation and the world into a more severe recession. We need fiscal discipline but not the old time religion.

A second set of policies is what I would call the middle-of-the-road or the consensus package. This set of policies, a great improvement over the old time religion, advocates a slight easing of monetary restraint, a more vigorous jaw-boning on wages and prices by the Federal Government, an expansion of public service jobs to help the unemployed, a tax cut for the poor, as well as other worthwhile proposals.

I support this consensus package and hope that it is the very least that we can get out of the economic summit.

But I am not sure this middle-of-the-road package is enough to break the inflationary psychosis that has the economy in its grip. I think we need to consider more drastic action, including credit allocation, reactivation of housing subsidies, tax credits tied to wage and price restraints, a wage-price freeze and a much tougher price-incomes policy, a new Secretary of Agriculture and a new set of agricultural policies, refusal to buy the OPEC oil above a certain price, establishment of constant purchasing power bonds, and the establishment of improved economic management and planning system in the Federal Government.[25]

Senator Humphrey set forth his economic philosophy, in terms that cannot but provide vivid contrast to the views of conservatives and Liberals as well, as follows:

ECONOMIC JUSTICE

This party has a long tradition of opposition against the increasing concentration of wealth and economic power. At the present time, a small number of the American people control most of our productive wealth. The rest of our population—including all working men and women—struggle to make ends meet in the face of rising prices and taxes.

We should repledge ourselves to combat those factors which tend to concentrate wealth and economic power. To that end, the next Democratic Administration should commit itself to the following policies.

The battleground for economic opportunity has shifted from the courtroom to the marketplace. The first and crucial step in that battle, as I have already indicated, is full employment for all those able, willing, and seeking jobs. A productive job means income and an opportunity for our workers to share in the abundance of our economic growth.

The next step is to move vigorously against the concentration of power within the business sector. Part of this can be accomplished by strengthening the anti-trust laws and enforcing these laws. We must do that. But we need to go beyond this negative remedy to a positive policy for encouraging the development of small business. . . .

The achievement of economic justice will also require a firm commitment to tax reform at all levels. In recent years there has been a shift in the tax burden from the rich to the working people in this country.

The Federal income tax code illustrates this with an "upside down" effect that distorts the distribution of tax benefits in favor of upper income groups. A 1974 study of taxes found that fully 53 percent of the tax benefits went to the 14 percent of taxpayers with incomes of $20,000 or more. As you can see, the Internal Revenue Code offers massive "tax welfare" to the wealthiest income groups in the population, and only higher taxes for the average citizen.

We should pledge ourselves to the long-run review of all special tax provisions to ensure that they are justified, that they work efficiently, and that they are distributed equitably among our citizens. . . .

For the immediate future a responsible Democratic tax reform program could save over $5 billion in the first year. Among the specific-reforms at the top of a Democratic tax reform agenda, I propose:

—To strengthen the minimum tax, so that every citizen pays at least some tax on all

his income, and cannot use loopholes in existing law to escape taxes altogether.
—To clamp down on the use of tax gimmicks in areas like oil and gas, farming, real estate and movies, which now allow wealthy individuals to receive excessive tax deductions in these areas to offset income from other sources.
—To eliminate inefficient tax incentives to business and substitute more effective incentives for capital formation, including improvements in the Investment Tax Credit.
—To end abuses in the tax treatment of income from foreign sources, such as repealing the tax deferral available to multinational corporations, and unjustified incentives that drains jobs and capital from the American economy in favor of foreign operation by U.S. corporations.
—To curb "expense account" living, by denying deductions for frills.

The Democratic Party should also make a reappraisal of the appropriate sources of Federal revenues. The historical distribution of the tax burden between corporations and individuals, and among the various types of Federal taxes, has changed dramatically in recent years. For example, the corporate tax share of Federal revenue has declined form 30 percent in 1954 to 14 percent in 1975.

Taxes are the price we pay for our collective efforts as a society, and I believe their burden must be shared more fairly if we are to make good on our commitment to economic justice.

The final step in achieving economic justice is to broaden the sharing of wealth in this country.

Total personal wealth in 1972 was $4.3 trillion. Nearly one-fourth of the $4.5 trillion of personally held assets were owned by the richest 1.0 percent of the population, while those with a gross estate greater than $60,000, who comprise just 6 percent of the population, own half of those assets. Most wealth is concentrated among a few people.

The U.S. is portrayed as a prosperous middle-class country, but a different picture emerges when it is understood that in 1972, 55 percent of household units had a net worth of less than $10,000 while 12 percent had less than $1,000. For most of our citizens just keeping significantly ahead of debts is not an easy matter.

I believe that the U.S. should develop programs that will spread newly created wealth each year more broadly among its citizens. Consideration must be given to programs that focus on broadening corporate stock ownership in America since it is the asset that holds the greatest potential for providing a broader base of wealth.[26]

Most indicatively of all, Humphrey has taken the firm position that:

The "market" left alone observes only profit criteria without considering desired social priorities. It must be remembered that even a decision to let the market allocate the available investment funds is a priority setting decision since we are well aware of what directions these decisions will follow, and have the power to alter these directions if we so desire.[27]

His proposals of Congressionally determined capital allocation, credit allocation, and constant purchasing power bonds are far more radical than the reader might be aware, implying the substitution of the government for private capital markets for much of the direction of capital deployment—it is difficult to imagine how much more radical someone might become, short of outright nationalization. It should be recalled that when Humphrey made these statements, he was very close to being the hope of what, prior to President Carter's nomination, used to be referred to as the "liberal mainstream of the Democratic party." If anyone supposes that the preceding quotes are at all idiocyncratic or are mere rhetoric, he would do well to examine the documentary record for himself.

Nor has the House been passed over by the winds of change. On the House side, Congressman Reuss, Chairman of the House Banking Committee, has also been a vigorous advocate of governmentally directed capital allocation and credit allocation. He has stated:

> The quickest way to generate the added purchasing power needed to counter the current recession is through tax reductions for low- and middle-income families, either by increasing the low-income allowance and the standard deduction or by reducing the regressive payroll tax. This should be financed as soon as possible by plugging income tax loopholes that primarily benefit the wealthy without any economic justification. Two immediate steps are needed to stimulate the flow of credit to vital economic sectors and thus reduce interest rates.
>
> Between July 1 and October 1, the Federal Resreve constricted the growth of the money supply to less than 2 percent per year at an annual rate, down from more than 7 percent growth needed to finance the long-run needs of the economy.
>
> This stop-and-go money policy of the Fed—sometimes too much, sometimes too little—has been a major cause of excessive inflation combined, now, with excessive unemployment. The Federal Reserve should bring money supply growth into the 4-6 percent range, and keep it there on a steady basis.
>
> But even with an adequate supply of credit . . . speculative and inflationary uses—ranging from conglomerate take-overs to gambling in foreign exchange or gold—. . . [should be turned] toward productive and anti-inflationary uses, such as housing, capital investment, agriculture, state and local governments.
>
> This will lower interest rates for productive uses and reduce inflationary pressures, while raising interest rates for speculative and inflationary purposes—just what is wanted.[28]

Congressman Reuss had been particularly active in an ongoing conflict with Arthur Burns and the Federal Reserve System. Reuss has made his position plain as follows:

> We believe that the legislation before the committee is needed in a congressional program to bring about lower interest rates, and thus combat the recession from which the Nation is suffering.
>
> We have seen mistakes by the Federal Reserve in administering the Nation's money supply in recent years. And the harm that has been done to the American economy during the last portion of 1972, during 1973, and during much of early 1974. The

Federal Reserve, over the repeated objections of many Members of Congress and others, expended money and credit at rates which we felt, and in the event proved so to do, would stimulate inflation.

The predictable result was the double digit inflation which still confronts the Nation. In the last 8 months, on the other hand, the Federal Reserve has abruptly reversed ground holding the money supply as expressed by M_1 to a growth rate of 1.6 percent during the last half of calendar 1974. The result of this abrupt reversal of policy was an increase in long-term interest rates affecting such vital areas as home mortgages, corporate borrowings for useful plant and equipment, and State and local governmental needs, to a historically high level.

Even though short-term interest rates have decreased in recent weeks, these long-term interest rates remain unconscionably high. Members of this committee have recently returned to Washington from a congressional recess where they were besieged with requests from their constituents asking what they intended to do to help revive the American economy.

The people made it clear to each of us that they want immediate action before economic tragedy engulfs us. Chairman Patman's subcommittee has recommended to the full committee that we act favorably on the two bills which are presently before us. Both of the bills were cosponsored by the entire majority membership of the committee. . . .

The first bill would require that the Federal Reserve so conduct monetary policy as to lower long-term interest rates and thus put men and women back to work. It leaves to the Federal Reserve the exact method to accomplish this goal, whether by increase in M_1, M_2, M_3, the bank credit proxy, or any other measure, whether by a change in the composition of the Federal Reserve's $82 billion portfolio, or by other methods.

The bill requires the Federal Reserve to report to the Congress each month on the action it takes to carry out the intent.

The second bill would nudge the available credit in this country away from inflationary areas and into national priority areas. It permits a voluntary program, whereby the major banks are given a framework in which they can demonstrate their responsiveness to the Nation's economic needs.

The legislation will permit responsible American bankers to show that they are concerned with the needs for low- and moderate-income housing, small business productive capital investment, and that these are needs which should command a higher priority, for example, rather than loans to produce more gambling casinos in the Bahamas, half-empty skyscraper office buildings in Manhattan, luxury condominiums in Florida, game preserves in Kenya, and speculation in foreign exchange.[29]

In the aforementioned luncheon held by the author for three leading Democrat economists and three Senate Antitrust Subcommittee lawyers, the sharp disagreement between the two groups over the extent to which administered pricing by powerful firms exercising large-scale market power caused inflation ended with one conclusion particularly worthy of note. It is reflected in the previously quoted exchange between Proxmire and Greenspan, at the point at which Proxmire queries Greenspan as to how it could be possible that, as the number one economic adviser to the President, he did not know the most basic information about the steel industry's costs, sufficient to form a judgment as to the basis of steel's pricing behavior. This theme, what might be called *the theme of information as power*, can be found at almost every juncture of the documentary record of the Congress, where Progressive and Liberal senators and congressmen seek to determine basic understandings of economic relationships. The manifestation of the theme, over and over again, is that, though Congress certainly has the power to demand information from the private sector to resolve basic questions of public policy, particularly macro-economic policy, the ideological balance of power in favor of the conservatives in Congress prevents that information from being obtained.

What was particularly striking at this luncheon was the agreement by all parties that (1) government did not now possess the information which would empirically settle the differences vis-à-vis the effects of concentration on inflation, and other key questions, that separated the Liberal economists from the congressional antitrust lawyers; and (2) they agreed that it would *not* be a difficult matter to contrive and enforce a uniform system of accounting on all firms, including the multinationals, that would resolve the outstanding issues between them by producing the necessary data.

This information issue has been manifest in many different disputes before the Congress, being the precondition of governmental control, including, prominently, the "line of business" reporting issue.[30] Senator Proxmire has been acutely aware of the overarching nature of the information-as-power theme, as the following shows:

Senator Proxmire. Let me get briefly into the line of business information.

You mention the line of business report program in your statement, something that you say that you have been very interested in. Obviously, it is impossible for us to understand the operations of an industry like, for example, General Electric, with its enormous variety of products, dominating in a particular area. We don't know what their profits are, what their costs are, what their operations are. But we know what their competitors' profits are. We don't have a picture of the industry because we don't have the particular factors involved. Now, you believe it is vital to carrying out the antitrust responsibilities of the FTC to have this kind of information. Specifically you stated it is vital to the selection process of the Commission.

Now, as you know, the House has passed restrictive language in the Agricultural Appropriations bill—I fought hard against it—which would prevent use of individual company data by the Federal Trade Commission for antitrust enforcement purposes. Do you not believe this language, if enacted, will severely handicap the Commission's case selection process? . . .

The House-passed language also prohibits the Federal Trade Commission in providing line of business information to any other agency of Government, which I thought was outrageous, because after all if the antitrust department should proceed with a case, they should do so on the basis of the facts. Do you think that the statutory prohibition would hamper other agencies of the Government which are involved in the fight against inflation, agencies such as the Council on Wage and Price Stability, in carrying out that fight effectively?[31]

Senator Proxmire draws the larger point as follows:

> *Business Week* has an article in a recent issue in which they analyze the very serious problem the whole economic profession faces and their demoralization because they don't seem to have any answers.
>
> One target of criticism is the validity of the present statistics we have, that is their relevance—not that they are not gathered in a very competent way—but their relevance with the effect of superinflation on them and especially the changing of the significance of these statistics as prices increase rapidly. For example, leading indicators tied to price performance may be giving us false signals.
>
> Now, can you give us, or do you know of any way we can get suggestions as to what we can do to make our statistic-gathering relevant to our present policy dilemma?
>
> Are you or is anyone you know trying to put together the most useful data that can inform the Congress and the President and policymakers in the private sector on changes in the economy?
>
> Can you tell us what is likely to happen to inflation and employment production and overall economic growth, so that we can have a better basis than the bad basis we in the past have had for making economic policy?[32]

Past resistance that business has offered to such Congressional inquiries, leads one to understand how implicative are such efforts to increase the informational power of the federal government vis-à-vis business.

The general theme, manifest in a number of the quotations given in this chapter, that much of the economy was structured by powerful economic forces that did not behave in accordance with market models of economics, was far more prevalent in the Congress than the author had begun to suspect prior to the interviewing and the systematic documentary analysis. The high point of this author's experience of the intensity and range of these Galbraithian convictions[33] about the nonmarket character of the behavior of the dominant economic forces, was driven home in interviewing a leading senator who many had predicted would become President, who described himself as a "moderate liberal," who was generally considered to the right of senators such as Kennedy, Humphrey, Mondale, and others. In his "hideaway" office under the Capitol dome, a perquisite accorded only most senior and powerful senators, in responding to the general question (number 2 in the interview schedule) about the market, he literally snapped out the reply, "There is no market." He was so emphatic, many of the usual follow-up questions that might have probed for some qualification of his response would have been out of place. He deeply believed that the laws of supply and demand do not operate to determine rationally what is invested in, what is produced, and what is consumed, but that an inherently asocial process, skewed by the implications of enormous concentration of wealth and of the control over capital deployment, determined economic events. This belief presages something that, under conditions of protracted economic crises and social dislocation, might imply something far different from what we learn from the print or electronic media, about the nature of opposition in the Congress.

The two themes that, overall, tie together the Progressive perspective are (1) the belief that the *agenda of social programs and needs* to be addressed by the action of government cannot be held in abeyance much longer without an irreparable rending of the American social fabric, and (2) that *economic growth* in the Liberal version of *untargeted aggregate growth* was incompatible with the pressing needs of the American people in a new age of scarcity.

Senator Adlai E. Stevenson has expressed what many of the Progressive Members interviewed for this study stated, and which can only be described as highly indicative of the character, programmatically, of the Progressive opposition, as follows:

> We need to ask how to want to use our resources and what we want to achieve. We need to focus debate on the quality of the nation's economic product.
>
> It is not enough to say our goal is full employment. If it were, we could put half the work force to work digging ditches and the other half to work filling them up again.
>
> It is not enough to say our goal is an end to inflation. The only time in this century that we had a zero rate of inflation was in the 'thirties in the depths of the Great Depression.
>
> And it is not enough to say that our goal is to maximize economic activity. Economic activity is not an end in itself; it is a means of achieving what we want to achieve, whether it consists of more goods or more services or more leisure.
>
> Conventional economic thinking fails to draw such distinctions. Economic goals are pursued in terms of statistical aggregates. The qualitative aspects are ignored. More growth is assumed to be better, regardless of the form it takes. In the national income accounts, a dollar spent for food, for housing or for clothing is the same as a dollar spent for electric toothbrushes, highways, or bombs. Yet, the way we employ our resources makes a difference to the real wealth and productivity of the country and the quality of life.[34]

Senator Stevenson's remarks were from an ordinary newsletter sent to his constituents. In his interview for this study, his views just quoted were amplified with intensity and specificity, as was the case in almost all of the interviewing. The distance between the views of the leading senators and congressmen who are generally identified as Liberal Democrat leaders, on the one hand, and Liberal economists, who prior to the crisis that began in 1973 or earlier, were the principal advisers to these same leaders, on the other hand, was surprisingly great. What came across vividly from the textures of the lengthy interviews in the Congress was a sense of crisis, of an unraveling within society, that was in no way evident among the economists and economic literature to which this investigator was exposed. When asked about what they foresaw if conservative policies dominated government for the next four or more years, the author was shocked to hear rather understated leaders volunteer the opinion that *we well might not have the same form of government ten years from now.* The Liberal economists seemed to think that though the "external shocks" of two devaluations, a quantum leap that quadrupled oil prices, and rapid food price increases made possible in part because of international market conditions had sent the economy into an unusually deep inflation and recession exacerbated by the Nixon-Ford policies, nonetheless, the recovery would occur much like other recoveries, and that the future would be more like than unlike the past.

Senator Church, on the other hand, stated what was not an unusual thought in the Congress, when he said in a book review in the *Washington Post*: "For I am convinced that not since the early 1930's has America been so ripe for a fundamental reconsideration of the relationship of corporate power and political responsibility."[35] The Progressive opposition is acutely aware that *capital* is needed in great abundance to develop new and alternative sources of energy, to check (let alone roll back) the many forms of pollution of the environment, to meet the already existing agenda of social needs, to confront the rising costs of raw materials and increased foreign competition for markets, and to modernize plant and equipment.[36] As the quote from Congressman Reuss indicates, many Progressive Members believe that a great deal of capital now flows into speculation, especially in foreign currencies since "the float," into bidding up the price of already highly valued properties, including securities, and into projects that enjoy little or no social value in a context of pressing social needs. They look to *reformed* government, more representative because of changes in campaign financing, voter registration, and other aspects of political reform, *to direct capital according to legislatively determined national priorities.* The magnitude of this change in terms of defining a programmatic opposition cannot be overestimated. The intensity of business reaction to what is perceived to be the encroachment, actual and threatened, of government into private-sector activities is not merely based on increased costs due to government activity in the worker, consumer, and environmental safety areas.[37] *Government-directed growth* through capital and credit allocation in line with a *legislatively determined agenda of social needs* represents programmatic opposition indeed. Moreover, spectacles such as major oil companies using large profits, not in further energy-related development, but to diversify, as Mobil did in buying the Montgomery Ward chain, and Atlantic Richfield did in buying Anaconda Copper, has added fuel to the fire of the Progressive opposition, as has the continuing flow of corporate mergers and ever-greater corporate concentration. But above all, the stubborn persistence of high levels of unemployment and inflation simultaneously, with fears that both will increase as petrodollars and American capital investment flow out of the American economy, creates pressures for a fundamentally new approach to economic reasoning, and to the politics of economic policy.

NOTES

1. Cf. Philip E. Converse, "Some Mass-Elite Contrasts in the Perception of Political Spaces," *Social Science Information* 14, nos. 3-4 (Summer 1975):49-83.

2. The concept of the "regime" used here, in conformity to its use generally by political scientists, is meant to be distinguished from a particular government, in the sense that there can be a change in governments, one group of people surrendering control of the institutions of the state, *without there also occurring any substantive change in operative policies.* A change in regime, that is, replacement by the opposition, does imply a large-scale change in policy.

Transaction Books has announced that Seymour Martin Lipset will soon publish *Socialism: Its Conspicuous Absence in American Politics,* stating that Lipset's "argument is premised on the degree to which American values already incorporate the highest aspirations of socialism" (Transaction Books Catalog Number 8, 1977-8, p. 2).

At least on first impression, some readers may find somewhat jarring a contention that implicitly entails that the value systems of opposing congressional coalitions are far more similar than dissimilar. Comparing legislators such as Senators Abourezk, Bayh, Church, Clark, Cranston, Culver, Durkin, Gary Hart, Haskell, Hathaway, Humphrey, Kennedy, McGovern, Metcalf, Muskie, Nelson, Proxmire, Ribicoff, Sarbanes, and Stevenson, and Vice-President Mondale, on the one hand, with Senators Allen, Baker, Bentsen, Harry Byrd, Jr., Robert Byrd, Curtis, Dole, Eastland, Garn, Goldwater, Hansen, Helms, Laxalt, Long, Lugar, McClellan, Morgan, Nunn, Packwood, Roth, Schmitt, William Scott, Stennis, Stevens, Talmadge, Thurmond, Tower, Wallop, and Zorinsky, on the other hand, it seems more than a little strange to think of an important core of shared policy values common to these two groups of senators. But there are analysts and commentators, on both the left and the right, who would assert that a common commitment to the "regime," that is, to the basic outlines of the American system of political economy, or of the existing public sector-private sector structures, rhetoric aside, binds apparently opposing forces in Congress. This claim must be more adequately specified and analyzed, in order to evaluate the significance of the finding of unidimensionality stated at the close of the previous chapter.

3. Cf. the extremely valuable article by Robert J. Samuelson, "Recession Forces New Look at Old Goals," *National Journal* 8, no. 34 (August 21, 1976):1173-82. In their abstract of this article in the beginning of this issue, the editors of this staid journal (which can be found in all congressional offices) in describing Samuelson's article, note:

> As the nation emerges from its bitterest economic recession in a generation, economists of all shades are taking a highly skeptical look at the standard economic orthodoxy of the 1960s. Keynesian theory appears to have left the economic community with egg on its face for failing to predict the recession or to come up with quick and easy proposals to end it. As a consequence, new ideas, both more conservative and more radical, are being given credence, and some major goals of public policy are undergoing significant reevaluation. Washington freelance writer Robert J. Samuelson, who specializes in economic affairs, looks at these new ideas and attempts to assess just where and why the vast majority of economists went wrong.

See also "Is Keynes Dead?" *Newsweek*, June 20, 1977, pp. 74-76, and "Review & Outlook: Keynes Is Dead," *Wall Street Journal*, 31 January 1977, p. 12.

4. John Kingdon, in an ongoing study of several different policy communities, will likely contribute a good deal to the understanding of how conceptions of the desirable and the feasible come about, and condition each other.

5. "An Age of Scarcity," *New York Times*, 4 April 1974, p. 16.

6. Elizabeth Drew, "A Reporter at Large: The Energy Bazaar," *New Yorker*, July 21, 1975, p. 35.

7. Cf. Davidson and Oleszek, *Congress Against Itself*.

8. Roger H. Davidson, "Breaking Up Those 'Cozy Triangles': An Impossible Dream?" (paper prepared for the symposium on Legislative Reform and Public Policy, University of Nebraska, Lincoln, Nebraska, March 11-12, 1976), pp. 30-31. Cf. the discussion of the Lowi distinctions in Chapter 2.

9. William Nordhaus and James Tobin, "Is Growth Obsolete?" and the discussion following in *Economic Growth* (New York: National Bureau of Economic Research and Columbia University Press, 1972), pp. 1-92.

10. For a recent and exemplary condensed statement of the Liberal economists' view of the market and the role of government, cf. Arthur M. Okun, *Equality and Efficiency: The Big Tradeoff* (Washington, D.C.: Brookings Institution, 1975). The classical conservative statement is Milton Friedman, *Capitalism and Freedom* (Chicago: University of Chicago Press, 1962). The Progressive view is most notably encapsulated in John Kenneth Galbraith, *Economics and the Public Purpose* (Boston: Houghton Mifflin, 1973).

11. Before or after each interview, either the author or his research assistant asked appropriate staff for press releases, constituency-targeted newsletters, speeches, testimony, and *Congressional Record* insertions on economic policy. Every effort was made to obtain this material before each interview. Moreover, before an interview, the *Congressional Quarterly Weekly Report's* index for the preceding months and years was searched to determine what issues the respondent had been "out front on," in order to expedite the interview. As a general matter, a far better grade interview will be obtained if a respondent feels one took the trouble to discover, and showed insight into, what he or she is concerned with. In general, these materials proved extremely valuable. In cases of several influential senators and House subcommittee and committee chairmen, several cartons of materials were sent to the author, in most cases, after a long discussion of the economic policy dispositions of the member with a key staff aide. A list of over thirty categories relevant to economic policy was drawn up. Each document was then systematically cross-indexed.

12. Schultze's testimony before the Senate Subcommittee on Unemployment was reprinted in part in the *Washington Post*, 7 June 1976, p. A23.

13. Arthur M. Okun, "Potential GNP: Its Measurement and Significance," in American Statistical Association, Proceedings of the Business and Economics Statistics Section (1962), pp. 98-104, reprinted in Okun, *The Political Economy of Prosperity* (Washington, D.C.: Brookings Institution, 1970), Appendix. Cf. also, Soma Golden, "Okun's Law on Jobless Seems to Prevail," *New York Times*, 2 July 1975, p. 43.

14. Arthur M. Okun, "Unemployment and Flat Tires," in *Capital Report* (Washington, D.C.: American Security Bank, January/February 1977), pp. 1-2.

15. Cited by Charles L. Schultze on the MacNeil/Lehrer Report, WETA-TV, Washington, D.C., March 8, 1977.

16. Cf. note 3, *supra*.

17. Cf. F. M. Scherer et al., *The Economics of Multi-Plant Operation* (Cambridge, Mass.: Harvard University Press, 1975). What is most striking is the recanting of the belief that the market model fits well the reality of the American economy by Charles Lindblom in his *Politics and Markets* (New York: Basic Books, 1977).

18. U.S., Congress, Joint Economic Committee, "Inflation Outlook," 93rd Cong., 3nd sess., 1974, pp. 13-15.

19. Press Release from the office of Senator William Proxmire, January 11, 1975.

20. U.S., Congress, Joint Economic Committee, *Inflationary Impact of Pricing by Concentrated Industries, Hearings,* 93rd Cong., 2nd sess., September 4 and 9, and October 7, 1974, pp. 61-62.

21. Ibid., p. 40.

22. Ibid., p. 41.

23. Ibid., p. 42.

24. *Congressional Record,* June 11, 1976, p. S9093.

25. U.S., Congress, Joint Economic Committee, "Inflation Outlook," pp. 3, 4.

26. *Congressional Record,* June 17, 1976, p. S9780.

27. U.S., Congress, Joint Economic Committee, *Long-Range Economic Growth, Hearings,* 94th Cong., 1st sess., October 23-24, 1975, p. 190.

28. U.S., Congress, Joint Economic Committee, *Inflationary Impact of Pricing by Concentrated Industries,* p. 40.

29. U.S., Congress, House, *To Lower Interest Rates: The Credit Allocation Act of 1975, Hearing.* Committee on Banking, Currency, and Housing, 94th Cong., 1st sess., February 19, 1975.

30. Cf. "Line-of-Business Reporting," *Issues on File,* Congressional Research Service, Library of Congress, update of March 21, 1977, 1B76040.

31. U.S., Congress, Joint Economic Committee, *Market Power, the Federal Trade Comission, and Inflation, Hearing.* Joint Economic Committee, 93rd Cong., 2nd sess., November 18, 1974, p. 71.

32. U.S., Congress, Joint Economic Committee, *Employment-Unemployment, Hearings.* Subcommittee on Priorities and Economy in Government, 93rd Cong., 2nd sess., July 5, August 2, September 6, and October 4, 1974, pt. 2, pp. 326-27.

33. For a valuable and interesting account of Galbraith's development, professional experiences, and training that shows the large continuity in his work, cf. Leonard Silk, *The Economists* (New York: Basic Books, Inc., 1976), pp. 97-150.

34. From "Senator Adlai E. Stevenson of Illinois, *Washington Report,* January 1976," a constituent newsletter.

35. (Senator) Frank Church, "Profits of Doom," *Washington Post,* 9 January 1975, p. F1.

36. Barry Bosworth, James S. Duesenberry, and Andrew S. Carron, *Capital Needs in the Seventies* (Washington, D.C.: Brookings Institution, 1975).

37. For one indication that the banking industry is feeling itself under something more than ordinary scrutiny, cf. excerpts of a speech by David Rockefeller in *MORE,* June 1977, p. 52. The accession of Senator Proxmire and Congressman Reuss to the chairmanship of their chambers' respective banking committees in the Ninety-fourth Congress did not, to say the least, delight the banking industry.

chapter 7

SUMMARY AND CONCLUSIONS: THE IDEOLOGICAL BALANCE OF FORCES

SUMMARY

In an era of growing and interrelated complexities in every policy area, and in the fabric of national and international politics, Congress, as never before, is being seen as the pivotal institution of American politics, rooted in the changing party system. But understanding Congress is very difficult, which inclines some to concentrate their attention on the relatively accessible manifestations of presidential power, despite constitutionally determined executive-legislative interdependence. No question is more central to understanding Congress and the presidency, than the question of the structure of power within Congress. The principal form that problem takes involves determining the nature of congressional coalitions.

Few controversies have been as persistent among both political scientists and political observers alike as the one over whether or not ideological coalitions, rooted in relationships of class to politics and economics, structure congressional and other elite politics. This book was written to reexamine empirically whether or not ideology structures congressional politics. This controversy has been an unusually heated one, for the ideological view necessitates accepting politics as involving deep and durable conflicts in society as well as in the polity. Quite understandably, many would prefer not to see such conflict as structuring their environment. Symptomatically, Clausen in his 1973 empirical study of Congress in the 1950s and 1960s, has disparaged the idea of ideological parties as being tied to "the bloody drama of ideological warfare."[1] Since it is inevitable that this study will be compared with Clausen's, it is worth noting that this study began with no such assumption that ideological conflict is inherently or inevitably violent.

Rather, this study, in the "responsible party model" tradition within the American Political Science Association, has assumed that ideological politics might, instead, take the form of democratically intense electoral conflict.

Clausen's study, with its principal findings that congressional coalitions *change* from one policy dimension to another (thus precluding valid use of ideological labels such as "liberal," "conservative," or "progressive"), might be seen as not inconsistent with the findings of this study. Clausen's study of the 1950s and 1960s covered a period of marked economic stability, low inflation, low unemployment, and a relatively stable and, for the United States, favorable international economic environment. This study, focusing as it does on the 1970s, reflects a period of relatively high inflation, high unemployment, international economic instability for the United States, and the effects of the Vietnam War. Perhaps in these differences might be found the source of discrepancy in findings. But even if that were so, it would not account for the persistence elsewhere of the disagreement over the role of ideology in the 1970s. In fact, as discussed previously, the differences in methodologies of this study and Clausen's are great enough that, for direct comparison, one would either have to apply the methods of this study to the period studied by Clausen, or vice versa, to decide whether changes over time in the real world, or the different methods, or both, accounted for the discrepancies in findings. This would be a worthwhile study for someone who knew both time periods well, and especially the policy reasoning of opposing congressional participants during both periods.

The principal features of this study can be summarized as follows. Chapter 2 specifies the concept of ideology used in this study, built squarely on the work of Converse, with several modifications suited to the needs of analyzing congressional coalitions. The chapter then separates out a number of different theories of pluralism, isolating the one that contradicts the ideological theory. The chapter closes with a specification of contrasting pluralist and ideological viewpoints on and studies of the nature of congressional coalitions.

Chapter 3 is based on 108 interviews on foreign policy with Members of the House of Representatives carried out during 1970. These interviews were highly structured and systematically coded. The particular emphasis on foreign policy in Chapter 3 reflects the fact that all past findings have shown foreign policy to be ideologically by far the most highly inconsistent issue area vis-à-vis other issue areas and, moreover, itself a multidimensional issue domain. The latter multidimensionality is contradicted by the findings of this chapter, which also lay the basis for findings of greater depth than would have been possible from roll call vote patterns alone regarding ideological consistency across foreign and domestic policy presented in Chapter 5. The liberal and conservative foreign policy perspectives are substantively delineated, and updated to 1977 in terms of continuities and change.

Chapter 4, by laying the groundwork for the central empirical chapter (Chapter 5), confronts a dilemma which has haunted empirical analyses of congressional coalitions, and proposes a theoretical basis for resolving that dilemma. The dilemma is stated as follows. Because of the need for a systematic basis of comparison, an analysis of congressional coalitions must rely on roll call analyses. But, for a variety of reasons, roll call votes are often false, misleading, or opaque as indicators of coalition structure. On the other hand, congressional documents and contextually rich analyses can be far more revealing of operative intentions and the real nature and bases of coalitions. But such documents and contextually rich accounts cannot be the basis from which to infer reliably any generalizations about behavior within each chamber of Congress, and across both, not even spatio-temporally bracketed generalizations, regarding coalition structures. A new contextualist approach to roll call data is proposed as a way between the horns of the dilemma. This new approach involves contextually validating each individual roll call vote using a number of new procedures and criteria which are theoretically as well as contextually derived.

Chapter 5 analyzes all roll call votes, Senate and House, of the Ninety-second Congress, first and second session (1971-72), and the Ninety-fourth Congress, first session (1975). Ideological consistency is tested among four dimensions: economic policy (including what Lowi has termed "distributive" legislation), race, civil liberties and democracy, and foreign policy. Foreign policy roll call data and the coded interview data from Chapter 3 were both used. A number of new coding techniques, including construction of a "class allocation index," were used. The coding of roll calls was subjected to an intercoder reliability test. Individual index scores were constructed for all senators and for House Members selected for one of two stratified random samples in each of the four policy dimensions. Rank order correlations (tau-b) were computed for all combinations of the four policy dimensions, and for a domestic liberalism index derived from the three domestic policy dimensions.

The results show very high ideological consistency among all policy dimensions. This finding is sharply different from previous findings. In substantive terms, the findings establish unidimensionality; that is, being strongly, moderately, or not at all liberal in one policy dimension corresponds very highly with being liberal or conservative to the same degree in all of the other dimensions, allowing ideological terms such as "progressive," "liberal," and "conservative" to be used validly to denote distinct ranges of senators and congressmen on a single liberal-conservative, or left-right, spectrum or dimension. Moreover, the results, it is argued, are underscored by a strong increase of predictability of congressional voting in the aggregate over previous studies, following an analysis by Weisberg. The results are compared with previous findings, notably those by Clausen, Matthews and Stimson, and earlier studies by Converse, MacRae, and others. The findings confirm the ideological theory and disconfirm the pluralist theory of congressional coalitions.

The single most unusual finding, sharply different form any known study from the 1950s on, is that foreign policy beliefs and the behavior of congressmen, although manifesting clear differences in basic philosophy and perceptions of the world, are no longer, if they were in the past, the basis of a crosscutting cleavage in the Congress. Rather, the foreign policy attitudes and behavior of congressmen and senators manifest a common coalition structure ("dimensional structuring") with domestic policy domains. One implication that follows is that the direction of U.S. foreign policy may be altered considerably according to whether liberals or conservatives dominate Congress and the presidency.

Chapter 6 delves into a difficulty presented by the results of Chapter 5. Given the truncated agenda of floor voting, which agenda reflects the dominance of the conservative coalition, it is ordinarily most difficult to tell what the minority liberals would do in economic policy terms if they became a majority. Confusion over this question has led many on both the left and the right to assert that, although there may be some systematic differences within Congress, these differences do not indicate fundamentally different philosophies or profoundly different policy proclivities. In Chapter 3 the substantive nature of foreign policy perspectives arising from the interview data showed qualitatively that distinctly different foreign policies would be realized if the minority liberals were to replace the conservatives as a majority. But with regard to economic policy and philosophy, differences in the Congress are not so easily made apparent. Conservative free market views are relatively well known, as are the general disposition of the liberals, who have also expressed a fundamental attachment to free market theories, but who would intervene in the economy in order to maintain high employment and to produce the revenues for their agenda of social programs. But these differences do not touch upon the more fundamental differences of perspective on macroeconomic policy. In particular, the effects of the economic crises of the 1970s on congressional liberals' views of the relationship between government and the private sector, and their changing views of market forces per se, need delineation, as do their derived views of inflation, unemployment, economic growth, capital allocation, and the relationship between the social policy agenda and macroeconomic policy alternatives. The question structuring this chapter is: Is there any fundamental opposition to the "regime" in the political scientists' sense of that term?

To answer this question the following data base, gathered during 1976, was utilized:

1. In-depth open-ended interviews were conducted with eleven liberal U.S. senators, eighteen key liberal Democratic congressmen, congressional staff experts, and leading Democratic economists, each lasting from one to three hours, often with much reinterviewing.

2. A luncheon was held by the author on the effects of economic concentration on inflation, involving three leading Democratic economists and three key staff members of the Senate Antitrust and Monopoly Subcommittee, all lawyers, and one other political scientist.
3. A systematic analysis of congressional document sources—over 200 different hearings, reports, and so on—plus debates in the *Congressional Record* on key economic conflicts in 1976 were carefully selected and analyzed in over thirty categories.

The results, meant to be suggestive rather than social scientifically conclusive in the manners of Chapters 3 and 5, indicate a surprisingly wide and deep ideological opposition among liberals, especially from what here are termed "Progressives" (with Galbraithian views) as opposed to "Liberals" (with views close to leading economists such as Arthur Okun and Charles L. Schultze). How much mainstream figures like Senators Bayh, Church, Cranston, Humphrey, Kennedy, Muskie, Proxmire, Sarbanes, and Stevenson, and Congressmen Bolling, Obey, Mikva, Reuss, and Udall have moved to the "progressive" category is indicated.

CONCLUSIONS: THE IDEOLOGICAL BALANCE OF FORCES AND ITS IMPLICATIONS

One major implication to be drawn from the findings of this study is that, in order to understand congressional behavior, one should understand the nature and balance of ideological forces and what those forces represent (1) in policy terms, and (2) in perspectives on society, economy, polity, and the international system. By doing so, as has been proved for the period of the early and mid-1970s, this study has made congressional voting behavior in the aggregate significantly more predictable than has been the case using different approaches. It also follows, *second*, that on the whole if one wishes to understand relations between a President and the Congress, understanding the nature and balance of ideological forces in Congress will likewise be a most useful tool for analysis.

A *third* implication involves the understanding of other factors in the legislative process. There have been many useful studies of Congress that have ignored ideology and concentrated on narrower variables to "explain" some aspect of congressional behavior. What is meant by "explanation" determines our understanding of those studies in relation to the findings here. If "explanation" corresponds to the set of seven criteria listed on page 148 then we must put a question to these studies: Are the relationships demonstrated in them either (1) the effects of variables that are actually surrogate variables for ideological dispositions, or (2) do they take the shape they do because of previously determined configurations of ideological forces which structure and constrain behavior within the period studied?

An example or two should suffice to make the point. If one wishes to study, for example, the effects of the interaction of members of state delegations, or state party delegations, on voting behavior within Congress, is one actually tapping ideological dispositions? The case of the Virginia state delegation before and after the election of two very liberal northern Virginia (metropolitan Washington, D.C.) Democratic congressmen, Representatives Joel Fisher and Herbert Harris, to the Ninety-fourth Congress, is a good case in point. The once intimate archconservative Virginia state delegation now had two members at the opposite end of the ideological spectrum. The discordant consequences on voting behavior within the Virginia delegation are apparent. Similar examples vis-à-vis other state party delegations' effects on voting have been analyzed with congruent findings.[2]

In the same vein, membership on the same committee can be similarly understood as a surrogate variable. Congressman (now Senator) Reigle was cited earlier in his description of how ideology determined to what committees a Member was assigned. If this is true, then to find voting behavior to correlate neatly with committee membership and infer the causal efficiency of committee norms is incorrect if one fails to note the determining fact of the ideological character of committee assignments.

As an example of structural relationships within the Congress that are determined by the ideological situation, or balance of forces, one need only think back on the changes in the seniority and committee systems that have occurred. I believe it is generally accepted that the influx of liberals in the House in the early and mid-1970s was the *sine qua non* of the reforms that took place. That they did not go further may be linked to the fact that the House did not become more liberal yet, and particularly did not become very "progressive." But that point is arguable.

A *fourth* major implication regards the research agenda on Congress and American politics and government. The findings of this study place at the center of the research agenda this question: What explains the existing balance of ideological forces in the Congress, and under what conditions would that balance change toward other configurations, and with what policy and societal consequences? As a corollary, the study of interest group influence in Congress and the electoral process, and indeed of pluralism, should be subordinated to a more general concern with, or awareness of, the *groups of interest groups* that directly or indirectly underpin the coalitions revealed in the findings of this study. It was not an idle aside that Larry O'Brien made when he described his experience as White House congressional liaison chief as being structured by battles involving:

> . . . two great armies. . . . One army . . . was led by the President and included . . . organized labor, the urban political leaders, the emerging black spokesmen, and many of the nation's intellectual luminaries. . . . [The other army] facing us was backed by the vast resources of the American business community, the major corporations and especially the oil industry, as well as the medical profession, and im-

portant elements or rural and suburban America. These two armies fought battle after battle on Capitol Hill.[3]

A *fifth* implication of the findings of this study flows directly from Converse's work, and though he has made it clear, it has not been widely appreciated.[4] It is that use of ideological labels, and the social dissemination of "what ideas go with what," and especially how a general issue may be found manifest in a particular issue, and vice versa, is a terribly important means of elite-mass communication. Much of practical political conflict occurs over efforts to clarify or obfuscate such elite messages to potential supporters. That American politics is now in the throes of the kind of political instability that attends the weakening of the party system is a state of affairs that places a premium on the effective dissemination of the ideological issues and choices confronting the electorate. There has been a virtual outpouring of commentaries, journalistic speculations, and papers at scholarly conventions, all about the consequences of the seeming demise of the present American party system. That demise itself is seriously questioned. Some analysts suggest that party realignment along ideological lines may occur, for better or for worse. Some who find that prospect good are tied to the responsible (or ideological) party model of the traditional American Political Science Association literature. The work of James MacGregor Burns is exemplary of this tendency.[5] But as Frank Sorauf has noted:

> Critics of such proposals for party government have concentrated on one insistent theme: The nonideological, heterogeneous, and pragmatic nature of American parties makes agreement on and enforcement of a coherent policy program very difficult, if not impossible. Yet the party organizations are becoming increasingly oriented toward programs and ideology—and thus toward the uses of governmental authority for specific policy goals.[6]

The findings presented in this study would seem to deny critics of party government their claim of the nonideological character of parties, since the ideological character of congressional parties, or factions within them, was implicitly confirmed by the findings of this study. Descriptions of the Democratic party especially are now generally couched in terms of distinct ideological factions, as described by Speaker O'Neill in the opening chapter. The findings of this study would seem to portend that American parties will become more, rather than less, ideological, given a context of "the new politics of resource constraints."

But most observers feel quite unsure of what forms party activity will take, especially given recent changes in the role of money in campaigns, and evidence of increased political demobilization of portions of the electorate. If so, it is even more essential to consider the manner of elite-mass communication. Converse notes:

> In most countries most of the time . . . it remains true that much of political competition can be organized comfortably and with at least crude precision in left-right terms. *More important still, perhaps, is the social fact that most political observers are highly dependent on this abstraction for efficient communication. . . .* [Italics added.][7]

Had the findings of this study been negative, that is, showed little or no ideological consistency, one might well have wondered what could validly be the basis of elite-mass communication, and whether ideology could possibly have anything to do with the evolution of either congressional or national parties. The findings of this study implicitly answer these questions in part.[8] It is tempting to ask: What if the general and specific nature of the ideological coalitions in Congress established in this study were communicated successfully to the electorate? Would voting behavior change significantly if such understandings were tied to issue debates, to specific candidates for Congress and the presidency, and to competing and ideologically distinct parties or factions within parties? And would the structure of the party system then change along ideological lines?

Sixth, if the legislative struggle can be described in terms of the balance of ideological forces, then Congress itself will be seen as a primary arena, if not *the* primary arena, of the nonviolent conflict over values. If so, then, perhaps the most important implication of the findings of this study is that a truly representative Congress embedded in a successful party system, might constitute a substantial third alternative to either "the market" or to government bureaucracy as the dominant center of both the authoritative allocation of values along classical democratic lines, and as the center of democratic legitimacy. Such a state of affairs would entail spreading widely and accurately a knowledge of specific and general issues and the reasoning and facts behind alternative positions, knowledge of candidates and their relation to issues, and, last, knowledge of how both issues and candidates are tied together in ideological factions and to the party system.

Seventh, and last of all, by understanding what central beliefs link the four policy dimensions of this study, we shall better understand political dispositions under changing circumstances and evolving issue saliencies. And by identifying what is common to all four policy dimensions, we shall enjoy a theoretical appreciation of why they are linked so consistently as the findings of this study establish. So the last task here must be to ask what is common to economic policy, including the narrower sort of special interest legislation which Lowi named "distributive," and foreign policy, race policy, and civil liberties and democracy issues.

It is best to begin with foreign policy. On the occasion of his return from a trip to Latin American conducted in 1969 for President Nixon, then Governor Nelson Rockefeller appeared before the Senate Foreign Relations

Committee to present his report. There occurred an exchange between Senator Church and Rockefeller which partially reveals the underlying rationales, or better, widely different perspectives that constitute, then as now, the fundamental ideological sources of conflict over American foreign policy in its more controversial aspects. That exchange is reproduced in part in note 9 of this chapter.[9] What is more striking in the transcript is the section marked "(Laughter)." That laughter indicated a failure to understand the underlying logic of Rockefeller's position, which does not emerge from the transcript as clearly as Church's view. The Rockefeller position can be stated as follows:

1. Ending the deprivations in the less developed countries (LDCs) entails economic development.
2. Economic development entails capital investment, only available from private capital markets in the advanced Western countries.
3. To attract such investment entails a favorable investment climate in the host country.
4. For there to be such a climate entails stability and a "friendly" regime.
5. Therefore, U.S. policy must be to aid regimes meeting those two criteria, irrespective of their nondemocratic character, which will in any case only evolve out of the economic development which brings with it a growing literate middle class capable of behaving as an informed electorate, insofar as any electorate can be truly informed.[10]

And even with regard to developed nations the same logic holds, since we are highly dependent on them as markets for the export of our products. Nonmarket economies, in this view, would be bound, over a shorter or longer period of time, to prove "unfriendly" at least to the United States in world markets, perhaps for political reasons.

Senator Church's position, and that of other liberal congressmen, is that private capital is not the only source of capital available to the LDCs. Without large increases in foreign aid, but rather by reallocating the funds now used to support and arm right-wing governments, the United States could contribute capital in significant amounts, predicated on responsible policies within recipient countries, that would have even greater long-term benefits.[11] In addition, more favorable terms of trade, technology transfer, access to U.S. markets, and other forms of international cooperation could diminish the problems of the LDCs. As to developed nations, whatever the nature of the mix of public sector and private sector a foreign country may have, economic nationalism will transcend the oversimplications derived from seeing everything as related to a capitalism-versus-communism-socialism struggle, in the views of senators such as Frank Church.

How is the logic of this dispute related to domestic ideological conflict? The answer is no farther from reach than one's daily newspaper. In their nationally syndicated column, Evans and Novak described, assumedly with authority, the perceptions of the Carter administration that its "biggest unspoken worry" [was] a "capital strike."

> That is the alarming description of sluggish capital investment that holds back economic recovery. Since this "strike" is bred essentially by fear of the new administration, much of it unthinking, Lance is attempting to reassure the financial community. . . .
>
> Wall street is on "strike" because it believes profitability is restricted by the tax structure, government regulation, and the new administration's attitude toward business. . . .
>
> Lance's rhetoric was impeccably orthodox as William Simon's, if not Andrew Mellon's: The Carter administration sees the route to recovery led by investors, not consumers.[12]

The same point is reinforced by the comments of a less sensationalist economic columnist for the *New York Times*, Leonard Silk. In a pre-1976 election column entitled "The Danger of Ideology," Silk stated:

> With so many genuine and difficult problems confronting the nation, it would be most unfortunate if the 1976 Presidential election should degenerate into an ideological slugfest.
>
> Governor Carter contributed to that danger in his acceptance of the Democratic nomination by indicating "a political and economic elite who have shaped decisions and never had to account for mistakes nor to suffer injustice." Similarly, on the Republican side, President Ford and Ronald Reagan . . . promptly sought to pin the leftist, big government, anti-business label on the Democratic party.
>
> Unity is in fact crucial to Mr. Carter's program for full economic recovery and a return to prosperity without inflation. . . . Mr. Carter's job will be to demonstrate that it is possible to construct a program that will serve the broad public interest in a way that will benefit, rather than hurt, diverse private interests.[13]

What does the knowledgeable Mr. Silk assume regarding domestic economics if not the theories of economic growth discussed in the previous chapter, which dovetail neatly with Rockefeller's basic reasoning.

To close the circle, the race and civil liberties dimensions are tied to the economic dimension. Many efforts to alleviate the injustices of racial inequality have required an expanded role for government in economic life (equal employment, federal subsidies for housing and health care, aid to cities and to education), which in a generalized way is anathema to conservatives. Moreover, the alliance of the Republicans and Southern Democrats in the Congress has tied race with conservative economics. The anti-union Southern states, with their "right-to-work" laws, drawing New England textile manufacturing to the South in an earlier period, and other investment in recent times, may maintain this relationship, unless the South is unionized. That is why so much attention has been focused in the press on the multi-million dollar effort by labor to unionize the vast J. P. Stevens textile firm.

This effort is seen by organized labor as a test case of the "possible" in the "new South."

The questions of civil liberties and democracy, as broken down into a more specific list of issues before the Congress in Chapter 5, will in that form and place be readily seen by the reader as tied to the other dimensions, without any need of further explanation. It should be understood that "democracy" is used here in an overtly political sense, implying political dissent, and the advantage gained by liberals if wider involvement in politics, along informed lines, takes place. Senator Cranston, the Senate majority whip, noted in a constituent newsletter: "A society created by and for the experts is a society of people with no stake in social survival." This quote is but one small indication of a great range of activities that show that democracy as an issue cuts very deeply within Congress. Congressional attitudes toward democracy, and issues before the Congress involving the most philosophically and practically intense aspects of concerns about democracy, would be worthy of book-length treatment by a team of political scientists.

In sum, the fundamental ideological conflict of our era is clearly emerging as one between those who primarily believe in the efficacy of the private sector and market forces, versus those who believe that the latter generates too much deprivation and injustice, and worse, deep systemic instability, and that only reformed democratic government can result in necessary investment and production of what is needed. In a nutshell, the conflict is between a market orientation and a social justice-democratic government orientation. We will inevitably see a vast refinement of this conflict in terms of far more sophisticated sets of issues and problems than structured the political agenda during the post-World War II economic prosperity in the United States and Europe, constrained by the cold war.

NOTES

1. Clausen, *How Congressmen Decide* (New York: St. Martins, 1973), p. 88.
2. Cf. Richard Born, "Cue-Taking Within State Party Delegations in the U.S. House of Representatives," *Journal of Politics* 38, no. 1 (February 1976): 71-94. Born concludes: "Therefore, a state party member . . . will probably end up voting in most cases no differently than were he not to have consulted within the delegation at all. His own policy predispositions are likely to lead him to like-minded experts . . ." (pp. 93-94).
3. Lawrence O'Brien, *No Final Victories* (New York: Ballantine Books, 1974), pp. 125-26.
4. Cf. Philip Converse, "The Nature of Belief Systems in Mass Publics," in David Apter (ed.), *Ideology and Discontent* (New York: Free Press, 1964), and his, "Some Mass-Elite Contrasts in the Perception of Political Spaces," *Social Science Information* 14, no. 3-4 (Summer 1975):49-83.
5. Cf. James MacGregor Burns, *Edward Kennedy and the Camelot Legend* (New York: Norton, 1976), pp. 302-7, "The Promise of Party."
6. Frank J. Sorauf, *Party Politics in America*, 2nd ed. (Boston: Little Brown, 1972), p. 305.
7. Converse, "Some Mass-Elite Contrasts," p. 49.

8. What *can* happen, nonetheless, is indicated by the interesting findings, as yet unpublished, by John Ellwood re. followers of George Wallace—comparing elite activitists and mass supporters. Ellwood has found that the two groups were sharply different. The elite activists were found to be virtually coterminous in issue orientations with other archconservatives among American political elites, whereas Wallace-ite mass supporters for the most part upheld traditional Democrat party orientations on economic issues, though a significant portion were conservative on foreign policy issues as well as race. I am grateful to Ellwood, now of the Congressional Budget Office, for making available to me a preliminary view of his findings, based on years of research. He interviewed Wallace elite activists extensively, and has interesting comparisons to make with Michigan C.P.S. data on other elites.

9. U.S., Congress, Senate, Committee on Foreign Relations, *Rockefeller Report on Latin America, Hearing,* before a subcommittee of the Committee on Foreign Relations, U.S. Senate, 91st Cong., 1st sess., 1969, pp. 12-19.

Senator Church. Then you recommend the expansion of the military assistance program for purposes of internal security.

Now, that means, to use the language of your report, that we will give very extensive military assistance to undemocratic governments for the purpose of internal security.

Governor Rockefeller. Not only these governments, all.

Senator Church. All governments. But most of these governments today—the biggest ones—are military dictatorships. . . .

Now, extending military assistance to foreign governments to help them obtain internal security is just a euphemism for maintaining internal order, and governments try to maintain internal order to keep themselves in control and prevent their own overthrow. Do you think we should extend this kind of assistance, say, to the Government of Haiti?

Governor Rockefeller. Well, I would say that basically it is essential that it be extended and that we cooperate with the training and the equipment hemisphere wide.

Senator Church. Then you would extend it to the Government of Haiti?

Governor Rockefeller. Well, I would want to be a little closer as a nation to some of these governments so that while we are cooperating in helping them to meet their problems, we are also talking to them on a very realistic basis about how they can take the steps to restore the democratic process.

Senator Church. Do you think you can talk 'Papa Doc' into restoring democracy in Haiti? (Laughter)

Governor Rockefeller. I will give you an answer and I think the answer is "Yes."

Now, you may not believe that. I do not think he is going to last very long. . . .

Outside, throughout the nation, there is nothing but degradation and poverty and an illiteracy rate of around 90-some percent and I do not know how any of us think you are going to build democracy under those conditions.

Senator Church. Governor, I am not talking about the advisability of extending economic aid that might be helpful to the people of Haiti. I am talking about extending guns, helicopters, radios, and command and control equipment to the present Government of Haiti for the purpose of helping it stay in power.

Governor Rockefeller. Well, if you will excuse me, Senator, the present Government is not there through my policies and I am not here to justify that Government. I am here to talk to you about how do we prevent that in the Government and how do we encourage the evolution of those countries to democracy.

Senator Church. But you are advocating a military assistance program.

Governor Rockefeller. Which is essential.

Senator Church. And you have indicated you would make it hemispherewide.

Governor Rockefeller. Yes, sir.

Senator Church. And the effect of this is to help such governments as the Haitian Government and other dictatorial governments stay in power.

I do not see what that has to do either with the American tradition, which is based on the peoples' right to revolt against despotism, or with improving the quality of life for the people of the hemisphere.

Governor Rockefeller. Senator, I have to challenge a basic assumption, that if we do not send aid and if we cut off our relations we are not going to achieve the goals of human dignity and freedom and opportunity which are our objectives. . . .

Senator Church. Governor, I do not want to cut you short on your answer, because I think there are particular countries where strong arguments can be made for particular programs. Uruguay, being a democratic country, may be one of them.

I simply take issue with the position that we should undertake, on a hemispherewide basis, to supply more military assistance to help all governments stay in power. I do not see what interest the United States has in trying to help a government like Duvalier's regime in Haiti to stay in power. I think that does us more damage in the long run than adhering to our national tradition of recognizing that other people have the right to revolt and to overthrow tyranny, even if it does not happen to wear a red cloak, even if it is not Communist tyranny. That is not the only kind of tyranny in the world.

I cannot reconcile this kind of sweeping recommendation, encompassing all the governments of Latin America, either with our traditional concepts as a nation or with our own national self-interest. . . .

Governor Rockefeller. But you keep repeating, "to help maintain governments in power." This is certainly a factor that will be used in some cases but the goals which you seek and which I seek which are opportunities for people, participation, freedom, democracy, cannot be achieved in the state of anarchy or chaos and I think you would agree with that yourself.

Senator Church. I am not sure I would agree with that, Governor. It seems to me the history of the world bears out that whenever significant internal change takes place, it is frequently accompanied by violence; in fact, more often than not.

That has not only been true in other countries; it has even been true in our own country.

I think there are some antiquated, feudal societies in Latin America where we can expect violence, where it becomes the only remedy for the people. I really find myself in basic philosophic disagreement with you on that score. . . .

It is not our policy or objective to insist that Latin America develop in our image. I understand that. We will have to deal with governments as we find them. But the question is whether we should adopt a program of giving arms, equipment, and training to keep these governments in power in their own lands. That is the question.

10. Cf. Robert Packenham's excellent analysis, *Liberal America and the Third World: Political Development Ideas in Foreign Aid and Social Science* (Princeton University Press, 1973).

11. For perhaps the most brilliant statement of the underlying logic of this position, cf. Stephen Hymer, "The Multinational Corporation and the Law of Uneven Development," in Jagdish N. Bhagwati, ed., *Economics and the World Order* (New York: Free Press, 1972).

12. Rowland Evans and Robert Novak, "Fear and Loathing on Wall Street," *Washington Post*, 6 April 1977, p. A23.

13. Leonard Silk, "The Danger of Ideology," *New York Times*, 20 July 1976, p. 31.

14. "U.S. Senator Alan Cranston Reports to Californians," March 1976, 94th Cong., 1st sess., no. 32.

appendix I

ROLL CALL VOTES BY CQ NUMBER

NINETY-FOURTH CONGRESS—SENATE—FIRST SESSION

Foreign Policy and Defense

66, 67, 73, 74, 195, 199, 201, 203, 204, 205, 206, 207, 213, 340, 374, 375, 393, 458, 459, 468, 470, 478, 479, 480, 482, 485, 486, 489, 493, 494, 497, 596, 601, 602

Civil Liberties and Democracy

14, 15, 16, 17, 18, 19, 20, 21, 22, 23, 25, 29, 30, 33, 38, 40, 42, 43, 45, 48, 49, 50, 51, 52, 53, 55, 129, 130, 141, 193, 265, 433, 454, 560

Upper Class

11, 12, 13, 56, 57, 58, 60, 61, 62, 63, 71, 72, 78, 79, 80, 83, 84, 85, 86, 87, 88, 89, 101, 106, 108, 109, 111, 118, 119, 120, 121, 122, 123, 124, 125, 126, 127, 128, 133, 134, 135, 136, 138, 160, 161, 164, 165, 166, 167, 219, 220, 262, 276, 282, 283, 284, 285, 287, 353, 355, 357, 359, 360, 361, 362, 364, 367, 368, 384, 385, 386, 387, 388, 395, 426, 427, 431, 432, 442, 443, 444, 445, 446, 447, 448, 449, 450, 451, 466, 523, 524, 527, 529, 530, 567

Middle-Lower Class

5, 9, 10, 28, 31, 69, 81, 82, 90, 94, 95, 102, 103, 107, 110, 112, 113, 114, 115, 116, 117, 132, 148, 153, 154, 155, 156, 157, 158, 169, 170, 171, 172, 173, 174, 175, 176, 177, 179, 180, 181, 182, 183, 184, 194, 196, 197, 198, 221, 271, 272, 281, 293, 294, 296, 331, 336, 337, 347, 348, 378, 389, 398, 399, 400, 401, 405, 406, 408, 413, 414, 422, 423, 429, 455, 456, 471, 472, 473, 475, 476, 481, 491, 495, 499, 500, 501, 502, 503, 504, 505, 506, 509, 510, 511, 512, 513, 515, 516, 517, 528, 531, 532, 533, 535, 536, 537, 538, 539, 540, 541, 542, 543, 544, 546, 547, 549, 550, 552, 553, 554, 555, 557, 562, 564, 565, 572, 573, 577, 582, 583, 584, 585, 589, 600

Lower Class

7, 91, 96, 150, 151, 163, 188, 189, 216, 236

Race

137, 191, 303, 306, 308, 309, 310, 311, 312, 313, 314, 315, 316, 317, 318, 319, 320, 321, 323, 324, 325, 326, 327, 328, 329, 377, 380, 381, 382, 396, 397, 402, 403, 404, 408, 409, 410, 411, 412, 415, 417, 418, 419

Excluded

1, 2, 3, 4, 32, 34, 35, 36, 37, 41, 46, 47, 59, 70, 75, 76, 77, 92, 93, 97, 98, 99, 104, 105,, 142, 143, 144, 145, 146, 152, 159, 178, 190, 192, 200, 208, 209, 210, 212, 218, 222, 223, 224, 225, 226, 228, 232, 233, 234, 235, 237, 238, 239, 241, 242, 243, 244, 245, 246, 247, 248, 249, 250, 251, 252, 253, 254, 256, 259, 260, 261, 264, 267, 268, 269, 270, 273, 277, 278, 279, 280, 286, 288, 289, 290, 291, 292, 299, 302, 304, 307, 335, 341, 343, 344, 345, 346, 349, 350, 351, 352, 354, 356, 358, 363, 365, 366, 369, 372, 373, 379, 391, 416, 428, 430, 434, 435, 436, 439, 440, 441, 452, 453, 461, 462, 463, 483, 484, 487, 488, 507, 514, 518, 519, 525, 526, 534, 545, 551, 561, 563, 566, 571, 574, 578, 586, 587, 588, 590, 591, 592, 595

NINETY-FOURTH CONGRESS—HOUSE—FIRST SESSION

Foreign Policy and Defense

14, 97, 105, 159, 160, 161, 164, 165, 166, 169, 221, 238, 241, 249, 264, 269, 289, 290, 298, 299, 330, 351, 383, 384, 406, 407, 409, 410, 421, 442, 460, 561, 562, 563

Civil Liberties and Democracy

8, 9, 10, 50, 72, 73, 74, 175, 226, 229, 230, 231, 275, 276, 296, 345, 423, 461, 462, 463, 464, 574

Race

182, 183, 184, 185, 186, 187, 189, 192, 294, 328, 403, 555, 556

Upper Class

5, 18, 19, 20, 21, 27, 32, 33, 34, 38, 46, 47, 86, 87, 119, 133, 138, 139, 140, 172, 194, 195, 198, 200, 202, 203, 204, 205, 206, 211, 212, 228, 232, 233, 234, 235, 242, 245, 246, 265, 285, 288, 300, 302, 308, 312, 313, 315, 335, 347, 348, 349, 350, 352, 353, 354, 355, 356, 366, 367, 368, 375, 388, 389, 390, 391, 392, 395, 396, 397, 398, 402, 404, 405, 408, 437, 452, 467, 468, 469, 471, 472, 485, 486, 487, 488, 546, 547, 548, 549, 550, 557, 558, 583, 584, 585, 586, 587, 588, 590, 600, 603, 604

Middle-Lower Class

6, 7, 11, 12, 13, 16, 17, 22, 23, 24, 25, 42, 44, 49, 52, 53, 54, 55, 56, 62, 63, 65, 66, 67, 83, 84, 111, 112, 113, 114, 115, 118, 120, 121, 122, 123, 124, 144, 145, 147, 156, 157, 162, 167, 168, 193, 196, 197, 207, 213, 219, 223, 224, 259, 260, 261, 266, 277, 281, 282, 283, 284, 293, 295, 301, 319, 321, 322, 323, 324, 325, 326, 339, 363, 364, 370, 371, 378, 379, 386, 400, 411, 430, 439, 444, 453, 454, 457, 476, 481, 482, 483, 492, 496, 497, 509, 512, 513, 514, 515, 516, 517, 518, 540, 541, 543, 551, 552, 553, 564, 568, 570, 572, 573, 580, 591, 592, 594, 597, 598, 599, 612

Lower Class

28, 29, 61, 64, 153, 188, 250, 251, 336, 420, 475, 534, 519

Excluded

1, 2, 3, 30, 35, 37, 39, 43, 45, 48, 51, 58, 59, 68, 70, 71, 85, 88, 91, 92, 94, 95, 98, 99, 100, 101, 102, 103, 104, 106, 107, 108, 110, 117, 143, 148, 149, 150, 151, 154, 170, 171, 173, 174, 178, 179, 180, 181, 190, 191, 225, 208, 209, 210, 214, 215, 216, 217, 218, 253, 254, 255, 256,

257, 274, 286, 291, 309, 310, 314, 318, 329, 331, 332, 340, 341, 342, 343, 344, 346, 357, 358, 359, 360, 361, 362, 369, 376, 393, 401, 417, 422, 424, 425, 426, 427, 428, 429, 431, 432, 433, 435, 436, 438, 440, 446, 447, 448, 449, 450, 455, 456, 458, 466, 470, 473, 478, 479, 480, 484, 507, 510, 529, 530, 537, 545, 554, 559, 576, 581, 582, 589, 593, 595, 596, 601, 608, 609, 610

NINETY-SECOND CONGRESS—SENATE—FIRST SESSION

Foreign Policy and Defense

53, 62, 67, 68, 69, 73, 75, 82, 83, 93, 96, 97, 98, 99, 100, 101, 102, 113, 138, 139, 147, 152, 174, 200, 201, 205, 206, 207, 208, 209, 210, 212, 213, 214, 215, 216, 217, 218, 219, 220, 221, 224, 225, 226, 227, 228, 229, 238, 239, 240, 241, 243, 244, 245, 246, 247, 248, 250, 251, 252, 254, 255, 271, 273, 274, 275, 276, 277, 278, 310, 314, 361, 363

Civil Liberties and Democracy

4, 5, 6, 7, 8, 9, 10, 11, 21, 30, 74, 86, 89, 108, 110, 132, 133, 134, 167, 168, 170, 172, 176, 177, 179, 180, 181, 301, 324, 325, 326, 327, 328, 329, 330, 332, 333, 334, 335, 336, 337, 344, 345, 346, 347, 348, 350, 351, 352, 353, 354, 382, 383, 384, 385, 393, 394, 395, 414, 417

Race

35, 36, 39, 42, 43, 44, 130, 135, 235

Upper Class

23, 54, 114, 127, 142, 144, 145, 146, 150, 151, 153, 155, 157, 164, 290, 297, 308, 318, 319, 321, 339, 340, 341, 356, 374, 377, 378, 379, 381, 397, 400

Middle-Lower Class

154, 156, 186, 230, 231, 233, 259, 260, 263, 265, 266, 267, 268, 289, 295, 302, 304, 307, 311, 312, 358, 388

Lower Class

25, 26, 27, 28, 29, 56, 63, 66, 112, 126, 148, 153, 159, 160, 173, 185, 193, 194, 195, 196, 197, 199, 281, 282, 283, 303, 306, 315, 316, 317, 342, 399, 406, 418

Excluded

15, 16, 19, 34, 37, 38, 40, 41, 46, 48, 49, 50, 51, 52, 58, 59, 60, 65, 71, 72, 78, 84, 87, 88, 90, 91, 92, 95, 104, 105, 107, 109, 111, 120, 124, 125, 131, 149, 162, 166, 169, 171, 178, 183, 184, 189, 190, 204, 211, 236, 242, 249, 253, 256, 272, 279, 280, 284, 285, 286, 288, 291, 292, 296, 300, 305, 309, 313, 320, 322, 331, 343, 349, 355, 357, 359, 360, 362, 364, 366, 373, 376, 391, 392, 403, 405, 413, 422

NINETY-SECOND CONGRESS—SENATE—SECOND SESSION

Foreign Policy and Defense

23, 26, 28, 121, 123, 124, 126, 127, 128, 129, 131, 132, 133, 134, 135, 154, 162, 167, 168, 172, 174, 185, 189, 198, 201, 205, 206, 223, 224, 227, 274, 277, 291, 295, 299, 301, 304, 306, 307, 308, 309, 310, 311, 312, 313, 314, 398, 399, 400, 401, 436, 437, 438, 439, 440, 441, 459, 461

Civil Liberties and Democracy

21, 57, 87, 88, 89, 90, 91, 92, 93, 94, 95, 97, 111, 112, 113, 114, 158, 160, 196, 204, 218, 219, 220, 341, 342, 379, 414

Race

3, 4, 5, 6, 8, 9, 10, 11, 12, 13, 14, 15, 16, 17, 20, 24, 33, 35, 36, 38, 39, 41, 44, 45, 46, 47, 48, 49, 50, 54, 55, 58, 59, 60, 61, 62, 64, 66, 68, 71, 72, 165, 166, 268, 343, 502, 503, 504

Upper Class

31, 115, 156, 163, 170, 197, 271, 288, 290, 292, 296, 321, 378, 382, 383, 419, 421, 424, 425, 426, 431, 442, 443, 450, 462, 486, 494, 495, 527

Middle-Lower Class

75, 78, 79, 82, 84, 85, 86, 98, 137, 143, 144, 145, 146, 147, 148, 161, 194, 195, 208, 209, 210, 211, 212, 213, 214, 215, 216, 230, 231, 232, 247, 248, 249, 287, 323, 334, 348, 357, 358, 371, 372, 375, 376, 385, 428, 432, 454, 469, 472, 473, 474, 475, 476, 477, 491, 497, 507, 508, 509, 510, 512, 514, 532

Lower Class

226, 228, 229, 239, 242, 243, 244, 245, 256, 257, 258, 262, 263, 264, 265, 266, 267, 270, 278, 279, 280, 282, 353, 354, 355, 369, 370, 405, 447, 453, 498, 499, 521, 522, 523

Excluded

22, 27, 29, 30, 51, 52, 56, 63, 65, 70, 77, 81, 83, 101, 102, 104, 105, 107, 117, 119, 138, 141, 149, 150, 151, 152, 153, 155, 157, 179, 180, 190, 207, 234, 238, 255, 273, 275, 276, 283, 284, 285, 286, 294, 300, 303, 320, 324, 325, 335, 336, 330, 331, 337, 338, 339, 340, 347, 345, 366, 367, 374, 380, 386, 387, 388, 389, 390, 391, 393, 394, 395, 396, 397, 411, 422, 423, 427, 434, 448, 449, 460, 463, 471, 479, 480, 481, 482, 484, 488, 489, 492, 493, 496, 506, 511, 516, 518, 520, 529, 530, 531

NINETY-SECOND CONGRESS—HOUSE—FIRST SESSION

Foreign Policy and Defense

24, 25, 79, 83, 84, 85, 86, 89, 90, 91, 92, 104, 107, 110, 116, 118, 161, 162, 166, 178, 205, 255, 267, 268, 269, 270, 271, 272, 291, 298, 320

Civil Liberties and Democracy

2, 4, 7, 33, 40, 41, 42, 105, 123, 135, 170, 171, 172, 211, 230, 245, 246, 278, 279, 280, 281, 282

Race

31, 53, 154, 173, 174, 216, 236, 237, 238, 239, 257, 258, 260, 313, 314, 317

Upper Class

14, 15, 51, 52, 63, 80, 101, 151, 152, 198, 199, 235, 247, 248, 249, 250, 266, 301, 306, 310

Middle-Lower Class

20, 30, 35, 36, 88, 103, 136, 140, 167, 187, 188, 190, 227, 228, 229, 232, 233, 295, 309, 311

Lower Class

58, 59, 67, 68, 69, 82, 112, 137, 138, 164, 165, 180, 181, 182, 183, 184, 185, 186, 201, 251, 252, 253, 259, 293, 297, 318

Excluded

1, 3, 5, 8, 9, 18, 21, 22, 23, 26, 27, 28, 29, 37, 38, 44, 48, 50, 61, 64, 65, 66, 71, 77, 78, 93, 98, 99, 100, 102, 119, 122, 125, 128, 130, 131, 134, 144, 145, 146, 150, 159, 160, 163, 175, 176,

179, 192, 195, 196, 206, 208, 209, 214, 215, 223, 225, 231, 234, 240, 241, 242, 244, 263, 273, 284, 286, 287, 288, 292, 296, 299, 300, 302, 303, 305, 307, 308, 315, 319

NINETY-SECOND CONGRESS—HOUSE—SECOND SESSION

Foreign Policy and Defense

9, 10, 11, 12, 76, 105, 155, 156, 157, 158, 159, 221, 223, 224

Civil Liberties and Democracy

22, 33, 108, 110, 116, 119, 148

Race

38, 39, 40, 93, 94, 129, 238, 240, 241, 242, 245

Upper Class

29, 55, 56, 57, 58, 60, 137, 138, 167, 193

Middle-Lower Class

26, 78, 79, 80, 139, 141, 142, 173, 187, 188, 189, 214, 217, 236

Lower Class

27, 28, 91, 95, 96, 97, 98, 99, 106, 107, 140, 166, 168, 177, 201, 233, 234, 235

Excluded

1, 3, 4, 6, 14, 15, 23, 24, 25, 30, 31, 34, 41, 45, 46, 47, 59, 61, 62, 69, 70, 71, 74, 82, 84, 87, 88, 92, 103, 104, 109, 117, 118, 120, 121, 122, 123, 131, 143, 145, 146, 147, 149, 150, 151, 153, 160, 161, 163, 164, 165, 170, 181, 186, 191, 192, 194, 195, 196, 204, 205, 208, 209, 210, 215, 216, 219, 222, 225, 232, 237, 243, 244, 247, 248

appendix II

RESPONSE PATTERNS OBTAINED IN THE CONGRESSIONAL INTERVIEWS ON FOREIGN POLICY*

QUESTION 1: VIETNAM CONSEQUENCES

"What do you think the *consequences* would be if there was to be a Communist takeover in all of Indochina, within the next two or three years, for the *security* of the United States" *Follow-up questions*: "Do you think there would be any domino effect outside of Indochina?" "Do you think there would be any domino effect outside of Indochina?" "Do you think there would be any psychological domino effect, that is, do you think Communist insurgencies in different parts of the world would be spurred by a Communist takeover in Indochina?" "You've said it would be bad for U.S. interests even though not vital to U.S. security; how would such a takeover hurt U.S. interests?" "Do you think a takeover would change the balance of power between the U.S. on the one hand and the Soviet Union and/or China on the other?"

Severe Consequences

". . . exclusion from world markets and raw materials, because of a general domino effect . . . wipe out all Western investment. If they take over, they won't want to do business with the free world."

". . . would force accommodation of all U.S. allies with Communist powers, because of the loss of credibility of U.S. pledges."

". . . shock wave repercussion."

". . . a bloodbath."

". . . a bloodbath, 3 million would be killed."

". . . a Dunkirk."

". . . a breakdown of the principle of collective security."

". . . a complete loss of U.S. influence throughout Asia . . . a threat to our large interests in the Orient."

*The response categories following each question begin with the conservative and go toward the liberal.

". . . a great defeat for us."
". . . disastrous."
". . . if not there, where; if not us, who."
". . . better there than the West Coast of the U.S."
". . . encourage military aggression."
". . . ominous, if aggression is not stopped."
". . . collapse of all treaties."
". . . credibility of the society of nations."
". . . Vietnam is the key to all of Asia."
". . . we'd soon be surrounded."
". . . free communism to devote more energy to aggression elsewhere."
". . . encourage insurgencies in many areas, as Magsaysay and Suharto said."
". . . test of our determination."
"I believe in the domino theory."

"If it appears that the President is compelled to withdraw by the pressures of U.S. public opinion, then Moscow and Peking will assume that the U.S. is a paper tiger and weaker nations will too, and will fall into line and make their accommodation with the Communist powers."

". . . a danger to the Philippines and Hawaii."

". . . endanger all the vital shipping lanes and air routes that we depend on, like the Straits of Malacca."

"India would be completely dominated; there would be political pressure on Mideast oil; Europe would then be threatened with economic and political chaos."

". . . vast raw materials lost to the Communist movement."
". . . they'll keep probing."
". . . seriously and adversely affect our interest all over the world."

". . . sever our lines of communication and our ability to maintain military installations abroad."

". . . affect seriously our foreign trade."

"The U.S. would give up any real influence abroad and the struggle for freedom and dignity of peoples everywhere."

". . . a shot in the arm to Reds all over the world."
". . . affect the stability of the whole Pacific area."
"The power stakes of the U.S. in the western Pacific would be greatly damaged."

". . . possibly a severe disruption in world relations, affecting U.S. relations in the Mideast and Europe as well as all of Asia."

". . . China and the Soviet Union will benefit in the balance of power."
". . . fail our allies. Even Australia would have serious doubts."

". . . certainly lessen U.S. influence in the world and the role of the U.S. as the leader of the free world."

". . . tremendous."

"Japan, Indonesia, the Philippines, Korea, Burma, Malaysia, and India would be threatened, undermined, seriously affected, and would go."

"We'd have to respond by expanding our policeman's role in many other places."

"Vietnamization is working, and therefore I don't think there will be a takeover there. I'm not willing to consider what would happen if Vietnamization fails, since I don't think it's going to fail."

"Where is it going to stop? We have to draw the line someplace."

[Re: Domino Effect]

"Definitely."
"Certainly."
"No question about it."

[Other members mentioned a variety of combinations of countries, primarily in East Asia and South Asia, as well as Southeast Asia, that they believed would fall, be endangered, threatened, and so on, as a consequence of a Communist takeover in Indochina. A few also added European countries. Only those who thought the effect would be limited to Thailand and Indochina were excluded from this coding category.]

Middle Response—Not Ascertainable

". . . not sure what the consequences would be."

". . . would affect the balance of power among the three superpowers, but I'm not sure how, it's hard to say. But the Soviet Union and China won't call the shots in Southeast Asia, but rather influence events."

". . . regrettable for U.S. security" [unable to elaborate].

"The Soviet Union and China will benefit from a takeover" [unwilling to elaborate further].

[Re: Domino Effect]

"Don't know."

"Can't say."

"I could see it both ways."

"A takeover in Vietnam would have some effect, but I am not sure what."

Little or No Consequences

"It's primarily a civil war."

"Neither the Soviet Union or China would want to see Vietnamese expansion. Thailand is solid."

"I don't accept the domino theory. They'd have to get across the water."

"We can hold up the Thais with military aid alone."

". . . not a major or significant minus to our national interest or security."

". . . wouldn't affect the balance of power among the U.S., the Soviet Union, and the People's Republic of China."

"I don't know any other areas of the world where it would have any great impact."

"The U.S. has been overly preoccupied with communism and a threat of communism."

"Conspiracy theories are all too convenient as a means of avoiding real problems."

"Southeast Asia is unique."

"A Communist Vietnam would be independent of China and would not be receptive to Chinese influence."

"Rice paddies can't turn out missiles."

"'Alignment' makes sense only in terms of missles."

"A Communist South Vietnam wouldn't be part of any international Communist conspiracy. The divisions among Communists are more significant."

"Only Thailand would be affected. I don't see any effect beyond that."

"A Communist South Vietnam would not be Communist as we understand it."

"It's really a nationalist movement."

"If we continue to support the Saigon government, it would need constant propping up and it's only a question of time till it falls."

"We can't prevent a takeover there, but we could touch off a holocaust."

"It's hard to have a middle where a revolution overthrows an oligarchy."

"Communism isn't a monolith."

"All revolutions aren't Communist takeovers."

"Nationalism is stronger. As nationalists they'd resist being part of any monolithic Communist structure."

"Not much of a threat to the U.S."

". . . no major consequences."

". . . of very little consequence."

". . . not even close to a foreign policy disaster."

"If countries fall, it's because of internal conditions and these would have their effect irrespective of the outcomes in Vietnam."

". . . not significant, given nuclear weapons."

"A Communist takeover is not irreversible."

". . . not relevant to U.S. security interests."

"I don't see the consequences that others see."

"It might lessen our influence but other ex-colonial powers have survived."

"It's ridiculous to think the U.S. is going to fall if Vietnam falls."

". . . strategically it's unimportant."

"It can't be worth saving, if not viable by now."

"We can coexist as well with a Communist Vietnam, as we have with other Communist countries."

"It would have an independent status, like Tito's Yugoslavia."

"Vietnam wouldn't be a puppet of either the Soviet Union or China. I don't see any domino effect even in Thailand."

[Re: Domino Effect]

"The dominoes themselves don't seem to perceive any threat."

"The dominoes aren't contributing to the war effort. If they saw any threat, they would. If they don't see any threat, why do we?"

QUESTION 2: VIETNAM: HOW FAR TO GO TO PREVENT A COMMUNIST TAKEOVER

"How far should the U.S. go to prevent a takeover by the Communists?" "How far should the U.S. government go after withdrawal from any combat role in providing support to the Saigon government to help it resist a Communist takeover?"

Remain for Political Objectives

". . . follow the President."

"I would have bombed Hanoi and Haiphong and closed Haiphong harbor."

"I would have devastated North Vietnam . . . opened the dikes."

"I am against the McGovern-Hatfield amendment."

"I am willing to give material support to South Vietnam for some time."

"I favor the Vietnamization policy of the Administration."

"We should give them air support and material assistance."

"If we stay in through 1971, there won't be a takeover."

"Attacks on the North may become necessary."

"We should be their arsenal."

"We must be willing to go the long mile."

"We must have an honorable peace."

"I'm in favor of using air power to interdict their movements."

"I think that the Cambodian effort was the first sensible thing we've done in years."

"We should stop this no win policy; either go in there and do the job, or get out. We could have won it. Our military has been shackled by politicians."

"I'd see more all out bombing all the way."

"I have no quarrel with having some residual force there for some time."

"I favor the Nixon Doctrine: lend material assistance, but not use American troops in a combat role."

"I never approved bombing Hanoi and Haiphong, but I'm for the bombing of the North, contrary to what the doves say."

Middle Position

". . . depends on conditions" [wouldn't care to amplify].

"Couldn't say."

"Public opinion wouldn't support our continuing effort there. Therefore we shouldn't bomb the North or reescalate the war."

"We're forced to withdraw because of domestic opinion."

"I'm for continued military and economic aid for fear of domestic recrimination, if there was a quick takeover after a sharp withdrawal, and if it was followed by a bloodbath. This could greatly increase domestic U.S. political polarization and lead as well to xenophobia and isolationism. But we must force Thieu to broaden his base. He must make reforms, if he's to stay in power. Massive firepower alone won't work. The military has always misled us on that."

Withdrawal from Political Objectives

"I'm in favor of a total withdrawal by a date certain, including an end to any kind of U.S. involvement there."

"I'm against any residual force."

"Nixon is keeping the commitment to Thieu and I oppose propping them up any more."

"A takeover will occur whether we stay or leave."

"We should accelerate our withdrawal."

"We should condition our support for the Thieu government on certain democratizing actions. If they don't democratize, I'd pull the plug."

"We're more endangered by staying in there than by getting out."

"I favor immediate and total withdrawal."

"I don't think massive firepower would work. When the rains come the planes would be grounded and the heads would pop up again."

"The idea of staying in there with any kind of significant force is insanity."

QUESTIONS 3-7: INTRODUCTION

"There has been controversy in Congress about U.S. support for a number of different regimes around the world—Greece, Cuba, Brazil, Rhodesia, Taiwan, and others. Looking at these. . . ."

QUESTION 3: MILITARY AID TO GREECE

"How do you feel about our military aid to Greece? Do you favor giving Greece military aid, or should it be withheld?" *Follow-up question*: [If respondent mentions regret about the anti-democratic character of the regime without going so far as to say that aid should be cut off to Greece] "Some members have stated that NATO-related considerations and conditions in the Mediterranean and the Mideast make it necessary to maintain our military aid to Greece, despite the character of the Greek government. How do you feel about that?"

For Giving Military Aid

"My interest is not in propping up the regime but in keeping Greece stable. I am concerned also for repercussions re: NATO and Mideast needs which require us to aid Greece."

"Our policy is the lesser of two evils. The Colonels are making progress toward democracy and providing stability."

"It's a friendly government. We can't refuse to deal with all the nations of the world whose ways of governing we don't like."

"It's not as friendly to Communists as other countries we give aid to. It's a strong anti-Communist government."

"I won't deny aid if it is to *our* advantage."

"We should support it because of the Mideast and Mediterranean situations, but we should make plain our displeasure with the regime and what is going on."

"We need to be pragmatic but we should work for and support non-dictators."

"Yes, we shouldn't involve ourselves in other countries' internal problems."

"I don't take the purist view. I prefer rather the nineteenth-century view. I'm not overwhelmed with the sinfulness of military regimes. They do lead to increased democracy and tend to be only temporary."

"Liking the Greek government or not is irrelevant. If once it was necessary to us, it still is for our own interest. We can't go around reforming the world."

"Yes, NATO considerations make it necessary."

"Yes, they are a NATO ally and therefore we have an obligation to them."

"Yes, because of Israel. Though because it's repressive, I could be talked out of it except for Israel."

"Yes, I've mixed feelings, but we're caught. We can't afford the luxury of worrying about the nature of the Greek government."

"Greece is important with regard to the situation with the Russians in the Mediterranean."

"I assume our government feels stability is in the making there, and is in the interest of Greece."

"Though I'm not happy about the junta, because of NATO defense needs, yes. I'm inclined to think a defensive justification could be made for it."

"Greece is the anchor of NATO and is badly in need of modernization of its defenses."

"My Greek friends accept what's going on there."

"The nature of the regime isn't relevant. Pressures could have been increased to push them towards democracy, but the people have no real experience of democracy and most important they have no middle class which is necessary if you are going to have democracy. I'm satisfied that we have to deal with imperfect governments in order to prevent communism."

"Greece, like Spain, is one of our best friends."

"As long as they only use it for NATO we should continue to help and not involve ourselves in trying to affect the nature of their government."

"The extent to which we're now giving is about right."

"We've had a military commitment to Greece for some time. This commitment should be kept. We should disregard the government's character. If the people are satisfied, so be it. We need to have a stable government there."

"We're *not* going to find many other democracies abroad. The alternative to not backing governments that aren't democracies is to retreat into Fortress America."

"I'm for the administration's aid level, but we should show that we deplore the loss of democracy in Greece."

"Soviet Mediterranean moves make it necessary despite the regime's character, the torture and the rest."

"There are those of liberal persuasion who feel that aid should only go to enlightened countries that have a democratic system of government. They frown on assistance to dictators and governments that are less than Simon Pure. The truth is that there are many governments, many countries in the world, where you just can't have a democracy, where they probably do better under some sort of limited dictatorship. As the people develop and grow to the point where they can carry on a democratic system. . . . It takes a great deal of expertise to run a country through the democratic process, as we are finding out in this country. I'm not sure we are mature enough here. So there are countries in Africa, Latin America and elsewhere where there is some doubt about it. I want to see a strong Greece, and I think therefore it would be democratic, but as long as the country is not in the hands of the opponents of the United States, I can't say we should rule out assistance just because we don't like the government."

Middle Ground: Not Ascertainable

"I don't know."

"I oppose military aid generally, as well as economic aid. I just don't believe in foreign aid."

"No, we should get out of the military aid business altogether."

For Refusing Military Aid to Greece

"I tend toward the view of no aid to an authoritarian government except to counter Soviet aid."

"It's a dictatorship. No."

"We should quit involving ourselves in other countries' internal conflicts. No."

"Not to repressive governments."

"No, we are propping up an autocracy."

"I'm particularly unhappy with the Greek government. Our aid possibly goes mostly for internal repression. I have no wish to arm totalitarian governments."

"Unless it became clear that it was necessary for NATO-related reasons, but I'd stop all arms at this time."

"No. Wrong kind of government."

"No, and a whole review of NATO is in order anyway."

"We should quit involving ourselves in other countries' internal conflicts. No."
external defense alone, so I oppose it."

"We should quit involving ourselves in other countries' internal conflicts. No."

"I'm against the regime and U.S. support of it, NATO needs notwithstanding."

"It is not necessary. There is no internal or external threat there."

"No. They'd use that aid internally."

"I'd restrict it to nothing. Anticommunism is always used as an excuse. Anticommunism is not the lesser of two evils. I say, let 'em go. Let's help the moderates rather than either extreme."

"We shouldn't bolster governments that aren't popular governments."

"I just doubt that the necessity for aid exists. I don't accept the argument that military aid to Greece is crucial to the defense of Western Europe."

"It's ironic that we do this sort of thing under the guise of upholding freedom."

"We can't support undemocratic regimes even if a left-wing takeover is threatened."

"Our support of the Greek government hurts us in Western Europe and elsewhere. The purpose is to defend free nations of the North Atlantic Alliance. The Colonels haven't the slightest intention of returning to free parliamentary democracy."

QUESTION 4: MILITARY AID TO BRAZIL

"There has been controversy in Congress about our aid to Brazil. The government there has been characterized as a particularly repressive one. But our aid levels there have been relatively modest, consisting largely of aid to their police forces and training of their military. Moreover, the situation there is potentially unstable and there is perhaps a danger of a leftist or of a Communist takeover. Given these considerations, or any others, do you favor continuing our aid to Brazil?"

For Continuing Aid

"Brazil had terrible inflation and anarchy and now the people are better off. I've been there. People are less nervous now than before, when they didn't know what was happening."

"It's better that they get these things from us than from others, like the Russians or French from whom they *will* get it anyway, if we don't supply them. At least this way we have some influence, especially once they need our spare parts. And this holds no matter, whether they have a democratic or repressive government. You can't distinguish military aid programs that affect internal versus external security. And since they're going to get the arms anyway, we at least get to keep communications open and maintain trade. Besides I don't think U.S. arms are crucial in domestic political balances."

"I look to exports on this sort of thing. It's necessary to take into account international considerations and American interests. At the moment I back foreign aid bills that include these things."

"Well, yes. It's a forced choice. I think it's necessary to be pragmatic. It's too easy to demogogue this sort of thing by saying 'cut it all off.'"

"I think you have to be pragmatic. I think it's the kind of situation where it's better to have a Batista than risk a Castro."

"I favor continuing it, even though the repression. I don't think we should meddle in the internal affairs of strong anti-Communist countries."

"It's the same principle as the Greek case. What we think about the government is irrelevant. I have no objection to this aid."

"I think they have a real internal security need and so despite its repressiveness and since they'd get it someplace else anyway, I'm for giving it to them."

"I think the present levels are necessary to keep it secure against Communist influence. Training of the army and police is important especially if the threat from Castro increases."

"I think we exaggerate the importance of our effort. It's primarily for security purposes and that's good."

"Stability to avoid revolutions requires, unfortunately, military aid."

"I support military aid to prevent the defeat of freedom anywhere. I follow the President and the Defense Department on the tactics of these things."

"The danger is from infiltration and subversion. I don't think we can afford to look too closely at the internal doctrines of people friendly to the United States. I wouldn't turn my back on a friendly dictator. If you get rid of a dictator, you may get a Red government."

"I support military aid for internal security in Latin America. I wouldn't cut off aid, but we should pressure governments to end aggression there, and release political prisoners, and restore constitutional freedoms."

"I'm for it. I think Latin America is very important to us and so I support it. I'm satisfied that we have to deal with imperfect governments to prevent communism. They allow private property, religion, and literature. Democracy isn't always possible."

"Our aid to Brazil is too small. It's better that we aid them, than someone else."

"I'm quite willing that they have it."

"We've got to keep up the aid to stop the infiltration from outside."

"So long as it's not unfriendly to the U.S. or acting contrary to U.S. security, it's OK. We can't spell out criteria for a government in ruling its own people."

"It's very important to us, and so we need to have a stable government there."

"It's in our interest to prevent anarchy. Even low-income people suffer from anarchy. And you can't give or take away this or that to force them to change their policy."

"I agree with the Rockefeller Report. There is a need for strong governments, and often the military provides the best means of a strong centralized government. I think we should continue our training programs, but we should keep a low profile of our own military there."

"We can't let it fall to a far-left government that undoubtedly would be Communist in the end. We'd like them to be democratic, but in the meantime, we have to give them whatever is necessary for them to maintain themselves."

"We're having very little effect. It doesn't bother me, and stability is important."

Middle Ground—Not Ascertainable

"We ought to use every bit of leverage we can to open up the regime, but we haven't used this leverage in any other case I know of. I don't know what should be done otherwise."

"I'd cut it all off. I'm against foreign aid, including military aid."

"We can't be the world's policeman, but we should meet a probe. I guess I don't know."

"Oligarchies are repressive, but it's hard to evaluate how great an effort they are making to bring about change, or if foreign subversion is a threat to U.S. security."

"Brazil's got a good Caucasian base, but the dictatorship and the church and others try to keep the status quo and impede development; yet if Brazil goes Red, it would be pivotal, so I don't have any firm conclusion on it."

For Discontinuing Aid

"I'm against all military aid to Latin America."

"I think in general we should cut back our military aid and increase our economic aid."

"I'd cut it all out. The effects of this kind of thing are either that we stimulate tensions among countries, or it's just wasted, or we fail to give democracy a chance due to the internal uses of our military aid. We invite polarization within these countries."

"I don't think we can impose our system of government, but I don't think we should give the military aid. I prefer to see the accent on economic assistance."

"Here again I think we're helping to prop up an unpopular government."

"In general, we should disengage from giving military aid to repressive regimes, and Brazil is increasingly repressive."

"It's a dictatorship and we should stop any assistance to it."

"We can't intervene in every uprising. Let the people decide. We're overextended. It should be cut back."

"We should cut off that aid. It's counterproductive. There could be no threat from Brazil under any conditions."

"No, we're not succeeding with our aid. The test should be whether there is human progress and reform."

"Our military aid to Brazil is indefensible."

"I'm not happy about Brazil. We shouldn't have given such total approval to the Castelo Branco government. The present government is far more repressive. If we cut off aid, we risk offending them and they're going to find it elsewhere. But we could end up on the wrong side when the chips fall the other way. I know they're going to buy Mystères, but I'm still glad we are not selling them jets."

QUESTION 5: MILITARY AID TO TAIWAN

"There was an intense argument on the floor last December about an appropriation of $50 million for F-4's for Taiwan. Do you recall how you voted on that and the basis on which you voted? How do you feel about our all-over military aid to Taiwan? Is it about right, is it inflated, or should they be getting more than they are now?"

FOR TAIWAN AID

"I supported F-4's for Taiwan in that vote. I think we have to sustain our commitment to that country. Force levels are about right."

"Their forces must be modernized. The Nationalist Chinese are our friends."

"Taiwan is a friendly government. We have few such loyal allies in the world today. I think you should spend on your friends. It's a good investment."

"We have a great obligation to Chiang. He's been our ally, and he's been out there helping to prevent the spread of communism."

"We've got to do all we can to support the Republic of China. It's a bulwark against communism and the only restraining influence against the tide of communism in that part of the world."

"Taiwan is our agent out there, part of our strategic network, and they've made remarkable progress economically."

"Well, I wouldn't *increase* the aid we're giving them, and I don't want to see them get an offensive capability that would allow them to drag us into something."

"We haven't been giving that much. I don't see it as a major issue."

"If we can't aid a country as dependable as Taiwan, who can we aid?"

"Taiwan is especially important now as a base given the loss of Okinawa."

"The Taiwan force neutralizes Red China."

Mixed Reactions and Nonascertainable Reactions

"I opposed the F-4's. They were not requested by the adminstration and the move was in a contrary direction to Nixon's attempt to open up relations with Mainland China. I don't know about our aid levels overall to Taiwan."

"I opposed the F-4's. They were introduced by Passman and friends for reasons that seemed emotional or self-interested, but I think our all-over aid levels to Taiwan are about right."

"I opposed F-4's. It was basically an emotional reaction to support the jet bill because Taiwan is our friend and because the Taiwanese are stalwart. But our aid levels to Taiwan are generally all right."

Against Taiwan Aid

"I opposed the F-4's going to Taiwan on substantive grounds. Taiwan didn't need them and generally is getting too much military aid anyway, since Taiwan can't defend herself anyway without U.S. military involvement. And if there was an attack on Taiwan, the U.S. would have to come into it, and once she did, that would be the whole story. Without U.S. direct involvement Mainland China could take Taiwan any time."

"The internal character of the regime there is bad. They have no real elections, and the native Taiwanese aren't represented really. It's a myth to think Chiang is going to retake the Mainland or that the Mainland is poised to strike at Taiwan. It just isn't. Nor is Taiwan a stabilizing force in Asia."

"Taiwan's security depends on the U.S. Its security doesn't depend on its military or on how many pushups they do on Taiwan."

"I've been against these inflated aid levels to Taiwan for the last quarter-century."

"They've got an oversized military establishment there and an authoritarian government that represses the native Taiwanese. The whole problem is an unfinished element in the Chinese civil war. Both sides say Taiwan is part of China. The Mainland Chinese have very little capacity now to invade Taiwan."

"The F-4's for Taiwan were sheer idiocy!"

"We've spent a whale of a lot of money on the Chiang government, far more than we needed to. We've not even used them in Vietnam."

"Those F-4's are a waste of money, and that money could have financed all the National Institutes of Health last year. They've got a Mickey Mouse military over there, and if there was a war, our forces would be required all the same."

"Any oppressive regime should be opposed."

"The levels of our aid there are surely inflated. I'm for a two-China policy."

"We should reorient our aid toward democracies only, which Taiwan is not."

"Taiwan isn't a bulwark of strength. When are they ever going to use their miltiary?"

"The F-4's was a knee-jerk issue. A bunch of Passman's friends decided over at *Madame Chennault's* that they were going to push this thing through, even though no one in Defense or the administration had asked for it. The whole buildup of Chiang's military has been excessive.

QUESTION 6: RELATIONS WITH CUBA

"Some Members have stated that we ought to begin to move toward normalizing our relations with Cuba, perhaps by moving toward ending the trade embargo toward Cuba. How do you feel about that?"

For Continuing the Embargo

"Cuba is a symbol and a sore spot in the American mind. It would be very much generally opposed by Members of Congress and certainly would be opposed by me. It's not appetizing at all."

"I'm worried about Cuba as a base for Soviet arms."

"We should strengthen the boycott of Cuba and intensify our effort to dispose of Castro."

"I'm against it. My sympathies are in the other direction. We should use economic pressures against them."

"Not unless the Cuban people go back to democracy and not until they stop exporting revolution all over Latin America."

"Only if there would be a *quid pro quo*. It would be good to decrease tensions *if* in return the Cubans recognize debts to U.S. industry because of previous expropriation and other debts. And they must cease and desist from exporting revolution though that is way down now, because Castro is broke. It's really a government by crony there. I feel sorry for the Cuban people. They were better off under the old dictator."

"First they'd have to stop their substantial subversion in Latin America."

"I'm unqualifiedly opposed."

"No! Why rescue Castro, when he's in economic trouble."

"No, we'd lose credibility."

"We shouldn't make it any easier for Castro."

"Castro's a ——— !"

"I'm against any change."

"I can't understand why. Cuba is a totally repressive society."

"No, under present conditions. A lot of the troubles of the U.S. flow from Cuba. These people are still dangerous."

"It's unlikely to happen. There's little to be gained for the U.S. Moves toward China are more important. Cuba is weak and any threat from her is down the road."

"No, not until Cuba is liberated and the Monroe Doctrine is back in effect."

"There's no reason to do that. The Castro regime is harsh in its attitude toward the U.S. and it's exporting revolution and subversion. There's no reason to soften our attitude. And he cooperates with hijackers."

"That's stupid. They're subverting Latin America."

"I doubt that there is any feasible way to improve relations."

"No, no unilateral change. They ought to be less hostile and their connection with Russia and their external policies all rule it out."

"I'm against it. I'm against anything that helps them spread revolution."

"We've had no offers from Castro. I don't see any willingness on his part. We've been trying to point out to other Latin American countries the dangers of Castro. He'd have to comply with the Hickenlooper Amendment."

Middle Ground—Not Ascertainable

"I favor expanding trade with Communist countries. It could be explored but depends on both sides making concessions." ["What concessions?"] "I really couldn't say."

For Ending the Embargo

"It's going to come. The quicker the less tensions there will be. The same for China."

"There is no advantage in the embargo. We trade with Russia. Why not Cuba."

"Yes, Cuban subversion in Latin America is not pronounced."

"American imperialism at its worst ran Cuba before Castro. It was held in bondage for years. There was human misery and squalor there, as you have never seen it. Our best interest and those of the Cuban people is to negotiate for peace." [Here respondent tells a long story of American absentee owners whom he knew and the massive extent of their holdings prior to Castro.]

"We use the threat of Castroite subversion as a straw man so as not to face deep long-lasting conditions which give rise to revolution and which are in part our responsibility and due to our neglect. It's so convenient to blame all evils on massive Communist conspiracies, while we tolerate and support regimes that fail their own peoples."

"If you trade together you don't war together. Cuba's not a threat. It's isolated. I favor a slow move toward a détente."

"I'd end the embargo. It's helpful to Castro to keep up a wall. I don't know if Castro is exporting revolution or not."

"The quicker we trade with everybody the better."

"I'd be willing to see that. Castro is here to stay, and we should normalize our relations with Cuba. We should have some limited trade as a good way to test the wind. There is real merit in that kind of policy."

"I'm for normalizing relations. I'm against the whole preoccupation with anticommunism. I don't know what ought to be the first steps—trade or what—but I see no reason to have enmity toward Cuba."

"The embargo just doesn't work."

"Yes!"

"Certainly."

"Yes. Increased trade would lead to increased influence in Cuba, so, yes, I favor such moves."

"I favor ending the embargo. I think you make friends and eliminate enemies by trading with each other."

"The Cuban takeover didn't hurt our security."

"I favored resumption of normal relations for some time. Increased contacts would encourage better policies on all sides and wean Cuba from the Soviet Union."

"It wouldn't bother me, but it wouldn't be any cure-all. We should accept the facts of life that Cuba exists, just as we should with China. Yes, I favor such moves. We should reach out to Cuba, just as we should to China. I don't see any reason for continuing the embargo. But I'm not eager to see Castro proselytizing all around."

"Yes, we ought to ease up, normalize, but Cubans ought to adopt a less Maoist attitude. The Latin American states seem to want a détente and trade. I'd like to see a discontinuing or a slackening off of his efforts to subvert other Latin countries, but Castro's efforts in Latin America aren't very important. They have much greater problems."

QUESTION 7: THE RHODESIAN EMBARGO

"Some Members have urged, for quite different reasons, that we move to end the trade embargo toward Rhodesia. They mention the price of chromium and our need for it, while others, opposing such a move, mention our commitment to uphold the U.N. sanctions and race relations within Rhodesia. Do you feel we ought to continue or end our embargo toward Rhodesia?"

For Ending the Embargo

"Sanctions are equal to meddling in the internal affairs of another country. What we want there is beside the point. I am against the use of sanctions. Rhodesia is not any worse than other African countries where black is against black. Where do you draw the line?"

"I've been a leader of the move to end that embargo. I've got sixty signatures of Members for a letter to the prime minister of Great Britain calling for an end to it. It's a terrific economic loss to us."

"It's unwise. I'd go completely on pragmatic self-interest."

"I am against it."

"It's in our own interest to end it. We need the chrome. I'm not particularly exercised about internal Rhodesian matters."

"I'm from a steel town. We need the chrome."

"We should end it. It makes no sense at all to try to inflict a form of government or a conscience on them. The big question is communism. They're not trying to put us down. The Communists are. We don't have sanctions against the Soviet Union. Why should we have them against Rhodesia?"

"I'd like to see better relations and increased trade with Rhodesia."

"We shouldn't have endorsed the embargo in the first place. They have a right to independence despite claims about racism."

"Sanctions were a mistake from the start. They are our friends: They have a stable government. I'd hope they'd be more representative, but their downfall would lead to chaos."

"I'm against the embargo. It's none of our business irrespective of our sympathies."

"We should end it for our national interest. Though it's a racist regime, we do business with Communist regimes. We should use influence to work for more enlightened policies."

"It's a hardship on the U.S. We buy our chrome form the Soviets who get it from Rhodesia anyway and then sell it to us at much higher prices while keeping the better grades for themselves. That doesn't make any sense at all. And then we're dependent on the Soviets for our chrome which is vital for steel production."

• "It's not our business to tell other countries to reform internally. The embargo doesn't accomplish anything. I have steel in my district. I feel the same way about Spain and Portugal."

Middle Ground

"Britain supports us in Vietnam. I think we have to continue supporting Britain in the embargo of Rhodesia." ["What if British policy changed?"] "I don't know what I would favor."

"The boycott hasn't been very effective. I don't know."

"What's immoral and what isn't? I don't know."

"We can't ignore regimes that aren't compatible with our values. I don't know."

For Continuing the Embargo

"Many specious arguments are heard. There are other chrome sources like Yugoslavia, that are now unused."

"I don't give a ——— about the price of chromium. We should be consistent with the U.N. Freedom and dignity are turned 180° around in Rhodesia, and it's just no good."

"I think we should avoid antagonizing black Africa. The chrome price is less important."

"I support the U.N. position."

"I'm for it, the chromium notwithstanding."

"Someone should stand up against them. I'm for continuing it."

"Rhodesian embargo is partly a sop to U.S. blacks and partly connected to our relations with other black African countries. It's small enough to be moral about. You can be moral, when you can afford to be moral."

"It's a repressive racist regime. I wouldn't end it. And there are blacks in my district who would want me to favor continuing it."

"We should strengthen the sanctions."

"The U.S. has to maintain a moral position. We have to continue it."

"It would be a great mistake to end it. We should frown on the regime there. There's been too little concern with Africa up to now. There's a basic humanitarian point of view at stake here."

"The Nixon administration has been doing a better job in Africa than was done before. I would favor continuing it, but I was glad of the U.S. veto of the U.N. resolution to demand Britain to use arms against Rhodesia."

"I feel strongly for the policy of sanctions. We should strengthen it for the rest of white Africa even though it probably won't lead to the fall of the Smith government. I'm not impressed by the argument that it hurts blacks the most. I talked with a black Rhodesian farmer in London who was all for the sanctions."

"I have mixed emotions. There is the question of human rights, but we can't remake the world. Yet the U.N. backs it, so I favor continuing the embargo. The chrome makes no difference. It's a question of U.S. foreign policy, not the interests of individual companies."

"We should strengthen the U.N. by abiding by its rules. Black Africa would be very unhappy if we didn't. And, on the merits, that's a real bad government. It makes likely that when and if a big war breaks out there that we'll end up on the wrong side, the white side."

"We shouldn't be too pushy about exporting democracy, yet it's one way mankind has to take a stand against racial superiority. The price of chrome doesn't impress me a lot. It's a way to a moral role for the U.S."

"We should be firm. Democracy is *the* consideration."

QUESTION 8: U.S. ARMS SPENDING

"There has been controversy in Congress about a number of different weapon systems—ABM and MIRV deployment, the B-1 bomber program, the goal of fifteen modernized aircraft carriers, and a number of others. Have you favored ABM deployment? How about MIRV deployment? Do you favor developing the B-1 bomber? How do you feel about the carrier program? Are there any other weapons systems with which you have some quarrel?"

For All Weapons Systems; No Quarrel with Any; for Strong National Defense

"I'm for a strong national defense."

"I can't think of any weapons systems I've opposed."

"ABM and/or MIRV deployment are necessary as a bargaining chip for SALT."

". . . leave the science of the thing to those who know."

"I follow the administration and the Joint Chiefs of Staff on this."

"I follow the Pentagon. I don't want to jeopardize the safety of this country."

"I defer to my friends on the Armed Services Committee."

"I respect the military. The voters wouldn't get the funds cut anyway."

"I'd rather do too much than too little."

"I believe we must lead from strength. No, I have no quarrel with any particular weapons system."

*Favor Cuts in Only One of Those Weapons Systems Mentioned**

*Favor Cutting Some and Leaving Others Intact—Not Ascertainable**

". . . must be some limits on spending."

*Favor Cuts in All But One of Those Mentioned**

Against All Weapons Systems Mentioned and/or for Cutting Military Budgets Heavily

"I'm for cutting the military budget significantly." [Respondent opposes all weapons systems mentioned.] "ABM, a tragic waste of money . . . unworkable . . . not a bargaining chip in SALT. . . . ABM is junk at jewelers' prices . . . MIRV . . . dangerously destabilizing."

"Carrier is obsolete. One missile can take it out."

"The B-1 bomber is unnecessary given the Polaris force."

"Our priorities are way out of line."

"I voted against the last few procurement bills. We can cut back significantly."

"Fifty percent of the military budget is waste."

"I'm quite willing to see military hardware cuts that are necessary for people-oriented programs."

"We have a general tendency toward fictitious races with the Soviets. We buy capabilities we don't use and don't need at the expense of domestic needs."

QUESTION 9: EXPROPRIATION

"There has been controversy in Congress about what posture the United States government should take toward regimes that expropriate the property of U.S. private investors. Clearly,

*In these categories responses were unexceptional.

there are different kinds of cases and situations, calling perhaps, for different kinds of responses—cases where there is no compensation, some inadequate compensation, full compensation; cases where expropriation takes place only in certain sectors of the economy, as with extractive industries, and so forth. Members of Congress have described to me two rough philosophies that seem to prevail among the Members. The first philosophy leans toward a relatively *harsh* response, coming down hard by imposing trade and aid sanctions with an eye out to discouraging this kind of thing wherever possible. The second philosophy is described as a tendency toward *leniency* in responding to expropriation, a willingness to take into account the development needs of the country, the profit record of the company, the manner in which the company entered the country, and so forth.

First, do you think this characterization of the two prevailing philosophies *does* describe a basic split among the Members, and second, would you describe yourself as leaning toward one or the other of these philosophies?"

Harsh

"I'm for the tough line. I'd go after them and very tenaciously to get fair treatment for our companies. Even if there were a change of regimes, I'd still hold the new regime responsible contractually."

"I'd sever economic relations until there was an agreement on all future economic relations. If there was a violation of existing agreements, I'd take economic action. I'd be harsh about it."

"We should be tough, though you must look at it case by case. I'd tend to be for harsh retaliation."

"I'd move in tough."

"I do think Congress can be described by those two philosophies. I lean to the harsher side, though sensibly. They've got to be civilized, too, and live up to controls. I'm for justice for our own people; I'm not for selling out our own people."

"I'm for the harsh view. I'd break relations and use trade sanctions: Crimes must be met with punishment."

"We should let it be known in no uncertain terms that we insist on adequate compensation. If none, then, yes, I'd use trade and aid sanctions."

"I've been instrumental in seeing that Venezuela gets no more arms. I believe you carry a big stick and fight their methods using a big stick."

"I wish we'd use much stronger trade and aid sanctions then we do now. I'm dissatisfied with our diplomats. They're almost apologetic. The greed of the local people must be answered."

"You can go too far in turning the other cheek as the government does now. We ought to use sanctions the same as you would domestically."

"We should use the fullest measures possible against criminal action."

"While I think capitalists have to take risks, I'd use trade and aid sanctions to the fullest extent."

"I think the Hickenlooper Amendment is right. It's a crowbar."

"I'm not for the Hickenlooper approach. It's too inflexible, but the State Department hasn't been as tough as it should be."

"I'm a strong supporter of the Hickenlooper Amendment, but it should have an escape clause."

"I'd cut off all aid. I wouldn't use trade sanctions. It wouldn't accomplish anything."

"We should require compensation for the continuation of aid."

"I lean toward jumping in hard, but we should take it on a case-by-case basis."

Middle Ground—Not Ascertainable

"To press a government too hard leads to anti-Americanism, but there are other factors, so you must look at each case."

"We have been very fortunate, and we have an insurance program which we've rarely used. Our posture now is correct. Most countries have great incentives to get along with the United States economically. They need to develop and need our markets. We need not be unduly nationalistic."

"I'm not afraid to retaliate in some manner, but we should know if the companies had been fair or deceptive, or if they had made spectacular profits."

"There are some cases where you might be less stringent."

"It depends on how effective you can be. It can be counterproductive. You don't want to give people political ammunition. I oppose the rigidity of the Hickenlooper Amendment. I think private market sanctions work sufficiently well."

"There are valid reasons why nations want to take back what belongs to them, but there is a danger of a domino effect, so we should make it difficult. So I'm for a tough approach. Yet they are not going to be willing to be bled dry."

"I'm against the Hickenlooper approach. It's too inflexible, but beyond that, it depends on many things."

"We've lacked an overarching economic policy. I'd be pragmatic about this sort of thing. The administration has handled Peru well."

"Maybe the companies took too much. I'd have clobbered the Peruvians for attacking our fishing vessels, though."

"The State Department and Commerce must decide in each instance. Congress can't decide. Perhaps investors have done badly by the people, or perhaps the people are merely vengeful toward the U.S."

Lenient

"I'm instinctively against cutting off aid and trade. Perhaps they don't want U.S. private investment, which leads me to question their interest in development. But so often we see Communist subversion in this, when it's really social justice that they want."

"I'd describe myself as closer to the lenient view. But I'd except the 200-mile limit imposed by Peru; that's going too far."

"The companies have to take their own chances."

"I'd prefer the use of diplomatic channels. Expropriating countries have an interest in being friendly with the U.S. and if not, sanctions won't accomplish much."

"I think we have to be magnanimous. Governments frequently are militant in order to stave off far *more* anti-American governments. Many countries traditionally have been exploited. There's something wrong with a government that doesn't want to get some of the action for its own people."

"We should try to get compensation. But these countries are inevitably going to take these over: Natural resources are *national* resources. On something like manufacturing plants I think they ought to pay. But I'm against the rigidity of the Hickenlooper Amendment. There should be international machinery to deal with this rather than foreign policy instruments."

"The Hickenlooper Amendment is counterproductive. I think we have to remember that we are dealing with proud peoples."

"I'd want to know was the advantage or the concession of the company obtained at too low a price, and how much had they taken out. It depends on the case."

"We should be as understanding as possible. We should avoid disruption that might hurt ourselves."

"Sanctions should be used with great restraint. They see these things as outside interference with domestic matters involving a loss of face."

"We shouldn't interfere in sovereign countries. U.S. government guarantees to U.S. investors is the main avenue to use."

"We should resort to the World Court. We should remember the cruelty that American industry has displayed, the savagery in the way it's worked its employees, like Coca Cola's treatment of migrant workers in Florida. The United Fruit Kingdom in Guatemala was like that. They should pay the people damages."

"We should be lenient. Sanctions only hurt the U.S. reputation in the world. We give substance to the model of the U.S. as an exploiting nation."

"We should be lenient, especially where an unrepresentative government is overthrown by a representative one that won't accept the former's commitments. But we should discourage such things as expropriation of World Bank loans."

"We've gutted and exploited those countries, taken everything out and put nothing back in. The countries are justified. You just can't have foreign interests having more power than the governments of some of those nations."

"Harsh moves might upset a government that would much more reflect the desires of the people of that country."

"We have a small part of the world population and much of the world wealth. We shouldn't be extracting as much as we can get, and giving back as little as possible. I can understand their frustration with U.S. dominance of their industry, when their people are starving."

"We should promote investment that is beneficial to both the investor and the country. If you invoke sanctions, who do you hurt? The leaders or the people you're trying to help? They should be invoked carefully, if at all. You have to consider that sometimes there's been rape of the host countries by the companies."

QUESTION 10: MILITARY AND ECONOMIC AID: GOALS AND LEVELS

"How do you feel about our military aid programs generally? Are they about right? Are they too high? Or should they be increased in any particular direction or areas?" *Follow-up questions*: "Are there any factors which you feel should lead the United States to cut or to increase its military aid?" "How about our economic aid programs, particularly development aid programs; are they too high, too low or about right?" "Is there anything in particular we should be doing more or less of?"

Support Neither Military nor Economic Aid Except at Vastly Reduced Levels

"Economic aid is completely ineffective and should be cut way back. I'm against military aid to all of Latin America. They can't use it. I'm against aid to Brazil. Our concern should be Western Europe."

"I'd cut it all out—all of it."

Support Military Aid at Roughly Present Levels and Economic Aid at Present or Lower Levels

"I'm not for outright contributions. I'd cut them all off. The World Bank gives easy credit when victims of a flood in my district can't even get a loan to rebuild their homes. Too much goes to bureaucrats and the military. I'd rather see it used at home. [But military aid to Greece is the lesser of two evils. I have no quarrel with aid to Brazil; they're better off now. I voted for the F-4's for Taiwan.]"

"Any left-leaning government, any revolutionary government, is going to be more receptive to Russian and Chinese domination of its military affairs to the point where they can be a military threat to the U.S. as a base or a source of revolutionaries as Cuba is. As far as economic aid is concerned, it's not well spent. They despise us anyway. I vote against it because of the waste and lack of policy. It should lead to the expansion of U.S. markets or some *quid pro quo*."

"Domestic needs come first, but we have obligations to other countries that we must fulfill lest our competitors move in. I wouldn't cut military aid. I wouldn't increase economic aid."

"Military aid is an instrument of national policy. It's not a 'do-good' instrument. Communists are everywhere ready to step in. I don't buy economic aid for 'do-good' purposes."

"We haven't been doing enough with military aid in countries threatened with internal or extreme threats of communism. We should have given more to Batista. I've been pushing for development of the STOL aircraft for jungle landings. And if they say they don't want them, we ought to say take 'em or else. We have been decreasing the economic aid, and we've reached bottom. A.I.D. does good in many areas, like malnutrition, but I wouldn't increase it."

"I'm not a strong advocate of development aid. We've spent $187 billion already. We can't get the results in the underdeveloped countries that we did in Europe. They haven't even been able to absorb what we've given them. It goes into the hands of a few, and we've won no friends with it. Military aid . . ." [mixed response; for aid to Taiwan and Brazil, but not to Greece; extreme anticommunism].

"If the Vietnam War ended, I *would* like to see an increase in economic aid. It leads to increased stability in these countries, and it's preferable to putting troops over there, *but* it should be *conditional* on other countries doing more. On military aid, given the commitment of Mainland China to militant world revolution and Cuba's efforts in trying to create revolution in this hemisphere, I support it."

"Stability to avoid revolution requires, unfortunately, military aid. Our development aid effort should be decreased. There is a lot of it wasted, and others must do more, in Asia, for instance."

"Atheistic aggressive communism is out for world domination, which requires us to defend freedom around the world and promote stability. I think foreign economic aid is a giveaway, and I'd cut it all the way back, despite the bleeding-heart liberals and idealists."

"I'm for military aid to strengthen the free world. If freedom is defeated anywhere, where is it to stop, Hawaii? Where do we draw the line? Development aid—I'd end it! It's overextended. There's too much support for governments and too little for people."

"As for economic aid, I don't favor helping people, who aren't helping me. A *quid pro quo* should be necessary, and there hasn't been much of that in a long, long time. Our military aid is about right."

"I oppose economic aid. I'm for cutting across the board. Let Japan and the others do more. Military aid lets us use mercenaries, instead of our boys. Dictatorships are natural to those people, so that shouldn't hold us back."

"If we don't supply military aid, they'll only turn to someone else. I'd cut back the economic aid a lot, which is why I voted against the foreign aid bill."

"I can't think of any cuts or increases I'd make in military aid. In economic aid, why, they're breaking the bank. The velocity of government is destroying us with giveaway socialism. You can't save people who won't save themselves."

"I think our military aid programs are very worthwhile and present levels are OK. I question the accomplishments of economic aid. I don't see a dime's worth of value in it. Loans should be hard loans on a business basis, not handouts."

"Our military aid has already been reduced wisely. I don't see our economic aid as sufficiently effective. Even if improved, I think Christian acts should be left to private giving."

"I don't know. I follow the administration on this sort of thing. I see a lot of waste in the economic assistance programs but 40 percent of my district is for foreign aid."

Support Economic Aid at Present Levels and Decrease Military Aid

"Ideally we ought to spend more on economic aid, but our domestic needs at home don't allow that. Direct economic aid has had a low payoff, so I'd like to see a larger portion of it go to multilateral agencies. Our military aid levels are too high overall. [Taiwan's is too high. We should get out of Korea. Continuing aid and advisers to South Vietnam is OK. We probably should cut aid to Greece.]"

Support Both Increased Economic Aid, and at Least Current Levels of Military Aid

[No identifiable reaction to military aid], "but I'm for increasing economic aid, *if* we are phasing out Vietnam. I'm not for the 1 percent goal. Domestic needs and foreign aid are competitive."

"I'm a former A.I.D. consultant. I think the 1 percent goal is a feasible target, though we should be more selective. We're beginning to recognize the limitations of military aid, but I really couldn't say where we could make cuts."

"I'm for increasing development aid, especially technical assistance. The 1 percent goal is reasonable. In military aid—you can't talk about it across the board. I'd be for cuts in Europe, if the European contribution increased."

"Military aid is too much *relative* to economic aid. I favor the 1 percent goal! But we should insist on land and tax reform and increased participation. But military governments can best promote development in some cases where there is a need for stability. [I would continue aid to Brazil because I don't think we should meddle in the internal affairs of strong anti-Communist countries.] I'd favor an increase in the proportion going to multilateral agencies."

"We should gradually increase economic aid. The LDCs can absorb much more aid. Military aid is about right now."

"Yes, absolutely, I'd favor increasing our development effort. Economic development is not necessarily the key to development; we have to look at the 80 percent of the people left out of the economy. I'd like to see an increase in the proportion going to multilateral agencies with a residue of bilateral aid. We should depoliticize the U.S. relationship as quickly as possible. We've asked the World Bank and the Inter-American Development Bank, 'How feasible is it for you to go into sector lending and straight grant programs?' As for military aid, it doesn't concern me one bit. We've reduced the number of our people in the military missions in Latin America by 50 percent. It's very low now."

"The levels and kinds of military aid we are at now are OK. I think the danger has been vastly exaggerated. An increase in development aid is well within our means. We should do more. We should get rid of Passman. He's demogogic. We could easily afford the 1 percent goal. Our aid appropriation process is essentially unreasoning."

"We're doing too little, and we're learning to do a better job in economic development. The rich nations have a responsibility to the poor nations. If the gap grows, it will lead to an unstable world. Yes, I favor the 1 percent goal, but I'm not enamored of the multilateral agencies: The Inter-American Development Bank is weak, and the Asian Development Bank is empire building; and I don't like the new McNamara soft-loan direction at the World Bank. We should stick to conservative banking principles and not try to be social workers. Military aid should follow the Nixon Doctrine of giving military aid, so as to lead to a lower profile for the U.S. abroad."

Support Increase in Economic Development Aid and Decrease in Military Aid

"I'd at least double it, though I think the 1 percent of the GNP goal is too high. I favor increasing the proportion going to multilateral agencies. I favor reducing military aid across the board. I oppose aid for internal security purposes except to counter Soviet aid, even if a leftist or Communist takeover were threatened."

"Our development aid is too low and should be increased substantially. The 1 percent goal is not appropriate. We must narrow the gap between the rich and poor nations despite the fact that we're creating future competitors. We should be cutting back our military aid."

"Economic aid has been cut back far too much. I'm not sure about the 1 percent goal, but we should do more and could do more by cutting military aid and using it for economic aid."

"I think we should give economic humanitarian and development aid *only*. Our military aid should be to democracies *only*! We shouldn't prop up autocracy or dictators."

"We spend too much on military aid and not enough on economic aid."

"Military aid is all that remains of foreign aid. We give India and Pakistan weapons, and they use them against each other. Our cuts of economic assistance is something which doesn't make me proud to be a member of this body. Chairman Passman does a great disservice. I support the 1 percent goal. It's little enough."

"I'm a Barbara Ward man. I'd greatly increase our development effort, especially through multilateral channels. Our military aid levels are way too high."

"I'd be for military aid to any democratic country with a bonafide threat to its national security—OK. But that's where I'd stop, and there aren't many countries today that fit that description. We have a long-term interest in the Third World, particularly countries where there is a good relationship between the people and the governments, that is, democratic in some functional form. These can provide the best underpinnings for an international community that could work; for some international scheme of peace. That's what our objective in the aid program should be. Sometimes, now, it's counterproductive. Our development aid effort should be at least double what it is. I support a 1 percent goal."

"Money alone isn't the answer, but I would like to see more money for development aid. Much of our foreign aid budget is Vietnam related. It should all be under the military budget, given its real nature. I support military aid for internal security in Latin America, but I favor a downward trend in it contrary to the Nixon Dictrine, which will increase it to make up for reducing other U.S. commitments. So often we assume subversion is communism when it really is an effort to reach social justice. I'm concerned that the U.S. has an image of being against change and social justice. We ought to provide more vigorous development aid to developing countries. Our anti-Communist instinct has been overdone."

"Military aid has maintained the stability of repressive right-wing government which I'd select out of the program. My district responded to a questionnaire on foreign aid, 87 percent saying less should be spent, but I've supported it. We should look on it in humanistic rather than purely political terms. We're not Number One among the world's aid-giving countries. I favor the 1 percent goal."

QUESTION 11: THREATS OF COMMUNISM

"When he first took office, President Kennedy, responding to a speech by Khrushchev about wars of national liberation, stated that the underdeveloped world had become a great battleground between East and West. He stated that outcomes there, whether or not these were Communist takeovers, could well determine the balance of power between East and West over the long run.

How do you feel about President Kennedy's vision of the place of the underdeveloped world in world politics? Is it essentially correct today, or do you think it does not apply?" *Follow-up questions*: "How do you view Soviet expansionist motives today? How about the Chinese; should we expect them to be seeking opportunities to expand?"

Large Threat

"There's been no change in Communist ambitions. They still are using subversion, and they still show limitless zeal in seeking world domination, though aggression is less frequent. It's still an ideological struggle."

"I believe in the domino theory. They use a country they take over for spreading subversion."

"I don't think there will be any reduction of tensions or any end to the cold war. I think President Kennedy's view is still essentially true. They're still trying to rule the world. It's still a question of whose view of man will predominate."

"They're still nibbling away. They're monolithic, disciplined, and have a long-term strategy, and they're ready to move in anywhere. They are constantly probing for Western weaknesses."

"I think there's the danger of the growth of economic blocs, if they take over in very many places and that would exclude the West from markets and raw materials as well as strategic sea and air routes."

"A lot of countries are dangerously unstable, and they will change their politics in the direction of the winner. [XYZ countries] couldn't survive without U.S. help."

"Mainland China has a deep commitment to militant world revolution and unlimited expansion. Why should it stop if it doesn't have to?"

"The Communist philosophy is fundamentally expansionist. The Communists will keep the pressure on all over the world. They present a ceaseless challenge, and they're seldom content to stop."

"The underdeveloped countries want a neutralist course, but they will accommodate to strength and aggression and the Communists move in to fill any vacuum."

"It's necessary for us to continue to deter aggression and if we don't, it's going to lead to world war."

"President Kennedy was right. I think they'll go on as far as they can."

Middle Ground—Not Ascertainable

"There is some significant threat of expansion, if they got a base for missiles in the Western Hemisphere, for example, and they seem to be seeking to expand in the Middle East. But I don't think that they are active in underdeveloped countries generally."

"I don't know if the domino theory is true or not."

"Not many countries are subverted, but a few are massively."

"There may be some economic alignments and competition, but I don't think there will be takeovers except in a few places."

"Subversion is being tried but trade is the answer."

"I don't know."

Little or No Threat

"I think that China [Russia, Cuba] is more internally preoccupied."

"The intensity of the split between China and Russia will continue to absorb them."

"The expansion of the Soviet philosophy depends on the strength of the democracies in meeting the needs of people."

"Both the Soviet Union and Communist China have become status quo powers. National communism is on the upswing. Communism isn't a monolith anymore. There are more tendencies to Tito-like independence. There is a momentum toward a breakdown of barriers, peaceful coexistence and East-West trade."

"I'm against the whole preoccupation of the U.S. with anticommunism. There are no irreversible alignments. President Kennedy was wrong. The less developed countries aren't concerned with communism or democracy but with their own needs. Losing a few countries to communism wouldn't be a catastrophe."

"The dominoes themselves don't perceive any threat. The Third World would be more of a liability than an asset in the balance of power. Egypt and Cuba are a drain on the Soviet budget. If Brazil went Communist, it wouldn't necessarily affect U.S. security; it would depend on if it spread."

"Territorial expansion of the Soviet Union is doubtful. Economic expansion is more important. Expansion is not inherent to communism. The takeover in Cuba didn't affect our security."

"The Soviet Union isn't as expansionist as it was. Communism isn't irreversible. The LDCs play off the superpowers against each other. We don't need them, and they do need us. The kind of government they have doesn't matter. We fail to see how Russia sees the world. Why should we deny or expect to be able to deny the Soviets' influence in the Mediterranean? It's not an American lake. Wars of national liberation aren't an extension of the cold war. Third World movements and ideologies are not an extension of Soviet or Chinese power. It's a mistake to think that revolutions can be externally generated. The external role in revolutions is minimal. Third World countries are so damn poor it doesn't matter whose side they're on. The Soviet Union is basically defensive in posture. Other problems than communism are more important in international politics: the gap between rich and poor nations, racial confrontation in Africa, international economic problems, economic competition from Japan and Germany."

"I see the threat from communism as being less than other people do. Anticommunism is often used as a cover-up for oligarchy and injustice. It's of little importance if they pick up a country or two, and even if a country goes Communist, it doesn't mean it's going to be dominated by Russia or China or that it will affect the balance of power. The LDCs are a common problem for the U.S. and the Soviets, not a source of competition. We can't keep propping up unpopular governments. Expansion leads to being overextended."

"The Soviets have tried to get takeovers in forty-three countries since World War II, and only five have succeeded. 'Alignment' is largely meaningless in a missile age. Revolutions don't necessarily lead to Communist takeovers."

"The dangers of Communist takeovers are minimal, if there is good government. And if there isn't good government, what we could do to avert a takeover would be largely useless. Nationalism is so strong we are just a marginal influence in any case."

"One of our mistakes is backing a regime which is friendly to us, but isn't accepted by its people, thus leading to the very instability we're trying to prevent."

SELECTED BIBLIOGRAPHY

The bibliography is divided into the following sections:

(1) Congress and the Presidency

(2) American Politics

(3) Foreign Policy

(4) Economic Policy

(5) Policy Analysis

(6) Methodology and Analytic Philosophy

(7) Ideology

(8) Theory and Comparative Politics

Except for exceptional instances, no items are cited here from congressional documents, the *Congressional Quarterly Weekly Report*, the *National Journal*, or daily newspapers.

1. CONGRESS AND THE PRESIDENCY

Asher, Herbert B. "The Learning of Legislative Norms." *American Political Science Review* 67 (June 1973):503.

Bach, Stanley. "Potential Mechanisms for Integrated and Comprehensive Policy Making by the House of Representatives." Unpublished manuscript, 10 August 1976.

Bardach, Eugene. "The Implementation Game: What Happens After a Bill Becomes a Law." Cambridge, Mass.: MIT Press, 1977.

Barnett, Marguerite Ross. "The Congressional Black Caucus." In *Congress Against the President*, edited by Harvey C. Mansfield, Sr. New York: Praeger, 1975, pp. 34-50.

Barone, Michael, Grant Ujifusa, and Douglas Matthews. *The Almanac of American Politics 1976: The Senators, the Representatives, the Governors— Their Records, States and Districts.* New York: E. P. Dutton, 1976. See also 1977 and 1978 editions.

Beckman, Norman. "Congressional Information Processes for Coordinating National Policies." Library of Congress, Congressional Research Service. Revised by Arthur G. Stevens, 26 March 1975.

______. "Use of a Staff Agency by the Congress: The Congressional Research Service." *The Bureaucrat*, vol. 3, no. 4 (January 1975):401-415.

Beer, Samuel H. "The Adoption of General Revenue Sharing: A Case Study in Public Sector Politics." *Public Policy*, vol. 24, no. 2 (Spring 1976): 127-196.

Belknap, George M. "Scaling Legislative Behavior." In *Legislative Behavior: A Reader in Theory and Research*, edited by John C. Wahlke and Eulau Heinz. Glencoe, Ill.: Free Press, 1959.

Bezold, Clement. "Voting on the House Floor: Information Seeking and Congressional Decision-Making." Center for Governmental Responsibility, University of Florida, May 1974.

Bibby, John F., and Roger H. Davidson. *On Capitol Hill: Studies in the Legislative Process*, 2d ed. Hinsdale, Ill.: Dryden Press, 1972.

Blanchard, Robert O. "A Profile of Congressional Correspondents." *Capitol Studies* (Fall 1975): 53-68.

______, ed. *Congress and the News Media*. New York: Hastings House, 1974.

Bolling, Richard. "Committees in the House." *Annals of the American Academy of Political and Social Science* 411 (January 1974): 1-14.

______. *House Out of Order*. New York: E. P. Dutton, 1965.

______. *Power in the House*. New York: E. P. Dutton, 1968.

Born, Richard. "Cue-Taking Within State Party Delegations in the U.S. House of Representatives." *Journal of Politics*, vol. 38, no. 1 (February 1976): 71-94.

Bowler, M. Kenneth. "The New Committee on Ways and Means: Policy Implications of Recent Changes in the House Committee." Paper prepared for the annual meeting of the American Political Science Association, Chicago, September 2-5, 1976.

Brady, David W., and Naomi B. Lynn. "Switched-Seat Congressional Districts: Their Effect on Party Voting and Public Policy." *American Journal of Political Science* 42 (August 1973): 528-543.

Brezina, Dennis W., and Allen Overmyer. *Congress in Action: The Environmental Education Act*. New York: Free Press, 1974.

Brown, Richard E. *The GAO: Untapped Source of Congressional Power.* Knoxville: University of Tennessee Press, 1970.

Bullock, Charles S. "Committee Transfers in the United States House of Representatives." *Journal of Politics* 35 (February 1973): 85-117.

Burnham, Walter Dean. "Insulation and Responsiveness in Congressional Elections." *Political Science Quarterly* 90 (Fall 1975): 411-435.

Burns, James MacGregor. *Congress on Trial: The Legislative Process and the Administrative State*. New York: Harper & Brothers, 1949.

______. *The Deadlock of Democracy*. Englewood Cliffs, N.J.: Prentice Hall, 1963.

______. *Edward Kennedy and the Camelot Legacy*. New York: Norton, 1976.

Cherryholmes, Cleo, and Michael Shapiro. *Representatives and Roll-Calls.* Indianapolis: Bobbs-Merrill, 1969.

Clapp, Charles L. *The Congressman: His Work As He Sees It.* Garden City, N.Y.: Doubleday, 1963.

Clausen, Aage R. *How Congressmen Decide: A Policy Focus.* New York: St. Martin's Press, 1973.

______, and Richard B. Cheney. "A Comparative Analysis of Senator House Voting on Economic and Welfare Policy: 1953-1964." *ASPR* vol. 44, no. 1 (March 1970): 138-152.

______, and Carl E. Van Horn. "Policy Trends in Congress and Partisan Realignment." Paper prepared for the annual meeting of the American Political Science Association, Chicago, 29 August-2 September 1974.

Cleaveland, Frederic N., et al. *Congress and Urban Problems.* Washington, D.C.: Brookings Institution, 1969.

Clem, Alan L. "Variations in Voting Blocs Across Policy Fields: Pair Agreement Scores in the 1967 U.S. Senate." *Western Political Quarterly,* vol. 23 no. 3 (1970): 530-551.

Cooper, Ann. "Mumbling It Through." *The Washington Monthly,* vol. 7, no. 10 (December 1975).

Cooper, Joseph. "The Origins of the Standing Committees and the Development of the Modern House." Rice University Studies 56 (1970).

______. "Strengthening the Congress: An Organizational Analysis." *Harvard Journal on Legislation,* vol. 12, no. 3 (April 1975): 307-368.

Cover, Al, and David Mayhew. "Congressional Dynamics and the Decline in Competitive Congressional Elections." In *Congress Reconsidered,* edited by Lawrence C. Dodd and Bruce I. Oppenheimer. New York: Praeger, forthcoming.

Cronin, Thomas E. *The State of the Presidency.* Boston: Little, Brown, 1975.

Dale, Edwin L., Jr. "Can Congress at Last Control the Money Tree?" *New York Times* Magazine (22 August 1976), p. 10.

Davidson, Roger H. "Breaking Up Those 'Cozy Triangles': An Impossible Dream?" Paper prepared for the Symposium on Legislative Reform and Public Policy, University of Nebraska, March 11-12, 1976.

______. "Congress in the American Political System." In *Legislatures in Developmental Perspective,* edited by Allan Kornberg and Lloyd D. Musolf. Durham, N.C.: Duke University Press, 1970, pp. 129-178.

______. "Congressional Committees: The Toughest Customers." *Policy Analysis,* vol. 2, no. 2 (Spring 1976): 299-323.

______. "Representation and Congressional Committees." *Annals of the American Academy of Political and Social Science* 411 (January 1974): 48-62.

______. *The Role of the Congressman.* New York: Pegasus, 1969.

______, and Walter Oleszek. *Congress Against Itself.* Bloomington: University of Indiana Press, 1977.

Davis, James W., and Delbert Ringquist. *The President and Congress: Toward a New Power Balance.* Woodbury, N.Y.: Barron's Educational Series, 1975.

Deckard, Barbara. "Political Upheaval and Congressional Voting: The Effects of the 1960's on Voting Patterns in the House of Representatives." *The Journal of Politics,* vol. 38, no. 2 (May 1976): 326-345.

______, and John Stanley. "Party Decomposition and Region: The House of Representatives, 1945-70." *The Western Political Quarterly,* vol. 27, no. 2 (June 1974): 249-264.

Dodd, Lawrence C. "Congress and the Quest for Power." Paper prepared for the annual meeting of the American Political Science Association, Chicago, September 2-5, 1976.

______, and Bruce I. Oppenheimer, eds. *Congress Reconsidered.* New York: Praeger, 1977.

Drew, Elizabeth. "A Reporter at Large (The Energy Bazaar)." *The New Yorker* (21 July 1975).

______. *Washington Journal: The Events of 1973-1974.* New York: Vintage Books, 1976.

Eckhardt, Bob, and Charles L. Black, Jr. *The Tides of Power: Conversations on the American Constitution*. New Haven: Yale University Press, 1976.

Ehrenhalt, Alan. "The AFL-CIO: How Much Clout in Congress?" *Congressional Quarterly Weekly Report*, vol. 33, no. 29 (19 July 1975): 1531-1539.

______. "Can the Democratic Party Survive Victory?" *Congressional Quarterly Weekly Report* 34 (31 July 1976): 2038-2039.

Ellwood, John W., and James A. Thurber. "The New Congressional Budget Process: Its Causes, Consequences, and Possible Success." Paper prepared for the Symposium on Legislative Reform and Public Policy, University of Nebraska, March 11-12, 1976.

Erikson, Robert S. "Is There Such a Thing As a Safe Seat?" *Polity*, vol. 8, no. 4 (Summer 1976): 623-632.

Eulau, Heinz. "Decisional Structures in Small Legislative Bodies." In *Comparative Legislative Behavior: Frontiers of Research*, edited by Samuel C. Patterson and John C. Wahlke. New York: John Wiley & Sons, 1972, pp. 107-140.

______. Review of John E. Jackson, "Constituencies and Leaders in Congress: Their Effects on Senate Voting Behavior." In *American Journal of Sociology*, vol. 81, no. 4 (January 1976): 953-955.

Farris, Charles D. "A Scale Analysis of Ideological Factors in Congressional Voting." In *Legislative Behavior: A Reader in Theory and Research*, edited by John C. Wahlke and Heinz Eulau. Glencoe, Ill.: Free Press, 1959, pp. 399-413.

Fenno, Richard F. *The Power of the Purse: Appropriations Politics in Congress*. Boston: Little, Brown, 1966.

______. *Congressmen in Committees*. Boston: Little, Brown, 1973.

______. "If, as Ralph Nader Says, Congress Is 'the Broken Branch,' How Come We Love Our Congressmen So Much?" In *Congress in Change*, edited by Norman J. Ornstein. New York: Praeger, 1975, pp. 277-287.

Ferejohn, John A. *Pork Barrel Politics: Rivers and Harbors Legislation 1947-1968*. Stanford: Stanford University Press, 1974.

Fiorina, Morris P. *Congress: Keystone of the Washington Establishment*. New Haven: Yale University Press, 1977.

______. *Representatives, Roll Calls, and Constituencies*. Lexington, Mass.: D.C. Heath, 1974.

Fishel, Jeff. *Party and Opposition: Congressional Challengers in American Politics*. (New York: David McKay, 1973.

Fisher, Louis. "Budget Concepts and Terminology: The Appropriations Phase." Library of Congress, Congressional Research Service, Government and General Research Division, HJ2005US 74-210 GGR, 21 November 1974.

______. *Presidential Spending Power*. Princeton: Princeton University Press, 1975.

Fitzgerald, Martin J. "The Expanded Role of the General Accounting Office: In Support of a Strengthened Congress." *The Bureaucrat*, vol. 3, no. 4 (January 1975): 383-400.

Flinn, Thomas A., and Harold L. Wolman. "Constituency and Roll Call Voting: The Case of Southern Democratic Congressmen." *The Midwest Journal of Political Science*, vol. 10, no. 2 (May 1966): 192-199.

Fox, Harrison W., Jr., and Susan Webb Hammond. *Congressional Staffs*. New York: Free Press, 1978.

Freund, Ernst. *Standards of American Legislation*. Chicago: Phoenix Books, University of Chicago Press, 1965.

Froman, Lewis A. *The Congressional Process: Strategies, Rules, and Procedures*. Boston: Little, Brown, 1967.

Frye, Alton. *A Responsible Congress: The Politics of National Security*. Published for The Council on Foreign Relations. New York: McGraw-Hill, 1975.

Goss, Carol F. "House Committee Characteristics and Distributive Politics." Paper prepared for the annual meeting of the American Political Science Association, San Francisco, September 2-5, 1975.

______. "Military Committee Membership and Defense-Related Benefits in the House of Representatives." *Western Political Quarterly* 25 (1972): 215-233.

Groennings, Sven, and Jonathan P. Hawley, eds. *To Be a Congressman: The Promise and the Power*. Washington, D.C.: Acropolis Books, 1973.

Harris, Richard. *Decision*. New York: Ballantine Books, 1971.

Hinckley, Barbara. "Policy Content, Committee Membership, and Behavior." *American Journal of Political Science*, vol. 19, no. 3 (August 1975).

______. *Stability and Change in Congress*. New York: Harper & Row, 1971.

______. "'Stylized' Opposition in the U.S. House of Representatives: The Effects of Coalition Behavior." *Legislative Studies Quarterly*, vol. 2, no. 1 (February 1977).

Holtzman, Abraham. *Legislative Liaison*. Chicago: Rand McNally, 1970.

Huitt, Ralph K., "The Internal Distribution of Influence: The Senate." In *The Congress and America's Future*, edited by David B. Truman. Englewood Cliffs, N.J.: Prentice-Hall, 1973, pp. 91-117.

______, and Robert Peabody. *Congress: Two Decades of Analysis*. New York: Harper & Row, 1969.

Humphrey, Hubert H. *The Education of a Public Man: My Life and Politics*. Garden City, N.Y.: Doubleday, 1976.

Huntington, Samuel P. "Congressional Responses to the Twentieth Century." In *The Congress and America's Future*, 2nd ed., edited by David B. Truman. Englewood Cliffs, N.J.: Prentice-Hall, 1973, pp. 6-38.

Jackson, John E. *Constituencies and Leaders in Congress: Their Effects on Senate Voting Behavior*. Cambridge: Harvard University Press, 1974.

Jasper, Herbert N. "A Congressional Budget: Will It Work This Time?" *The Bureaucrat*, vol. 3, no. 4 (January 1975): 429-443.

Johannes, John R. "The President Proposes and Congress Disposes—But Not Always: Legislative Initiative on Capitol Hill." *Review of Politics* 36 (July 1974): 356-70.

Jones, Charles O. *Every Second Year: Congressional Behavior and the Two-Year Term*. Washington, D.C.: Brookings Institution, 1967.

______. "Why Congress Can't Do Policy Analysis (Or Words to That Effect)." *Policy Analysis*, vol. 2, no. 2 (Spring 1976): 251-264.

______, and Randall Ripley. *The Role of Political Parties in Congress*. Tucson: University of Arizona Press, 1966.

Kampelman, Max M. "Congress, The Media, and the President." In *Congress Against the President*, edited by Harvey C. Mansfield, Sr. New York: Praeger, 1975.

Kantor, Arnold. "Congress and the Defense Budget: 1960-70." *American Political Science Review*, vol. 66, no. 1 (March 1972): 129-143.

Karns, David A. "Legislative Context and Roll Call Analysis: Foreign Policy Voting Behavior in the Senate." Unpublished manuscript, Cornell University, November 1972.

Keefe, William J., and Morris S. Oqul. *The American Legislative Process: Congress and the States*, 4th ed. Englewood Cliffs, N.J.: Prentice-Hall, 1977.

Keith, Robert. "The Use of Unanimous Consent in the Senate." *Congressional Research Service*. Unpublished manuscript, Summer 1976.

Kernall, Samuel. "Is the Senate More Liberal Than the House?" *Journal of Politics*, vol. 35, no. 2 (May 1973).

Kesselman, Mark J. "Presidential Leadership in Congress on Foreign Policy." *Midwest Journal of Political Science*, vol. 5, no. 3 (August 1961): 284-289.

______. "Presidential Leadership in Congress on Foreign Policy: A Replication of a Hypothesis." *Midwest Journal of Political Science*, vol. 9, no. 4 (November 1965): 401-406.

King, Susan B., and Robert L. Peabody. "Control of Presidential Campaign Financing." In *Congress Against the President*, edited by Harvey C. Mansfield, Sr. New York: Praeger, 1975, pp. 180-195.

Kingdon, John W. *Congressmen's Voting Decisions*. New York: Harper & Row, 1973.

Kostroski, Warren L. "Party and Incumbency in Postwar Senate Elections." *American Political Science Review* 67 (September 1973): 838-854.

"Labor, Liberal Groups Score Election Wins." *Congressional Quarterly Weekly Report*, vol. 32, no. 45 (November 1974): 3077-3085.

Lehnen, Robert G. "Behavior on the Senate Floor: An Analysis of Debate in the U.S. Senate." *The Midwest Journal of Political Science*, vol. 11, no. 4 (November 1967): 505-521.

Lenchner, Paul. "Partisan Realignments and Congressional Behavior: Some Preliminary Snapshots." *American Politics Quarterly*, vol. 4, no. 2 (April 1976): 223-236.

Lutzker, Paul. "The Behavior of Congressmen in a Committee Setting: A Research Report." *Journal of Politics* 31 (February 1969): 140-66.

MacNeil, Neil. *Forge of Democracy*. New York: David McKay, 1963.

MacRae, Duncan. *Dimensions of Congressional Voting: A Statistical Study of the House of Representatives in the Eighty-First Congress.* (Berkeley: University of California Publications in Sociology and Social Institute, 1958).

______. *Issues and Parties in Legislative Voting: Methods of Statistical Analysis* (New York: Harper & Row, 1970).

Malbin, Michael J., and Michael A. Scully. "Our Unelected Representatives." *The Public Interest*, no. 47 (Spring 1977), pp. 16-48.

Manley, John. "The Conservative Coalition in Congress." *American Behavioral Scientist*, vol. 17, no. 2 (November/December 1973): 223-248.

______. *The Politics of Finance: The House Committee on Ways and Means.* Boston: Little, Brown, 1970.

Mansfield, Harvey C., Sr. "The Congress and Economic Policy." In *The Congress and America's Future*, edited by David B. Truman. Englewood Cliffs, N.J.: Prentice-Hall, pp. 141-178.

______. "The Dispersion of Authority in Congress." In *Congress Against the President*, edited by Harvey C. Mansfield, Sr. New York: Praeger, 1975, pp. 1-19.

Matthews, Donald R. *U.S. Senators and Their World.* Chapel Hill: University of North Carolina Press, 1960.

______, and James A. Stimson. *The Decision-Making Approach to the Study of Legislative Behavior: The Example of the U.S. House of Representatives.* Paper delivered at the annual meeting of the American Political Science Association, New York, September 2-6, 1969.

______. "Decision-Making by U.S. Representatives: A preliminary model" in S. Sidney Ulmer, *Political Decision-Making*. New York: Van Nostrand-Reinhold, 1970.

______. *Yeas and Nays: Normal Decision-Making in the U.S. House of Representatives.* New York: John Wiley & Sons, 1975.

Mayhew, David R. *Congress: The Electoral Connection*. New Haven: Yale University Press, 1974.

______. *Party Loyalty Among Congressmen: The Difference Between Democrats and Republicans, 1947-1962.* Cambridge: Harvard University Press, 1966.

Melsheimer, John T. "Congressional Veto of Executive Actions." Library of Congress, Congressional Research Service, Issue Brief IB 76006, 3 February updated 15 June 1976.

Miller, A. *The Impact of Committees on the Structures of Issues and Voting Coalitions: The U.S. House of Representatives 1955-1962.* Unpublished Ph.D. dissertation, University of Michigan, 1971.

Miller, Clem. *Member of the House: Letters of a Congressman*. New York: Charles Scribner's Sons, 1962.

Moe, Ronald C. "Senate Confirmation of Executive Appointments: The Nixon Era." In *Congress against the President*, edited by Harvey C. Mansfield, Sr. New York: Praeger, 1975, pp. 141-152.

______, and Steven C. Teel. "Congress as Policy-Maker: A Necessary Reappraisal." *Political Science Quarterly*, vol. 85, no. 3 (September 1970): 443-470.

Moyer, Wayne. "House Voting on Defense: An Ideological Explanation." In *Military Force and American Society*, edited by Bruce M. Russett and Alfred Stepan. New York: Harper & Row, 1973, pp. 106-141.

Murphy, James T. "Political Parties and the Porkbarrel: Party Conflict and Cooperation in House Public Works and Committee Decision Making." *American Political Science Review*, vol. 68, no. 1 (March 1974): 169-185.

Nathan, Richard P. "The Administrative Presidency." *The Public Interest*, no. 44 (Summer 1976), pp. 40-54.

Neustadt, Richard. "The Constraining of the President." In *Perspectives on the Presidency*, edited by Aaron Wildavsky. Boston: Little, Brown, 1975, pp. 431-447.

______. "Politicians and Bureaucrats." In *The Congress and America's Future*, edited by David B. Truman. Englewood Cliffs, N.J.: Prentice-Hall, 1973, pp. 118-140.

______. *Presidential Power*, 2d ed. New York: John Wiley & Sons, 1976.

Ogul, Morris S. *Congress Oversees the Bureaucracy: Studies in Legislative Sueprvision*. Pittsburgh: University of Pittsburgh Press, 1976.

Oleszek, Walter J. "Toward a Stronger Legislative Branch: Congress Proposes Committee and Oversight Reforms." *The Bureaucrat*, vol. 3, no. 4 (January 1975): 444-461.

Olson, David H. "District Party Organization and Legislative Performance in Congress." *Journal of Politics* 36 (May 1974): 482-488.

Olson, David M., and Cynthia T. Nonidez. "Measures of Legislative Performance in the U.S. House of Representatives." *The Midwest Journal of Political Science*, vol. 16, no. 2 (May 1972): 269-277.

Orfield, Gary. *Congressional Power: Congress and Social Change*. New York: Harcourt Brace Jovanovich, 1975.

Ornstein, Norman. "Causes and Consequences of Congressional Change: Subcommittee Reforms in the House of Representatives, 1970-73." In *Congress in Change*, edited by Norman J. Ornstein. New York: Praeger, 1975, pp. 884-114.

______. *Information, Resources and Legislative Decision Making: Some Comparative Perspectives on the U.S. Congress*. Unpublished Ph.D. dissertation, University of Michigan, 1972.

______. "Legislative Behavior and Legislative Structure." Paper presented at the Seminar on Mathematical Models of Congress, Aspen, Colorado, June 1974.

______, ed. "Changing Congress: The Committee System." *Annals of the American Academy of Political and Social Science* 411 (January 1974, special issue).

______. *Congress in Change: Evolution and Reform*. New York: Praeger, 1975.

______, and David W. Rohde, "Seniority and Future Power in Congress." In *Congress in Change*, edited by Norman J. Ornstein. New York: Praeger, 1975, pp. 72-87.

Patterson, Samuel C. "Congressional Committee Professional Staffing: Capabilities and Constraints." In *Legislatures in Developmental Perspective*, edited by Allan Kornberg and Lloyd D. Musolf. Durham, N.C.: Duke University Press, 1970, pp. 391-428.

______, ed. *American Legislative Behavior: A Reader*. Princeton, N.J.: D. Van Nostrand, 1968.

______, and John Wahlke. "Trends and Prospects in Legislative Behavior." In *Comparative Legislative Behavior: Frontiers of Research*, edited by Samuel C. Patterson and John C.

Wahlke. New York: John Wiley & Sons, 1972, pp. 289-304.

Peabody, Robert L. *Education of a Congressman: The Newsletters of Morris K. Udall, Member of Congress, Second District of Arizona.* New York: Bobbs-Merrill, 1972.

______. *Leadership in Congress: Stability, Succession, and Change.* Boston: Little, Brown, 1976.

______. Jeffrey M. Berry, William G. Frasure, and Jerry Goldman. *To Enact a Law: Congress and Campaign Financing.* New York: Praeger, 1972.

______, and Nelson W. Polsby, eds. *New Perspectives on the House of Representatives.* Chicago: Rand McNally, 1963.

______. "Political Finance: Reform and Reality." *Annals of the American Academy of Political and Social Science* 425 (May 1976).

Polsby, Nelson W. *Congress and the Presidency*, 3d ed. Englewood Cliffs, N.J.: Prentice-Hall, 1977.

______. "Goodbye to the Senate's Inner Club." In *Congress in Change*, edited by Norman J. Ornstein. New York: Praeger, 1975, pp. 208-215.

______. "The Institutionalization of the U.S. House of Representatives." *American Political Science Review* 62 (1968): 144-168.

______. "Legislatures." Chapter 4 in *Government Institutions and Processes, Handbook of Political Science* 5, edited by Fred I. Greenstein and Nelson W. Polsby. Reading, Mass.: Addison-Wesley, 1975, pp. 257-319.

______. "Policy Analysis and Congress." *Public Policy*, vol. 18, no. 1 (Fall 1969): 61-74.

______. "Two Strategies of Influence: Choosing a Majority Leader, 1962." In *New Perspectives on the House of Representatives*, 2d ed., edited by Robert L. Peabody and Nelson W. Polsby. Chicago: Rand-McNally, 1969.

______, ed. *Congressional Behavior.* New York: Random House, 1971.

______, Miriam Gallagher, and Barry Rundquist. "The Growth of the Seniority System in the U.S. House of Representatives. *American Political Science Review* 63 (1969): 787-807.

Price, David E. *Who Makes the Laws?: Creativity and Power in Senate Committees.* Cambridge: Schenkman, 1972.

Price, H. Douglas. "Congress and the Evolution of Legislative 'Professionalism.' " In *Congress in Change*, edited by Norman J. Orstein. New York: Praeger, 1975, pp. 2-23.

______. "The Congressional Career: Then and Now." In *Congressional Behavior*, edited by Nelson W. Polsby. New York: Random House, 1972.

______. "The Electoral Arena." In *The Congress and America's Future*, edited by David B. Truman. Englewood Cliffs, N.J.: Prentice-Hall, 1973, pp. 39-62.

Reedy, George E. *The Twilight of the Presidency.* New York: World Publishing, 1970.

Reichley, A. James. *Conservatives in the White House: Policy Formulation and Decision-Making Under Nixon and Ford, 1969-77.* Washington, D.C.: Brookings Institution, forthcoming.

Riegle, Donald, with Trevor Armbrister. *O Congress.* New York: Popular Library, 1972.

Rieselbach, Leroy. *Congressional Politics.* New York: McGraw-Hill, 1973.

______. *Congressional Reform in the Seventies.* Morristown, N.J.: General Learning Press, 1977.

Ripley, Randall B. *Congress: Process and Policy.* New York: W. W. Norton, 1975.

______. *Majority Party Leadership in Congress.* Boston: Little, Brown, 1969.

______, and Grace A. Franklin. *Congress, Bureaucracy, and Public Policy.* Homewood, Ill. Dorsey, 1976.

______, and William B. Moreland, "Party Loyalty and Policy Success in Congress 1933-72: A Roll Call Analysis of the Relations Between Party Leaders, Committee Leaders, and Rank-and-File Members." Paper presented at the Conference on Mathematical Models of Congress, Aspen, Colorado, June 16-23, 1974.

Ritt, Leonard. "Committee Position, Seniority, and the Distribution of Government Expenditures." *Public Policy*, vol. 24, no. 4 (Fall 1976): 463-489.

Roberts, Charles, ed. *Has the President Too Much Power?* New York: Harper's Magazine Press, 1974.

Robinson, James A. "Staffing the Legislature." In *Legislatures in Developmental Perspective*, edited by Allan Kornberg and Lloyd D. Musolf. Durham, N.C.: Duke University Press, 1970, pp. 366-390.

Robinson, Michael J. "A Twentieth Century Medium in a Nineteenth Century Legislature: The Effects of Television on the American Congress." In *Congress in Change*, edited by Norman J. Ornstein. New York: Praeger, 1975, pp. 240-261.

Rohde, David W. "Committee Reform in the House of Representatives and the Subcommittee Bill of Rights." *Annals of the American Academy of Political and Social Science* 411 (January 1974): 39-47.

______, Norman J. Ornstein, and Robert L. Peabody. "Political Change and Legislative Norms in the United States Senate." Paper prepared for the annual meeting of the American Political Science Association, Chicago, 29 August-2 September 1974.

Rosenbloom, David L. *Electing Congress: The Financial Dilemma.* New York: Twentieth Century Fund, 1970.

Rudder, Cathy, "Rules Changes and the Revenue Committees." In *Congress Reconsidered*, edited by L. Dodd and B. Oppenheimer. New York: Praeger, 1978.

Rundquist, Barry S. "Congressional Influences on the Distribution of Prime Military Contracts." Unpublished Ph.D. dissertation, Stanford University, 1973.

______, and David E. Griffith. "The States, Congressional Committees, and Military Spending: Longitudinal Observations of the Distributive Theory of Policy Making." Paper prepared for the Conference on Mathematical Models of Congress, Aspen, Colorado, June 16-23, 1974.

Rundquist, Paul S. "Recent Filibuster Trends." Library of Congress, Congressional Research Service 7 January 1976.

______. "Senate Personal Committee Staff: A First Year Appraisal." Paper prepared for the annual meeting of the American Political Science Association, Chicago, September 2-5, 1976.

Saloma, John S., III. *Congress and the New Politics.* Boston: Little, Brown, 1969.

Schick, Allen. "The Appropriations Committees versus Congress." Paper prepared for the annual meeting of the American Political Science Association, San Francisco, September 2-5, 1975.

______. "The Battle of the Budget." In *Congress Against the President*, edited by Harvey C. Mansfield. New York: Praeger, 1975, pp. 51-70.

______. "The Budget Bureau That Was: Thoughts on the Rise, Decline and Future of a Presidential Agency." In *Perspectives on the Presidency*, edited by Aaron Wildavsky. Boston: Little, Brown, 1975, pp. 339-361.

______. "Budget Reform Legislation: Reorganizing Congressional Centers of Fiscal Power." *Harvard Journal on Legislation* 2 (February 1974): 303-350.

______. "Complex Policy-Making in the United States Senate." Library of Congress, Congressional Research Service. Unpublished manuscript prepared for the Committee on the Operation of the Senate, 10 June 1976.

______. "The Congressional Budget Act of 1974 (P.L. 93-344): Legislative History and Analysis." Library of Congress, Congressional Research Service, HJ 2005 US 75-945, 26 February 1975.

______. "The Congressional Budget and Impoundment Act (P.L. 34-344): A Summary of Its Provisions." Library of Congress, Congressional Research Service, HJ 8 U.S. A 75-335, 5 February 1975.

______. "The Impoundment Control Act of 1974: Legislative History and Implementation." Library of Congress, Congressional Research Service, HJ 8 U.S. A 76-45 S, 27 February 1976.

______. "The Supply and Demand for Analysis on Capitol Hill." *Policy Analysis*, vol. 3, no. 2 (Spring 1976): 215-234.

______. "The Taking of OMB: The Office of Management and Budget During the Nixon Years." Paper presented at the Princeton University Conference on Advising the President, 31 October 1975.

Schlesinger, Arthur J. "Congress and the Making of Foreign Policy." In *Perspectives on the Presidency*, edited by Aaron Wildavsky. Boston: Little, Brown, 1975, pp. 231-261.

Schneier, Edward. "The Intelligence of Congress: Information and Public Policy Patterns." *Annals of the American Academy of Political and Social Science* 388 (March 1970): 14-24.

Seidman, Harold. *Politics, Position, and Power: The Dynamics of Federal Organization*. New York: Oxford University Press, 1975.

Shannon, W. Wayne. *Party, Constituency and Congressional Voting: A Study of Legislative Behavior in the United States House of Representatives.* Baton Rouge: Louisiana State University Press, 1968.

______. "Review-Article: Congressional Party Behavior—Data, Concept and Theory in the Search for Historical Reality." In *Polity*, vol. 3, no. 2 (Winter 1970): 280-284.

Siff, Ted, and Alan Weil. The Ralph Nader Congress Project, *Ruling Congress: A Study of How the House and Senate Rules Govern the Legislative Process.* New York: Penguin Books, 1975.

Singer, James S. "Labor Wields Influence on Capitol Hill." *National Journal*, vol. 8, no. 17 (24 April 1976): 549-555.

______. "Labor Lies Low in GOP Administration." *National Journal*, vol. 8, no. 21 (22 May 1976): 698-703.

Smith, Donald. "Unrealized Expectations: Congressional Budget Office Under Fire." *Congressional Quarterly Weekly Report*, vol. 34, no. 3 (5 June 1976): 1430-1432.

Smith, Frank E. *Congressman from Mississippi.* New York: Capricorn Books, 1964.

Southwick, Thomas P. "Congressional Veto: Constitutionality Challenged." *Congressional Quarterly Weekly Report*, vol. 34, no. 13 (31 July 1976): 2029-2031.

Stevens, Arthur. "Subcaucuses and the Move to Reform." In *Congress Reconsidered*, edited by Lawrence C. Dodd and Bruce I. Oppenheimer. New York: Praeger, 1977.

Stewart, Geoffrey S. "Constitutionality of the Legislative Veto." *Harvard Journal on Legislation*, vol. 13, no. 3 (April 1976): 593-619.

Stewart, John G. "Central Policy Organs in Congress." In *Congress Against the President*, edited by Harvey C. Mansfield, Sr. New York: Praeger, 1975.

Stimson, James A. "Teller Voting in the House of Representatives: The Conservative Screening Hypothesis." *Polity* 8 (Winter 1975): 317-25.

Stone, Clarence N. "Issue Cleavage Between Democrats and Republicans in the U.S. House of Representatives." *Journal of Public Law*, vol. 14, no. 2 (1965): 343-358.

Sundquist, James L. "Congress and the President: Enemies or Partners?" In *Setting National Priorities: The Next Ten Years*, edited by Henry Owen and Charles L. Schultze. Washington, D.C.: Brookings Institution, 1976.

______. *The Decline and Resurgence of Congress.* Washington, D.C.: Brookings Institution, forthcoming.

______. "Reflections on Watergate: Lessons for Public Administration." *Public Administration Review*, vol. 134, no. 5 (September-October 1974): 435-461.

Tacheron, Donald G., and Morris K. Udall. *The Job of the Congressman.* Indianapolis: Bobbs-Merrill, 1970.

Thurber, James A. "Congressional Budget Reform and New Demands for Policy Analysis." *Policy Analysis*, vol. 2, no. 2 (Spring 1976): 197-214.

Truman, David B. *The Congressional Party: A Case Study.* New York: John Wiley and Sons, 1959.

______, ed. *The Congress and the America's Future*, 2d ed. Englewood Cliffs, N.J.: Prentice-Hall, 1973.

Turner, Julius. *Party and Constituency: Pressures on Congress*, revised by Edward V. Schneier, Jr. Baltimore: Johns Hopkins Press, 1951, 1970.

Vogler, David. *The Third House: Conference Committees in the United States Congress.* Evanston, Ill.: Northwestern University Press, 1971.

Wahlke, John C., and Heinz Eulau, eds. *Legislative Behavior: A Reader in Theory and Research.* Glencoe, Ill.: Free Press, 1959.

Walker, Jack L. "Setting the Agenda in the U.S. Senate: A Theory of Problem Selection." Prepared for the annual meeting of the American Political Science Association, Chicago, September 2-5, 1976.

Weaver, Warren, Jr. *Both Your Houses: The Truth About Congress*. New York: Praeger, 1972.

Wilson, Woodrow. *Congressional Government: A Study in American Politics.* Cleveland: World Publishing, 1956.

Wolfinger, Raymond E., ed. *Readings on Congress*. Englewood Cliffs, N.J.: Prentice-Hall, 1971.

Worthley, John A., ed. *Comparative Legislative Information Systems: The Use of Computer Technology in the Public Policy Process.* Washington, D.C.: National Science Foundation, 1976.

Yacker, Marc D. "Congressional Reform—House of Representatives (94th Congress)." Library of Congress, Congressional Research Service, Government Division, Issue Brief No. IB75015, 25 February 1975; updated 25 May 1976.

______. "Congressional Reform—Senate (94th Congress)." Library of Congress, Congressional Research Service, Government Division, Issue Brief No. IB75016, 5 March 1975; updated 2 June 1976.

2. AMERICAN POLITICS

Adamany, David W., and Agree, George E. *Political Money*. Baltimore and London: Johns Hopkins University Press, 1975.

Broder, David S. *The Party's Over*. New York: Colophon Books, 1972.

Burnham, Walter Dean. *Critical Elections and the Mainspring of American Politics.* New York: W.W. Norton, 1970.

______. "Theory and Voting Research: Some Reflections on Converse's 'Change in the American Electorate.'" *American Political Science Review*, vol. 68, no. 3 (September 1974): 1002-1023.

Campbell, Angus, Philip E. Converse, Warren E. Miller, and Donald E. Stokes. *The American Voter*. New York: John Wiley & Sons, 1964.

______, eds. *Elections and the Political Order*. New York: John Wiley & Sons, 1966.

Chambers, William Nisbet, and Walter Dean Burnham, ed. *The American Party Systems: Stages of Political Development.* New York: Oxford University Press, 1967.

Converse, Philip E. "Change in the American Electorate." In *The Human Meaning of Social Change*, edited by Angus Campbell and Philip E. Converse. New York: Russell Sage, 1972.

______. "Information Flow and the Stability of Partisan Attitudes." In *Elections and the Political Order*, edited by Angus Campbell, et al., New York: John Wiley & Sons, 1966.

______. "Public Opinion and Voting Behavior." In *Handbook of Political Science*, Vol. 4, edited by Fred I. Greenstein and Nelson W. Polsby. Reading, Mass.: Addison-Wesley, 1975, pp. 75-169.

Dahl, Robert A. "On Removing Certain Impediments to Democracy in the United States." Paper delivered at the annual meeting of the American Political Science Association, Chicago, September 2-5, 1976.

Evans, Rowland, and Robert Novak. *LBJ: The Exercise of Power*. New York: New American Library, 1966.

Gelb, Joyce, and Marian Lief Palley. *Tradition and Change in American Party Politics*. New York: Thomas Y. Crowell, 1975.

Harris, Louis. *The Anguish of Change*. New York: W. W. Norton, 1973.

Heclo, Hugh. *A Government of Strangers: Executive Politics in Washington*. Washington, D.C.: Brookings Institution, 1977.

______. "OMB and the Presidency—the Problem of 'Neutral Competence,'" *The Public Interest*, no. 38 (Winter 1975), pp. 80-98.

Huntington, Samuel P. "Paradigms of American Politics: Beyond the One, the Two, and the Many." *Political Science Quarterly*, vol. 89, no. 1 (March 1974): 1-26.

James, Judson L. *American Political Parties: Potential and Performance*. New York: Pegasus, 1969.

Jennings, M. Kent, and L. Harmon Zeigler, eds. *The Electoral Process*. Englewood Cliffs, N.J.: Prentice-Hall, 1966.

Kearns, Doris. *Lyndon Johnson and the American Dream*. New York: Harper & Row, 1976.

Kirkpatrick, Evron. "Toward a More Responsible Two-Party System: Political Science or Pseudoscience?" *American Political Science Review* 65 (December 1971): 965-990.

Ladd, Everett Carl, Jr., and Charles D. Hadley. *Transformations of the American Party System*. New York: W. W. Norton, 1975.

Lane, Robert E. "The Effects of the Market Economy on Political Personality." Paper delivered at the annual meeting of the American Political Science Association, Chicago, September 2-5, 1976.

______. *Political Life*. New York: Free Press, 1959.

______. *Political Man*. New York: Free Press, 1972.

Lockard, Duane. *The Perverted Priorities of American Politics*. New York: Macmillan, 1971.

McConnell, Grant. *Private Power and American Democracy*. New York: Alfred A. Knopf, 1967.

Miller, Arthur H., Warren E. Miller, Alden S. Raine, and Thad A. Brown. "A Majority Party in Disarray: Political Polarization in the 1972 Election." *American Political Science Review*, vol. 70, no. 3 (September 1976): 753-778.

Miller, Warren E., and Teresa Levin. *Leadership and Change: The New Politics and the American Electorate*. Cambridge: Winthrop, 1976.

Mueller, John E. "Trends in Popular Support for the Wars in Korea and Vietnam." *American Political Science Review*, vol. 65, no. 2 (June 1971): 358-375.

Natchez, Peter. "Images of Voting: The Social Psychologists." *Public Policy*, vol. 18, no. 4 (Summer 1970).

O'Brien, Lawrence. *No Final Victories: A Life in Politics—from John F. Kennedy to Watergate*. New York: Ballantine, 1974.

Page, Benjamin I., and Richard A. Brody. "Policy Voting and the Electoral Process: The Vietnam War Issue." *American Political Science Review*, vol. 66, no. 3 (September 1972): 979-995.

Parenti, Michael. "Ethnic Politics and the Persistence of Ethnic Identification." *American Political Science Review*, vol. 61, no. 3 (September 1967).

Pennock, J. Roland. "Comments on Gerald M. Pomper's 'Toward a More Responsible Two-Party System? What Again?'" *The Journal of Politics*, vol. 34, no. 3 (August 1972): 952-955.

Pomper, Gerald M. "Toward A More Responsible Two-Party system? What, Again?" *The Journal of Politics*, vol. 33, no. 4 (November 1971): 916-940.

Porter, William E. *Assault on the Media: The Nixon Years*. Ann Arbor: University of Michigan Press, 1976.

Pressman, Jeffrey L., Dennis G. Sullivan, and F. Christopher Arterton. "Cleavages, Decisions, and Legitimation: The Democrats' Mid-Term Conference, 1974." *Political Science Quarterly*, vol. 91, no. 1 (Spring 1976): 89-107.

Ranney, Austin. *Curing the Mischiefs of Faction: Party Reform in America*. Berkeley: University of California Press, 1975.

______. *The Doctrine of Responsible Party Government*. Urbana: University of Illinois Press, 1962.

RePass, David E. "Issue Salience and Party Choice." *American Political Science Review*, vol. 65, no. 2 (June 1971): 389-401.

Rogin, Michael P. *Intellectuals and McCarthy: The Radical Spectre*. Cambridge: MIT Press, 1969.

Rosenberg, Milton J., Sidney Verba, and Philip E. Converse. *Vietnam and the Silent Majority: The Dove's Guide*. New York: Harper & Row, 1970.

Rubin, Richard L. *Party Dynamics: The Democratic Coalition and the Politics of Change*. New York: Oxford University Press, 1976.

Schattschneider, E. E. *Party Government*. New York: Farrar and Rinehart, 1942.

Stewart, John G. *One Last Chance: The Democratic Party, 1974-76*. New York: Praeger, 1974.

Stimson, James A. "Belief Systems: Constraint, Complexity, and the 1972 Election." *American Journal of Political Science*, vol. 19, no. 3 (August 1975): 393-417.

Stokes, Donald E. "Some Dynamic Elements of Contests for the Presidency." *American Political Science Review*, vol. 60, no. 1 (March 1966).

______. "Spatial Models of Party Competition." In *Elections and the Political Order*, edited by Angus Campbell, Philip E. Converse, Warren E. Miller, and Donald E. Stokes. New York: John Wiley & Sons, 1966.

Sundquist, James L. *Dynamics of the Party System: Alignment and Realignment of Political Parties in the United States*. Washington, D.C.: Brookings Institution, 1973.

______. "The New Deal Issues Still Exist." Interview in *National Journal* (31 May 1975), p. 809.

______. *Politics and Policy: The Eisenhower, Kennedy, and Johnson Years*. Washington, D.C.: Brookings Institution, 1968.

______, with David Davis. *Making Federalism Work*. Washington, D.C.: Brookings Institution, 1969.

"Toward a More Responsible Two-Party System: Report of the Committee on Political Parties." *American Political Science Review* 64 (September 1950).

Truman, David B. "The American System in Crisis." *Political Science Quarterly* (December 1959): 481-497.

Turner, Julius. "Responsible Parties: A Dissent from the Floor." *American Political Science Review*, vol. 45, no. 1 (March 1951): 143-152.

Verba, Sidney, and Norman H. Nie. *Participation in America: Political Democracy and Social Equality*. New York: Harper & Row, 1972.

Wellford, Harrison. *Sowing the Wind*. New York: Bantam, 1973.

Wildavsky, Aaron. *The Revolt Against the Masses*. New York: Basic Books, 1971.

Zeigler, L. Harmon, and Wayne G. Peck. *Interest Groups in American Society*. Englewood Cliffs, N.J.: Prentice-Hall, 1972.

3. FOREIGN POLICY

Ball, George W. "Cosmocorp: The Importance of 'Being Stateless.'" In *World Business: Promise and Problems*, edited by Courtney C. Brown, New York: Macmillan, 1970, pp. 330-338.

Barnet, Richard J., and Muller, Ronald E. *Global Reach: The Power of the Multinational Corporations*. New York: Simon and Schuster, 1974.

Berg, Alan. "The Trouble with Triage." *New York Times* Magazine (15 June 1975), pp. 26-35.

Bergsten, C. Fred. "Coming Investment Wars?" Brookings General Series Reprint 299. Washington, D.C.: Brookings Institution, 1975.

———. "Crisis in U.S. Trade Policy." *Foreign Affairs*, vol. 47, no. 4 (July 1971): 619-635.

———. "Let's Avoid a Trade War." *Foreign Policy*, no. 23 (Summer 1976), pp. 24-31.

———, Thomas Horst, and Theodore H. Moran. *American Multinationals and American Interests.* Washington, D.C.: Brookings Institution, 1978.

———, and Lawrence Krause. *World Politics and International Economics.* Washington, D.C.: Brookings Institution, 1975.

Brown, Seyom. *New Forces in World Politics.* Washington, D.C.: Brookings Institution, 1974.

Bundy, William P. "Dictatorships and American Foreign Policy." *Foreign Affairs*, vol. 54, no. 1 (October 1975): 50-60.

Cooper, Richard N. "Economic Interdependence and Foreign Policy in the Seventies." *World Politics*, vol. 24, no. 2 (January 1972): 159-181.

Cottam, Richard W. *Competitive Interference and Twentieth Century Diplomacy.* Pittsburgh: University of Pittsburgh Press, 1967.

deVries, Tom. "Jamaica, or the Non-Reform of the International Monetary System." *Foreign Affairs*, vol. 54, no. 3 (April 1976): 577-605.

Gelb, Leslie. "The Essential Domino: American Politics and Vietnam." *Foreign Affairs*, vol. 50, no. 3 (April 1972): 459-475.

Grant, James P. "Development: The End of Trickle Down?" *Foreign Policy*, no. 12 (Fall 1973), pp. 43-65.

Grassmuck, George L. "Sectional Biases in Congress on Foreign Policy." The Johns Hopkins University Studies on Historical and Political Science, series 68, no. 3 (1951), pp. 1-181.

Green, Philip. *Deadly Logic.* New York: Schocken, 1967.

Hayter, Teresa. *Aid as Imperialism.* Baltimore: Penguin, 1971.

Heilbroner, Robert L. "Counterrevolutionary America." *Commentary*, vol. 43, no. 4 (April 1967): 31-38.

Hoffman, Stanley. "Will the Balance Balance at Home?" *Foreign Policy*, no. 7 (Summer 1972), pp. 60-86.

Hymer, Stephen. "The Multinational Corporation and the Law of Uneven Development." In *Economics and World Order: From the 1970's to the 1980's*, edited by Jagolish N. Bhagwati. New York: Free Press, 1972, pp. 113-140.

Kaysen, Carl. "The Computer That Printed Out W*O*L*F*." *Foreign Affairs*, vol. 50, no. 4 (July 1972): 660-668.

Kennan, George F. "A Plea by Mr. X 30 Years Later." Article in "Outlook," *The Washington Post* (11 December 1977), p. D1.

Kennedy, Edward M. "The Persian Gulf: Arms Race or Arms Control." *Foreign Affairs*, vol. 54, no. 1 (October 1975): 14-36.

Keohane, R. O., and Nye, J. S., eds. *Transnational Relations and World Politics.* Cambridge: Harvard University Press, 1972.

Lake, Anthony, and Roger Morris. "The Human Reality of Realpolitik." *Foreign Policy*, vol. 1, no. 4 (Fall 1971).

Manning, Bayless. "Goals, Ideology and Foreign Policy." *Foreign Affairs*, vol. 54, no. 2 (January 1976).

Moran, Theodore H. "New Deal or Raw Deal in Raw Materials." *Foreign Policy*, no. 5 (Winter 1971-72), pp. 119-136.

Moynihan, Daniel P. "The United States in Opposition." *Commentary* (March 1975), pp. 31-44.

Nathan, James, and James K. Oliver. *United States Foreign Policy and World Order.* Boston: Little, Brown, 1976.

Osgood, Robert, and Robert Tucker. *Force, Order, and Justice.* Baltimore: Johns Hopkins Press, 1967.

Owen, Henry. "Foreign Policy Premises for the Next Administration." *Foreign Affairs*, vol. 42, no. 4 (July 1968): 699-712.

Packenham, Robert A. *Liberal America and the Third World: Political Development Ideas in Foreign Aid and Social Science.* Princeton, N.J.: Princeton University Press, 1973.
Podhoretz, Norman. "Making the World Safe for Communism." *Commentary*, vol. 61, no. 4 (April 1976).
Rosenau, James N. *Domestic Sources of Foreign Policy.* New York: Free Press, 1967.
______. "Intervention As a Scientific Concept." *Journal of Conflict Resolution*, vol. 13, no. 2 (June 1969): 149-171.
Rostow, Eugene V., and George W. Ball. "The Genesis of the Multinational Corporation." In *Global Companies: The Political Economy of World business*, edited by George W. Ball. Englewood Cliffs, N.J.: Prentice-Hall, 1975, pp. 4-10.
Rothschild, Emma. "Food Politics." *Foreign Affairs*, vol. 54, no. 2 (January 1976): 285-307.
Schelling, Thomas C. *The Strategy of Conflict.* Cambridge: Harvard University Press, 1960.
Sigmund, Paul E. "The Invisible Blockade and the Overthrow of Allende." *Foreign Affairs*, vol. 52, no. 2 (January 1974): 322-340.
Sunkel, Oswaldo. "Big Business and 'Dependencia.'" *Foreign Affairs* 50 (April 1972): 515-531.
Strauss-Hupe, Robert, et al. *Protracted Conflict.* New York: Harper, 1959.
Szulc, Tad. "Lisbon and Washington: Behind Portugal's Revolution." *Foreign Policy*, no. 21 (Winter 1975-76), pp. 3-63.
Tucker, Robert W. *The Radical Left and United States Foreign Policy.* Baltimore: Johns Hopkins Press, 1971.
Ullman, Richard H. "Washington versus Wilson." *Foreign Policy*, no. 21 (Winter 1975-76), pp. 97-124.
Vernon, Raymond. "The Multinational Enterprise: Power versus Sovereignty." *Foreign Affairs*, vol. 49, no. 4 (July 1971).
______. *Sovereignty at Bay: The Multinational Spread of U.S. Enterprises.* New York: Basic Books, 1971.
Vershbow, Alexander R. "The Cruise Missile: The End of Arms Control?" *Foreign Affairs*, vol. 55, No. 1 (October 1976): 133-146.
Willick, Daniel H. "Foreign Affairs and Party Choice." *American Journal of Sociology*, vol. 75, no. 4, pt. 1 (January 1970): 530-549.
Wolfers, Arnold. *Discord and Collaboration.* Baltimore: Johns Hopkins Press, 1962.

4. ECONOMIC POLICY

Blair, John. *Economic Concentration: Structure, Behavior and Public Policy.* New York: Harcourt Brace Jovanovich, 1972.
Bluestone, Barry. "Economic Crises and the Law of Uneven Development." *Politics and Society*, vol. 3, no. 1 (Fall 1972): 65-82.
Bosworth, Barry, James S. Duesenberry, and Andrew S. Carron. *Capital Needs in the Seventies.* Washington, D.C.: Brookings Institution, 1975.
Crockett, Andrew D., and Morris Goldstein. "Inflation Under Fixed and Flexible Exchange Rates." *International Monetary Fund Staff Paper* (November 1976).
Denison, Edward F. *Accounting for United States Economic Growth 1929-1969.* Washington, D.C.: Brookings Institution, 1974.
Friedman, Milton. *Capitalism and Freedom.* Chicago: University of Chicago Press, 1962.
Galbraith, John Kenneth. *Economics and the Public Purpose.* New York: Signet, 1975.
Goodwin, Crawford D. *Exhortation and Controls: The Search for a Wage-Price Policy, 1945-1971.* Washington, D.C.: Brookings Institution, 1975.
Heilbroner, Robert L. "Radical Economics: A Review Essay." *American Political Science Review* 66 (September 1972): 1017-1020.
Hirsch, Fred. *Social Limits to Growth.* Cambridge: Harvard University Press, 1976.
Kaldor, Nicholas. *Essays on Value and Distribution.* London: Duckworth, 1960.

Kindleberger, Charles P. *American Business Abroad: Six Lectures on Direct Investment.* New Haven: Yale University Press, 1969.

______. "The Multinational Corporation in a World of Militant Developing Countries." In *Global Companies: The Political Economy of World Business.* Englewood Cliffs, N.J.: Prentice-Hall, 1975, pp. 70-84.

Krause, Lawrence B., and Walter S. Salant, ed. *Worldwide Inflation: Theory and Recent Experience.* Washington, D.C.: Brookings Institution, 1977.

Kuznets, Simon S. *Population, Capital and Growth.* New York: W. W. Norton, 1973, p. 342.

Lebergott, Stanley. *The American Economy: Income, Wealth, and Want.* Princeton, N.J.: Princeton University Press, 1976.

Lekachman, Robert. *Economists at Bay: Why the Experts Will Never Solve Your Problems.* New York: McGraw-Hill, 1976.

______. *Inflation: The Permanent Problem of Boom and Bust.* New York: Vintage, 1973.

Lindblom, Charles E. *Politics and Markets: The World's Political Economic Systems.* New York: Basic Books, 1977.

Means, Gardiner C., and John M. Blair, et al., *The Roots of Inflation: The International Crisis.* New York: Burt Franklin, 1975.

Morgan, Dan. "Giant Global Commodity Firms Losing Cloak of Obscurity." In *Congressional Record,* vol. 122, no. 15 (6 February 1976): S1483 ff.

Nordhaus, William, and James Tobin. "Is Growth Obsolete?" and the discussion following. In *Economic Growth.* New York: National Bureau of Economic Research and Columbia University Press, 1972, pp. 1-81.

Okun, Arthur M. *Equality and Efficiency: The Big Trade-off.* Washington, D.C.: Brookings Institution, 1975.

______. *The Political Economy of Prosperity.* New York: W. W. Norton, 1970.

______. "A Postmortem of the 1974 Recession." In *Brooking Papers on Economic Activity,* edited by Arthur M. Okun and George L. Perry. Washington, D.C.: Brookings Institution, 1975.

______. "Upward Mobility in a High Pressure Economy." In *Brookings Papers on Economic Activity* 1. Washington, D.C.: Brookings Institution, 1973.

______, ed. *The Battle Against Unemployment: An Introduction to a Current Issue of Public Policy,* rev. ed. New York: W. W. Norton, 1972.

Pechman, Joseph A. "Business Doesn't Need More Tax Breaks." *New York Times,* 20 July 1975, p. 19.

______. "Making Economic Policy: The Role of the Economist." Brookings General Series Reprint 311. Washington, D.C.: Brookings Institution, 1976.

______, and Benjamin A. Okner. *Who Bears the Tax Burden.* Washington, D.C.: Brookings Institution, 1974.

Perry, George L. "If Not Oil Taxes, Then What?:" Statement of January 29, 1975, before the Joint Economic Committee. *The Brookings Bulletin* 12 (Spring 1975).

______. "Inflation and Unemployment." Reprint. Washington, D.C.: Brookings Institution, 1970.

Roosa, Robert V. "Economic Planning: A Middle Way." *New York Times,* 8 February 1975, p. F14.

Samuelson, Paul A. "Candidates' Economics." *Newsweek* (29 May 1972), p. 69.

Samuelson, Robert J. "Economists up in the Air over How to Keep Inflation and Unemployment Down." *National Journal,* vol. 8, no. 34 (21 August 1976): 1173-1182.

Scherer, Frederic M. *Industrial Market Structure and Economic Performances.* (Chicago: Rand McNally, 1970.

______, Alan Beckenstein, Erich Kaufer, R. Dennis Murphy, with the assistance of Francine Bougeon-Maassen. *The Economics of Multi-Plant Operation: An International Comparisons Study.* Cambridge: Harvard University Press, 1975.

Schultze, Charles L. "The Economics of the Full Employment and Balanced Growth Act of 1976 (S. 50)." Statement before the Senate Committee on Public Welfare, Subcommittee on unemployment, poverty, and migratory labor, 14 May 1976.

______. "Is Economics Obsolete? No, Underemployed." *Brookings General Reprint.* Washington, D.C.: Brookings Institution, 1972.

______. *The Public Use of Private Interest.* Washington, D.C.: Brookings Institution, 1977.

Shanahan, Eileen. "'Equal Time' for Economic Ideas." *New York Times,* 1 September 1974.

Solomon, Robert. *The International Monetary System, 1945-1976: An Insider's View.* New York: Harper Row, 1977.

Solow, Robert M. "Is the End of the World at Hand?" In *The Economic Growth Controversy,* edited by Andrew Weintraub, Eli Schwartz, and J. Richard Aronson. White Plains, N.Y.: International Arts & Sciences Press, 1973, pp. 39-61.

Surrey, Stanley S. *Pathways to Tax Reform: The Concept of Tax Expenditures.* Cambridge: Harvard University Press, 1973.

Thurow, Lester C. *Generating Inequality: Mechanisms of Distribution in the U.S. Economy.* New York: Basic Books, 1975.

______. *Poverty and Discrimination.* Washington, D.C.: Brookings Institution, 1969.

Winslow, John F. "The Bankers' Attack on Free Enterprise." *Washington Monthly* (June 1976), pp. 34-38.

______. *Conglomerates Unlimited: The Failure of Regulation.* Bloomington: Indiana University Press, 1973.

Wriston, Walter B. "Blue Eagles and Deja Vu." Speech before the Society of American Business Writers, Washington, D.C., 5 May 1975.

5. POLICY ANALYSIS

Blechman, Barry M., Edward M. Gramlich, and Robert W. Hartman. *Setting National Priorities: The 1976 Budget.* Washington, D.C.: Brookings Institution, 1975.

Campbell, Angus, Philip E. Converse, and Willard L. Rogers. *The Quality of American Life: Perceptions, Evaluations, and Satisfactions.* New York: Russell Sage, 1976.

Davis, Karen. *National Health Insurance: Benefits, Costs, and Consequences.* Washington, D.C.: Brookings Institution, 1975.

Fried, Edward R., Alice M. Rivlin, Charles L. Schultze, and Nancy H. Teeters. *Setting National Priorities: The 1974 Budget.* Washington, D.C.: Brookings Institution, 1973.

Ginzberg, Eli, and Robert M. Solow. *The Great Society: Lessons for the Future.* New York: Basic Books, 1974.

Goodwin, Leonard. *Can Social Science Help Resolve National Problems? Welfare, A Case in Point.* New York: Free Press, 1975.

Haveman, Robert H. "Policy Analysis and the Congress: An Economist's Views." *Policy Analysis,* vol. 2, no. 2 (Spring 1976): 235-250.

Kneese, Allen V., and Charles L. Schultze. *Pollution, Prices and Public Policy.* Washington, D.C.: Brookings Institution, 1975.

Levitan, Sar A., and Robert Taggart. *The Promise of Greatness.* Cambridge: Harvard University Press, 1976.

Lynn, James T., and Charles L. Schultze. *The Federal Budget: What Are the Nation's Priorities?* Washington, D.C.: American Enterprise Institute for Public Policy Research—Rational Debate Series, 1976.

Natchez, Peter B., and Irwin C. Bupp, "Policy and Priority in the Budgetary Process." *American Political Science Review,* vol. 67, no. 3 (September 1973): 951-963.

Orfield, Gary. "How to Make Desegregation Work: The Adaptation of Schools to Their Newly-Integrated Student Bodies." Brookings General Series Reprint 312. Washington, D.C.: Brookings Institution, 1976.

———. *Must We Bus? Segregated Schools and National Policy*. Washington, D.C.: Brookings Institution, 1978.

Orshansky, Mollie. "How Poverty Is Measured." *Monthly Labor Review*, vol. 92, no. 2 (February 1969): 37-41.

———. "The Shape of Poverty in 1966." *Social Security Bulletin*, vol. 31, no. 3 (March 1968).

Owen, Henry and Charles L. Schultze, eds. *Setting National Priorities: The Next Ten Years.* Washington, D.C.: Brookings Institution, 1976.

Palley, Marian Lief, and Howard A. Palley. *Urban America and Public Policies.* Lexington, Mass.: D. C. Heath, 1977.

Polsby, Nelson W. "Policy Initiation in the American Political System." In *Perspectives on the Presidency*, edited by Aaron Wildavsky. Boston: Little, Brown, 1975, pp. 222-230.

Schneider, Jerrold E. "Making Government Work: Political versus Technical Obstacles to Social Accounting." *American Behavioral Scientist*, vol. 17, no. 4 (March/April 1974): 585-608.

———. "Review Article: Harrison Wellford's, 'Sowing the Wind' ": International Journal of Health Services, vol. 4, no. 1 (1974): 189-195.

Schultze, Charles L., Edward R. Fried, Alice M. Reuben, and Nancy H. Teeters. *Setting National Priorities: The 1973 Budget.* Washington, D.C.: Brookings Institution, 1972.

Wildavsky, Aaron. "The Analysis of Issue-Contexts in the Study of Decision Making." In his *The Revolt Against the Masses*. New York: Basic Books, 1971.

6. METHODOLOGY AND ANALYTIC PHILOSOPHY

Aberbach, Joel D., James D. Chesney, and Bert A. Rockman. "Exploring Elite Political Attitudes: Some Methodological Lessons." *Political Methodology* 2 (1975): 1-28.

Alker, Hayward R., Jr. *Mathematics and Politics*. New York: Macmillan, 1965.

———. "Statistics and Politics: The Need for Causal Data Analysis." In *Politics and the Social Sciences*, edited by S. M. Lipset. New York: Oxford University Press, 1969.

Anderson, Lee F., Meredith W. Watts, Jr., and Allen R. Wilcox. *Legislative Roll Call Analysis.* Evanston, Ill.: Northwestern University Press, 1966.

Axelrod, Robert. *Structure of Decisions: The Cognitive Maps of Political Elites.* (Princeton, N.J.: Princeton University Press, 1976.

Blalock, H. M., and Ann B. Blalock, eds. *Methodology in Social Research*. New York: McGraw-Hill, 1968.

Blalock, Hubert M., Jr., *Causal Inference in Nonexperimental Research.* Chapel Hill: University of North Carolina Press, 1961.

———. *Theory Construction: From Verbal to Mathematical Formulations.* Englewood Cliffs, N.J.: Prentice-Hall, 1969.

———, ed. *Causal Models in the Social Science*. Chicago: Aldine, 1971.

Brunner, Ronald D. "Intentionality, Contextuality and Research Methods in the Study of Public Opinion." Paper delivered at the annual meeting of the American Sociological Association, Montreal, August 25-29, 1974.

Cannell, Charles F., Sally A. Lawson, and Doris L. Hausser. *A Technique for Evaluating Interviewer Performance*. Ann Arbor: University of Michigan Press, 1975.

Casstevens, Thomas W. "Linear Algebra and Legislative Voting Behavior: Rice's Indices." *Journal of Politics* 32 (November 1970): 769-783.

Cattell, Raymond B., "Factor Analysis: An Introduction to Essentials," "I. The Purpose and Underlying Models," *Biometrics*, March 1965, pp. 190-215. "II. The Role of Factor Analysis in Research," *Biometrics*, June 1965, pp. 405-435.

Chisholm, Roderick M. "The Contrary-to-Fact Conditional." In *Readings in Philosophical Analysis*, edited by Herbert Feigl and Wilfred Sellars, eds. New York: Appleton-Century-Crofts, 1949.

Clausen, Aage R. "Measurement Identity in the Longitudinal Analysis of Legislative Voting."

American Political Science Review, vol. 61, no. 4 (December 1967): 1120-1235.

______. "The Measurement of Legislative Group Behavior." *Midwest Journal of Political Science*, vol. 2, no. 2 (May 1967): 212-224.

______. "Subjectivity and Objectivity in Dimensional Analysis: Illustrations from Congressional Voting." *Mathematical Applications in Political Science*, edited by James F. Herndon and Joseph L. Bernd. Charlottesville: University of Virginia, 1974, pp. 15-39.

______, and Carl E. Van Horn. "How to Analyze Too Many Roll Calls." Paper prepared for Conference on Mathematical Models of Congress, Aspen, Colorado, June 16-23, 1974.

Converse, Philip E. "The Problem of Party Distances in Models of Voting Change." In *The Electoral Process*, edited by M. Kent Jennings and L. Harmon Zeigler. Englewood Cliffs, N.J.: Prentice-Hall, 1966, pp. 175-207.

______. "Survey Research and the Decoding of Patterns in Ecological Data." In *Quantitative Ecological Analysis in the Social Sciences*, edited by Mattei Dogan and Stein Rokkan. Cambridge: MIT Press, 1969, pp. 459-486.

Coombs, Clyde H. *A Theory of Data*. New York: John Wiley & Sons, 1964.

Costner, Herbert L. "Criteria for Measures of Association." *American Sociological Review*, vol. 30, no. 3 (June 1965):341-353.

Crane, Wilder, Jr. "A Caveat on Roll Call Studies of Party Voting." *Midwest Journal of Political Science* 4 (1960): 237-249.

David, Paul T. "How Can an Index of Party Composition Best Be Derived?" *Journal of Politics*, vol. 34, no. 2 (May 1972): 632-637.

Davidson, Donald, J.C.C. McKinsey, and Patrick Suppes. "Outlines of a Formal Theory of Value." *Philosophy of Science* 22 (1955): 140-160.

Dodd, Lawrence C. "'Like a Bridge Over Troubled Waters'—or How Not to Analyze Legislative Coalitions in Four Easy Lessons." Paper prepared for the Mathematical Models of Congress Seminar, Aspen, Colorado, June 16-23, 1974.

Everitt, Brian. *Cluster Analysis*. New York: John Wiley & Sons, 1974.

Fiorina, Morris P. "The Voting Decision: Instrumental and Expressive Aspects." *The Journal of Politics*, vol. 38, no. 2 (May 1976): 390-413.

Fishbein, Martin, ed. *Readings in Attitude Theory and Measurement*. New York: John Wiley & Sons, 1967.

Galtung, Johan. *Theory and Methods of Social Research*, rev. ed. New York: Columbia University Press, 1969.

Goodman, Leo A., and William H. Kruskal. "Measures of Association for Cross Classification." *Journal of the American Statistical Association*, vol. 49, no. 268 (December 1954): 723-764.

Goodman, Nelson. "The Problem of Counterfactional Conditionals." In *Fact, Fiction and Forecast*. London: University of London-Athlone Press, 1954.

Grumm, John G. "The Systematic Analysis of Blocs in the Study of Legislative Behavior." *Western Political Quarterly* 18 (June 1975): pp. 350;362.

Hampshire, Stuart. "Critical Notice: 'The Concept of Mind,' by Gilbert Ryle," *MIND 59* (1959): 237-255.

Hart, H.L.A., and A.M. Honore. *Causation in the Law*. Oxford: Clarendon Press, 1959.

Hartigan, John A. *Clustering Algorithms*. New York: John Wiley & Sons, 1975.

Heise, David R. "Separating Reliability and Stability in Test-Retest Correlations." *Causal Models in the Social Sciences*, edited by H. M. Blalock. Chicago: Aldine-Atherton, 1971, pp. 348-363.

Hempel, Carl G. *Aspects of Scientific Explanation*. New York: Free Press, 1965.

______. *Fundamentals of Concept Formation in Empirical Science*. Chicago: University of Chicago Press, 1952.

Herndon, James F. "Conflict and Consensus in a Legislative System." In *Mathematical Applications in Political Science* 4, edited by Joseph L. Bernd. Charlottesville: University Press of Virginia, 1969.

Holsti, Ole R. *Content Analysis for the Social Sciences and Humanities.* Reading, Mass.: Addison-Wesley, 1969.

Jackson, John E. "Modeling and Measuring Political Attitudes: A Question of Unobserved Variables." Paper prepared for the annual meeting of the American Political Science Association, San Francisco, 3 September 1975.

Kahn, Robert L., and Charles F. Cannell. *The Dynamics of Interviews: Theory, Technique, and Cases.* New York: John Wiley & Sons, 1957.

Kaplan, Abraham. *The Conduct of Inquiry: Methodology for Behavioral Science.* San Francisco: Chandler, 1964.

Kelley, E. W. "Techniques of Studying Coalition Formation." *Midwest Journal of Political Science,* vol. 12, no. 1 (February 1968): 62-84.

———. "Utility Theory and Political Coalitions: Problems of Operationalization." In *The Study of Coalition Behavior: Theoretical Perspectives and Cases From Four Continents,* edited by Sven Groennings, E. W. Kelley, and Michael Leiserson. New York: Holt, Rinehart, and Winston, 1970, pp. 474-477.

Kim, Jae-On. "Multivariate Analysis of Ordinal Variables." *American Journal of Sociology,* vol. 81, no. 2 (September 1975): 261-298.

Kish, Leslie. "Some Statistical Problems in Research Design." *The Quantitative Analysis of Social Problems,* edited by Edward R. Tufte. Reading, Mass.: Addison Wesley, 1970, pp. 391-406.

Lazarsfeld, Paul F. "Evidence and Inference in Social Research." In *Evidence and Inference,* edited by Daniel Lerner. Glencoe, Ill.: Free Press, 1958.

Leege, David Calhoun. "Is Political Science Alive and Well and Living at NSF: Reflections of a Program Director at Midstream." Paper delivered at the annual meeting of the American Political Science Association, San Francisco, September 2-5, 1975.

Levine, Mark S. "Standard Scores as Indices: The Pitfalls of Not Thinking It Through." *American Journal of Political Science,* vol. 17, no. 4 (November 1973): 431-440.

Lewis, Anthony Dexter. *Elite and Specialized Interviewing.* Evanston, Ill.: Northwestern Union Press, 1970.

Lewis, Clarence Irving. *An Analysis of Knowledge and Valuation.* LaSalle, Ill.: Open Court, 1946.

MacRae, Duncan Jr. "Indices of Pairwise Agreement Between Justices or Legislators." *Midwest Journal of Political Science,* vol. 10, no. 1 (February 1966): 138-141.

———. *Issues and Parties in Legislative Voting: Methods of Statistical Analysis.* New York: Harper & Row, 1970.

———. "A Method for Identifying Issues and Factions from Legislative Votes." *American Political Science Review,* vol. 58, no. 4 (December 1965).

———. "Spatial Models for the Analysis of Roll-Call Data." *Mathematical Applications in Political Science V,* edited by James F. Herndon and Joseph L. Bernd. Charlottesville: University Press of Virginia, 1971), pp. 51-69.

———, and Hugh D. Price. "Scale Positions and 'Power' in the Senate." *Behavioral Science* 4 (1959): 212-218.

———, and Susan Barker Schwarz. "Identifying Congressional Issues by Multidimensional Models." *Midwest Journal of Political Science,* vol. 12, no. 2 (May 1968): 181-201.

Muehl, Doris, ed. *A Manual for Coders.* Ann Arbor: Survey Research Center, 1961.

Pool, Ithiel De Sola. *Trends in Content Analysis.* Urbana: University of Illinois Press, 1959.

Przeworksi, Adam, and Henry Teune. *The Logic of Comparative Social Inquiry.* New York: John Wiley & Sons, 1970.

Quine, Willard Van Orman. *Word and Object.* Cambridge: MIT Press, 1960.

Reynolds, H. T. *Making Causal Inferences with Ordinal Data.* Working Papers in Methodology, no. 5. Chapel Hill: University of North Carolina Institute for Research in Social Science, 1971.

Rice, Stuart A. "Measuring Cohesion in Legislative Groups." In *Legislative Behavior: A Reader in Theory and Research*, edited by John C. Wahlke and Heinz Eulau. Glencoe, Ill.: Free Press, 1959, pp. 372-376.

Riker, William H. "A Method for Determining the Significance of Roll Call Votes in Voting Bodies." In *Legislative Behavior: A Reader in Theory and Research*, edited by John C. Wahlke and Heinz Eulau. Glencoe, Ill.: Free Press, 1959, pp. 377-383.

Selvin, Hanan C. "A Critique of Tests of Significance in Survey Research." *The American Sociological Review*, vol. 22, no. 5 (October 1957).

Shepard, Roger N., A. Kimball Romney, and Sara Beth Nerlove, eds. *Multidimensional Scaling: Theory and Applications in the Behavioral Sciences* (vol. 1: Theory; vol. 2: Applications). New York: Seminar Press, 1972.

Sullivan, John L. "Multiple Indicators: Some Criteria of Selection." In *Measurement in the Social Sciences: Theories and Strategies*, edited by H. M. Blalock, Jr. Chicago: Aldine, 1974, pp. 243-269.

Survey Research Center-Institute for Social Research, University of Michigan. *Interview's Manual*. Ann Arbor: University of Michigan, 1976.

Symposium Proceedings. *Approaches to Elite Analysis*. Washington, D.C.: Mathematica, June 11-12, 1975, Report 5-1.

Tryon, Robert C., and Daniel E. Bailey. *Cluster Analysis*. New York: McGraw-Hill, 1970.

Tufte, Edward R. "Improving Data Analysis in Political Science." In *Quantitative Analysis of Social Problems*, edited by Edward R. Tufte. Reading, Mass.: Addison Wesley, 1970, pp. 437-449.

Tukey, John W., and M. B. Wiek. "Data Analysis and Statistics: Techniques and Approaches." In *Quantitative Analysis of Social Problems*, edited by Edward R. Tufte. Reading, Mass.: Addison Wesley, 1970, pp. 370-390.

Weisberg, Herbert. *Dimensional Analysis of Legislative Roll Calls*. Unpublished Ph.D. dissertation, University of Michigan, 1968.

______. "Dimensionland: An Excursion into Spaces." *American Journal of Political Science*, vol. 18, no. 4 (November 1974): 743-776.

______. "The Inherent Predictability of Legislative Votes: The Perils of Successful Predication." California Institute of Technology, *Social Science Working Papers*, April 1976.

______. "Models of Statistical Relationship," *American Political Science Review* 67 (December 1974): 1638-1655.

______. "Scaling Models for Legislative Roll Call Analysis." *American Political Science Review* 66 (December 1972): 1306-1315.

______. "Theory Development in Congressional Research." Paper delivered at the Research Seminar on Mathematical Models of Congress, Aspen, Colarado, June 16-23, 1974.

Wilcox, Allen R. "Indices of Qualitative Variation and Political Measurement." *Western Political Quarterly*, vol. 26, no. 2 (June 1973): 326-343.

Wilson, Thomas P. "Critique of Ordinal Variables." In *Causal Models in the Social Sciences*, edited by H. M. Blalock, Jr. Chicago: Adline Atherton, 1971, pp. 415-431.

______. "A Proportional-Reduction-in-Error Interpretation for Kendall's Tau-B." *Social Forces*, vol. 47, no. 3 (March 1969): 340-342.

Wright, G. H. von. *Explanation and Understanding*. Ithaca, N.Y.: Cornell University Press, 1971.

7. IDEOLOGY

Brown, Steven R. "Consistency and the Persistence of Ideology: Some Experimental Results." *Public Opinion Quarterly* 34 (Spring 1970): 61-68.

Converse, Philip. "The Nature of Belief Systems in Mass Publics." In *Ideology and Discontent*, edited by David E. Apter. New York: Free Press, 1964.

______. "Some Mass-Elite Contrasts in the Perception of Political Spaces." *Social Science Information*, vol. 14, nos. 3, 4 (Summer 1975): 49-83.

Coveyou, Michael R., and James E. Piereson. *Ideological Perceptions and Political Judgment: Some Problems of Concept and Measurement.* Paper delivered at the annual meeting of the American Political Science Association, San Francisco, September 2-5, 1975. Copyright 1975, the American Political Science Association.

Diggins, John P. "Ideology and Pragmatism: Philosophy or Passion." *American Political Science Review*, vol. 64, no. 3 (September 1970).

Hart, Gary (Senator), "Big Government: Real or Imaginary?" *Vital Speechs of the Day*, 42, no. 16 (1 June 1976): 495-498.

Hickel, Gerald Kent. *Beyond The Polls: Political Ideology and Its Correlates.* Lexington, Mass.: Lexington Books, D. C. Heath, 1973.

Insko, Chester A. *Theories of Attitude Change*. New York: Appleton-Century-Crofts, 1967.

Kendall, Willmoore, and George W. Carey, eds. *Liberalism vs. Conservatism: The Continuing Debate in American Government.* Princeton, N.J.: D. Van Nostrand, 1966.

Ladd, Everett Carll, Jr. *Ideology in America: Change and Response in a City, a Suburb, and a Small Town.* New York: W. W. Norton, 1972.

Lane, Robert. "Patterns of Political Beliefs." In *Handbook of Political Psychology*, edited by Jeanne N. Knutson. San Francisco: Jossey-Bass, 1973.

______. *Political Ideology*. New York: Free Press, 1967.

______. *Political Thinking and Consciousness: The Private Life of the Political Mind.* Chicago: 1969.

La Palombara, Joseph. "Decline of Ideology: A Dissent and Interpretation." *American Political Science Review*, vol. 60, no. 1 (March 1966): 5-16.

Lipset, Seymour Martin. "Some Further Comments on the End of Ideology." *American Political Science Review*, vol. 60, no. 1 (March 1966): 17-18.

Lodge, George C. *The New American Ideology.* New York; Alfred A. Knopf, 1975.

Lowi, Theodore. "American Business, Public Policy, Case-Studies and Political Theory." *World Politics* 16 (July 1964): 677-715.

______. *The End of Liberalism: Ideology, Policy, and the Crisis of Public Authority.* New York: Norton, 1969.

______. "The Public Philosophy: Interest Group Liberalism." *American Political Science Review* 61 (March 1967): pp. 5-24.

Luttbeg, Norman J. "The Structure of Beliefs Among Leaders and the Public." *Public Opinion Quarterly* 32 (Fall 1968): 398-409.

Marcus, George E., David Tabb, and John L. Sullivan. "The Application of Individual Differences Scaling to the Measurement of Political Ideologies." *American Journal of Political Science* 18 (May 1974): 405-420.

McClosky, Herbert. "Consensus and Ideology in American Politics." *American Political Science Review* 58 (1964): 361-382.

______. "Conservatism and Personality." *American Political Science Review* 52 (1958): 27-45.

______. "Personality and Attitude Correlates of Foreign Policy Orientation." In *Domestic Sources of Foreign Policy*, edited by James N. Rosenau. New York: Free Press, 1967, pp. 51-110.

______, and P. Hoffman, and R. O'Hara. "Issue Conflict and Consensus Among Party Leaders and Followers." *American Political Science Review* 54 (1960): 406-427.

______, and J. Schaar. "Psychological Dimensions of Anomy." *American Sociological Review* 3 (1965): 14-39.

Minar, David. "Ideology and Political Behavior." *Midwest Journal of Political Science*, vol. 5, no. 4 (November 1961).

Mullins, Willard A. "On the Concept of Ideology in Political Science." *American Political Science Review*, vol. 66, no. 2 (June 1972): 498-510.

Naess, Arne. *Communication and Argument: Elements of Applied Semantics.* Totowa, N.J.: Bedminster Press, 1965.

______. *Democracy, Ideology and Objectivity.* Oslo, Norway: Oslo University Press, 1956.

Powell, B. Bingham, Jr. "Political Cleavage Structure, Cross-Pressure Processes, and Partisanship: An Empirical Test of the Theory." *American Journal of Political Science,* vol. 20, no. 1 (February 1976): 1-23.

Putnam, Robert D. *The Beliefs of Politicians: Ideology, Conflict, and Democracy in Britain and Italy.* New Haven: Yale University Press, 1973.

Rae, Douglas W., and Michael Taylor. *The Analysis of Political Cleavages.* New Haven: Yale University Press, 1970.

Russett, Bruce M., and Elizabeth C. Hanson. *Interest and Ideology: The Foreign Policy Beliefs of American Businessmen.* San Francisco: W. H. Freeman, 1975.

Sartori, Giovanni. "Politics, Ideology, and Belief Systems." *American Political Science Review,* vol. 63, no. 2 (June 1969): 398-411.

Seliger, Martin. *Ideology and Politics.* New York: Free Press, 1976.

Sullivan, John L. "Ideological Distance Between Candidates: An Empirical Examination." *American Journal of Political Science,* vol. 20, no. 3 (August 1976): 439-468.

"Symposium: What Is a Liberal—Who Is a Conservative?" *Commentary,* vol. 52, no. 3 (September 1976).

Waxman, Chaim I., ed. *The End of Ideology Debate.* New York: Simon & Schuster, Clarion Books, 1969.

8. THEORY AND COMPARATIVE POLITICS

Bachrach, Peter. *The Theory of Democratic Elitism.* Boston: Little, Brown, 1967.

______, and Morton S. Baratz. "Two Faces of Power." In *Political Power: A Reader in Theory and Research,* edited by Roderick Bill, David Edwards, and R. Harrison Wagner. New York: Free Press, 1969.

Beer, Samuel H. *British Politics in the Collectivist Age.* New York: Alfred A. Knopf, 1965.

______. "Tradition and Rationality: A Classic Revisited." *American Political Science Review,* vol. 68, no. 3 (September 1974): 1291-1295.

Bell, David. *The Coming of Post-Industrial Society: A Venture in Social Forecasting.* New York: Basic Books, 1973.

Bendix, Reinhard, and Seymour Martin Lipset, eds. *Class, Status, and Power: Social Stratification in Comparative Perspective,* 2d ed. New York: Free Press, 1968.

Brandt, Richard B. *Ethical Theory.* Englewood Cliffs, N.J.: Prentice-Hall, 1959.

Centers, Richard. *The Psychology of Social Classes: A Study of Class Consciousness.* Princeton, N.J.: Princeton University Press, 1949; New York: Russell & Russell, 1961.

Dahl, Robert A. *Polyarchy: Participation and Opposition.* New Haven: Yale University Press, 1971.

______, and Charles E. Lindblom. *Politics, Economics and Welfare.* New York: Harper & Brothers, 1953.

Dahrendorf, Ralf. *Class and Class Conflict in Industrial Society.* Stanford: Stanford University Press, 1959.

Deutsch, Karl W. *The Nerves of Government: Models of Political Communication and Control.* New York: Free Press, 1963.

Dodd, Lawrence C. *Coalitions in Parliamentary Government.* Princeton, N.J.: Princeton University Press, 1976.

Eulau, Heinz. *Micro-Macro Political Analysis: Accents of Inquiry.* Chicago: Aldine, 1969.

Fairfield, Roy P., ed. *The Federalist Papers.* Garden City, N.Y.: Anchor Books, 1961.

Germani, Geno. "Fascism and Class." In *The Nature of Fascism,* edited by S. J. Woolf. New York: Vintage Books, 1969.

Green, Philip. "Science, Government, and the Case of RAND: A Singular Pluralism." *World Politics*, vol. 20, no. 2 (January 1968): 301-326.

Heclo, Hugh. "Frontiers of Social Policy in Europe and America." *Policy Sciences* 6 (1975): 403-421.

Heilbroner, Robert L. *Business Civilization in Decline*. New York: W. W. Norton, 1976.

Hinckley, Barbara. "Party As Coalition in Legislative Settings: Possible Impermeability to External Effects." Paper presented at the annual meeting of the American Political Science Association, San Francisco, September 1975.

Huitt, Ralph K. "Political Feasibility." In *Cases in Public Policy-Making*, edited by James E. Anderson. New York: Praeger, 1976.

Huntington, Samuel P. "Political Development and Political Decay." *World Politics*, vol. 17, no. 3 (April 1975): 386-430.

Jackson, J. A., ed. *Social Stratification*. New York: Cambridge University Press, 1968.

Janowitz, Morris. *Social Control of the Welfare State*. New York: Elsevier, 1976.

King, Anthony. "Modes of Executive-Legislative Relations: Great Britain, France, and West Germany." *Legislative Studies Quarterly*, vol. 1, no. 1 (February 1976): 11-36.

Kingdon, John W. "Some Reflections on Models of Legislative Voting." Paper prepared for delivery at the Conference on Mathematical Models of Congress, Aspen, Colorado, June 16-23, 1974.

Kornberg, Allan, and Lloyd D. Musolf, eds. *Legislatures in Developmental Perspective*. Durham, N.C.: Duke University Press, 1970.

Lipset, Seymour M., and Stein Rokkan, eds. *Party Systems and Voter Alignments: Cross National Perspectives*. New York: Free Press, 1967.

McFarland, Andrew S. *Power and Leadership in Pluralist Systems*. Stanford: Stanford University Press, 1969.

Nettl, J. P. *Political Mobilization: A Sociological Analysis of Methods and Concepts*. New York: Basic Books, 1967.

Padover, Saul K. *To Secure These Blessings: The Great Debates of the Constitutional Convention of 1787, Arranged According to Topics*. New York: Washington Square Press/Ridge Press, 1962.

Pitkin, Hanna Fenichel. *The Concept of Representation*. Berkeley: University of California Press, 1972.

Riker, William H. *The Theory of Political Coalitions*. New Haven: Yale University Press, 1962.

Rogin, Michael. "Nonpartisanship and the Group Interest." In *Power and Community*, edited by Philip Green anbd Sanford Levinson. New York: Vintage Books, 1970, pp. 112-141.

Rundquist, Barry S., and John A. Ferejohn. "Observations on a Distributive Theory of Policy-Making." In *Comparative Public Policy*, edited by Craig Liske, William Loehr, and John McCamant. New York: John Wiley, 1975.

Schick, Allen. "The Constitutional Matrix: Toward a Reconstruction of the Bureaucratic State." Paper presented at the annual meeting of the American Political Science Association, New York City, September 2-6, 1969.

Schlesinger, Arthur J. "Parliamentary Government." *The New Republic* 31 August 1974, pp. 13-15.

Shapiro, Michael J. "Rational Political Man: A Synthesis of Economic and Social Psychological Perspectives." *American Political Science Review*, vol. 63, no. 4 (December 1969).

Silvert, Kalman H., ed. *Expectant Peoples: Nationalism, and Development*. New York: Vintage Books, 1967.

______. *The Reasons for Democracy*. New York: Viking, 1977.

______, and Leonard Reissman. *Education, Class, and Nation*. New York: Elsevier, 1976.

Truman, David B. *The Governmental Process: Political Interests and Public Opinion*. New York: Alfred A. Knopf, 1951.

Verba, Sidney. "Some Dilemmas in Comparative Research." *World Politics*, vol. 20, no. 1 (October 1967): 111-127.

SUBJECT INDEX

AFL-CIO COPE, 56
American Bar Association, 128
American Political Science Association, 194, 199
Angola, 69, 79, 83, 87, 94

Balance of Ideological Forces, 197, 198-200
Black Caucus, 66
Brazil, 49, 60, 219-221
Brookings Institution, xv, 119
Brown University, xvi

Chile, 69
Civil liberties issues, 124-125, 128, 203
Class, 23-33
- class allocation index, 118-123, 159. *See* Methodology, "refraction," theoretical
- economic theories, 118-119

Congress
- Bolling-Martin Select Committee on Committees of the House, 9
- changes in, 14
- Culver Commission on the Operation of the Senate, 9
- institutional capacity of, 7, 144
  - and cueing, 29, 118, 119, 144
- integrated policy making in, 6-7
- membership turnover, 108-109, 149
- new era of resource constraints, 163-165
- Obey Commission on Administrative Review (of the House), 9
- oversight of the bureaucracy, 144
- projection of new role, 189, 200
- staff in, 6, 7, 20, 98
- Stevenson-Brock Temporary Select Committee to study the Senate Committee System, 9
- tensions with Executive Branch, 7, 197

Congressional coalitions
- abstract conceptual structure for analysis—Sundquist's treatment, 148
- analysis of, a dilemma, 91-102
- civil liberties and democracy issues, 124-125, 189
- economic (including "distributive") issues, 159-191, 193
- foreign policy, 62-80
- interpretations of, based on pre-1971 recorded-teller-vote-reform votes, 107-108
- parties and, 4, 38, 109, 159, 182-183, 199
- perspectives on, 3-9
- pluralism vs. ideology, dispute over, 27-30
- political feasibility and, 20
- potential coalitions, 13
- race issues, 123-124
- unidimensionality and its significance, the principal finding, 147-148

Cuba 49, 59

Defense spending, 49, 64, 70, 71, 72
Delaware, University of, xv
Democracy, 37, 64, 124-125, 189

Economic policy, 159-192
  and complexities in understanding congressional coalitions, 5, 6
  economic concentration, 182, 185-186, 188, 190
  economic growth, 164, 175, 188
  fiscal policy and the social agenda, 165, 175-176
  inflation, 168-175, 176-182
    and Phillips Curve, 174
  interview schedule, 166-167
  Keynesian economics, 161, 190-191
  monetary policy, 184-185
  Okun's law, 171
  scarcity and the new congressional context, 163-165
  theories of market economics, 37, 165, 183, 160-191
  unemployment, 168-173, 176-182
  unequal public presentation of elite economic policy controversies, 40

Federal Reserve System, 184-185
Foreign Policy, 45-90
  Bretton Woods system, end of, 18
  Communism, perceptions of the threats of, 45-47, 59, 69, 73-75, 79, 82-83
    and counter-intervention, 74, 77
  expropriation, 50-53, 61, 64, 71-72
  foreign aid, 50, 53-54, 61, 70-71
    and human rights, 68
  foreign competition, 48
  interview schedule, 47-50
  multinational corporations, 5, 65-67, 72, 75, 79, 87
  new foreign policy agenda, 18, 48, 71-73, 75-80
  North-South hemisphere tensions, 75
  nuclear proliferation, 78-79
  protectionism, 48
  raw materials, 48, 85, 163
  regimes, attitudes toward left-wing and right-wing, 47-50, 53, 59, 64, 65, 69, 78, 88-89

Greece, 49, 62

Humphrey-Hawkins Full Employment and Balanced Growth Act, 168-169

Ideologies
  Conservatives
    civil liberties and democracy, 124-125, 128
    definition of, 147-148, 159-160, 165, 174, 200-203
    economic policy, 165, 181, 160-191
    foreign policy, 65-66, 67-80, 82-83, 88-90, 181-182, 190
    race, 123-124
  Liberals
    civil liberties and democracy, 124, 128
    definition of, 147-148, 159-160, 165, 200-203
    economic policy, 181-182, 160-191
    foreign policy, 63-65, 67-80, 88-90
    race, 123-124
  Progressives
    definition of, 147-148, 154-160, 165, 200-203
    economic policy, 176-190
    foreign policy, 67-80
Ideology, 11, 20, 92
  and conflict, 26-27, 141-142
  Converse's model, 14-16
    "centrality," 14
    "constraint" (attitude consistency with functional interrelationships among attitudes), 14
    "contextual grasp," 14, 15
    "crowning postures," 15
    fully developed ideologies—four main functions, 14-15
    "levels of conceptualization," 14
    "range," 14
  functions of the concept, 11-13
  inferences to behavior, 12

Lowi distinctions—"distributive," "regulative," and "redistributive," 30-33, 164

Marxism, 12
Methodology
  coding procedures, 109-115
  comparisons with past studies, 136-148
  contextual, 18-20, 33, 50, 110
  contrary-to-fact conditional claims, 8

dispersion around a group mean versus pairwise comparisons of all possible pairs, 116
dispositional vs. causal claims, 102, 105
excluded votes, 111-115
focused interview coding technique, 58, 85
index construction, 116
intercoder reliability test—Converse's technique, 125-127
item direction assignment, 110
Kelley, E. W., on operationalizing ideology, 148
law of anticipated response, 8
longitudinal versus cross-sectional studies, 99-100
measurement of cohesion, 115-118
policy cutpoints procedure, 16-18, 33, 50, 110
"refraction," theoretical, 19
sampling, 55-57, 110, 140
sources of complexity, 5-9
surrogate variables, 197-198
Weisberg's "inherent predictability of congressional voting," 136-138

National Endowment for the Humanities, xv

People's Republic of China, 47, 64
Pluralism
and class, 23-25
and conflict avoidance, 25-27
and concentration of power, 21
and interest group focus, 21
as interest group theory of political coalitions, 22
Madisonian pluralism, 22
and social pluralism, 21

Race issues, 123-124
Responsible Party Model (also ideological or parliamentary party model), 38, 141, 194, 199
Rhodesia, 49, 60, 61, 62-63, 66, 224-226
Role of government, 6, 163, 189, 200

Structural functionalism, 12

Taft Hartley law, 8-9
Taiwan, 49, 60, 221-222
Tunney Amendment (on Angola), 94-95

Union of Soviet Socialist Republics, 47, 64

Vietnam, 46, 47, 48, 54-55, 60, 64, 65, 66-67, 70, 83, 108, 127, 135, 213-217

World Bank, 51, 52, 53, 84

INDEX OF NAMES

Aberbach, Joel D., 58, 85, 252
Abourezk, Senator James, 190
Ackley, Gardner, 86
Adamany, David W., 245
Agree, George E., 245
Aiken, Senator George, 95
Alker, Hayward, 41, 155, 252
Allen, Senator James B., 190
Anderson, Kristi, 35, 146, 157, 158
Anderson, Lee, 139, 153, 157, 158, 252
Andrews, Congressman George, 84
Aristotle, 25
Arterton, Christopher, 246
Asher, Herbert B., 235
Axelrod, Robert, 37, 252

Bach, Stanley, 10, 236
Bachrach, Peter, 36, 257
Bailey, Daniel E., 255
Baker, Senator Howard, 69, 152, 190
Ball, George W., 5, 9, 247, 249
Banta, Henry, xvi
Bardach, Eugene, 236
Barnet, Richard J., 9, 247
Barnett, Marguerite Ross, 236
Barthelmas, Wes, xvi
Bayh, Senator Birch, 152, 190, 197
Beall, Senator J. Glenn, 84
Beard, Charles A., 103
Beer, Samuel H., 36, 38, 112, 151, 236, 257
Belknap, George M., 81, 82, 146, 147, 158, 236
Bell, Daniel, 257
Bendix, Reinhard, 39, 257
Bentsen, Senator Lloyd M., 152, 190
Berg, Alan, 87, 247
Bergsten, C. Fred, xvi, 9, 83, 86, 89, 247-248
Berry, Jeffrey M., 242
Bezold, Clement, 236
Bibby, John F., 236
Biden, Senator Joseph R., Jr., 152
Black, Charles, Jr., 238
Blair, John, 249, 250
Blalock, Ann B., 252
Blalock, Hubert M., Jr., 103, 105, 154, 155, 252
Blanchard, Robert O., 236
Blechman, Barry M., 86, 251
Bluestone, Barry, 249
Bolling, Congressman Richard, 104, 197, 236
Bonner, R. E., 154
Born, Richard, 203, 236
Bosworth, Barry, xvi, 86, 192, 249
Bowler, M. Kenneth, 103, 236
Boyd, Richard W., 145, 158
Brademas, Congressman John, 122
Brady, David W., 236
Brams, Steven, xiv, 148

Brandt, Richard B., 257
Brezina, Dennis W., 236
Brock, Senator Bill, 52
Broder, David S., 245
Brody, Richard A., 246
Brown, Lester R., 87
Brown, Richard E., 236
Brown, Seyom, xv, 9, 37, 86, 88, 89, 248
Brown, Steven R., 35, 255
Brown, Thad A., 35, 246
Brunner, Ronald D., 252
Buckley, Senator James, 87
Bullock, Charles S., III, 236
Bumpers, Senator Dale, 152
Bundy, William P., 86, 248
Bupp, Irwin C., 251
Burnham, Walter Dean, 38, 236, 245
Burns, Arthur, 39, 119, 184
Burns, James MacGregor, 151, 157, 199, 203
Butz, Earl, 71
Byrd, Senator Harry, Jr., 190
Byrd, Senator Robert, 8, 190

Califano, Joseph A., 6, 9, 148
Campbell, Angus, 38-39, 245, 251
Cannell, Charles F., 252, 254
Cannon, Lou, 149
Carey, George W., 256
Carlucci, Ambassador Frank, 82
Carron, Andrew S., 192
Carter, President Jimmy, 4, 6, 46, 68, 75, 109, 168, 202
Casstevens, Thomas W., 150, 252
Cattell, Raymond B., 154, 252
Carron, Andrew S., 249
Centers, Richard, 257
Chambers, William Nisbet, 245
Charles, Joseph, 39
Cheney, Richard B., 150, 237
Cherryholmes, Cleo H., 137, 150, 236
Chesney, James D., 58, 85, 252
Chiles, Senator Lawton, 152
Chisholm, Roderick, xvi, 10, 252
Church, Senator Frank, 54, 69, 88, 89, 188, 189, 190, 192, 197, 201, 204-205
Clapp, Charles, 237
Clark, Senator Richard, 32-33, 71, 143, 190
Claude, Inis, 119
Clausen, Aage R., 16, 27, 28, 29, 30, 35, 39, 40, 45-46, 80-81, 82, 91, 105, 108, 111, 112, 113, 114, 115, 137-141, 148, 149, 150, 151, 153, 167, 193, 194, 195, 203, 237, 252-253
Cleaveland, Frederic N., 237
Clem, Alan L., 150, 237
Cohelen, Congressman Jeffrey, 84
Colby, William E., 88
Conlon, Richard, xvi
Converse, Philip, xv, 14-15, 17, 27, 31-32, 33, 35, 36, 38-39, 40, 41, 58, 62, 63, 81, 85, 106, 114, 117, 125-126, 144, 145-146, 152, 154, 156, 157, 159, 190, 194, 195, 199, 203, 245, 247, 251, 253, 255, 256
Cook, Stuart W., 105
Coombs, Clyde H., 117, 253
Cooper, Joseph, 237
Cooper, Richard N., 248
Costner, Herbert L., 154, 253
Cottam, Richard W., 248
Cover, Al, 237
Coveyou, Michael R., 35, 256
Crane, Wilder, Jr., 150, 253
Cranston, Senator Alan, 8, 10, 190, 197, 203, 205
Crittenden, Ann, 87
Crockett, Andrew D., 86, 249
Cronin, Thomas E., 237
Culver, Senator John, 70, 190
Cunningham, Noble E., 39
Curtis, Senator Carl, 152, 190

Dahl, Robert A., 36, 37, 90, 245, 257
Dahrendorf, Ralf, 257
Dale, Edwin L., Jr., 237
Daniel, Clifton, 103
Dauer, Manning J., 39
David, Paul T., 253
Davidson, Donald, 253
Davidson, Roger H., xv, 10, 103, 104, 164, 191, 236, 237
Davis, David, 247
Davis, James W., 237
Davis, Karen, 251
Deckard, Barbara, 38, 112, 151, 157, 237
DeCubas, Jose, 52, 84
Denison, Edward, xvi, 249
Derthick, Martha, xv
Destler, I. M., 87
Deutsch, Karl W., 12, 34, 257
deVries, Tom, 37, 86, 248
Diggins, John P., 256
Dirksen, Senator Everett, 30

Dodd, Lawrence C., 10, 237, 253, 257
Dole, Senator Robert, 72, 87, 190
Drew, Elizabeth, 51, 163, 191, 237
Duesenberry, James S., 192, 249
Durkin, Senator John A., 190

Eastland, Senator James, 32, 33, 143, 152, 190
Eckhardt, Congressman Bob, 238
Eckholm, E. P., 87
Egan, Jack, 157
Ehrenhalt, Alan, 38, 238
Ellsworth, Robert F., 86
Ellwood, John, 204, 238
Eulau, Heinz, 100-101, 104, 238, 257
Evans, Rowland, 201, 205, 246
Everitt, Brian, 104, 253

Farris, Charles D., 81, 158, 238
Fellner, William, 164
Fenno, Richard F., Jr., 10, 103, 238
Ferejohn, John A., 238, 258
Fiorina, Morris P., 238, 253
Fishbein, Martin, 253
Fishel, Jeff, 238
Fisher, Congressman Joel, 198
Fisher, Louis, 10, 238
Fitzgerald, Martin J., 238
Flanagan, Robert J., 86
Flinn, Thomas A., 150, 238
Ford, President Gerald R., 70, 75, 127-128, 202
Form, William H., 157
Fox, Harrison W., Jr., xvi, 10, 157, 238
Franklin, Grace A., 31, 40
Fraser, Congressman Donald M., 47, 68
Freund, Ernst, 238
Fried, Edward R., 84, 89, 119, 155, 251, 252
Friedman, Milton, 87, 119, 121, 122, 164, 191, 249
Froman, Lewis A., Jr., 103, 238
Frye, Alton, 238

Galbraith, John Kenneth, 119, 121, 122, 160, 191, 192, 249
Gallagher, Miriam, 242
Galtung, Johan, 58, 85, 101, 104, 253
Garn, Senator Jake, 152, 190
Gelb, Joyce, 246
Gelb, Leslie H., 86, 87, 88, 248
George, Alexander L., 115, 153
George, Juliet L., 153
Germani, Geno, 257
Ginzberg, Eli, 251
Goldberg, Arthur S., 104
Golden, Soma, 191
Goldman, Jerry, 242
Goldstein, Morris, 86, 249
Goldwater, Senator Barry, 69, 190
Goodman, Leo A., 253
Goodman, Nelson, 10, 253
Goodwin, Crawford D., 249
Goodwin, Leonard, 251
Goss, Carol F., 239
Gramlich, Edward M., 251
Grant, James P., 248
Grassmuck, George L., 248
Gravel, Senator Mike, 152
Green, Philip, 36, 248, 258
Greenspan, Alan, 177-178, 185
Greenstein, Fred I., 27, 150
Groenning, Sven, 239
Grumm, John G., 150, 253
Gunnell, John G., 104

Haberler, Gottfried, 164
Halleck, Congressman Charles, 30
Hammond, Susan Webb, 10, 157, 238
Hampshire, Stuart, 105, 253
Harriman, Ambassador W. Averell, 82, 87
Harris, Congressman Herbert, 198
Harris, Louis, 246
Harris, Richard, 239
Hart, H. L. A., 253
Hart, Peter D., 129
Hart, Senator Gary, 152, 190, 256
Hart, Senator Phillip A., 69
Hartigan, John A., 253
Hartman, Robert W., 251
Harvey, Paul, 157
Haskell, Senator Floyd K., 190
Hathaway, Senator William D., 190
Haveman, Robert H., 251
Hawley, Jonathan P., 239
Hays, William L., 154, 155
Hayter, Teresa, 248
Heclo, Hugh, xv, 246, 258
Heilbroner, Robert L., 89, 248, 249, 258
Heise, David R., 253
Heller, Walter, 164
Helms, Senator Jesse A., 190
Hempel, Carl G., 34, 105, 253

Herndon, James F., 253
Hickel, Gerald Kent, 36, 256
Hinckley, Barbara, xv, 35-38, 239, 258
Hirsch, Fred, 249
Hoagland, Jim, 89
Hoffman, Paul, 35, 256
Hoffman, Stanley, 84, 248
Holsti, Ole R., 85, 254
Holt, Pat, 83
Holtzman, Abraham, 239
Honore, A. M., 253
Hopkins, Raymond, 87
Horst, Thomas, 9
Hubbard, Henry, 4, 9
Huber, Joan, 157
Huitt, Ralph K., 13, 35, 37, 239, 258
Humphrey, Senator Hubert H., 68, 70, 89, 129, 152, 168, 178, 180-184, 190, 197, 239
Huntington, Samuel P., 24, 25, 39, 239, 246, 258
Hymer, Stephen, 205, 248

Insko, Chester A., 256

Jackson, John A., 39, 258
Jackson, John E., 36, 103, 104, 239, 254
James, Judson L., 246
Janowitz, Morris, 258
Jasper, Herbert N., 239
Javitz, Senator Jacob, 152
Jennings, M. Kent, 246
Johannes, John R., 239
Johnson, President Lyndon B., 26, 29, 120
Jones, Charles O., 4, 239

Kahn, Robert L., 254
Kaldor, Sir Nicholas, 249
Kampelman, Max, M., 239
Kantor, Arnold, xv, 239
Kaplan, Abraham, 254
Karns, David A., xv, 83, 104, 150, 239
Karns, Margaret, xv
Kaufman, Herbert, xv
Kaysen, Carl, 248
Kearns, Doris, 39, 246
Keefe, William J., 239
Keenan, Edward L., 88
Keith, Robert, 103, 239
Kelley, E. W., 148, 150, 153, 254
Kendall, Willmoore, 256
Kennan, George F., 90, 248
Kennedy, President John F., 29, 50, 98
Kennedy, Senator Edward M., 52, 70, 86, 151, 152, 190, 197, 248
Keohane, R. O., 248
Kernall, Samuel, 239
Kesselman, Mark J., 239
Kim, Jae-On, 254
Kindleberger, Charles P., 51, 84, 250
King, Anthony, 258
King, James P., Jr., xvi
King, Margaret P., xvi
King, Susan B., 240
Kingdon, John, xv, 27, 28-29, 30, 36, 39, 40, 150, 191, 240, 258
Kirkpatrick, Evron, 246
Kish, Leslie, 86, 139, 157, 254
Kissinger, Henry, 82, 95, 135
Kneese, Allen V., 10, 153, 251
Koehler, David, 148
Kornberg, Allan, 258
Krause, Lawrence B., 86, 250
Kruskal, William H., 253
Kuznets, Simon S., 250

Ladd, Everett Carl, Jr., 246, 256
Lake, Anthony, 248
Lane, Robert E., 24, 28, 35, 37-38, 39, 246, 256
La Palombara, Joseph, 34, 256
LaPort, Robert, Jr., 84, 85, 86
Lasswell, Harold, 123
Laxalt, Senator Paul D., 152, 190
Lazarsfeld, Paul F., 105, 254
Leahy, Senator Patrick J., 152
Lebergott, Stanley, 250
Leege, David C., 104, 254
Lehnen, Robert G., 240
Leiserson, Michael, 148
Lekachman, Robert, 250
Lenchner, Paul, 240
Lenin, V. I., 119
Levine, Mark S., 150, 254
Levitan, Sar A., 251
Lewis, Clarence Irving, 254
Lindberg, Leon, xv
Lindblom, Charles E., 36, 191, 250, 257
Link, Mary, 157
Lipset, Seymour Martin, 34, 39, 155, 190, 256, 257, 258
Lockard, Duane, 246

Lodge, George C., 256
Long, Senator Russell, 190
Lowi, Theodore J., 22, 23, 25, 30-31, 32, 33, 38, 39, 40, 97, 106, 256
Lugar, Senator Richard G., 190
Luttbeg, Norman J., 35, 256
Lutzker, Paul, 240
Lynn, James T., 251

Machiavelli, Niccolò, 25
Mackleprang, Lon, 150
MacNeil, Neil, 240
MacRae, Duncan, Jr., 31, 40, 81, 112, 114, 117-118, 139, 146-147, 150, 151, 152, 154, 157, 158, 195, 240, 254
Madden, Congressman Ray, 151-152
Madison, James, 22, 23, 24, 25, 38, 39, 116
Malbin, Michael J., 240
Manley, John, 240
Mann, Thomas E., 153, 154
Manning, Bayless, 37, 248
Mansfield, Harvey C., Sr., 10, 31, 33, 40, 240
Marcus, George E., 35, 256
Mathias, Senator Charles McC., 69
Matthews, Donald R., 27, 28, 29, 30, 34, 39, 40, 108, 137, 138, 142-145, 149, 157, 195, 240
Mayhew, David, 237, 240
McClellan, Senator John, 190
McClosky, Herbert, xv, 27, 35, 256
McClure, Robert D., 39
McConnell, Grant, 36, 246
McCracken, Paul, 164
McFarland, Andrew S., 36, 258
McGovern, Senator George, 190
Means, Gardiner C., 250
Mellon, Andrew, 202
Melsheimer, John T., 240
Metcalf, Senator Lee, 190
Mikva, Congressman Abner J., 197
Miller, Arthur H., 35, 153, 244
Miller, Clem, 240
Miller, Warren E., 35, 126, 156, 245, 246
Minar, David W., 17, 36, 256
Moe, Ronald C., 241
Mondale, Vice-President Walter F., 69, 72, 87, 152, 190
Moran, Theodore H., 9, 85, 248
Morgan, Dan, 69, 190, 250
Morgenthau, Hans, 88-89
Morris, Roger, 248
Moyer, Wayne, 241
Moynihan, Senator Daniel P., 83, 248
Mueller, John E., 246
Muller, Ronald E., 9, 247
Mullins, Willard A., 256
Murphy, James T., 241
Muskie, Senator Edmund S., 70, 152, 190, 197
Musolf, Lloyd D., 258

Nader, Ralph, 162
Naess, Arne, 257
Nagorski, Zygmunt, Jr., 89
Nakamura, Robert, xv
Natchez, Peter, 246, 251
Nathan, James A., 82, 156, 248
Nathan, Richard P., 241
Nathan, Robert R., 119
Nelson, Senator Gaylord, 190
Nettl, J. P., 258
Neustadt, Richard, 241
Nie, Norman H., 35, 146, 157, 158, 247
Niemi, Richard J., 155
Nixon, President Richard M., 18, 67, 114, 127, 128, 135
Nordhaus, William, 191, 250
Novak, Robert, 201, 205, 246
Nunn, Senator Sam, 152, 190
Nye, Joseph S., 248

Obey, Congressman David, 197
O'Brien, Lawrence F., 29, 30, 40, 198, 203, 246
Ogul, Morris S., 10, 241
Okun, Arthur, xvi, 119, 120, 121, 122, 124, 155, 156, 160, 164, 171-173, 180, 191, 197, 250
Oleszek, Walter J., 10, 103, 191, 241
Oliver, James K., xv, 82, 86, 126, 156, 248
Olson, David, 150, 241
O'Neill, Speaker Thomas P., 4, 9, 149, 199
Oppenheimer, Bruce, 10
Oqul, Morris S., 239
Orfield, Gary, xv, 10, 37, 156, 166, 241, 251, 252
Ornstein, Norman J., 10, 32, 41, 104, 148, 241
Orshansky, Mollie, 252
Osgood, Robert, 248
Overmyer, Allen, 236
Owen, Henry, 252

Packenham, Robert, 205, 249
Packwood, Senator Bob, 190
Padover, Saul K., 39, 258
Page, Benjamin I., 246
Paletz, David L., 151
Palley, Howard, 252
Palley, Marion L., xv, 156, 246, 252
Parenti, Michael, 246
Patterson, Samuel C., 241
Patterson, Thomas E., 39
Paul, Roland, 83
Peabody, Robert L., 9, 10, 32, 41, 103, 104, 240, 241, 242
Pechman, Joseph A., 250
Pell, Senator Claiborne, 87
Pennock, J. Roland, 246
Perry, George A., 250
Petras, James F., 84, 85, 86
Petrocik, John, 157
Pierce, John C., 35
Pierson, James E., 35, 256
Pitkin, Hanna Fenichel, 258
Plato, 25
Podhoretz, Norman, 82, 249
Polsby, Nelson W., 24, 27, 28, 29, 30, 102, 106, 242, 252
Pomper, Gerald M., 246
Pool, Ithiel De Sola, 254
Porter, William E., 39, 246
Powell, G. Bingham, Jr., 148, 257
Pressman, Jeffrey L., 246
Price, David E., 242
Price, H. D., 242, 254
Proxmire, Senator William, 176-180, 185-187, 190, 192, 197
Przeworski, Adam, 104, 254
Puchala, Donald, 87
Putnam, Robert D., 92, 102, 257

Quine, W. V. O., 105, 254

Rae, Douglas W., 148, 257
Raine, Alden S., 35, 246
Ranney, Austin, 247
Reagan, Ronald, 157, 202
Reedy, George E., 15, 35, 242
Reichley, A. James, 242
Reigle, Senator Donald, 97, 103, 198, 242
RePass, David E., 40, 82, 247
Reuss, Congressman Henry, 89, 151, 184, 189, 192, 197
Reynolds, Henry, xv, 127, 154, 155, 254
Rhode, David W., 32, 41
Ribicoff, Senator Abraham, 152, 190
Rice, Stuart A., 255
Rich, Spencer, 152
Riegle, Senator Donald, 83
Rieselbach, Leroy, 242
Riker, William, 148, 255, 258
Ringquist, Delbert, 237
Ripley, Randall B., 31, 40, 239, 242
Rivlin, Alice M., 84, 89, 119, 155, 251
Roberts, Charles, 243
Robinson, James A., 243
Robinson, Michael J., 243
Rockefeller, David, 192
Rockefeller, Nelson, 4, 9, 54, 65, 84, 88, 200-201, 204-205
Rockman, Bert A., 58, 85, 252
Rogers, Willard, 251
Rogin, Michael, 36, 247, 258
Rohde, David W., 104, 241 243
Rokkan, Stein, 258
Roosa, Robert V., 250
Rose, Douglas D., 35
Rosenau, James N., 249
Rosenberg, Milton J., 35, 247
Rosenbloom, David L., 243
Rostow, Eugene V., 249
Roth, Senator William, 190
Rothschild, Emma, 87, 251
Rubin, Richard L., 247
Rudder, Cathy, 243
Rundquist, Barry S., 242, 243, 258
Rundquist, Paul S., 243
Russell, Bertrand, 94
Russett, Bruce M., 257
Ryle, Gilbert, 105

Salant, Walter S., 86, 250
Saloma, John S., 243
Samuelson, Paul A., 250
Samuelson, Robert J., 164, 190, 250
Sanderson, Fred H., 87
Sarbanes, Senator Paul, 190, 197
Sartori, Giovanni, 34, 257
Schattschneider, E. E., 247
Schelling, Thomas C., 249
Scherer, F. M., 191, 250
Schick, Allen, xvi, 10, 103, 243-244, 258
Schlesinger, Arthur, 104, 244, 258
Schmitt, Senator Harrison H., 190

Schneier, Edward, 244
Schultz, George, 71
Schultze, Charles L., xvi, 10, 84, 86, 89, 103, 119, 143, 153, 155, 157, 168-171, 173, 174, 176, 180, 191, 197, 251, 252
Schwarz, Susan Borker, 150, 254
Schweiker, Senator Richard S., 152
Scott, Senator William L., 190
Scully, Michael A., 240
Seidman, Harold, 244
Sekiguchi, Sueo, 86
Seliger, Martin, 34, 257
Selltiz, Claire, 105
Selvin, Hanan C., 85, 86, 255
Shanahan, Eileen, 40, 160, 251
Shannon, W. Wayne, 244
Shapiro, Michael J., 137, 150, 236, 258
Shepard, Roger N., 255
Shulman, Marshall D., 88
Siegal, Sidney, 153, 154, 157
Siff, Ted, 103, 244
Sigmund, Paul E., 85, 86, 249
Silk, Leonard, 192, 202, 205
Silvert, K. H., xv, 258
Simon, William, 202
Sinclair, Barbara Deckard. *See* Deckard, Barbara
Singer, James S., 244
Smith, Donald, 244
Smith, Congressman Frank E., 244
Solomon, Robert, 251
Solow, Robert M., 251
Sorauf, Frank J., 199, 203
Sorensen, Theodore, 46, 129
Southwick, Thomas P., 157, 244
Stafford, Senator Robert T., 84
Stanley, John, 38, 112, 151
Steinberg, Brian, xv
Stennis, Senator John, 152, 190
Stevens, Senator Ted, 190
Stevens, Arthur G., Jr., 103, 153, 244
Stevenson, James S., 192
Stevenson, Senator Adlai E., 188
Stewart, Geoffrey S., 244
Stewart, John G., 244, 247
Stimson, James A., 27, 28, 29, 30, 34, 35, 39, 40, 108, 137, 138, 142-145, 149, 157, 195, 240, 244, 247
Stokes, Donald E., 24, 35, 39, 156, 245, 247
Stolley, Paul D., xvi
Stone, Clarence N., 244
Strauss-Hupe, Robert, 249
Sullivan, John L., 35, 105, 255, 256, 257
Sundquist, James L., 10, 148, 153, 244, 247
Sunkel, Oswaldo, 249
Suppes, Patrick, 253
Surrey, Stanley S., 251
Szulc, Tad, 82, 84, 249

Tabb, David, 35, 256
Tacheron, Donald G., 244
Taft, Senator Robert, 84
Taggart, Robert, 251
Talmadge, Senator Herman E., 190
Taylor, Michael, 148, 257
Taylor, Richard, xvi
Teeters, Nancy H., 84, 89, 119, 155, 251, 252
Teune, Henry, 104, 254
Thurber, James A., 238, 244
Thurmond, Senator Strom, 190
Thurow, Lester, 119, 251
Tobin, James, 191, 250
Tolchin, Martin, 153
Tower, Senator John G., 69, 190
Truman, David, 24, 36, 45, 81, 244-245, 247, 258
Tryon, Robert C., 255
Tucker, Robert, 248, 249
Tukey, John W., 255
Tufte, Edward R., 56, 255
Turner, Julius, 245, 247

Udall, Congressman Morris K., 197, 244
Ullman, Richard H., 249
Ulman, Lloyd, 86
Uslaner, Eric, 148

Van Horn, Carl E., 105, 111, 113, 115, 151, 237, 253
Verba, Sidney, 34, 35, 104, 157, 247, 258
Vernon, Raymond, 119, 249
Vershbow, Alexander R., 249
Vogler, David J., 104, 151, 245

Wahlke, John C., 158, 241, 245
Walker, Jack L., 245
Wallace, Governor George C., 204
Wallop, Senator Malcolm, 190
Warnke, Paul, 46, 129
Watts, Meredith W., Jr., 153, 252
Waxman, Chaim I., 36, 257
Weaver, Warren, Jr., 245

Weber, Max, 25
Weisberg, Herbert F., xv, 17, 35, 36, 137-138, 142, 147, 149, 150, 153, 154, 157, 158, 195, 255
Wellford, Harrison, xvi, 247
Wicker, Tom, 157
Wilcox, Allen R., 150, 153, 252, 255
Wildavsky, Aaron, 104, 247, 252
Willick, Daniel H., 249
Wilson, President Woodrow, 245
Wilson, Thomas P., 155, 255
Winslow, John F., 251
Wolfers, Arnold, 119, 248
Wolfinger, Raymond E., 245
Wolman, Harold L., 150, 238
Worthley, John A., 245
Wright, G. H. von, 255
Wriston, Walter B., 251

Yacker, Marc D., 245

Zeigler, L. Harmon, 36, 246, 247
Zorinsky, Senator Edward, 190

ABOUT THE AUTHOR

Jerrold E. Schneider began this study as a Research Fellow at the Brookings Institution, and several years later completed it as a Brookings Guest Scholar and National Endowment for the Humanities Fellow. He is a member of the political science faculty at the University of Delaware.